Take it from the travel experts,
Literary Trips is indispensable

"A great idea, wonderfully executed. The stories in *Literary Trips* will send you madly off in all directions out into the world of travel, back into the books themselves. Same destination, of course."
— Charles Foran, author of *The Story of My Life So Far*
and *The Last House of Ulster*

"A fascinating feast of brilliantly evocative tales delicately salted with practical information. Crisp, amusing, and displaying a deft touch in casual portraiture, the lives of literary luminaries, and their favored haunts are most beautifully met in *Literary Trips*."
— Christopher P. Baker, author of Lonely Planet and Moon guidebooks

"This book is the next best thing to making the pilgrimages yourself."
— Douglas Fetherling, author of
Running Away to Sea: Round the World in a Tramp Freighter

"You'll love this book's twist of life: insider details—favored digs, author hangouts, useful Web sites—that let you mix your own pilgrimages."
— Vicki León, author of the *Uppity Women in History* series

"This collection of captivating and informative tales will enrich the experience of the traveler to these destinations."
— C. Steen Hansen, publisher, *Specialty Travel Index*

"A guided tour to literature's landscapes and imaginings, and a practical guide to experiencing the tastes, sights, and smells that have stirred some of the world's best writings."
— Ian Gill, author of *Haida Gwaii: Journeys Through the Queen Charlotte Islands*

"Finally a book that captures the reasons why we travel. It sets a new trend in North American travel writing, raising it to literary standards as it reaches out to touch the emotions of the readers and tell a story rather than bore them with guidebook and tourist-board promotional hype. This is what travel is all about and what travel writing should be, without exception. Let the transformation begin!"
— Donna S. Morris, travel editor of *Autoroute* magazine
and editor of *DreamScapes* and *The Professional Traveller* magazines

Literary
TRIPS

Following in the Footsteps of Fame

Editor: Victoria Brooks
Foreword by Paul Bowles
Introduction by Bob Shacochis
Illustrations by Alex Ignatius

Ah, yes!

HOT, HOT, HOT-
HUMID! YEAST-
3 Aug 2001

GreatestEscapes.com
PUBLISHING

00 01 02 03 04 5 4 3 2

First published in 2000 by
GreatestEscapes.com Publishing
730–800 West Pender Street
Vancouver, British Columbia
Canada V6C 2V6
www.literarytrips.com
www.greatestescapes.com

Canadian Cataloguing in Publication Data

Main entry under title:

Literary trips

Includes index.
ISBN 0-9686137-0-5

1. Literary landmarks—Guidebooks. I. Brooks, Victoria. II. Ignatius, Alex.
PN164.L57 2000   910.2'02   C99-911149-3

Series editor: M. R. Carroll
Text and cover design: Carty Design Inc.
Maps and illustrations: Alex Ignatius
Cover photo by Marianne Grondahl/Photonica
Distributed in the United States by Words Distributing Company
Distributed in Canada by Sandhill Book Marketing Ltd.
Printed and bound in Canada by Friesens

Contents

Each time I go to a place I have not seen before, I hope it will be as different as possible from the places I already know. I assume it is natural for a traveler to seek diversity, and that it is the human element which makes him most aware of difference. If people and their manner of living were alike everywhere, there would not be much point in moving from one place to another.

Paul Bowles
Their Heads Are Green and Their Hands Are Blue

Foreword

A GREAT PART of the fascination exerted by the unknown comes from the joy of meeting it face-to-face for the first time. The excitement of finding something strange consists precisely in noting its strangeness. The less one knows about the subject to be examined, the better-equipped one is to have significant reactions to the many unique deviations presented.

When one begins to look for and find and love these innumerable distinguishing characteristics, one falls under the spell of a place. As in all processes of learning, the more one discovers, the more conscious one is of the great amount of material not yet learned.

A fairly common phenomenon is the fanatic intent on extracting the essence of the subject that obsesses one. Particularly interesting to me is the fact that the subject need not exist in reality. Witness Edgar Allan Poe, for whom the impossibly lovely (on occasion monstrous) landscapes offered him by his unconscious mind preoccupied him all his life. What did he find at that "ultimate dim Thule"?

Paul Bowles

Tangier, Morocco
July 1999

Acknowledgments

MY THANKS GO OUT to these indispensable companions on my journey: Guy Brooks, whose research work and companionship I cannot do without; Kathryn Means, who came up with the title of this book, and for her unfailingly good advice and support on every aspect of the project; M. R. Carroll, for his trusted advice, support, and talented editing; the late Paul Bowles, for spending time with me and lending his name to what must have seemed a relatively unknown quantity; Bob Shacochis, for contributing his talent; Dr. David and Katherine Friesen (my parents), for gathering information unbidden and for adding their support; Matt Midboe, for tracking down the elusive Mr. Bowles in Tangier; and once again, my husband, Guy, and Brian Buchanan, two talented businessmen who took this project public and raised funds.

As for what follows in the pages you are about to read, it should be noted that all prices quoted in the book are in U.S. dollars unless otherwise specified. At the time of writing, prices were calculated at the prevailing exchange rate which, of course, is always subject to change. So make sure you double-check all such information before booking anything. Hotel rates, as listed in **The Writer's Trail** sections at the end of each essay, are coded as follows: Extremely expensive—more than $300 per night based on double occupancy; Expensive—$200 to $300; Moderate—$100 to $200; Inexpensive—under $100.

Bon voyage, and good reading!

Victoria Brooks

West Vancouver, British Columbia
October 1999

Introduction

IN THE ETERNAL HIERARCHY of travelers, the first among equals are the dreamers, the circumnavigators of the imagination, visionaries who set out on their armchair voyages of discovery, the very act of their explorations creating and embellishing and re-creating the world, and all the many splendid and sordid textures of life within it. I am speaking, of course, of writers and readers, those pilgrims of literature who share humanity's most divine curse and most enduring lust: the need to savor experience, if not physically, then in spirit; the need to wander toward a horizon of mystery, if not with the body, then certainly through the soul.

Alongside the prophets and queens, storytellers—dreamers, travelers, thinkers, life's legendary witnesses—are mankind's original celebrities, the ones we have carried with us in our hearts throughout the ages, cherishing their works, teaching their names to our children and our children's children: Virgil, Homer, Ovid, Plato, Dante, William Shakespeare, Jane Austen, Charlotte and Emily Brontë, Leo Tolstoy, Federico García Lorca, to name but a handful from the canon. Their fame is inseparable from Western civilization's glory, though that bond between writer and society seems to fade with each passing year.

Quick, take a street-corner poll. Who won the Booker Prize last year? Who won the Pulitzer Prize or Governor General's Award for fiction? Nobody knows, not many care, and everything clicks by too fast to worry about it. The days, not so long ago, when reporters queued at the dock or train station to badger Oscar Wilde, or rushed to the airport to greet F. Scott Fitzgerald or S. J. Perelman returning from Europe, are over. And good riddance, perhaps, if not for the subsequent devaluation of writing itself.

So it's oddly nostalgic, I think, and wonderful, to have here before us *Literary Trips*:

Following in the Footsteps of Fame, an end-of-an-era reminder that, however much Hollywood now speaks for the global culture, however much the culture is increasingly influenced and defined by the visual image rather than the written word, however much we pay homage to big-screen actors over those who create in solitude, and measure success by bank accounts and sheer visibility rather than achievement, there still exists among the ever-growing horde of consumers, and perhaps always will, those who understand that there is no true collective life of the mind, and no common destiny that is not capricious, until it is written down.

My own beginnings as a traveler arrived in just this way—dreaming, dreaming—courtesy of an unlikely dream machine, the United States Department of Defense, where my father worked for the navy for 30 years. Throughout history soldiers and sailors have played the role of heroic travelers, their expeditions and escapades providing us not only with the first but, outside of religious texts, the only stories of travel and discovery for centuries—until Marco Polo saddled up. I was not raised a military brat, whisked from post to post around the Cold War planet, but instead spent my childhood and adolescence in the suburbs of Washington, D.C. One day in the late 1950s, my father, a quintessential bureaucrat, brought home the first of what would become about a dozen small travel books published by the U.S. armed forces for distribution among the troops. It was called *A Pocket Guide to North Africa*, and I took it to the sanctuary of my room and read its opening sentences:

> Your tour of duty in North Africa can be a rewarding experience or an irksome chore. It all depends on you. You won't find the region at all like the U.S.A.—or the people like those on Main Street back home. But by taking the trouble to learn a little about North Africa and the North Africans, you'll find the things that are strange to you becoming pleasantly different rather than distressingly odd.

Naive banalities for an adult in 1999, but for a young boy in the 1950s, the words were magic. I still have the pocket guide, and several others—relics of my innocence, and America's. I was eight or nine at the time and had never heard of Paul Bowles, who by then was well established in Tangier, nor did I hold more than a thimbleful of knowledge about writers, and knew nothing of their lives except the vague notion they were somehow important to the way we lived. But for the first time, with the military's *A Pocket Guide to North Africa* in hand, I knew about Morocco, I stared at pictures of Berber girls unveiled, I learned about such exoticisms as mosques and evil eyes, and I fell asleep at night swaddled in white robes for protection against the Saharan sun and blowing sands as I followed ancient trade routes across the endless golden desert.

A Pocket Guide to Japan followed, then one called *South of the Border*, brimming with references about conquistadors and pirates, palm trees and volcanoes, the myriad imagery that lures us from our quotidian lives on Main Street toward the mystique of the Other, and from which emerges the robust inner life of the seeker. There my memory of the individual guides ends, but by the time I was 10, seven years before I went flying overseas, I had traveled the world from top to bottom with the GIs and infected myself with a gnawing restlessness for other landscapes, other tribes than my own, that has been well exercised over the decades without ever being exhausted. Like hunger, like sex, it is an appetite that cannot be truly diminished but only temporarily assuaged—by foot, bicycle, horse; by planes and trains and boats, surely; and just as surely by books, those dreams that we hold in our hands and linger with page by page, for books are both a ticket to a destination and the destination itself, both the traveler and the journey, and no other road can offer such intimacy.

I have, like so many other readers, been drawn to Ernest Hemingway's grave in Idaho, and Robert Frost's in Vermont. Before I turned 21, I had already stepped in awe through the rooms of Tolstoy's house in St. Petersburg, and Shakespeare's in Stratford-upon-Avon. I have paid my respects to William Faulkner in Oxford, Mississippi, to Virgil in Mantua, Italy, to W. B. Yeats in Dublin, to Mark Twain in Hannibal, Missouri, to Gertrude Stein in Paris. I can't tell you why—there is no answer beyond the gift of coincidence—but for almost three decades I have found myself crossing paths with another wanderer, D. H. Lawrence, first in the gloomy coal-mining districts of Nottingham, England; then in Taormina, Sicily, where my wife and I, in the midst of a quarrel, made a pilgrimage to the house where Lawrence had lived—and fought famously—with his wife, Frieda; and now in the Sangre de Cristo Mountains of northern New Mexico where I have a cabin a short distance from Lawrence's ranch.

There is a sense of continuity, no matter how tenuous, created by such path-crossings, and the crossings themselves feel like the gentlest of blessings. However fragile the connection, the dead stream through it into the light and give us their eyes, their lusts, and leave us spellbound with their secrets. To perhaps see as they saw, love as they loved, grieve as they grieved, to advance or complete some subliminal line of understanding, if only for an everlasting moment. As the U.S. military advised its men and women on the eve of their travels: *It all depends on you.*

What do I want from the world? To know it. What do I want from life? To taste it. And what do I want from writers? To take us there, and serve it forth, and make us turn the page.

Bob Shacochis

Cañada de los Alamos, New Mexico
October 1999

NORTH
AMERICA

PACIFIC

OCEAN

ATLANTIC

OCEAN

AFRICA

SOUTH
AMERICA

T H E

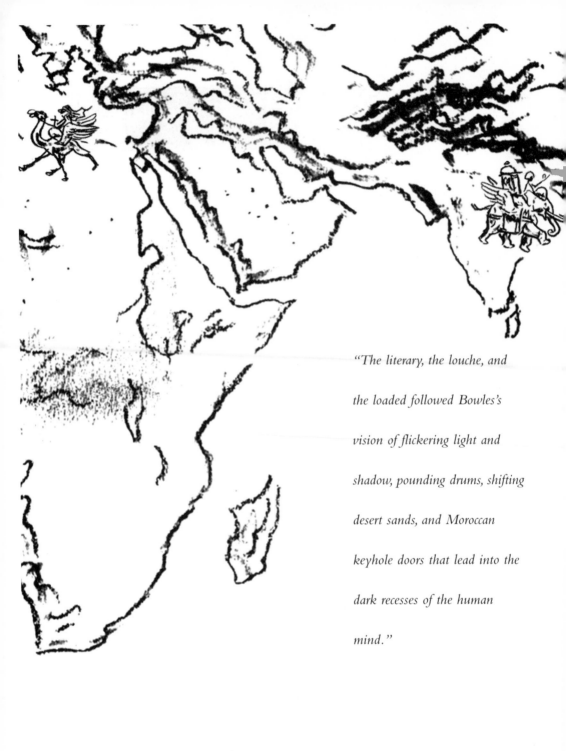

"The literary, the louche, and the loaded followed Bowles's vision of flickering light and shadow, pounding drums, shifting desert sands, and Moroccan keyhole doors that lead into the dark recesses of the human mind."

1   Africa to Australasia

Paul Bowles
Dreaming in Tangier

Victoria Brooks

It is a balmy night. A night of 1,001 stars. Outside her suite overlooking the mosque is a sitting room shaped like a cupola. She has thrown the windows wide to the sounds of the ancient Medina, to the drums of the women, to the ancient and reverent song of the muezzins—to her dreams. When the 4:00 a.m. call of the muezzins comes, she dreams of a young man who invites her to a concert held in a large, timeless garden edged with sunset splashes of fragrant mimosa and purple bougainvillea. The garden is shaded by date palms that sway like belly dancers and is flanked by high walls washed in white. Above, the sky is a sea of shimmering blue.

The young man in her dream is well spoken and elegant. He exudes brilliance as if it were a hot white light. She wonders if he is the actor Steve McQueen. She knows he is famous. His words to her evoke mystery and promise, maybe even wisdom. As he speaks, the garden becomes a yellow desert filled with the sound of flutes and drums. He speaks gently of his passions: travel, music, literature, and Morocco. She gazes at him, marveling at the oceanic depth of his teal eyes, his gaze as profound and entrancing as an Arabian sheikh's. Moving closer, he gently kisses her mouth.

She awakens. The experience has begun.

JUST A 20-MINUTE WALK from Place de France in Tangier, Morocco, is Paul Bowles's three-and-a-half-room flat, located in a nondescript suburban four-story building. The apartments sit atop a convenience store stocked with detergent, Coca-Cola, and plastic bottles of Sidi Ali and Olmos mineral water. Today the store is closed and the cheap goods are protected by rolling aluminum shutters. The entrance to the building is in the rear. The small metal elevator that brings visitors and pilgrims to Bowles's door creaks as it ascends. The safe, middle-class street outside is empty, except for a few neighborhood children playing jacks. Bowles lives alone, looked after by a trusted manservant. Born in 1910, the dreamer will soon be 89. His blue eyes are as cloudy as milky tea, but his memories are vivid.

When I first see the author, I find him wrapped in an old brown housecoat and woolen blankets on his monastic single bed. Around him are the items usually found in a sickroom: Kleenex, aspirins, sinus medicine, a glass with a straw, books and papers he can no longer see. Outside his comfortable, lived-in apartment, tall palms housing twittering birds shudder slightly in the cool Atlantic air of spring, much as his lungs do when he breathes. In his still-agile spectator's mind, he is aware of the details of life beyond his window. He was, is, the ultimate dreamer—a transcendent creator, a wizard of the written word. His brilliance remains untouched by the heavy cloak of age he is forced to wear. His brilliance is still a hot white light that pierces the veneer of humanity.

At Port de Tangier, just a few miles from where the old dreamer rests, a ferry opens its white painted metal mouth to expel trucks, cars, campers, Land Rovers, workers, and passengers. Waiting like an expectant horde of mosquitoes are the touts. Ragged and unshaven, they loll and wait and smoke, stubbing their cigarettes on the litter-strewn ground. The ferry made no sound as it slid through the Strait of Gibraltar, but they know it has arrived. The knowledge coils them like springs. The tourists have arrived. The litany of the touts begins.

"Come with me. Come with me," one cries.

"You will lose your way. You may be robbed," another shouts.

Like barracuda, they follow the tourists warily but aggressively with their hungry, shifty eyes. "A room at a good hotel, first-class, clean, cheap," several cajole.

"I will guide you through the Casbah," others promise. "Come with me. Come with me."

This is Port de Tangier, where the ferries arrive from Algeciras, Spain, where touts slouch and wait, where crumpled Marvel and Gitane packs cover the customs house floor just as they did when Nelson Dyar, Paul Bowles's protagonist in the nightmarish novel *Let It Come Down*, first arrived.

It is a humid late-summer day in 1947. A parade of porters, dressed like poor physicians in stained blue cotton, carry the traveler's burden through the tight knots of touts to a fleet of ancient, beatup Mercedes, Citroën, and Renault cabs. In the cavernous boots of the old-fashioned taxis, the sweating porters deposit 13 trunks, one of which is a makeshift library heavy with books. The others are treasure chests stuffed with elegant clothes: a few pale tropical suits of silk and linen; a straw hat woven in Panama, still in its narrow wooden box; and, for lounging, a striped silk-and-cotton djellaba purchased by the dreamer

The narrow, twisting lanes and alleys of Tangier lead one into the mystery that is Morocco. Victoria Brooks

in a market in Fez, where he had spent most of that summer. Carefully wrapped in the clothes is a heavy tape recorder, along with notebooks and pens for writing. The dreamer has truly arrived. He is young and handsome, blond and blue-eyed, slim and elegant. He is the still-youthful Paul Bowles.

The dreamer gropes in his pockets for coins for the porters. He looks up and admires the whiteness of the sky. It is like the inside of an oyster shell, like the painted houses of Tangier that are capped by ceramic-tiled roofs whose color and shape mimic the waves and hue of the sea.

From 1923 to 1956, Tangier was an international zone, a twilight one-night stand that danced with naked abandon to the dubious tune of resident diplomatic agents from nine nations: France, Spain, Britain, Portugal, Sweden, Holland, Belgium, Italy, and the United States. Its special status meant it was a free-money market and almost no one was denied entry. It was an anything-goes town. It was what author William Burroughs called the "Interzone." Its wide-open nature attracted the wealthy and the louche, the artist and the exile. And some were all of these.

Paul Bowles was lured to Morocco by a vivid dream on a balmy New York City evening in 1947, the smell of spring, of change itself, tangible in the air. It was a dream that took him back to Tangier where he had spent a deliciously exotic summer 16 years earlier in 1931 with composer Aaron Copland, his friend and mentor. The dream had been launched in France on the advice of novelist Gertrude Stein, who had told Bowles, "Go to Tangier." Nearly 70 years later, Bowles says to me in his apartment, "It was to be a lark, a one-summer stand."

Bowles had purchased passage for Copland and himself from Marseilles to Tangier, but just before they sailed, the captain of the *Imérethie II* announced an itinerary change to Ceuta, a Spanish possession in Morocco on a peninsula that juts into the Mediterranean Sea 75 miles northeast of Tangier. The 20-year-old Bowles stood alone on the ferry's planked deck at dawn, imagining the summer heat of Tangier "like a Turkish bath" as he leaned against the salt-sprayed rail deep in thought. His sharp young eyes were trained on the rugged scribble of the mountains of Algeria, and he was filled with a sense of excitement. Then, as he writes in his autobiography *Without Stopping*, his dreamer's vision turned inside out as he gave form to his "unreasoned conviction that certain areas of the earth's surface contained more magic than others." This conviction, this view of himself, initiated his self-exile in Tangier. To Bowles, his flight was akin to escaping from a prison whose bars were the conventions and confines of the Western world.

On that first trip in 1931, Bowles and Copland disembarked for their summer lark in Ceuta with so much luggage that they needed a small detachment of porters. As soon as they could, the pair boarded a narrow-gauge train for

Tangier. On arrival they booked into El Minzah, a new deluxe hotel, when they couldn't get a room at the Grand Hôtel Villa de France, which Gertrude Stein had recommended.

To this day, Bowles wonders about the reason for the change in the ship's itinerary. "It's still unknown to me," he tells me with a shake of his head, his old eyes misted with the past and the mystery of the unknown.

The change in destination did nothing to transform his destiny, however. Bowles's initial look at the North African landscape became the first few strokes on a paper canvas that was soon sealed and signed with the indelible ink of his existence in Tangier and his travels throughout Morocco. The first time he saw Tangier, he says, "I loved it more than any place I'd seen in my life."

Still, it wasn't until 1947 that Bowles was able to settle in Tangier. He had already gained a considerable reputation as a stage composer, having written scores for Tennessee Williams's *The Glass Menagerie* and *Summer and Smoke*; William Saroyan's *Love's Old Sweet Song*; Lillian Hellman's *The Watch on the Rhine*; and *Horse Eats Hat*, directed by Orson Welles for the Federal Theater Project.

His short story "A Distant Episode" had been published by the *Partisan Review* in January 1947 and was critically acclaimed. The story tells of a condescending American linguistics professor whose tongue is cut out by nomads when he wanders off the tourist path. The professor becomes a captive and is paraded through the North African desert, miming obscene gestures taught to him by those he once thought he was superior to. It is a tale that renders the so-called civilized world and all its intellectual trappings meaningless, an account of the perils that may face Westerners who stray into uncharted territories. Tangier was, and is, such a place. The central conceit of "A Distant Episode" is Bowles's recurring theme, his trademark and his warning.

After his talent was recognized, Bowles was offered an advance by the U.S. publisher Doubleday for a yet-to-be-written novel that he would eventually title *The Sheltering Sky*. On the brink of literary success, he booked a one-way passage in June 1947 from New York to Morocco. The writer Jane Auer Bowles, his wife since 1938, was to follow in six months. She was a lesbian, he a homosexual.

But it wasn't only the Bowleses who were enticed by the exotic allure of Tangier. European émigrés, American expatriates, and literary renegades of every stripe descended on the sybaritic city where anything could be had for very little money, where homosexuality was accepted, where use of the local *kif* (cannabis and tobacco) and *majoun* (hashish jam) were commonplace, where the lifestyle was decadently delicious, sometimes even depraved.

As Bowles notes in *Without Stopping*, Tangier struck him as a dream city: "Its topography was rich in prototypal dream scenes: covered streets like corridors . . . hidden terraces high above the sea, streets consisting only of steps . . . as well as the classical dream equipment of tunnels, ramparts, ruins, dungeons and cliffs."

Bowles wrote as he traveled in Morocco, constructing his first novel from within his soul, layering it with the details and textures of North Africa. Much of his writing was done while lying in French pension beds. But in the autumn of 1947 he purchased a villa in Tangier for $500 and settled down to complete *The Sheltering Sky*.

Paul and Jane Bowles would always travel often and far, but their hearts would remain caught in the gossamer web of Morocco. The dreamer's talented and tempestuous wife often flitted like a nervous butterfly from Connecticut or New York and back, following her whims and women (New York ladies and Berber country girls). In between she practiced her craft (the novel *Two Serious Ladies*, the play *In the Summer House*, and a short-story collection *Plain Pleasures*). Jane Bowles, too, belonged to Tangier. After a long illness, though, she died of a stroke in 1973 at the age of 56.

Cecil Beaton, Truman Capote, Gore Vidal, James Baldwin, and Tennessee Williams all visited Tangier during Bowles's first few years in the city. David Herbert, second son of the Earl of Pembroke, who was once described by guest Ian Fleming as the "Queen Mother of Tangier," and Woolworth heiress Barbara Hutton held court in the city, where expatriates were nicknamed *tangerinos* and natives were dubbed *tanjawis*.

After her third divorce in 1946, Hutton purchased a stone palace inside the Casbah, the fortress that stands within the walls of the old Arab quarter known as the Medina. Hutton threw parties featuring camels, snake charmers, belly dancers, and "blue men" brought in from Morocco's High Atlas Mountains. The blue men are a tribe of tall, handsome nomads whose skin is stained indigo from the dye in their turbans and flowing desert robes. The "poor little rich girl" entertained like a nomad queen in a Hollywood extravaganza, wearing glittering Moroccan caftans while seated on a throne. When not in a party mood, she retired to her bedchamber, and disappointed guests went in search of pleasure elsewhere.

More than a half century later, Bowles shares a memory of her with me: "Barbara Hutton was so weak from reducing and pills she had to be carried through the streets of the Medina when she left her palace." He "was not impressed with her dramatics," her messy life, and preferred to distance himself from the decadent fray. Over the years, his desire for solitude has been frequently

All over Morocco, timeless scenes are re-created every day. Here, on the outskirts of Tangier, Bedouin live the dream. Victoria Brooks

interrupted by the parade of socialites, artists, exiles, and escape artists who have passed through Tangier's revolving door and thrust Bowles into the role of the city's unofficial, often reluctant ambassador.

In the 1950s, a motley crew of literary renegades, including Beat writers Allen Ginsberg and Jack Kerouac and their godfather William Burroughs, made the scene. In 1954 Burroughs followed Bowles to Tangier after reading *The Sheltering Sky*, a novel written in a dazzling, visionary stream-of-consciousness style with more than a few echoes of the work of Albert Camus and Edgar Allan Poe, the authors Bowles most admired. Bowles's masterpiece of three American postwar travelers adrift on an emotional voyage in the desolate yet beautiful North African Sahara explores their creator's powerful theme: the dream/nightmare that awaits the culturally and morally estranged.

Doubleday, which had already paid Bowles an advance, refused to accept the book "for not being a novel," so the manuscript began a yearlong journey across publishers' desks before its release in September 1949 by the English publisher John Lehmann. A month later an American edition was put out by New Directions, and soon after the novel became an international bestseller and received powerful critical praise. In 1959 Norman Mailer wrote in *Advertisements for Myself*: "Paul Bowles opened the world of Hip. He let in the murder, the drugs, the incest, the death of the Square . . . the call of the orgy, the end of civilization; he invited all of us to these themes."

The Sheltering Sky's mystique was heightened by the fact that Bowles had put himself into a *majoun*-induced state to write his character Port Moresby's grippingly horrific death scene. Local drugs were often used by the Tangier literary set to tap into their subconscious minds and write in the "proper style."

Burroughs, whom the locals called El Hombre Invisible, lived in Tangier for four years. In a small room in the city's Hôtel El Muniria, he wrote his hallucinatory satire *Naked Lunch*, a fictional rendering of his own descent into the hellish world of the heroin addict. Later, when Bowles and I rendezvous on the outskirts of Tangier, he conjures up an image of Burroughs: "He was always dressed to his fingertips in black, with black gloves that he would slowly and theatrically peel off, one finger at a time, like an undertaker." In the beginning, Bowles was aloof with Burroughs, but later, he admits, he came to "admire his humor."

In *Let It Come Down*, Bowles writes that "If a man was not on his way anywhere . . . then the best thing for him to do is sit back and be." The literary, the louche, and the loaded followed his vision of flickering light and shadow, pounding drums, shifting desert sands, and Moroccan keyhole doors that lead into the dark recesses of the human mind. Over mint tea, sherry, *kif*, and Marlboroughs, sybarites and eccentrics reclined low in the scuffed brown leather chairs of the Café de Paris on Place de France, basking in the intense light of Bowles's oracle.

Now, outside the café, I watch the continuing pageant in Rue de la Liberté: beggars with outstretched, unwashed palms etched with want; darkly handsome men, both young and old, in brightly hued pantaloons or tassel-hooded djellabas; Berber women with round peasant faces obscured by the shade of their wide-brimmed straw hats, black pom-poms dancing to the soft beating of their bare feet as they walk their wares to the souks; and Arab women swaddled from shining midnight eyes to pale toes in voluptuous white cotton. It's an ageless procession of Arab commerce and culture, and all of it unfolds just as it did in Bowles's heyday. During one of our meetings, he told me gnomically: "If we weren't eccentrics, we wouldn't have been here." And now I see what he meant. All around me are shopkeepers selling faux antiques, boxes of camel bones from the Sahara encrusted with amber and silver, and leather slippers from Fez as soft and yellow as butter. The shopkeepers are entirely men, and they place their carved wooden chairs strategically on the street, vying for attention among the beggars in cheap Western garb and old men in fezzes and stained caftans.

The Tangier of past and present become one, then separate. The hours still pass as if in a dream, but today the Café de Paris is no longer an appropriated salon where the Bowleses and the literary renegades discuss their muses. These days it brims with gloomy unemployed Arab men who hover over mint tea in glasses that are stormy with milk.

The renegades, infidels, and exiles took everything they could from Tangier. And when the Moroccan oasis no longer offered the free status of an international zone, they scattered. For them it was a place to use like a cheap, exciting prostitute, a place to take selfish pleasure for a night, a year, or until the thrill was gone. But Bowles stayed, and he, and the City of the Dream, still mesmerize.

Yes, the Master remained, centered in his own vision, to write more novels and stories and to translate the works of talented Moroccan authors, continuing to offer his revelations to the world, his rare gift wrapped in sunlight and shadow, extreme beauty and disturbing discovery.

She dreams again. This time she lies sleeping in Tangier's famous Hôtel El Minzah in a suite overlooking the waters of the Strait of Gibraltar and the sleek ferries from Algeciras that slide into the harbor like a hallucination from Paul Bowles's world.

The experience has begun. It is Sunday. She dreams she is riding in an aged Mercedes taxi down Boulevard Pasteur, down a long, empty avenue lined with bougainvillea and palms, the outstretched, sun-baked fronds of the latter reaching heavenward as if seeking Allah's benediction. Her driver is named Ali. The sun shines high and clear. The sky is as translucent and white as a pearl. Abruptly she tells Ali to stop.

She has spotted the old dreamer perched on a folding stool at the side of the deserted road. Leaving the taxi and approaching him, she sits beside his stool: she, a child, a convert, a pilgrim; he, her oracle. Birds chirp discreetly in the trees, while on a distant hill a herd of goats bleat, the sounds fading away like old memories.

He regales her with his travels to Sri Lanka, Santiago de Cuba, Panama, Berlin, Mexico, and Central America. He tells her of New York and his dislike of large cities, then, when she asks him what wisdom he has acquired during his decades in Tangier, he replies, "Patience." Then he adds, "This is as good a place as any. It has been good to me."

He is elegant, even more so than when she dreamt about him as Steve McQueen. His eyes are as deep and mysterious as his soul, as entrancing as a sheikh's. He has wisdom, charm, humor. She loves him. He is Paul Bowles. She knows she is blessed just by sitting near him. She puts her hand over his. He rises with difficulty, then walks in the sunlight like some old god, stopping to rest on the folding stool when he tires. Too soon the manservant notes his master's exhaustion and tells her they must go.

She gives Bowles a gentle lover's kiss on his soft old mouth. As she watches his battered gray Citroën drive slowly away, she vaguely remembers something important he once wrote in Without Stopping: *"I had always been vaguely certain that sometime during my life I should come into a magic place which, in disclosing its secrets, would give me wisdom and ecstasy, perhaps even death."*

She raises her eyes to the pale horizon and sees Tangier like a scrawl of mauve ink on a page of his dream. It is his Tangier, refracted like a diamond through her veil of tears.

(Note: A few weeks before his 89th birthday, Paul Bowles died on November 18, 1999, of heart failure in the Italian Hospital in Tangier. I had planned to return to Morocco to present him with a copy of *Literary Trips*, with this story in it. If only I could have sat by his narrow bed and held his gnarled old hand one last time.)

Many have come and gone, the famous and the infamous, but Paul Bowles endured in Tangier for more than 50 years. Victoria Brooks

The Writer's Trail

Following in the Footsteps

Destination: Morocco's raffish port city Tangier is down-at-the-heels but fascinating. In 1949 Truman Capote called it "that ragamuffin city." Since then its decaying atmosphere has put many tourists off, but if you're looking for truly memorable experiences in your travels, this is the place to visit. The wide-open bars of Tangier's international-zone days where the notorious and the famous could be seen enjoying a "walk" on the wild side don't exist anymore (after Moroccan independence in 1956, alcohol was banned in the Medina), but Paul Bowles's City of the Dream is still a feast for the senses. Marvel at the splendid Moorish architecture and the intricate labyrinth of the Medina. Haggle with hawkers in the souks. Drink in the sight of Arab women and men in velvet, silk, cotton, or brightly colored rayon djellabas moving through tangled streets bursting with all that life has to offer. Enter the Dream.

Location: Tangier is on Morocco's northern coast at the west end of the Strait of Gibraltar. It is an ocean's breath away from Europe; only nine miles of sea separate it from Spain.

Getting There: Royal Air Maroc is the magic carpet to Morocco and flies from North America and major cities around the globe. There is usually a stopover in Casablanca, Air Maroc's hub. For information call 1-800-344-6726 or the airline's New York City office at (212) 974-3850. In Canada call (514) 285-1937. Air Maroc's Web site is *www.royalairmaroc.com*. Iberia, British Airways, and Air France also fly from Spain, London, or Paris to Tangier. If you go by sea, there are ferry routes (passenger and vehicle) from Spain, France, and Gibraltar. Some routes also feature hydrofoils. From Algeciras, Spain, it is two and a half hours by car ferry to Tangier. You can also take a ferry from Algeciras to the Spanish duty-free territory of Ceuta (one and a half hours). From Sète, in southern France, the crossing to Tangier takes 36 hours. There are also ferries from Almería (six and a half hours) and Málaga (seven hours) in Spain to the Spanish duty-free port of Melilla. Tickets can be purchased from travel agencies or from ferry-company offices at port terminals (unreliable on weekends) in all these places. Avoid the ferries, if at all possible, in July and August when they are packed with migrant workers. Passports must be stamped before disembarkation. Longer routes usually warrant reservations. Call your local Moroccan tourist board for schedules and contact numbers.

Orientation: Tangier's Grand Socco (Large Square) is located just outside the walls of the Medina (Arab quarter) and links the old city with the Ville Nouvelle (European section). The Medina straddles a nearby hill. Its main street, Rue es Siaghin, leads to the Petit Socco (Small Square) in the heart of the Medina. The Petit Socco, bordered by cafés and old residences, is where the literary renegades hung out and where the action still is. Walk downhill (southeast) to the port from here. The Casbah is on a cliff in the northwest corner of the Medina. Follow Rue des Chrétiens and its continuation, Rue Ben Raisouli, until you arrive at the lower gate of this unique section of the city. The Ville Nouvelle is west and south of the Medina. The international airport is eight miles (about a 30-minute drive) from the center of Tangier.

 Tip: Keep in mind poet Allen Ginsberg's definition of hip: "innately understanding and all-tolerant."

Getting Around: Wander by foot in the Medina. For trips in the Ville Nouvelle, to the beaches, or to the Grottes d'Hercule, take one of the cheap and plentiful taxis. Car rental is expensive, but you'll want a vehicle to travel cross-country. Offices of the international companies (Hertz, Avis) can all be found in Tangier, but local agencies are cheaper.

Literary Sleeps

Hôtel El Minzah: This famous Moorish-style, 142-room, 17-suite hotel was built in 1930 and is well situated near the Medina. Paul Bowles stayed here on his first trip to Tangier in 1931. The Grand Hôtel Villa de France, where Gertrude Stein told him to stay, is now boarded up. A suite at El Minzah will reward you with a fabulous view of Tangier, the Strait of Gibraltar, and even Spain on a clear day. The swimming pool, gardens, workout room, and spa are welcome havens from the hustle of Tangier. 85 Rue de la Liberté. Tel.: (212-9) 93 58 85. Fax: (212-9) 93 45 46. Expensive.

Hôtel Continental: Atmospheric and friendly 60-room hotel in the Medina where some scenes of the film version of *The Sheltering Sky* were shot (ask in the hotel shop to see photos taken during

Tangier's whiteness, as reflected in buildings such as Hôtel El Muniria, adds to the city's shimmering translucency. Victoria Brooks

the filming). The hotel's seductive character makes up for its worn-around-the-edges quality. One of the hotel bellmen has worked in the hotel since he was a child and will regale you with stories of the past. Ask for a room overlooking the port. Book ahead; the hotel is sometimes packed with tour groups or film crews. 36 Rue Dar El Baroud. Tel.: (212-9) 93 10 24. Fax: (212-9) 93 11 43. Inexpensive.

Hôtel El Muniria: This is the small hotel in the Ville Nouvelle where, in room 9, William Burroughs wrote *Naked Lunch*. The establishment is English-owned and has rooms with showers. Some rooms have excellent views (numbers 7 and 8). Trendy bar with superb view is either crowded with young Moroccans or empty. 1 Rue Magellan. Inexpensive.

Hôtel Palais Jamai, Fez: If you make it to Fez, and you should, stay where Paul and Jane Bowles did. Jane freaked out on *majoun* in one of the 19th-century hotel's suites and never touched the stuff again. The building was beautifully redone in 1999, but for the most authentic experience ask for a suite in the old palace. The 115-room, 25-suite hotel and its beautiful gardens and pool area overlook Fez El Bali, the most fascinating Medina in Morocco. You'll have no trouble hearing the calls of the muezzins at 4:00 a.m. here. Bab Guissa, Fez El Bali. Tel.: (212-5) 63 43 31. Fax: (212-5) 63 50 96. Extremely expensive.

Literary Sites

Café Central: This café, at the end of Rue es Siaghin in the Petit Socco, is where William Burroughs was inspired to begin *Naked Lunch*. If you linger long enough here, or at any of the nearby cafés, you'll probably be approached by a Moroccan selling *kif*.

Café de Paris: Located on Place de France in the Ville Nouvelle, this is the spot to sip and people-watch. In mid-afternoon, the café is still something of a gay hangout, but unless you're aware of this, you won't notice. Mint tea is dirt-cheap and the old leather chairs are comfortable.

Tip: Tangier is rife with pilferers. Never let any valuables, including your sunglasses, leave your hand.

Casbah: Located inside the walls of the Casbah is Sidi Hosni, Barbara Hutton's stone palace. Here she threw lavish parties for guests Charlie Chaplin, Maria Callas, Cecil Beaton, Aristotle Onassis, Claudette Colbert, Greta Garbo, and the literary set, which included Paul and Jane Bowles. Hutton's former palace is located opposite a café with a psychedelic wall painting. You may need a guide. The Woolworth heiress actually had certain streets in the Casbah widened to accommodate her Rolls-Royce. North of the *mechouar*, or courtyard, of Dar El Makhzen (the former sultan's palace and now a museum) is the Rue Riad Sultan where, near the Sultan's Gardens, you'll find a door that leads to Le Détroit, an upstairs café. When it was the exclusive Thousand and One Nights Restaurant, it was owned by writer Brion Gysin, who entertained his famous friends, including the Rolling Stones (Brian Jones once produced a record here) and Paul Bowles. It was also notable for the trance musicians who played here in the 1960s. The view is sensational, but the restaurant is overrun with tour groups.

Grottes d'Hercule: These natural limestone caves are six miles from Tangier. Cecil Beaton held a notorious beach party here for his literary friends. In one cave, champagne was served, and in the other, hashish. Although you can no longer imbibe decadent pleasures, unless you bring your own, the caves have a spectacular view and are well worth the trip. In classical mythology, Hercules is said to have rested here after creating the so-called Pillars of Hercules: Gibraltar and Ceuta.

Fez: In 1931 Paul Bowles told Gertrude Stein that this city "is full of flies and dust, and rats knock everything over on the tables at night. It is quite dirty and very beautiful." The ancient Medina hasn't changed a bit. In a letter to a friend, Bowles wrote: "Fez I shall make my home some day!" He never did. Tangier claimed him instead. But if you only have time for one other city in Morocco, make it Fez.

Tip: Before you take photographs of people, ask their permission, and don't be surprised if they insist on payment.

Icon Pastimes

Wander the warren of streets and alleys of Tangier with Paul Bowles's vision as your guide. Enjoy the never-ending pageant of the city and watch the many parts that its citizens play. Sit for as long as you want in the Café de Paris or any of the *salons de thé* where Bowles once spent long hours with his wife, Jane, and other writers and artists, both foreign and Moroccan. Purchase a djellaba in a souk, and don't forget to bargain. It's part of the Moroccan experience and is expected.

Contacts

Moroccan Tourist Office: In New York City call (212) 557-2520/1/2 or fax (212) 949-8148. In Canada call (514) 842-8111/2 or fax (514) 842-5316. Web site: *www.tourism-in-morocco.com*. In Tangier contact the Morocco National Tourist Board: 29 Boulevard Pasteur. Tel.: (212-9) 93 82 39.

In a Literary Mood

Books

Bowles, Paul. *The Collected Stories of Paul Bowles: 1939–1976.* Santa Rosa, CA: Black Sparrow Press, 1991. This sweeping compendium includes some of the finest short stories ever written.

_____. *A Hundred Camels in the Courtyard.* San Francisco: City Lights, 1986. These four tales dwell on *kif*, not alcohol, as the socially accepted drug. The work is also available as a two-CD audiobook from Cadmus Editions (*www.cadmus-editions.com*). Bowles, of course, reads his own stories.

_____. *In Touch: The Letters of Paul Bowles.* Edited by Jeffrey Miller. New York: Farrar, Straus, and Giroux, 1994. Six decades of absorbing, fascinating correspondence with Gertrude Stein, Allen Ginsberg, Aaron Copland, and many other famous personalities.

_____. *Let It Come Down.* Santa Rosa, CA: Black Sparrow Press, 1997. Exotic, violently gripping novel with Tangier as the protagonist during the time it was an anything-goes international zone. Although Bowles states in his introduction that "The city celebrated in these pages has long ceased to exist," Tangier still feels like a decadent, seamy place from the razor edge of Bowles's incredible mind. As for the novel, the story is both intriguing and terrifying. Hold on tight to reality while you read it.

_____. *The Sheltering Sky.* New York: Vintage International, 1990. The novel that elevated Bowles to cult status. Utterly compelling, brilliant, and hallucinatory story about three young Americans of the postwar generation who fall into North Africa's psychological heart of darkness.

_____. *The Spider's House.* London: Sphere Books, 1991. The chasm between Arab and Western cultures is dramatized in this novel with brutal honesty against the backdrop of the 1954 Moroccan nationalist uprising in Fez.

_____. *Without Stopping: An Autobiography*. Toronto: Longmans Canada, 1972. Bowles's own story is elusive and full of wisdom, just like the great author himself.

Burroughs, William S. *Naked Lunch*. New York: Grove Press, 1990. Burroughs's best-known book, written between 1954 and 1957 in Tangier, had to be rescued from his hotel-room floor by Allen Ginsberg. First published in Paris in 1959 by the notorious Olympia Press, it was finally released in the United States in 1962. The landmark obscenity trial that ensued served to help end literary censorship in America.

Dillon, Millicent. *A Little Original Sin: The Life and Works of Jane Bowles*. New York: Holt, Rinehart and Winston, 1981. This is the only biography about Paul Bowles's fascinating wife. Tennessee Williams called her "the most important writer of prose fiction in modern American letters."

_____. *You Are Not I: A Portrait of Paul Bowles*. Los Angeles: University of California Press, 1998. This is the latest Bowles biography, but it's also something of a memoir about him, too. The author has had a long relationship with Bowles and has been involved in a number of books concerning him and his wife, Jane.

Green, Michelle. *The Dream at the End of the World: Paul Bowles and the Literary Renegades in Tangier*. London: Bloomsbury, 1991. Excellent account of the people who made Tangier a magnetic city when it was an international zone.

Sawyer-Lauçanno, Christopher. *An Invisible Spectator: A Biography of Paul Bowles*. New York: Weidenfeld & Nicolson, 1989. Bowles dislikes this biography and advises against reading it. You might want to judge for yourself.

Guidebooks

Gordon, Frances Linzee, Damien Simonis, and Dorinda Talbot. *Morocco*. 4th ed. Hawthorn, Australia: Lonely Planet Publications, 1998. The only guide appropriate for budget travelers.

Knopf Guides. *Morocco*. New York: Alfred A. Knopf, 1994. This guide's easy-read format makes it a practical traveler's companion. It also features great color photographs. Paul Bowles's elusiveness is revealed by a reference on page 125 that erroneously states the author died in 1986.

Stannard, Dorothy, ed. *Morocco*. London: APA Publications, Insight Guides, 1998. Written by local writers, this guide includes interesting Tangier tidbits such as "The Novelist as Tourist" and a description of Barbara Hutton's infamous Tangier parties by the late David Herbert. Also contains beautiful photography and artwork.

Films/Videos

Aldrich, William, and Jeremy Thomas (producers). *The Sheltering Sky*. Bernardo Bertolucci (director). Warner Bros., 1990. Warner Home Video. Cast: John Malkovich, Campbell Scott, and Debra Winger. Paul Bowles's classic tale of three Americans adrift in the brutal North African landscape is narrated by the author himself, who also makes a cameo appearance. Although Bowles likes Winger's interpretation of her role, he is unhappy with Malkovich's and calls the movie's ending "unforgivable."

Baichwal, Jennifer, and Nick de Pencier (producers). *Let It Come Down: The Life of Paul Bowles*. Jennifer Baichwal (director). Documentary. Canada: Requisite Productions, 1998. Distributed by Zeitgeist Films. A profile of the writer-composer in his 88th year that features candid interviews with him in his Tangier home, as well as a recording of a final rendezvous with friends Allen

Ginsberg and William Burroughs in New York (1995) when Bowles was honored by a Lincoln Center presentation of his music by the Eos Orchestra.

Conklin, Gary (producer and director). *Paul Bowles in Morocco.* Documentary. U.S.: Mystic Fire Video, 1986. Conversations with Bowles about the lifestyle of Tangier's famous expatriates and the author's belief that an undercurrent of magic exists in Morocco. Video can be purchased at *www.mysticfire.com/TBBowles.html.*

Warnow, Catherine, and Regina Weinrich (producers and directors). *Paul Bowles: The Complete Outsider.* Documentary. U.S.: First Run Features, 1994. Available on video.

Web Sites

Paul Bowles: *www.charm.net/~brooklyn/People/PaulBowles.html.* There are no official Bowles Web sites, but this unofficial one has interesting links to the Beat writers who were close to Bowles.

Cadmus Editions: *www.cadmus-editions.com.* A miscellany of Bowles material can be found here.

T. E. Lawrence
Arabian Nights in Jordan

Joyce Gregory Wyels

A SENSE OF DÉJÀ VU creeps over me as desert shadows lengthen. Where have I seen this stark landscape before? Then a camel ambles across my line of vision and I remember: Omar Sharif led Peter O'Toole through shimmering stretches of this moonscape in the film *Lawrence of Arabia*.

Ziad, our Jordanian guide, confirms that the movie was shot in Wadi Rum, the vast southern desert that spills across Jordan into Saudi Arabia. Pointing at the ground for emphasis, he adds, "I tell you something. The real Lawrence, he also rode with the Arabs, right here."

Real and unreal, past and present blend effortlessly in the otherworldly landscapes of Jordan. Half-remembered names from the Bible reemerge as the settings for daily headlines. The ruins of Roman cities, Byzantine churches, Islamic and Crusader castles lie jumbled together with little regard for timelines. Thomas Edward (T. E.) Lawrence, known to millions as Lawrence of Arabia, captures the feeling in his epic *Seven Pillars of Wisdom*: "Past and future flowed over us like an uneddying river."

My first glimpse of this historical disarray takes place in Amman. Climbing Jebel al-Qala'a, one of the city's seven hills, or *jebels*, my companions and I reach the Citadel, where T-shirted youngsters chase a soccer ball around fallen pillars. Below us a Roman amphitheater spreads out fanlike amid boxy modern buildings. Only since World War I has Amman, known as Rabbath Ammon in the Old Testament and Philadelphia during Greco-Roman times, gained prominence as the capital of the Hashemite Kingdom of Jordan.

Modern Jordan, in fact, traces its beginnings to the era of the Great War. By 1914 the Ottoman Turks had ruled the Arab lands that now constitute Jordan and its neighbors for nearly 400 years. When the Ottoman Empire allied itself with Germany, the British offered support for a long-simmering Arab drive for independence. Following the successful Arab Revolt (and subsequent political shenanigans), Transjordan—now Jordan—was carved out of the Arabian Desert.

East of Amman, our party of four photographers explore hunting lodges and caravansaries with names like Qasr al-Kharanah and Quseir Amra, creations of the nomadic eighth-century Islamic Umayyads. Even farther east, on the road to Iraq, we come upon a crumbling complex of black basalt in the former oasis of Azraq, where the chronicle of human habitation extends back to the Paleolithic period. More recently, Qasr al-Azraq sheltered Lawrence and his Arab companions as they waged guerrilla strikes against Turkish targets.

Entering the ruins, I am startled to see a man standing in the shadows of the otherwise empty fort. He introduces himself as Nader, a member of the local Druse community. The Druse, Nader informs me, were members of a religious sect that had started in 11th-century Egypt and spread eastward. Showing me around the gutted rooms, he pauses at the southern gate tower and declares, "Here Colonel Lawrence and his men sat at night around the fire." Perhaps sensing some skepticism on my part, he adds, "Men of my village camped here with Lawrence in the winter of 1917. It was a cold winter."

Lawrence himself, in *Seven Pillars of Wisdom*, writes: "On stormy nights we brought in brushwood and dung and lit a great fire in the middle of the floor. About it would be drawn the carpets and the saddle-sheepskins, and in its light we would tell over our own battles, or hear the visitors' traditions. . . . We dreamed ourselves into the spirit of the place; sieges and feasting, raids, murders, love-singing in the night."

With Azraq as their base, Lawrence and his men conducted their own raids, blowing up bridges and dynamiting the railroad that snaked from Damascus in the north to Medina, far to the south. Their hit-and-run strikes disrupted Turkish communications and provided support to the main British army.

Lawrence threw himself into the task with great enthusiasm. Toward the end of 1916, after a meeting with the Arab leader Feisal, he wrote to a fellow officer in Cairo: "The situation is so interesting that I think I will fail to come back. I want to rub off my British habits and go off with Feisal for a bit." Resplendent in white silk Arab robes, he did just that. Later he wrote home: "It is by far the most wonderful time I have had. I have become a monomaniac about the job in hand, and have no interest or recollections except Arabian politics just now."

At the main door to the fortress, Nader asks me, smiling, "Can you close this?" Try as I might, I can't budge the thick stone slab. Even Lawrence remarked that "it took a great effort to start swinging, and at the end went shut with a clang and crash which made tremble the west wall of the old castle."

Prominent among Lawrence's fellow raiders was Sherif Ali ibn el Hussein; in Lawrence's words, "His beauty was a conscious weapon. He dressed spotlessly, all in black or all in white; and he studied gesture. Fortune had added physical perfection and unusual grace. . . . They made obvious the pluck which never yielded, which would have let him be cut to pieces, holding on." For me—and no doubt for countless other movie fans—Sherif Ali will always be the darkly handsome Omar Sharif.

By the time of his Azraq forays, Lawrence had already cemented his reputation as a brilliant, unconventional strategist, largely on the strength of his capture of Aqaba. Turkish forces, expecting a naval attack on the Red Sea port, had trained their artillery seaward. When Lawrence and his camel-mounted cohorts thundered in from the desert, the surprised Turks surrendered. The fall of Aqaba in July 1917 represented a major turning point for the British and for Lawrence personally. "After the capture of Aqaba," he later wrote, "things changed so much that I was no longer a witness of the Revolt, but a protagonist in the Revolt."

We plan to travel to Aqaba by way of the King's Highway, the 5,000-year-old route mentioned in the Bible. But first Ziad detours to the Roman city of Jerash. En route, he peppers us with questions about English words—*closer, farther, pretend, religion*—scribbling impromptu translations on a Kleenex box that he keeps on

The remains of the ancient Roman city of Jerash stand as a silent testament to the passage of time and the impermanence of empires. Joyce Gregory Wyels

the dash. "Let me to remember," Ziad says when a word eludes him. When our attention flags, he demands, "Look to me!" A barrage of gestures that sometimes requires his abandoning the steering wheel altogether accompanies "I don't know the word, but I try to make you understand." In our own self-interest, when he asks, "You understand me?" we chorus "Yes!"

Ziad sweetly undertakes to tutor me in spoken Arabic. *"Marhaba,"* he greets me each morning. *"Shukran,"* I say, thanking him as he performs little courtesies. Dutifully I practice the usual "I'm hungry/thirsty/tired" phrases. But lacking Ziad's linguistic bravado, I take refuge in the disclaimer *"Ana ma bifam Arabi,"* which Ziad assures me means "I don't speak Arabic."

Lawrence's knowledge of Arabic made him an invaluable liaison between the British and the Arabs. According to a member of the Imperial Camel Corps, "He was just a natural guerrilla leader, with a knowledge of the country, its people, its languages, its customs."

In May 1917, Lawrence drew praise from a Colonel Wilson: "His services have been of great value to me and the work he has carried out required both pluck and endurance." Only six months earlier, Wilson had pronounced him "a bumptious young ass."

S. C. Rolls, who later served as Lawrence's driver, described his first meeting with the idiosyncratic officer vividly: "The Egyptian foreman turned round and pointed with his whip at a group of Arabs. . . . I saw that the leader of the convoy was making his camel kneel. He came shuffling up to me, and I said: 'Allah yalla imshi—buzz off.' And he parted his kofia and I saw that his face was red . . . his eyes were blue grey, and there was a smile on his face. And he said, 'Is your captain with you?' I said, 'Yes, sir, certainly sir.' I was flabbergasted. That was Colonel Lawrence."

Years later, Lawrence's contempt for convention bedeviled his *Seven Pillars of Wisdom* editor. "Jeddah and Jidda used impartially throughout," the editor noted in one exchange. "Intentional?" Lawrence's reply was "Rather!" "Sherif Abd el Mayin . . . becomes el Main, el Mayein, el Muein, el Mayin, and el Muyein," the editor scolded. "Good egg," Lawrence parried. "I call this really ingenious." The problem, as Lawrence put it, was that "Arabic names won't go into English, exactly. . . . There are some 'scientific systems' of transliteration, helpful to people who know enough Arabic not to need helping, but a wash-out for the world. I spell my names anyhow, to show what rot the systems are."

From the King's Highway, my companions photograph landscapes reminiscent of the Grand Canyon. In Madaba—Medeba in the Bible, Madeba in *Seven Pillars*— we study the mosaic map of Jerusalem and the Holy Land in the Greek Orthodox Church of St. George. Stunning Byzantine mosaics also cover interior surfaces of a church on nearby Mount Nebo, overlooking the Dead Sea, said to be the site where Moses first glimpsed the Promised Land.

Just south of the Dead Sea, Lawrence fought perhaps the only "conventional" battle of his career. In January 1918, at the mountain village of Tafileh, Arab forces repelled a Turkish attack in what one historian called a "miniature masterpiece." Lawrence, on the basis of his report of the battle, won a military decoration. Self-mockingly, he wrote: "We should have more bright breasts in the Army if each man was able, without witnesses, to write out his own despatch." An Arab historian later disputed Lawrence's role in the battle, ascribing the victory to the Arab commander.

I am reminded of more recent hostilities when we stop at the Dead Sea. A young Palestinian mistakes me for one of a contingent of Italians merrily floating in the salt-laden water while humming snatches of French can-can music. When Abdullah discovers I am American, he delivers a short but impassioned speech. "We are all the same—Americans, Jordanians, Palestinians—all brothers under the skin. We want to live in peace." In a more subdued tone, he concludes, smiling, "Welcome to Jordan."

Not far from the Dead Sea, a ruined fortress rises on a craggy plateau 4,300 feet above sea level. Twelfth-century Crusaders built the castle known as Kerak to guard approaches to Jerusalem. With a group of schoolgirls on a field trip, we wander through rooms and subterranean passages occupied first by medieval knights and later by their conquerors under Saladin.

At Shobak, an imposing shell of a castle on an isolated peak, a tall, white-robed desert dweller with ebony skin proffers a silent greeting. In *Seven Pillars*, Lawrence describes a solitary journey to this castle in the winter of 1918, an icy odyssey that tested both camel and rider.

The two Crusader castles remind me of Lawrence's passion for medieval history and architecture. Starting at an early age, he traversed England, Wales, and France, exploring castles and fortresses. Even before the Arab Revolt, he journeyed through the Middle East as an archaeologist—possibly a cover for his espionage activities as a British intelligence officer.

That was certainly the case when he undertook a mapping expedition in the Sinai Peninsula, ostensibly to trace the route of the Israelites during their 40 years in the desert. Lawrence wrote to his mother: "We are obviously only meant as red herrings, to give an archaeological colour to a political job." In 1914, three years before he captured Aqaba, Lawrence visited the local Turkish governor, who forbade him, as he put it, "to photograph or archaeologize." Lawrence stated later: "I photographed what I could, I archaeologized everywhere."

Both the map of Jordan and *Seven Pillars* are peppered with *wadis*—Wadi Sirhan, Wadi Safra, Wadi Musa—a term that denotes a watercourse or valley. Thus our route southward parallels the Wadi Araba, which cuts a swath from the

Dead Sea (at 1,300 feet below sea level, the lowest point on the planet) to the Gulf of Aqaba, and extends to Africa's Great Rift Valley. Driving along the King's Highway, Ziad stops at a small shop, then hurries us out the back door. "You will see," he assures us when we ask why. The ground drops off steeply behind the building; it is simply the best place in the Wadi Araba to view the desert sunset, a silent light show of reds, yellows, oranges, and purples that foreshadows the vivid landscapes between Shobak and Aqaba.

In *Seven Pillars*, Lawrence makes frequent reference to dramatic sunsets. Riding west from Wadi Rum to Aqaba, he reflects upon his "outcast life among these Arabs" while facing the sunset: "fierce, stimulant, barbaric; reviving the colours of the desert like a draught."

Aqaba seems like a mirage when it appears. No doubt the Red Sea resort seemed even more surreal to Lawrence, whose tribal warriors had swept through town and splashed victoriously in the waters of the Gulf of Aqaba. Today those warriors would first have to skirt modern beach hotels built for the international divers who converge on the reef that stretches to Eilat on the Israeli side and south to Saudi Arabia. In an ultimate irony, cruise ships now disgorge passengers at Aqaba for excursions to Petra, the ancient Nabataean capital that eluded discovery by outsiders for centuries.

Petra sparkles as the gem of Jordan's tourist circuit. "Brilliant Petra," Lawrence called it; he once stationed troops there to protect the position of the old warrior Auda Abu Tayi (played by an impassioned Anthony Quinn in *Lawrence of Arabia*).

But more than Petra, even more than Azraq and Aqaba, the place most closely associated with Lawrence is Wadi Rum. His description, "vast, echoing, and God-like," still fits. "Our little caravan grew self-conscious," he wrote, the first time he crossed its expanse, "and fell dead quiet, afraid and ashamed to flaunt its smallness in the presence of the stupendous hills." Later he expressed his resentment at the intrusion of British troops in "the cliffs which had been my private resort."

My companions succumb to the sea and sand at Aqaba. But I covet one last desert sunset, this time from the vantage point of a hot-air balloon over the Wadi Rum. It is already late afternoon when Ziad points out the tracks of the Hejaz Railway, the one that Lawrence targeted so often and so successfully.

Ziad then leads me beyond the Wadi Rum Rest House to a low-slung black tent where a few hobbled camels nose about next to a pickup truck. Inside, he introduces me to some of the modern Bedouin who still pitch their goat-hair tents in the desert backcountry. Descendants of the tribesmen who rode with Lawrence, they serve us strong coffee in keeping with what Lawrence called "the splendid hospitality of the east."

Finally we reach the balloon staging area where an immense inflatable bag

Chiseled out of solid rock in the desert, centuries-old Petra now lures tourists the way it once attracted merchants and religious worshippers more than 2,000 years ago. Joyce Gregory Wyels

lies spread across the desert floor. The balloon wobbles into an upright position as the sun slips below the horizon, suspending the surroundings between daylight and dark in a brief desert twilight. Blues and purples merge with the day's hot colors, and I climb into the gondola. Our ascent affords a top-down view of the convoluted rock formations that rise from the flat desert floor like magnified brain coral.

Toward the end of his two years in Arabia, Lawrence was plagued by guilt. Although he had rallied the desert tribes in the name of Arab unity and freedom, he knew that England, France, and Russia were already plotting their postwar spoils: "I salved myself with the hope that, by leading these Arabs madly in the final victory I would establish them, with arms in their hands, in a position so assured (if not dominant) that expediency would counsel to the Great Powers a fair settlement of their claims."

But while Lawrence urged rival Arab leaders to unite in the final drive to Damascus, Britain signed secret agreements that would splinter Arab lands into Western-dominated fragments. Disillusioned, Lawrence sought solace in Wadi Rum: "Later, when we were often riding inland my mind used to turn me from the direct road to clear my senses by a night in Rumm, and by the ride down its

A Bedouin appears to guard the approach to Kerak, one of the many ruins of Crusader castles that dot Jordan.
Joyce Gregory Wyels

dawn-lit valley toward the shining plains, or up its valley in the sunset . . ."

Still, despite two years of physical and emotional hardships, military setbacks and political machinations, Lawrence achieved his goal. Arab armies, equipped by the British and led by Lawrence, drove the Turks from their territory. *Seven Pillars of Wisdom*, Lawrence's personal and historical treatise, is subtitled *A Triumph*.

Because my attention is fixed on the receding rocks, the sun's second coming takes me by surprise. Suddenly the fiery orb reappears above the western mountains. Two sunsets in one day! Lawrence would have loved it.

The Writer's Trail

Following in the Footsteps

Destination: Like neighboring Israel, the Hashemite Kingdom of Jordan is a crossroads of biblical history. Numerous archaeological sites testify to the civilizations that have swept across its desert terrain. Jordan is probably the most Westernized of the Arab states; nevertheless, since most of the population is Muslim, modesty in dress is advised.

Location: Jordan is bordered by Israel to the west, Syria to the north, Iraq to the northeast, and Saudi Arabia to the south and east. Aqaba is its only outlet to the Red Sea.

Getting There: Royal Jordanian Airline flies to Amman from New York City, Chicago, and Detroit. You can call Royal Jordanian in the United States at 1-800-223-0470; Canada 1-800-363-0711. The airline's Web site is *www.rjair.com*. Several other airlines, including KLM/Northwest Airlines, British Airways, Air France, Alitalia, and Lufthansa, fly to Jordan. You can also fly on Royal Jordanian from Tel Aviv to Amman. Queen Alia International Airport is 21 miles south of Amman. Traveling to Jordan overland is a little trickier. Reasonably frequent government-run buses connect Damascus (Syria), Baghdad (Iraq), Riyadh (Saudi Arabia), and Tel Aviv (Israel) with Amman. There is a weekly train from Damascus to Amman. You can also take a bus/ferry from Cairo, Egypt, to Aqaba, or a car ferry from Nuweiba in Egypt to Aqaba.

Orientation: Amman, the capital and major city, is within five hours' drive to anywhere in Jordan. Most major sites are south of Amman.

Tip: Don't wander alone in Wadi Rum or other desert regions.

Getting Around: Daily nonstop flights operate from Amman and Aqaba. Buses run from Amman to Petra and Aqaba for about $14 for a round trip, $46 for an excursion. Taxis are available in the cities. Major rental-car agencies (Avis, Budget, Hertz) have offices in Amman. Rates are $35 to $50 per day for an economy car, and up to $115 per day for a luxury car.

Literary Sleeps

Amman: The five-star Intercontinental is a longtime favorite. Tel.: (962-6) 564-1361. Fax: (962-6) 564-5217. Expensive. In the same general area is the small Hisham Hotel, which features a pleasant terrace restaurant. Tel.: (962-6) 464-2720. Fax: (962-6) 464-7540. Moderate.

Aqaba: This town is filled with beach hotels—those on the beach somewhat more expensive, those inland more modestly priced. Many have water sports available. The Coral Beach is a popular beach hotel. Tel.: (962-3) 201-3521. Fax: (962-3) 201-3614. Moderate. Three good hotels in the three-star range are the Aquamarina 1, 2, and 3. Only the first is on the beach. Tel.: (962-3) 201-6250. Fax: (962-3) 201-5169. Moderate.

Petra: Although newer hotels have been built to accommodate tourists in Petra, the Petra Forum is the best-placed for seeing the ruins. Tel.: (962-3) 215-6266. Fax: (962-3) 215-6977. Expensive. Another good bet is Taybet Zaman Village, about five and a half miles from Petra. A restored 19th-century village forms the basis for this attractive complex. Expensive.

Tip: Unless you stay in a one-star hotel, plan to budget an additional 20 percent for room tax and service.

Literary Sites

Azraq: Sixty miles east of Amman, this oasis town possesses the only water in the entire eastern desert. The castle here, which dates back to the 13th century, was used by T. E. Lawrence as his headquarters in 1917 during the Arab Revolt.

Petra: Everyone makes a grand entrance in Petra. The only way in is through a cleft (*siq*) in the mountains, hundreds of feet high but only a few feet wide. The narrow gorge winds through the mountains for a mile or so before it ends opposite one of Petra's most striking buildings, the Treasury. As early as 400 B.C., Petra was the capital of a flourishing Nabataean culture. The Nabataeans were nomads from western Arabia who prospered by commandeering profits from trade caravans that passed through their territory. For more than 1,000 years, Petra was forgotten until it was redis- covered by a 19th-century explorer.

Wadi Rum: T. E. Lawrence had a special affection for the spectacular desert landscape found here. Instead of sand dunes, Wadi Rum features towering rock formations called *jebels*. A mile or so southwest of the village of Rum, there is a spring called Lawrence's Well.

Icon Pastimes

Savor the colors of a desert sunset from the Wadi Rum, Wadi Araba, or Wadi Musa. Petra Moon Tourism Services places travelers with a Bedouin family, facilitates camping, and arranges camel, jeep, or hiking trips. You can literally follow in the footsteps of T. E. Lawrence by participating in their camel ride from Wadi Rum to Aqaba, a trip of four days and three nights.

Contacts

Jordan Tourism Board North America: 3504 International Drive NW, Washington, D.C. 20008 U.S. Tel.: (202) 244-1451. Fax: (202) 966-3110. Web site: *www.jordanembassyus.org/tourism.htm*.

Petra Moon Tourism Services: P.O. Box 129, Wadi Musa, Petra, Jordan. Tel.: (962-3) 215-6665. Fax: (962-3) 215-6666. Web site: *www.petramoon.com*.

In a Literary Mood

Books

Belt, Don. "Lawrence of Arabia: A Hero's Journey." *National Geographic*, January 1999. This article, with maps and historical explanations, is especially useful for clarifying political boundaries in the Middle East from 1914 to the present.

Brown, Malcolm, and Julia Cave. *A Touch of Genius: The Life of T. E. Lawrence*. New York: Paragon House, 1989. The authors, producers of two BBC documentaries on Lawrence, offer a balanced portrait of the man—a well-documented analysis that falls somewhere between the public adulation accorded Lawrence of Arabia and the negative backlash that followed. It includes an extensive bibliography and photos taken by Lawrence himself.

Graves, Robert. *Lawrence and the Arabs*. New York: Doubleday, 1928. First published in England in 1927, Graves's popular biography is said to have been written with considerable assistance from Lawrence himself.

Knightley, Phillip, and Colin Simpson. *The Secret Lives of Lawrence of Arabia*. New York: McGraw-Hill, 1970. The authors base their exposé on the release, in 1968, of government documents as well as on letters by Lawrence's brother, Professor A. W. Lawrence. Among the aspects of his private life that they highlight are the fact of his illegitimate birth and an alleged tendency toward masochism. In his career, they maintain, he played a dual role in the Arab Revolt all along, duping the Arabs and scheming to ensure Britain's imperial role in the Middle East.

Lawrence, A. W., ed. *T. E. Lawrence by His Friends.* London: Cape, 1937. This compilation of essays and remembrances was solicited by Lawrence's brother, Arnold, and features contributions by, among many others, George Bernard Shaw and his wife, Charlotte; Lady Astor; Lord Allenby; Lord Halifax; Lowell Thomas; and Winston Churchill. An abridged version of this book was published in 1954.

Lawrence, T. E. *Revolt in the Desert.* London: Wordsworth Editions, 1998. Originally published in 1927, this book is a shorter account by Lawrence of his involvement in the Arab Revolt. Winston Churchill said it was among "the greatest books ever written in the English language."

_____. *Seven Pillars of Wisdom.* New York: Doubleday, 1935. Lawrence's own epic account of his desert campaigns leading the Arab Revolt against the Turks was originally privately printed in 1926.

Mack, John E. *A Prince of Our Disorder.* Boston: Little, Brown, 1976. The American author, a psychiatrist, explores the confluence of Lawrence's unique personality and aptitudes with the world events that produced a 20th-century crusader for Arab independence.

Thomas, Lowell. *With Lawrence in Arabia.* New York: Century, 1924. It was Thomas, the American newscaster, who promoted the matinee-idol image of Lawrence of Arabia. For the rest of his life, Lawrence tried doggedly to escape his celebrity status. Twice, under assumed names, the former colonel enlisted at the lowest rank, first in the Royal Air Force, then in the Army Tank Corps. Before his death, he had returned to the RAF under the legally adopted name T. E. Shaw, giving rise to the nickname Tes among his friends.

Guidebooks

Ellis, Michael. *Insight Guide Jordan.* Singapore: APA, 1999. Makes frequent references to Lawrence in essays such as "Lawrence of Arabia and the Arab Revolt."

Shaw, Tahir. *Spectrum Guide to Jordan.* New York: Interlink Books, 1999. Comprehensive and current, with numerous photos.

Simonis, Damien, and Hugh Finlay. *Jordan and Syria: A Travel Survival Kit.* 3rd ed. Hawthorn, Australia: Lonely Planet Publications, 1997. Lonely Planet offers its usual well-rounded guide for the independent traveler, containing practical information plus history, cultural context, and useful Arabic phrases.

Films/Videos

Pasolini, Uberto, David Puttnam, Brenda Reid, and Colin Vaines (producers). *A Dangerous Man: Lawrence After Arabia.* Christopher Menaul (director). Anglia Films/WNET/Sands Films/Thirteen, 1990. Video Treasures. Cast: Ralph Fiennes, Dennis Quilley, and Alexander Siddig. TV movie set during the 1919 Paris Peace Conference provides a dramatic, and different, look at the political T. E. Lawrence. It's hard to shake the image of Peter O'Toole as Lawrence, but Fiennes does a fine job in counterpoint with Siddig's memorable portrayal of Feisal.

Spiegel, Sam (producer). *Lawrence of Arabia.* David Lean (director). Columbia, 1962. Columbia Tristar Home Video. Cast: Alec Guinness, Peter O'Toole, Anthony Quinn, Omar Sharif. The classic film won seven Academy Awards and made international stars of O'Toole and Sharif. An American journalist sets the tone for this interpretation: "He was a poet, a scholar, and a mighty warrior. He was also the most shameless exhibitionist since Barnum and Bailey." The production, featuring sweeping panoramas of camel-mounted Arab warriors, took more than two years to film, largely in the Wadi Rum desert of Jordan.

Web Sites

Jordan: *www.accessme.com/tourism*; *www.arabia.com/Jordan.*

T. E. Lawrence: *www.castle-hill-press.com/tefile/home.htm.*

Rohinton Mistry
Chasing Ghosts in Bombay

Margaret Deefholts

AT 10 A.M. THE STREET is a tumult of double-decker buses, taxis, cars, scooters, and pedestrians. Motorcyclists rev their engines and truck drivers lean on their klaxons as they edge past obstinate bullock carts. Sidewalk vendors bawl above the din, and the smell of spices, dust, and thronging humanity hangs over everything. The scene is both dizzying and exhilarating.

Not surprising. I am in Bombay, India's most diverse, gritty, and compelling city. Officially known as Mumbai since 1996, Bombay is home to 16 million people, give or take a few hundred thousand slum squatters who have escaped the census polls. More than any other Indian metropolis, it is a *mirchi-masala* city—a tangy mixture of cultures, religions, and languages.

It is also a city that has many worlds crammed into its all-encompassing fist. It has clawed at the consciousness of writers who once called it home and turned their experiences into literature, from Salman Rushdie's grotesque, inverted *Midnight's Children* to Vikram Chandra's portrayal of a complex and sophisticated society in *Love and Longing in Bombay*.

Bombay is also Canadian Rohinton Mistry's landscape, the canvas on which he paints the details of his characters' anguish, joy, and pathos. Mistry's tales, drawn from his own background, center around the small, tightly knit community of Parsis, whose ancestors fled Persia in the wake of religious persecution and settled along the west coast of India in the eighth century. Their culture is as unique to this City by the Sea as are the Towers of Silence on Malabar Hill and the Fire Temples where they worship, mourn, and rejoice.

I pore over maps of Bombay and talk to Parsi friends. "Where," I ask, "is Mistry's Firozsha Baag and Khododad Building?"

"They are fictional composites," they say, "but take a look at the Parsi enclave on Grant Road."

So I do. And, standing at the entrance to the apartments, the ghosts of Mistry's characters—underpaid bank clerks, tellers, bookkeepers, and their families—seem to leap out at me from the walls. The buildings are streaked with mildew—the legacy of several monsoons—and the whitewash is peeling off in leukoderma-like patches. The blocks are eerily reminiscent of the apartments with leaky ceilings and flimsy partition walls that Mistry describes in his novel *Such a Long Journey* and his compilation of short stories, *Tales from Firozsha Baag*.

An old car slows near the building entrance, and I peer at the driver, a mustachioed, bespectacled gentleman wearing a crisp white cotton *dugli*, a bow tied neatly at the base of his throat. Is he that great teller of tales, Nariman Hansotia? Perhaps not, but someone very like him probably took shape in Mistry's imagination when he wrote *Tales from Firozsha Baag*.

Although this section of Grant Road has an air of shabby respectability, the street fringes on Bombay's underworld of cheap prostitution, gambling dens, illicit booze, and petty crime. Like Tar Gully, the impoverished lane alongside Mistry's Firozsha Baag apartment complex, fetid alleyways slink between shops and ramshackle residential blocks.

I consult my map again and take a cab to Chor Bazaar in Bombay's inner-city sprawl. The vehicle threads through a snarl of traffic. Cows meander across the road, goats chew rubbish in the gutters, and stray dogs, tongues lolling, sit in the shade of shop awnings. This is a predominantly Muslim area, and *burkha*-shrouded women throng the sidewalks like flocks of crows.

The Chor Bazaar, or Thieves' Market, a warren of narrow, winding lanes, is filled with a river of humanity: people swirling, eddying, and surging past shops and stalls. This is where Gustad Noble in *Such a Long Journey* finds the fanatically loyal secret agent, Ghulam Mohammed, who acts as a messenger between Noble and the latter's old friend, Jimmy Billimoria. It is also, according to the locals, the place where people buy back their own pilfered goods. Whatever the truth, Chor Bazaar is the place to find anything and everything: secondhand crockery, auto parts, computer hardware, old windup gramophones, and so-called antiques. It is noisy, chaotic, and utterly irresistible.

I buy an old bottle with a marble in its throat for 25 cents and find several

If you happen to lose something while in Bombay, it may end up in the Chor Bazaar, or Thieves' Market.
Makarand Shiraskar

bookstalls, one of which has Captain Marvel comics and books by Rafael Sabatini. I ask for a copy of the *Complete Works of Shakespeare*, just as Noble did, and the shopkeeper produces a book with a flourish. He thumps the cover, raising a cloud of dust, before handing it to me. "Very good book, madam. First edition. Guaranteed!" It's actually a copy of *Lamb's Tales from Shakespeare*, published in the 1920s, but it has a fine leather cover, so after some bargaining I purchase it for the equivalent of $1.50.

On the main street, I wait at a bus stop to catch a ride to Crawford Market. A red double-decker bus pulls up, and there is a frantic scrimmage of bodies dodging and shouldering one another to get inside. But getting on is easier than I'd thought: the press of humanity behind me bears me on board like flotsam. A conductor squeezes through the crowd, clicking his ticket puncher, his khaki uniform sweat-patched at the armpits. The bus lurches down Mohammed Ali Road and drops me off near Crawford Market.

The market is much emptier than I'd expected. There are no hunks of raw meat hanging from the ceiling. Gone, too, are the butchers in bloodstained vests hacking at bone and gristle that so repulsed Gustad Noble. They have been moved to another location in New Bombay, and Crawford Market is now filled with fruit and vegetable booths. Stalls loaded with pyramids of produce line the aisles, and the cavernous, shedlike building echoes with the sound of vociferous haggling. As I step gingerly along the floor, which is slippery with fruit skins and vegetable waste, vendors heft old-fashioned scales, iron weights on one side and produce on the other.

Just outside the main building, the bird market is noisy with the flutter and squawk of parrots, budgerigars, and pigeons. A perplexed Noble stood here inexpertly trying to choose a chicken to take home for a special celebratory dinner—a meal that turns into a disaster and marks a turning point in his relationship with his rebellious son, Sohrab.

Close to Crawford Market is St. Xavier's Boys School, which features in several of Mistry's short stories. From across the street, I crane to catch glimpses of the building between passing traffic. Are Patla Babu and Jhaaria Babu ("The Collectors") still selling exercise books and stamps to students at the gates? Sitting against the school boundary wall is a sidewalk barber, and nearby a man cleans a client's ears. But there is no sign of Mistry's sidewalk entrepreneurs.

Yet some things haven't changed. It is almost lunchtime, and a tiffin carrier balancing a long, narrow crate on his head lopes through the school gates. The crate holds several cylindrical metal containers with home-cooked lunches, and the man is probably heading toward the drillhall/lunchroom (smelling of stale, rancid curry), which Mistry describes in "Lend Me Your Light."

The magnificent bulk of Victoria Terminus, with its ornate Gothic spires, domes, and gargoyles, is a short walk away. I stroll over to the main-line platforms where Noble would have boarded his train to Delhi in *Such a Long Journey*. Coolies wearing red turbans and shirts bawl "Side! Side!" as they carry boxes and bedding rolls on their heads. Tea vendors crowing *"Chai, garam chaaaai"* weave past sellers of hot gram and cold drinks. Families squat on the platform waiting for their trains, some staring ahead blankly, others stretched out asleep, oblivious to the confusion around them. Women cook rotis on portable stoves. Bare-chested holy men, *sadhus*, with matted dreadlocks, stand in a group to one side, and young soldiers on their way to an army camp sit patiently on their kit bags. Above the hissing of locomotives, the public-information loudspeaker crackles with incomprehensible announcements.

That night I have dinner with Parsi friends in their modern apartment near Bombay Central Station. We talk about Mistry's books and Bomi says, "I enjoyed his first two books, but the last one, *A Fine Balance*, was targeted more toward a foreign audience than an Indian one. It was just too exaggerated, especially the end."

"And those low-class tailors!" his wife Freny interrupts. "Who can believe that any respectable Parsi lady would have them living in the same flat, eating and drinking from the same plates and cups, using the same bathroom and all. Cheee!"

The conversation turns to the dwindling Parsi community in Bombay. "Not like the old days," says Freny. "Our young people are all going abroad and many are moving away from the old traditions. But," she adds, her face brightening, "I'm told by my friends in Canada that they still cook *dhansak* and *sali-boti*. At least their palates are still Parsi, even if their brains aren't."

After dinner, Bomi drives us through the red-light district of Kamathipura. These are Bombay's "cages," so-called because the huddled brothels have barred windows. It is the neighborhood where the Nobles' family doctor has his practice and where Ghulam Mohammed's "House of Cages" is located.

We cruise the dimly lit lanes where madams sit like dark bloated spiders at the entrances to their brothels, chewing *paan* and winking at passersby while extolling the charms of their "girls." Women lean out of upper-floor windows, beckoning and rolling their kohl-rimmed eyes seductively. Others, wearing sequined dresses and smoking cigarettes, lounge against the entrance doors, their faces like celluloid masks. Some of them are little more than children who, as Bomi tells me, have been lured from remote villages with the promise of respectable domestic employment. Although the brothels are legal and the women supposedly undergo medical checkups on a regular basis, AIDS is rampant throughout the red-light area.

Flora Fountain, where there is no flora and the fountain is erratic, owes its name to a stone monument depicting the goddess Flora. This is the commercial core of the city and where international banks and mercantile firms have their offices. Noble and his friend Dinshawji would have worked in one of the dignified Victorian buildings lining the streets that radiate from Flora Fountain's central hub.

Sunlight falls in sharp, hard lances between the buildings, and the air feels like damp flannel against my skin. I seek a patch of shade under an awning to listen to the patter of hawkers selling everything from small appliances to ghetto blasters. The sidewalks are lavish with displays of ready-made garments and an assortment of plastic toys and cheap gilt jewelry. Cars, buses, scooters, and motorbikes roar around the fountain's circle, and people swarm antlike along the sidewalks.

Few cities in the world have the power to stir the emotions of its citizens the way Bombay does, and Mistry's story "Lend Me Your Light" evokes the ambivalence felt by expatriates who revisit old neighborhoods. Jamshed, the young Parsi who has immigrated to the United States, regards Flora Fountain with disdain: "'Terrible, isn't it, the way these buggers think they own the streets—don't even leave you enough room to walk. The police should drive them off, break up their bloody stalls, really.'" And then later he says: "'God, what a racket! I'll be happy when it's time to catch my plane back to New York.'" By contrast, Mistry's alter ego in the story, also home after a sojourn in Toronto, and viewing the same scene, thinks to himself: "These people were only trying to earn a meagre living by exercising, amidst a paucity of options, this one; at least they were not begging or stealing."

I go west along Veer Nariman Road, and in a lane alongside Churchgate Railway Station, I find an Irani restaurant. It is typical of its kind, and Mistry used a similar eatery as the setting for Noble's tête-à-tête with Laurie Coutino, the delectable bank manager's secretary in *Such a Long Journey*.

Mistry is at his wry best in this scene: the smirking waiter ushering Gustad and Laurie into the privacy of the cubicle; Laurie confessing her unease at Dinshawji's ribald pun on her name, and Gustad—titillated at being alone with Laurie, but alarmed at Dinshawji's indiscreet behavior—offering his assurances that he will take matters in hand. However, his subsequent talk with Dinshawji has unforeseen repercussions and causes Gustad agonies of conscience.

The Irani restaurant is crowded, and small boys armed with soggy rags swipe table surfaces, cleaning off crumbs, sticky residues of spilt tea, and wet circles left by cold-drink bottles. Waiters bawl out to the kitchen, *"Ek plate samosa,"* or *"Do chai."* A large iron cooking pot near the entrance sizzles with fried *bhajias*, and my stomach does an appreciative growl in response to the smell of onions, cumin, and chilies. I follow a waiter up a rickety flight of steps to a cubicle. The air conditioner is noisily asthmatic, but the room is cool and shadowed—a welcome relief from the afternoon humidity and glare.

I order an ice-cold *lassi*-yogurt drink and a plate of *aloo-mutter*, accompanied by a *roti* and a crisp, deep-fried *papad*. The straw in my *lassi* is as soft as an overcooked noodle and keeps collapsing when I draw on it, the plate has a grimy crack running across the surface, and the only cutlery is a tin teaspoon. But the food is marvelous—spicy and fresh. What's the point of getting typhoid and hepatitis shots if they aren't put to the test?

Recipe for Dhansak

(Courtesy of Vera Irani, Richmond, British Columbia)

1 chicken cut into pieces, or 2 lb. (1 kg) of mutton (lamb) leg cut into pieces
2 cups of washed and cleaned red lentils (*masoor-dal*)
1 onion finely chopped
1 tomato finely chopped
1 bundle of finely chopped green cilantro (coriander or *hara dhania*)
1 bundle of finely chopped green fenugreek (*methi*), alternatively a
    teaspoon of dried fenugreek
1 tablespoon of fresh pulped ginger
1 tablespoon of fresh pulped garlic

Mix the following spices with water into a paste.

1 teaspoon of hot chili powder
1 teaspoon Madras curry powder
1 teaspoon cumin powder
1 teaspoon coriander powder
1/2 teaspoon garam masala (a mixture of powdered cinnamon, cloves,
    cardamom, and black pepper)
4 tablespoons oil
salt to taste

*Add the lentils, onions, tomato, cilantro, and fenugreek to 4 cups of boiling water and
simmer until the lentil grains are soft and pulpy. Put into a blender for about a minute,
or until the mixture is creamy and thick. Set aside. Heat the oil in a large cooking pot.
Add the ginger and garlic and stir briskly for half a minute. Add the above paste of spices
and stir for another minute. Add the chicken (or mutton) and fry well along with the
spices. Pour in the lentil mixture, add salt, and keep adding enough water to prevent
the* dhansak *mixture from sticking to the bottom of the pot. Simmer for half an hour or
until the meat is tender. Serve with fried rice and a salad of chopped onions, tomatoes,
chilies, and wedges of lemon.*

Earlier in my visit to Bombay, I had been asked to tea by Parsi friends to meet
Dr. Rustom Manek, a priestly Dastoorji. He is a bearded gentleman, dignified
in his white cotton robes, and suddenly I find myself thinking about the Parsi
rituals for the dead described by Mistry in *Such a Long Journey*:

The incline of the hill levelled off. The procession had arrived at the Tower. The *nassasalers* halted and placed the bier on the stone platform outside. They uncovered the face one last time and stood aside. It was time for the last farewell to Dinshawji.

The men approached the stone platform, still linked in twos and threes . . . and bowed three times in unison without letting go of the white kerchiefs. Then the four [*nassasalers*] shouldered the bier again and climbed the stone steps to the door leading inside the Tower. They entered and pulled it shut behind them. The mourners could see no more. But they knew what would happen inside: the *nassasalers* would place the body on a *pavi*, on the outermost of three concentric stone circles. Then, without touching Dinshawji's flesh, using their special hooked rods they would tear off the white cloth. Every stitch, till he was exposed to the creatures of the air, naked as the day he had entered the world.

As Dr. Manek takes a sip of his tea, I ask him about the rituals. "Zoroastrianism is an ancient religion that predates the birth of Christ by about six centuries," he says, looking directly at me, his eyes magnified through thick spectacles. "Because we revere the four elements of earth, air, fire, and water, we do not

Imagine Rohinton Mistry, one of his characters, or Rudyard Kipling haggling over fruit and vegetables in Crawford Market. It's not hard. Makarand Shiraskar

pollute the earth by burying our dead. Nor do we allow fire, the most sacred and mystical of all our religious symbols, to be defiled by corpses. Instead we lay our cadavers out on the roof and allow nature to take its course." He pauses to wipe biscuit crumbs from the corners of his mouth and adds, "To some this may seem a bizarre practice—allowing the flesh of our loved ones to be consumed by vultures—but is this any different from bodies being eaten by worms and contaminating the earth into the bargain?

"But things are changing. Many of our people have gone abroad and mingled in the larger world. Nowadays some Parsi families choose other, more expedient means of disposing of their dead. I suppose that is inevitable. After all, Zoroastrianism, too, must move with the times." Despite his words, regret edges his voice.

Non-Parsis aren't permitted to enter the Fire Temples, or the Towers of Silence at Doongerwadi on Malabar Hill, so I ask my cabdriver to drive past the elegant Fire Temple on Princess Street, and then we swing via a flyover onto Marine Drive toward the Hanging Gardens and the Towers of Silence. A blood-orange sun is beginning to dip into the sea, and a breeze has sprung up off the water.

The Hanging Gardens are pleasantly shady in the early evening, but the contingent of muscular bodybuilders that young Jehangir envied in Mistry's story "Exercises" aren't strutting their stuff. There are no lust-driven lovers, either. Perhaps the shadows need to lengthen into twilight before they make their appearance. Instead families stroll along the pathways, while their children chase one another with little chirrups of glee around the trees and benches. Above me, specks of vultures drift on the wind and then begin to descend sharply toward the shrubbery at the far end of the Hanging Gardens. Down, down, circling, wheeling, toward the adjacent bastions of the Towers of Silence, shrouded behind a thick cover of trees.

The evening is cooler now and the dying day has a scent of marigolds and *mogra* flowers, wistful as old memories and whispered regrets. In one of the most poignant chapters in *Such a Long Journey*, Noble thinks sadly:

> Dinshawji dismantled. And after the prayers are said and the rituals performed at the Tower of Silence, the vultures will do the rest. When the bones are picked clean, and the clean bones gone, no proof will remain that Dinshawji ever lived and breathed. Except his memory.
>
> But after that? After the memory is lost? When I am gone, and all his friends are gone. What then?

I have no answers to Noble's questions about the evanescence of life. As the brief Indian twilight thickens into dusk, I leave the Hanging Gardens and look down at the now brilliantly lit curve of Marine Drive, which lies like a glittering choker against the throat of the dark sea.

The road from the Hanging Gardens winds past the elite mansions of Malabar Hill. I take a taxi to Chowpatty Beach, which is mentioned in several of Mistry's short stories, and I'm catapulted into a celebration of life at its most exuberant—an abrupt transition from the somber Towers of Silence.

It is now dark. The beach is partly neon-lit, and hissing kerosene lanterns illuminate some of the vendors' booths. Music from the latest Bollywood film blares from a loudspeaker, and at one corner of the beach a hand-cranked contraption with four tumbling boxes is filled with shrieking, delighted children. The sands are thick with people, strolling, chatting, laughing, and pausing to treat themselves to Bombay's specialty, *bhel-puri* (a spicy mixture of puffed rice, chopped onions, coriander leaves, green chilies, and tamarind juice), or to sample *kulfi* ice cream from vendors' carts. Within my first two minutes on the beach, I am offered a pony ride, a horoscope reading, and a chance to try my skill at cards. A masseur at my elbow is persistent. "Brain massage, memsahib? No? Okay, then you like to try body massage?" I shake my head. A small packet tied with thread is waved in front of me. "This very good medicine, memsahib. Fine for roly-poly with your mister. Hundred times better than Viagra [he pronounces it *bhaiayagra*]. Guaranteed!"

The beach is littered with shredded paper, cardboard containers, and plastic bags. To one side is a bright red barrel that proudly announces: Utility Multi-Advantageous Fibreglass Waste Bin. It is completely empty.

Bombay is reputedly home to one of the worst slums in Asia—possibly in the world. Although not mentioned by name, Dharavi is not unlike the shantytown colony in which the two tailors, Omprakash and Ishvar, rent a hut in *A Fine Balance*.

My taxi driver, a burly, turbaned Sikh, raises his eyebrows when I tell him my destination. "You shouldn't go there, memsahib. Too dangerous for lady alone."

It is broad daylight, and I don't intend going through the alleyways of Dharavi. "It's okay," I say. "You wait for me. I won't be long."

He shrugs and grinds his gears into action. We drive north through the city suburbs, weaving in and out of a tangle of motor vehicles, animals, pedestrians,

Dharavi, in Bombay, may well be Asia's—perhaps the world's—worst slum. Makarand Shiraskar

and hand-drawn carts, the last carrying furniture, sacks of grain, and blocks of ice wrapped in jute.

Whatever Freny and Bomi might say, Mistry's description of the slum in *A Fine Balance* isn't exaggerated. Dharavi is a putrefying stretch of marshland, and the conglomeration of shacks—such as the tailors lived in—are built of rusty corrugated tin sheets, tarpaulin, plastic sheets, old sacking, and cardboard. The stench of human and animal excrement mingles with the acrid fumes of a nearby tannery. Men squat outside their huts, some lolling on string charpoy beds playing cards, others passing around bottles of hooch. Women fill pots with water from communal taps, the flow reduced to a trickle. A crowd gathers around me—half-naked children with distended bellies and sore-encrusted eyes. A thickset man pushes his way to the front. "What you are wanting here, madam?" he demands. His manner is belligerent. "You think these people are monkey performers for your camera? You must pay them money. Pay me money also."

The taxi driver materializes at my side. *"Arre, kya?"* he says placatingly. "Don't get upset. The memsahib is going now. She won't take any more photos."

I turn away meekly and follow the driver back to the taxi. The thickset man stands irresolute, glowering, and a group of men gather quickly behind him. The driver reverses and pulls onto the street, his wheels churning up clouds of dust.

"That is small boss," he explains. "He works for the big boss, the slum land-lord." He clashes his gears and narrowly skins past an auto-rickshaw. "Inside Dharavi, small-small gullies are there. Drug dealers, prostitute bosses, *matka* rings, murderers, and thieves—they all live there. Not safe even for me to go inside. If someone not like my face, they will just put knife into my stomach—*bhup!* And nobody, not even the police, will ask any questions."

By contrast, Mount Mary's Church in Bandra is tranquil. Like Noble and his friend Malcolm, I stop to look at the collection of wax limbs—arms, legs, heads, toes, fingers, and whole torsos—neatly displayed in rows on several carts at the gates of the church. I buy a conventional white taper. Inside the church, a few people kneel in pews, rosaries clasped in their hands, their lips moving silently.

Near the altar, a profusion of tiny bobbing flames from a cluster of candles punctuates the shadows. Wraiths of smoke spiral upward. I light my taper, set it down, kneel, close my eyes, and inhale the smell of burning wax. There is an orange glow behind my eyelids.

Afterward, I ride back to Churchgate Station from Bandra by commuter train and look out of the grilled window of the ladies' compartment as the train clatters over the Mahim Causeway. The stations fly past—Dadar, Parel, Mahalaxmi—and I note the changing scene beyond: skyscrapers, hovels, alley-ways, boulevards, shards of sea glinting between buildings, then an expanse of grass in front of the gymkhana complexes on Marine Drive. My gaze sweeps over the streets carrying the sick, the destitute, the maimed, the sophisticates, the humble, the pious, and the profane—all part of a great city that throbs to the heartbeat of its masses.

Rohinton Mistry celebrates this landscape—his landscape—with all its kaleidoscopic shifts of color, its harsh contrasts, and its nuances of mood. A city whose vitality is fueled by dreams and desperation. An unquenchable city. A city unlike any other in the world.

(Note: The names of all persons mentioned in this essay are pseudonyms and should not be ascribed to any actual person or persons in Bombay or elsewhere.)

Glossary

Aloo mutter: Potatoes and chickpeas

Arre, kya: Expression meaning "Oh, what does it matter?"

Bhajias: Onions, potatoes, or other vegetables coated in spicy chickpea flour and deep-fried in oil

Bhel-puri: A Bombay sidewalk specialty that combines crisp noodles, miniature rounds of deep-fried flat bread, puffed rice, green coriander, chopped chilies, chopped onions, and tamarind juice

Burkha: A one-piece garment worn by Muslim women that covers the body from head to toe

Do chai: Two teas

Dugli: Loose thin white cotton coat worn by Parsis

Ek plate: One plate

Garam chai: Hot tea

Gram: Any of several leguminous plants (as a chickpea) grown for their seeds

Kulfi: A rich creamy ice-cream specialty

Matka: Lottery game

Mirchi-masala: A blend of chili pepper and other spices

Nassasalers: Corpse handlers at the Towers of Silence in Bombay

Paan: An aromatic leaf stuffed with spices and condiments

Papad: Crisp, fried flat bread made of spiced chickpea flour

Paratha: Fried flour or wheat flat bread

Pista-badaam: Pistachio-almond

Roti: Flour or wheat flat bread

Sadhus: Hindu holy men

Samosa: Spicy snack of potatoes, peas, and onions wrapped in chickpea pastry and deep-fried

Tiffin: British term for a light midday meal

The Writer's Trail

Following in the Footsteps

Destination: Bombay is India's most affluent and cosmopolitan city, but it also contains some of Asia's poorest slums. Industrialists and entrepreneurs from all over the subcontinent have gravitated here, turning it into a dynamo of commercial activity. The poor, too, have their dreams, and the influx from rural areas has swelled the city's population to the bursting point (more than 16 million). Nicknamed Bollywood, Bombay is also the film capital of India. It churns out about 200 features a year.

Location: Situated on the central-west coast of India along the Arabian Sea, Bombay is the capital of the state of Maharashtra.

Getting There: Bombay's Sahar International Airport (20 miles from the city center) is served by most international airlines, with connections through New York City, London, Singapore, and Hong Kong. Santa Cruz Airport (15 miles from the city center) is served by a comprehensive network of domestic flights. Air India can be contacted in New York City at (212) 407-1300; in Toronto at (416) 865-1030; in London at (44-181) 745-1000; and in Bombay at (91-22) 202-4142. The airline's Web site is *www.airindia.com.* Bombay Central Station and Victoria Terminus are major railway junctions, and train routes fan out across the entire subcontinent. Indian Railways can be visited at *www.indianrailway.com.* Long-distance buses arrive and depart from the state road transport terminal opposite Central Station.

Orientation: The best time to visit Bombay is between November and January. The city was once seven islands, which the British, through land reclamation in the 18th and 19th centuries, consolidated into a single island that is now more of a peninsula. The southern end of the peninsula/island, Colaba, is where many of the city's better restaurants and hotels are found. Here, too, one will experience an explosion of vendors, hawkers, snake charmers, and touts, all of whom can be found swirling around the Gateway to India, the yellow basalt arch that was erected on the Apollo Bunder (a square) by the British in 1924 to commemorate King George V's visit to the city in 1911. North of Colaba is the Fort area, thus named because of the British fort that once stood there. Victoria Terminus, Churchgate Railway Station, and Flora Fountain are located here. Just north of Victoria Terminus is Crawford Market, and north of there, in Kalbadevi, is the Chor Bazaar. West of the Fort Area is Marine Drive, which curves around Back Bay to connect Nariman Point's skyscrapers, Chowpatty Beach, and Malabar Hill, where the Hanging Gardens and the Towers of Silence are found. The slum Dharavi, Mary Mount's Church in Bandra, and Bombay's airports are north of Malabar Hill.

Tip: Whenever the local politicians run out of things to do, they change the name of yet another road or landmark. The Maharashtra Tourism Development Corporation (see **Contacts**) at Nariman Point hands out free tourist maps that list the old and new names of the main roads.

Getting Around: Public transport is inexpensive, but not always the quickest means of getting around Bombay, due to crippling traffic congestion. Taxis are convenient and affordable. Fares are metered. However, since the meters are out-of-date, cabdrivers carry a fare card with conversion rates; fares are roughly 10 times the amount shown on the meter. If in doubt, ask to look at the fare card. To get from Sahar International Airport to the city center, use the services of the prepaid taxi booth at the airport. Shuttle buses from both airports are frequent. Bombay's buses are plentiful, but schedules are elastic. The destination marked on the front of the bus is in Marathi, the language of Bombay (along with Hindi), while the English equivalent is on the side panel. Avoid the rush-hour stampede. Suburban train service to and from Greater Bombay is frequent and regular at both Bombay's Victoria Terminus and Churchgate Station. During rush hours, it is impossible to get on or off the trains without the combined talents of a juggler, a contortionist, and an acrobat.

Literary Sleeps

Oberoi Hotel: Five-star lodgings with a terrific view of Back Bay. Marine Road, Nariman Point. Tel.: (91-22) 202-5757. Fax: (91-22) 204-1505. Extremely expensive.

Oberoi Towers Hotel: Like its sister hotel, this establishment has lots of glitz, but not much personality. Marine Road, Nariman Point. Tel.: (91-22) 202-4343. Fax: (91-22) 204-3282. Extremely expensive.

Taj Mahal Intercontinental Hotel: The old wing of the Taj is unbeatable for elegance, comfort, and Old World charm. Apollo Bunder (near Gateway of India). Tel.: (91-22) 202-3366. Fax: (91-22) 287-2711. Expensive.

President Hotel: 90 Cuffe Parade, Colaba. Tel.: (91-22) 215-0808. Fax: (91-22) 215-1201. Moderate.

Ascot Hotel: 38 Garden Road, Colaba. Tel.: (91-22) 284-0020. Fax: (91-22) 287-1765. Inexpensive.

Bentley's Hotel: 17 Oliver Road, Colaba. Tel.: (91-22) 284-1474. Fax: (91-22) 287-1846. Inexpensive.

Chateau Windsor Hotel: 86 Veer Nariman Road, Fort. Tel.: (91-22) 204-3376. Fax: (91-22) 202-6459. Inexpensive.

Hotel Godwin: 41 Garden Road, Colaba. Tel.: (91-22) 287-2050. Fax: (91-22) 287-1592. Inexpensive.

Tip: If you're in the vicinity of either Victoria Terminus or Churchgate Railway Station around noon, look for a daily occurrence unique to Bombay. Scores of *dabba-wallahs* pushing handcarts stacked with tiffin containers emerge from the stations and fan out across the city delivering up to 100,000 home-cooked lunches to offices. The *dabba-wallahs* are illiterate, but a series of colored dots and dashes on each tiffin container acts as a guide to its destination.

Literary Sites

Chowpatty Beach: Located off Marine Drive between Nariman Point and Malabar Hill, this ultimate people place comes alive at night. Bombay's citizens venture here in the thousands to meander among the fruit and nut vendors, balloon sellers, and buskers. During the Ganesh Chaturthi Festival in August/September, giant likenesses of the elephant-headed god are submerged in Back Bay.

Crawford Market: Built in 1871, this indoor market is just north of Victoria Terminus and serves as a last reminder of the British Raj before you enter the free-for-all of the bazaars in Kalbadevi. Besides its associations with Rohinton Mistry's fiction, the fruit and vegetable market has connections with Rudyard Kipling. His father, Lockwood, created the bas reliefs that cover the Norman-Gothic exterior of the market. And, if you look real hard at the center of the place, you should be able to spot the fountain Lockwood designed. It's usually obscured by old fruit boxes. Incidentally Rudyard Kipling was born in 1865 just south of Crawford Market at the school of art where his father was a teacher.

Flora Fountain: In the Fort area of Bombay, all roads seem to meet at the fountain, the commercial hub of Bombay's frenetic day-to-day business. Surrounded by some of the city's most impressive Victorian Italian Gothic buildings, the fountain named after the Roman goddess of flowers is where everyone in Bombay, fictional or real, ends up sooner or later.

Malabar Hill: Once upon a time, the British reigned here from on high in colonial bungalows, now replaced by the apartment complexes and mansions of Bombay's newly rich. The hill forms the northern promontory of Back Bay and boasts the Hanging Gardens, an elaborate topiary from which you can seemingly view all the city has to offer. Nearby are the Parsi Towers of Silence where the dead are exposed to the elements. The towers are closed to the public, of course, but armed with Rohinton Mistry's *Such a Long Journey* you can easily visualize what they are like.

Icon Pastimes

The two most passionate activities enjoyed by Rohinton Mistry's characters as well as by the real-life citizens of Bombay are shopping and eating. Bombay's most interesting buys are found along its sidewalks. Check out "Fashion Street" on Mahatma Gandhi Road (near Flora Fountain) for inexpensive cotton garments; the secondhand books displayed on the pavement at Flora Fountain; belts, handbags, shoes, and accessories on Colaba Causeway; fruit and vegetables at Crawford Market; and gold and silver jewelry at Zaveri Bazaar—and just about anything you can think of at Chor Bazaar—in Kalbadevi. For handicrafts visit the air-conditioned World Trade Centre at Cuffe Parade, or the Khadi Village Industries Emporium on Dadabhoy Naoroji Road. Bombay's restaurants range from upscale establishments such as the Tanjore in the Taj Mahal Hotel to no-frills Irani restaurants (owned or run by Iranian settlers in Bombay). Udipi restaurants feature South Indian vegetarian meals for about $3 or less. Or try a Bombay "frankie" (curried chicken wrapped in an egg *paratha*) on Colaba Causeway. And the *pista-badaam* or *kesar kulfi* at New Kulfi Centre (a street stall opposite Chowpatty Beach) are to die for. When you've had your fill of food and shopping, you can take in cricket matches at Wankhede and Brabourne Stadiums, just off Marine Drive, or cheer the horses (from November to April) at Mahalaxmi Racecourse.

Contacts

Government of India Tourism Office: 1270 Avenue of the Americas, Suite 1808, New York, New York 10020 U.S. Tel.: (212) 586-4901. Fax: (212) 582-3274. Web site: *www.tourindia.com*. 60 Bloor Street West, Suite 1003, Toronto, Ontario M4W 3B8 Canada. Tel.: (416) 962-3787. Fax: (416) 962-6279.

Maharashtra Tourism Development Corporation: Nirmal Building, 11th floor, Nariman Point, Bombay 400021 India. Tel.: (91-22) 202-6481. Fax: (91-22) 202-6022.

In a Literary Mood

Books

Chandra, Vikram. *Love and Longing in Bombay.* New York: Little, Brown, 1997. Five stories linked by a common narrator take the reader from neighborhoods haunted by ghosts, murders, and secretive deeds into the drawing rooms of Bombay's elite.

Forbes, Leslie. *Bombay Ice.* New York: Bantam Doubleday Dell, 1999. Forbes is a Canadian journalist who melds Bollywood with film noir in a literate thriller that crackles with wordplay and allusion.

Hancock, Geoff. "An Interview with Rohinton Mistry." *Canadian Fiction Magazine* 65 (1989). At the moment there is still a shortage of biographical material about Mistry, but this interview provides at least a few insights into the author's personality during his early years as a writer.

James, Clive. *The Silver Castle.* New York: Random House, 1999. Part *Candide*, part *Oliver Twist*, this tragicomic novel recounts the rise and fall of a Bombay street child named Sanjay.

Mistry, Rohinton. *A Fine Balance.* Toronto: McClelland & Stewart, 1995. Mistry's second novel is set in the mid-1970s soon after the Indian government declares a state of emergency, but the book reaches back in time to present an interlocking epic of four Bombay people's lives: a widowed seamstress, a displaced student from the Himalayan foothills, and two tailors from the subcontinent's interior.

_____. *Such a Long Journey.* Toronto: McClelland & Stewart, 1991. Set in 1971, the year India went to war with Pakistan over the fate of what eventually became Bangladesh, this novel focuses on the physical, emotional, and spiritual plight of Bombay bank teller Gustad Noble. Combining high comedy with poignant drama, Mistry creates an unforgettable cast of characters.

_____. *Tales from Firozsha Baag.* Markham, ON: Penguin, 1987. This collection of Mistry short stories launched his career and introduced the reading public to his wonderful assortment of Bombay Parsis.

Rushdie, Salman. *Midnight's Children.* New York: Penguin, 1995. Before Rohinton Mistry's books, Rushdie's first major novel, a Booker Prize winner originally published in 1981, was the seminal Bombay novel in English. Rushdie's genius lies in blurring the edges between reality and fantasy. He uses Bombay as a backdrop for satirical lampoons of thinly disguised politicians, Bollywood film stars, and industrialists.

_____. *The Moor's Last Sigh.* New York: Pantheon, 1997. Almost banned in Bombay, this novel shows Rushdie is still a literary force to be reckoned with. With a protagonist who speaks from the grave in Spain and a narrative that seems bent on encompassing all that is India, you know you are in for a mind-bending ride.

Vakil, Ardashir. *Beach Boy.* New York: Scribner, 1998. A perceptive Parsi novel of troubled adolescence set in an upper-class Bombay suburban neighborhood.

Guidebooks

India. 8th ed. Hawthorn, Australia: Lonely Planet Publications, 1999. Superbly researched, this guidebook is the only one you'll ever need on India. Don't leave home without it. Also check out Lonely Planet's other guides on different regions of India.

Films/Videos

Jindal, Suresh, and Simon MacCorkindale (producers). *Such a Long Journey.* Sturla Gunnarsson (director). The Film Works/Amy International Artists, 1998. Distributed by Optimum Releasing. Cast: Sam Dastor, Om Puri, and Roshan Seth. Seth plays Gustad Noble with sensitivity and compassion in a faithful adaptation of Mistry's novel.

Kennedy, Tatania (producer). *The Sixth Happiness.* Waris Hussein (director). BBC Films/British Film Institute, 1997. Cast: Souad Faress, Firdaus Kanga, and Khodus Wadia. Adaptation of Firdaus Kanga's acclaimed 1990 semiautobiographical book *Trying to Grow.*

Nair, Mira (producer and director). *Salaam Bombay!* Cadragee/Le Sept Cinéma/Mirabei Films/NDFC-Doordarshan, 1988. Cast: Chanda Sharma, Shafiq Syed, and Hansa Vithal. A richly textured tale that looks at Bombay's red-light district through the eyes of a homeless boy.

Web Sites

Bombay: *www.hotelbook.com*; *www.india-travel.com/cityhotel.com*; *www.lonelyplanet.com*; *www.mumbai-central.com.*

India: *www.india.travel.com*; *www.india-travel.com*; *www.indolink.com*; *www.mapsofindia.com*; *www.tourtravelindia.com.*

Rohinton Mistry: *www.nlc-bnc.ca/events/readings/emistry.htm.*

Parsi Cuisine: *www.altavisions.com/recipes.*

Bruce Chatwin
Walkabout in Australia

Richard Taylor

EVEN BEFORE I LEFT Canada for Australia, I had quickly jotted down some questions posed in the jacket copy of Bruce Chatwin's Australian odyssey, *The Songlines*, which I now pondered: "Why is man the most restless, dissatisfied of animals? Why do wandering people conceive the world as perfect whereas sedentary ones always try to change it? Why have the great teachers—Christ or the Buddha—recommended the Road as the way to salvation?"

Because my wife, Dale, had already gone to work and my youngest daughter, Quinn, was sick and still in bed, my 11-year-old daughter, Sky, sat eating breakfast alone with me. Down in the bay, huge swells of the Coral Sea were rolling in, and the morning air just outside our veranda was filled with the melodious warbling chaos of swooping magpies, lorikeets, galahs, and parrots. On the breakfast table beside the messy pile of my notes were two books I had been reading for pleasure and plunder: Gretel Ehrlich's *The Solace of Open Spaces* and Susannah Clapp's *With Chatwin: Portrait of a Writer*.

Clapp had been the editor of Chatwin's first classic travel book, *In Patagonia*, and in the process had become a close friend. Her memoir is an intimate look at a remarkable, contradictory man. On the front cover of the British edition, Chatwin sits bolt upright on a paint-spattered wooden chair, his hands resting tentatively on his knees. A startled, pretty-boy face with the penetrating, horizon-crazed eyes of a 19th-century explorer stares straight out. Wearing old jeans, well-worn moccasins, and a rugged traveling shirt, he is alone in a bare, pine-floored corner of a room that recalls Vincent van Gogh's painting of his lonely, empty bedroom.

Between heaping spoonfuls of her cereal, oblivious to the vast glory of the open sea view outside our veranda window, Sky looked down at Chatwin's picture and asked, "Why would anyone want to read a book about him?"

I told her that Chatwin was one of the world's most famous travelers who, in a very short career of 10 years, produced a handful of beautifully crafted works, and that I was writing about him in my ongoing book, *Memories of a Crazed Househusband.*

Sky dropped her spoon in her cereal and said, "Dad! You're putting *him* into your book, but you won't put Narmeen into it."

I assured Sky that I would mention her best friend in Canada, Narmeen, in my book somewhere. What I didn't tell Sky, because it was too complicated and would have upset her too much, was that the restless roving of a dead travel writer was one of the reasons we were living in a beach house on the northeast New South Wales coast of Australia. How, for example, could I have possibly explained to a homesick child the malaise suffered by romantic wanderers who feel most at home with themselves when they are away from home? How could I explain that all travelers want to get away from the routine of their lives to reinvent themselves for a time and perhaps find Paradise?

It was mid-January 1997, the glorious beginning of a long, lazy summer at the bottom of the world. Inadvertently, because of a teachers' exchange, we had hit the jackpot and gotten parachuted into a beach house along one of the last unspoiled classic surf breaks. During the day, Dale taught English at Byron Bay High school, while our two daughters attended Lennox Head Primary School. I stayed at home to surf the Point and begin writing my new book. The view from my desk was white-maned surf rolling on a blue sea into an empty golden beach. Humped in the distance was the coastal rainforest of Broken Head. As I tapped the keys of my laptop, delicious salt air blew the spicy rustle of eucalyptus gum trees into my face.

Each night in our beach house I read *The Fatal Shore*, Robert Hughes's phantasmagoric tome about crime and punishment and the founding of Australia. It recounts the fate of the thousands of convicts transported from England to Australia from 1787 to 1868. Reading Hughes's book left me more sleepless than the thought of all the sharks I would surf and swim with in the ocean. His early chapters with their vivid descriptions of the strange isolation of this primeval continent and its enigmatic Aboriginals held me breathless, listening for white demons outside our bedroom window.

A little more than 200 years ago there was no such thing as "white"

The author, seen here, has surfed some of the world's best beaches, but the waves and ambience at Australia's Byron Beach are hard to beat. Dale Taylor

Australia. All there was Down Under was a big prehistoric island with eternal waves breaking against a tree-fringed coastline of great beauty and mystery, a lost world where Aboriginals roamed, hunted, and gathered, minding their own business and living off the sacred land.

At the time of the European invasion, there were more than 500 Aboriginal tribes, each linked by its own religion, language, and family relationships. The Aboriginals had no writing, but relied on a complex structure of spoken and sung myths passed on by elders. They were incredibly proficient nomads who flourished on a seemingly empty, inhospitable continent, without money, property, "work," houses, clothes, kings, priests, or slaves. Right from the beginning, when white men first offered trinkets in exchange for what little the Aboriginals seemed to possess, they resented the spiritual oneness these indigenous people had with the land. The Aboriginals were in tune with their environment and the cosmos long before aromatherapy, secondhand religions, mutual funds, facelifts, expensive chocolate-chip cookies, big-screened televisions, and the World Wide Web.

Ever since Dale and I got married in 1975, we had been living a life of travel that can only be described as fabulous. In all those years, as I struggled to become a writer and Dale became a teacher, and later when I stayed at home to take care of our girls from the time they were babies, we never had two full incomes. We scrimped, we budgeted, and we sold coin and stamp collections, family heirlooms, paintings, and first editions of books. In short, we garage-saled everything the second it outgrew its usefulness. We did without big-screened televisions, CD players, dining-room sets, and a big house with a couple of cars in the driveway—things that a couple who have been married for more than two decades usually aspire to, material things that family and friends have constantly urged us to acquire. A long time ago, though, like Chatwin, we decided to use our money, time, and energy for travel. We never stay still for very long. Every few years, as romantic nomads, we've managed to rid ourselves of our material possessions so that we can travel to the most amazing places on Earth.

Over the years as I read Chatwin's books, I actually felt, much as anyone does who gets a writer into his metabolism, that I knew Bruce personally. Each book was a message from a long-lost friend. I soon discovered that what I liked best about him was his jaunty, wistful quality, his endlessly curious intellect and comic angle of vision. And although he could be neurotic, his profound optimism in the face of nearly everything revealed a stout heart. Still, for someone who appeared in print to be so upbeat and on the move, there was also something doomed and static about him, tendencies that were confirmed the day I heard about his premature demise.

Chatwin died in 1989 at 48, supposedly from a rare bone fungus after eating a so-called thousand-year-old black egg somewhere in China. Actually, though, he died very unglamorously of AIDS in Nice, France, and was buried in an unmarked grave next to a 10th-century Byzantine chapel on Greece's Peloponnese Peninsula. If Chatwin and his wife, Elizabeth, had managed to have the kids they had claimed they wanted, and Chatwin had stayed at home to look after them and travel the world the way I do, perhaps he might be alive today. And he might have even penned a book similar to the one I'm writing.

Instead, Chatwin's unconventional marriage had perhaps allowed him too much leash. He was childless and unencumbered by an all-consuming domestic life. Besides being an obsessive traveler and an insatiable romantic, he was a promiscuous bisexual, a connoisseur of the extraordinary, and a brilliant amateur photographer. For better or worse, he was the quintessential Peter Pan. He could be annoyingly pretentious, chauvinistic, metaphysically suspect, and down-right flighty, but his boyish Robert Louis Stevenson charm, his rampant enthusiasm and talent as a writer, usually won the day.

When his first book, *In Patagonia*, turned the world of travel writing on its ass in 1979 and became an instant classic, Chatwin was able to become a full-time writer and a wanderer with a mission. What no one could have predicted was that he would inspire a generation of travelers to break loose and roam the planet with their pens.

In 1997, after rereading *The Songlines*, Dale and I decided to hit the road again and travel down to Byron Bay, a small coastal town of 3,000 Australian souls near the Queensland–New South Wales border. A chronic wanderer who can't settle down, I longed to write my own anatomy of restlessness. Like Chatwin, Dale and I wanted to get away from the noise of the late 20th century and see if it was possible to have one last blazing adventure before permanent domestic imprisonment closed in. So we clawed our way out of our former life in Ottawa to go on a 12-month walkabout in search of *mana*, the sacred, magical power of the primitive that promises hope, freedom, and escape. To many friends at the time, I must have seemed like a crazed, burnt-out, middle-aged Huckleberry Finn with a surfboard tucked under one arm. But I saw our journey as a romantic desire to temporarily give my family a safe harbor from the modern world, a kind of Dreamtime versus Machinetime.

As early as 1970, even before Chatwin considered himself a writer, he had dug up evidence to validate the itch to wander. In an early *Vogue* article, "It's a Nomad Nomad NOMAD World," he said that brain specialists who took encephalographic readings of travelers found that changes of scenery and awareness of the passage of seasons throughout the year stimulated the rhythms of the brain, contributing to a sense of well-being and an active purpose in life. Monotonous surroundings and tedious, regular activities wove patterns that produced fatigue, nervous disorders, apathy, self-disgust, and violence. So, Chatwin argued, it wasn't surprising that people protected from the cold by central heating and from the heat by air-conditioning should feel the need for journeys of mind or body, for drugs, sex, and music. After all, he wrote in the *Vogue* piece, "We spend far too much time in shuttered rooms."

Being an incurable nomad himself, Chatwin spent a couple of decades try-ing to breathe life into a "big" book about nomads that he wanted to call *The Nomadic Alternative*. After he gave up his cushy job as one of the youngest-ever directors of the London auction house Sotheby's of London, after terminated his intensive research and field studies in archaeology, he decided to write and travel as much as he could. When he left Sotheby's, Chatwin wanted to get rid of his horror of expensive art objects that had to be assessed, sent for, put up, possessed, and sold, so he set out to study nomads. Two sweeping statements he came up with were that the Bible is about the conflict between nomads and settlers and that religion is the travel guide for settlers. Instead of hunting objects, he decided to hunt for stories. As he once put it, "To have your fingers twitch for a notebook is better than having them twitch for a checkbook anyday."

Leaving only a cryptic telegram that said "Gone to Patagonia for six months," Chatwin embarked on the first of many journeys that led to a half-dozen extraordinary books. *In Patagonia* was an attempt to limn a Cubist picture of that remote part of southern Argentina that is peopled by expatriates and exiles. Although the book avoids introspection, it is full of deeply personal material— a blend of fiction and the oddest facts imaginable, a collage of impressions, memories, histories, and stories that takes into account Elizabethan sea voyages, Butch Cassidy, the revolutionary uprisings of Indians, the lonely farms of Welsh Patagonians, and a possible source of the Ancient Mariner.

After he published the exquisitely bizarre *The Viceroy of Ouidah* and a haunting novel, *On the Black Hill*, Chatwin felt driven once more to write the nomad book. It was to be a wildly ambitious work that would enlarge on Blaise Pascal's dictum about humans being unable to sit quietly in a room. The contention in *The Songlines* would be that man had acquired, together with his straight legs and striding walk, "a migratory drive or instinct to walk long distances through the seasons." Chatwin wanted to trace the longings of civilized people for the natural life of nomads and other primitive peoples. He had a nostalgia for Paradise, a belief that all those who have resisted or remained unaffected by civilization have a secret happiness the civilized have lost. Such notions were bound up in the idea of the Fall of Man, utopias, and the Myth of the Noble Savage.

Chatwin insisted that we are travelers from birth, that our mad obsession with technological progress is a response to barriers impeding our geographical progress. Movement, he felt, is the best cure for melancholy, and all our activities are linked to the idea of journeys. According to Chatwin, our brains have an information system that relays our orders for the road, and that this is the mainspring of our restlessness. Early on people discovered they could release this information all at once by tampering with the chemistry of the brain. They could fly off on an illusory journey or an imaginary ascent. Consequently, Chatwin asserted, "Settlers naively identified God with the vine, hashish, or a hallucinatory mushroom, but true wanderers rarely fell prey to this illusion. Drugs are vehicles for people who have forgotten how to walk."

So, in December 1982, he packed up his old nomad notebooks, which he had kept after he burned an earlier unpublishable manuscript. These notebooks

Giants may have once roamed here: a view of Lennox Point, near Byron Bay, from the author's beach house at Seven Mile Beach. Dale Taylor

contained a mishmash of nearly indecipherable jottings, thoughts, quotations, brief encounters, travel sketches, and notes for stories. He brought all this material to Australia because he planned to wander the desert, away from libraries and other writers' works, and wanted to take a fresh look at what his notebooks contained.

After arriving in Sydney, Chatwin succumbed to total hedonism at a beach house at Bondi Beach. Then, from Adelaide, he traveled to the outback and on to the Aboriginals' Red Centre where he visited Alice Springs and Uluru (Ayers Rock) in Northern Territory, searching for proof to validate his nomad theories. A couple of years later, while he attended the Adelaide Writers' Festival with Salmon Rushdie, he made a second important visit to Alice Springs and Uluru. In a four-wheel-drive Toyota, he and Rushdie toured the outback, talked about life and literature, and climbed Ayers Rock. All told, Chatwin's time in the heart of Australia amounted to a mere nine weeks.

A few years after that, however, he produced *The Songlines*, which became a literary bestseller. In the book, Chatwin and his eccentric friend Arkady set out to discover the paradoxical meanings of the invisible pathways that meander all over Australia, trails known to Europeans as Dreaming Tracks or Songlines (the latter popularized by Chatwin) and to the Aboriginals as the Footprints of the Ancestors or the Way of the Law.

Two-thirds of *The Songlines* deals with this Don Quixote/Sancho Panza–like quest of two holy fools—Chatwin and Arkady—as they travel the desert to investigate nomadic Aboriginal culture that had been operating for nearly 50,000 years. On this journey, they speak a profound and silly dialogue concerning both sides of Chatwin's own inner conversation about restlessness. Arkady (a name that deliberately suggests poetry and an ideal, rustic paradise) is actually an invented character inspired in part by the outback dialogues Chatwin had had with Rushdie. But more important, Arkady's character is modeled on Anatoly Sawenko, an Australian-born son of a Ukrainian immigrant. Sawenko worked as a consultant to the Central Australian Land Council; his job was to make sure the proposed railroad line from Alice Springs to Darwin didn't interfere with any sacred Aboriginal sites. Hooking up with Sawenko gave Chatwin an inside access to indigenous desert culture.

The remaining third of *The Songlines* consists of Chatwin's loosely connected scribblings and quotations about the book of nomads he had originally intended to write. It isn't until the middle of his Australian book that Chatwin confesses he had a presentiment that the traveling phase of his life might be over and that before the malaise of settlement creeps over him, he wants to shed light on what is for him the question of questions: "the nature of human restlessness."

"Why," he asks by way of Pascal, "must a man with sufficient to live on feel drawn to divert himself on long sea voyages? To dwell in another town? To go off in search of a peppercorn. Or go off to war and break skulls."

Like all unencumbered male writers, Chatwin would probably have been severely cramped by a nagging mortgage and a couple of snarling kids. Be that as it may, *The Songlines* drew me into a walkabout with its author, and along the way I was given the opportunity to experience wild Australia and the wounded Aboriginals' collision with the white man's burden. Chatwin, via arresting images and a perfect ear for dialogue, speaks of the wandering Aboriginals' seasonal return to sacred places to make contact with ancestral roots established in the Dreamtime. And, as usual, he slips out of the back door of his own unfinished story—neither settler nor true nomad.

Some Australians feel Chatwin exploited Aboriginal culture in what they contend amounts to a literary hoax, while others believe he articulated something profound. Australian writer Thomas Keneally who wrote the novel *Schindler's Ark* (the basis of the film *Schindler's List*) claimed, in an interview, that *The Songlines* was a truly cosmic book. Keneally added: "Australians were raised to think that at the heart of Australia there was a dead heart. Australia is not European-sensibility friendly and it took a mad desert freak like Chatwin, a sort of literary T. E. Lawrence, to go to places like that. To realize that far from

Australia having a dead heart, there was a map, there had always been a map."

While gathering material for *The Songlines*, Chatwin actually stayed up in the hills above Byron Bay, near where my family and I lived. Unable to get his nomad book moving and utterly depressed by his unending quest for heightened reality, he only found solace in ocean windsurfing. Even though he read books, surfed, swam, and experimented with health food and magic mushrooms, by all accounts his restlessness irritated everyone he met.

Many of the travelers I encountered on the beaches and hiking trails in Byron Bay who weren't reading *The Fatal Shore* or Marlo Morgan's *Mutant Message Down Under* were devouring *The Songlines*. The Chatwin nomadic itch has inspired many to take off, despite the fierce umbilical pull of "shuttered rooms" in houses filled with stress-filled belongings that tie people down. Wandering may have settled some of Chatwin's natural curiosity and urge to explore, but he was always tugged back by a longing for a real home he never found. He had a strong compulsion to roam and perhaps an equally strong need to return, a homing instinct like that of a migrating bird. An unfortunate irony, given Chatwin's death shortly after *The Songlines* was published, is illustrated on the last page of the book when he says the mystics believed the ideal man will walk himself to a "right death" because he who has arrived "goes back."

Although at times Chatwin wasn't of this earth even when he was alive, he isn't really dead. Each of his books is still an invitation to a higher plane of romance and travel. Since 1989 a river of posthumous words continues to be published by and about Chatwin. And now that more than 10 years have passed since his death, I associate him with my longing to return to our beach house in Australia. Like all wanderers caught up in the necessary delusions of any number of fools' paradises, Chatwin, a little doomed by yearnings that could never be truly satisfied, is perhaps best summed up by something Robert Louis Stevenson once wrote: "You must remember that I will be a nomad, more or less, until my days are done."

As for my family and me, now that we've returned to Canada from our third sublime Australian walkabout, we're sort of thinking about settling down. But who knows?

The Writer's Trail

Following in the Footsteps

Destination: Australia is an island slightly smaller in size than all 48 conterminous U.S. states put together. With only 18 million people in a dozen cities that fringe its coastline, it is one of the last frontiers of the imagination. Australians are famous for their good-natured, sarcastic humor, colorful buggering of the English language, and happy-go-lucky outlook on life. After more than two centuries of European oppression, Australia's indigenous people and their fascinating culture are slowly gaining dignity through the Land Rights movement and attention from the rest of the world. For better or worse, the farther you stray from the coast the closer you'll get to the center of what Australia is really all about. But don't feel you have to leave the shore if you love the lure of the sea, because the best beaches in the world are in Australia.

Location: Australia is situated south of Indonesia and Papua New Guinea and between the Indian and Pacific Oceans.

Getting There: Many airlines and charter companies fly from Europe and North America to Australia. Qantas, Australia's number-one airline, can be reached in North America at 1-800-227-4500, or check out its Web site at *www.qantas.com*. Qantas's mailing address in the United States is Level 4, 841 Apollo Street, El Segundo, California 90245. No matter how you do it, though, your flight will be very expensive and long, given the distance involved, so it's probably advisable to make at least one stopover on your way to Australia, say, in Hawaii, Fiji, Tahiti, Tonga, or New Zealand. And don't forget that the seasons are opposite Down Under. September to November (spring) and March to June (fall) are generally quite pleasant in Australia and are good times to visit the country. Of course, with Sydney hosting the 2000 Summer Olympics, it may seem as if the whole world is planning to go to Oz at the beginning of the new millennium.

Tip: Although Australians prefer Canadians to Americans and Britons, they are easy to please if you refrain from showing them up.

Orientation: From east to west, Australia measures about 2,500 miles, while north to south it's around 2,000 miles. The country's major cities are Canberra (the capital), Sydney, Melbourne, Brisbane, and Perth. Sydney and Melbourne each have more than three million people, while Brisbane and Perth have populations exceeding one million. Most of Australia's people live along the coastal plain that fringes the island, with the greatest concentration on the southeastern coast. The interior, or outback, is largely flat, arid, and sparsely populated. The country is divided into six states and two territories: Western Australia, South Australia, Queensland, New South Wales, Victoria, Tasmania, Australian Capital Territory, and Northern Territory. Byron Bay, the easternmost point of mainland Australia, is in the northeast corner of New South Wales, near the Queensland border. Bondi Beach is found near Sydney, 500 miles south of Byron Bay. Uluru (Ayers Rock) and Alice Springs are in Northern Territory in what the Aboriginals call the Red Centre, literally the middle of the country.

Getting Around: Because Australia is so large, air travel is generally the best way to get around the country. There is a daily train from Sydney to Byron Bay, which takes about 12 hours, and there are plenty of buses connecting the two places. Qantas and Ansett are the two main domestic air carriers, and you can easily get flights to Alice Springs and Uluru (Ayers Rock). Greyhound Pioneer Australia is the country's national bus service, but long-distance travel by bus or train is something you should probably avoid. Rent a car instead. All the usual agencies (Hertz, Avis, et cetera) have offices in Sydney and there are numerous Australian companies, many of which are cheaper. Because gas is so expensive Down Under, traveling by car won't be cheap, but it will be a lot more comfortable and convenient.

Literary Sleeps

Alice Springs: There are plenty of places to stay here, from top-end hotels on the east side of the Todd River to a vast range of bed-and-breakfasts and backpacker hostels everywhere. Of particular note, though, is the Bond Springs Homestead 15 miles north of town. You can't beat this actual working cattle station for Aussie atmosphere, especially if you like taking your evening meals around a huge table in a ranch kitchen. Bond Springs Station, just off Stuart Highway. Tel.: (61-8) 8952-9888. Fax: (61-8) 8953-0963. E-mail: *bondhmst@alice.aust.com.* Inexpensive to expensive. The Todd Tavern will keep you in the thick of things—it's about as centrally located as you can get—but the bar bands that play on weekends may keep you awake. 1 Todd Street. Tel.: (61-8) 8952-1255. Inexpensive. However, if you want to actually bunk somewhere Bruce Chatwin did, check out the extremely popular Melanka Lodge. The hostel has everything from eight-bed dorms to single and double rooms, and it's bar, the Waterhole, is a great place to meet fellow travelers. 94 Todd Street. Tel.: 1-800-815-066 in Australia. Fax: (61-8) 8952-4587. Inexpensive.

Byron Bay: As in Alice Springs, accommodation possibilities abound here. Bruce Chatwin spent a relatively miserable time between Christmas and New Year's Day in Byron, staying at a house in the junglelike hills above the town. Chatwin felt strangled by the rainforest, and you can, too, at Taylors, set amid a riot of fig trees and camphor laurel above Byron. McGettigans Lane, Ewingsdale. Tel.: (61-2) 6684-7436. Fax: (61-2) 6684-7526. Expensive. Most people will want to stay near the beaches, though. Those with money to burn should find On the Bay Beach House to their liking, though children under 15 aren't welcome. 44 Lawson Street. Tel.: (61-2) 6685-5125. Fax: (61-2) 6685-5198. Expensive. Backpacker hostels, caravan parks, and beach motels are everywhere, but to keep in the Chatwin spirit of things, you can't go wrong with Nomads Byron Bay, a clean and friendly hostel with dorms and doubles. Lawson Street. Tel.: (61-2) 6685-8695. Inexpensive. And if you don't want to share your space with others but would rather not splurge, there's the Great Northern Hotel on Jonson Street. Tel.: (61-2) 6685-6454. Inexpensive.

 Tip: If you do get out on a walkabout in the outback, be careful. Intense sunlight and heat can dehydrate you rapidly, so wear a hat and carry plenty of water. And watch out for poisonous spiders and snakes. There are all kinds.

Uluru (Ayers Rock): You can't actually bed down right at the Rock, but you'll find a good range of lodgings in Yulara, about 12 miles north of the Aboriginal sacred site. According to Bruce Chatwin's biographer Nicholas Shakespeare, Chatwin and Salman Rushdie stayed in something called the Inland Motel, so you might want to search it out. At the very top end of things is the Desert Gardens Hotel, which has partial views of Uluru from balconies on the second floor of the newer portion of the hotel. Tel.: (61-8) 8956-2100. Extremely expensive. The slightly less pricey Outback Pioneer Hotel and Lodge has a good lookout point for sunset views of the Rock. The complex also has a very economical 20-bed dorm hostel and cabin-style rooms. Tel.: (61-8) 8956-2170. Inexpensive to expensive. The Spiniflex Lodge, near Yulara's visitors' center, will be kind to your pocketbook, but the in-room cooking facilities are limited and the bathrooms are communal. Tel.: (61-8) 8956-2131. Inexpensive.

Literary Sites

Alice Springs: As the base of the Arrernte (or Aranda) Aboriginal people, the largest town near Ayers Rock, and a convenient jump-off point into the outback, the Alice is a magnet for all those seeking to learn something about the culture of Australia's indigenous population. The white town was founded in the 1870s at the confluence of the usually dry Charles and Todd Rivers. A number of old buildings (Stuart Gaol, Old Courthouse) dating back to the early 1900s are found in the town's compact center. Visit the John Flynn Memorial Museum in Adelaide House on Todd Street. Flynn was the founder of Australia's famous Royal Flying Doctors, who have a base on Stuart Terrace that you can also take a look at. Bruce Chatwin used the work and theories of Professor Theodor Strehlow extensively in *The Songlines*, and the Strehlow Research Centre on Larapinta Drive houses the most extensive collection of Aboriginal spirit items in Australia (not open to the public) and features displays that focus on Strehlow's work and the culture of the Arrernte (Tel.: [61-8] 8951-8000; open daily 10:00 a.m. to 5:00 p.m.). After all that touring, you can eat an authentic Australian meal at the Red Ochre Grill opposite Adelaide House, complete with bush tucker (wattle seeds, yams, warrigal greens, bush tomatoes) or, if you're a carnivore, try "territory food" such as buffalo, kangaroo, and camel at the Overlander Steakhouse at 72 Hartley Street.

Byron Bay: Any town that names many of its streets after writers (Ben Jonson, Andrew Marvell, Robert Browning, Samuel Butler, to name some) has got to be author-friendly. Although it is odd that classic British authors get the nod rather than Australian writers. The other obvious literary connection here is that Captain James Cook named the place after Lord Byron's grandfather. Beaches are the big draw in this town—an incredible selection that ranges from miles of empty sand to tiny, secluded coves. When you get tired of sun and surf, take a stroll around Cape Byron Lighthouse, the most powerful beacon on the Australian coastline. It's on Lighthouse Road and is open daily from 8:00 a.m. to 5:30 p.m. This is also a good spot to hang-glide and whale-watch. If you're looking for a place to get a hearty breakfast with a sensational view of Clarks Beach and the possibility of dolphin sightings, head for the Beach Café. Or if you're really hungry after a long day of swimming and surfing, try the Raving Prawn in the Feros Arcade between Lawson and Jonson Streets.

Uluru (Ayers Rock): The Rock is located in Uluru-Kata Tjuta National Park in the heart of what Aboriginals call the Red Centre. A UNESCO World Heritage Site, Uluru has deep cultural and spiritual significance for the local Aboriginal people. The 1,140-foot-high weathered sandstone formation rises abruptly from the surrounding pancake-flat scrub. At dawn and sunset the Rock is stained scarlet and crimson in what has to be one of the world's greatest light shows. Various guided walks around the site are available.

Tip: To the local Aboriginal people, the Anangu, climbing Uluru is a desecration of the Rock. Many tourists still do so, but lately there's been a growing movement to refrain, symbolized by the sale of T-shirts that state: I Didn't Climb Ayers Rock.

Icon Pastimes

When Bruce Chatwin was on the coast, particularly at Sydney's Bondi Beach, he indulged in swimming, surfing, and windsurfing. At Byron Bay you can also hang-glide, scuba-dive at Julian Rocks a couple of miles offshore, and try your hand at trapeze flying at the Byron Bay Beach Club a couple of miles west of town. Byron Bay may well be the Alternative Lifestyle Capital of Australia, which is borne out by the many flotation-tank places and massage and acupuncture parlors. Quintessence Healing Sanctuary ([61-2] 6685-5533) at 8/11 Fletcher Street offers the New Age gamut from clairvoyance to sports massage. In Alice Springs, hot-air ballooning and camel rides are popular, or if you're lucky maybe an Aboriginal will show you how to carve and paint your own didgeridoo.

Contacts

Australian Tourist Commission: Level 4, 80 William Street, Woolloomooloo, Sydney, New South Wales 2011, Australia. Tel.: (61-2) 9360-1111. Fax: (61-2) 9331-2538. E-mail: *www.aussie.net.au.*

Northern Territory Tourism Commission: GPO Box 1155, Darwin, Northern Territory 0801, Australia. Tel.: (61-8) 8999-3900. Fax: (61-8) 8999-3888. E-mail: *www.nttc.com.au.*

Tourism New South Wales: GPO Box 7050, Sydney, New South Wales 2001, Australia. Tel.: (61-2) 9931-1111. Fax: (61-2) 9931-1424. E-mail: *www.tourism.nsw.gov.au.*

In a Literary Mood

Books

Chatwin, Bruce. *Anatomy of Restlessness: Selected Writings 1969–1989.* Edited by Jan Born and Matthew Graves. New York: Viking, 1996.

_____. *In Patagonia.* London: Picador, 1979. Chatwin deconstructed travel writing with his first book—a wonderful compendium of fact, fiction, and exotica rooted in Argentina's fabled southern region.

_____. *On the Black Hill.* London: Picador, 1983. All his life Chatwin wrestled with the nature of fiction and nonfiction. In his first novel, set on the Welsh border, he tackled fiction. But is it?

_____. *Photographs and Notebooks.* Edited by David King and Francis Wyndham. Toronto: Alfred A. Knopf Canada, 1993.

_____. *The Songlines.* London: Picador, 1988. Truth or fiction? In his attempt to get at the heart of nomadic existence and the mysteries of Australia's Aboriginals, Chatwin melded the two in such a way that it's as if he invented a new genre.

_____. *Utz.* New York: Viking, 1989. An evocative novel about an antique porcelain collector in Cold War Prague who has kept his priceless collection intact despite the ravages of Hitler and Stalin only to find himself a prisoner of his own mania.

_____. *The Viceroy of Ouidah.* New York: Summit, 1980. Quintessential Chatwin in its quirky focus on an off-the-beaten-track place—Dahomey—and an eccentric Portuguese slaver who founded a dynasty there that exists to this day.

_____. *What Am I Doing Here?* New York: Viking, 1989. An excellent collection of Chatwin's essays, travelogues, and portraits.

Clapp, Susannah. *With Chatwin: Portrait of a Writer.* London: Cape, 1997. Informative personal memoir by one of Bruce Chatwin's editors.

Davidson, Robyn. *Tracks.* London: Cape, 1980. Young Australian woman's inspiring journey across the outback with four camels and a dog.

Hughes, Robert. *The Fatal Shore.* New York: Vintage, 1988. The harrowing but fascinating story of white Australia's dark, epic beginnings.

Morgan, Marlo. *Mutant Message Down Under.* New York: HarperCollins, 1994. Fictional account of American woman's spiritual odyssey in Aboriginal Australia.

Morgan, Sally. *My Place.* New York: Seaver Books, 1988. A Western Australian woman describes how she discovered her Aboriginal roots in a book that put indigenous Aussie writing on the map.

Shakespeare, Nicholas. *Bruce Chatwin*. London: Harvill Press, 1999. This first definitive biography of Chatwin was authorized by the author's widow and family.

Guidebooks

Daly, Margo, Anne Dehne, David Leffman, and Chris Scott. *Australia: The Rough Guide*. 3rd ed. London: Rough Guides, 1997. This is my personal favorite guide to the country, although there are more than a dozen different ones to choose from.

Finlay, Hugh, and others. *Australia*. 9th ed. Hawthorn, Australia: Lonely Planet Publications, 1998. Since Australia is Lonely Planet's home turf, it's not surprising it does a good job of covering the country. Check out the company's many regional and city guides, too, including *Northern Territory*, *Bushwalking in Australia*, *New South Wales*, and *Sydney*.

Films/Videos

Crawford, Henry (producer). *A Town Like Alice*. David Stevens (director). Anchor Bay Entertainment, 1981. Available on video. Cast: Bryan Brown, Helen Morse, and Yuki Shimoda. Epic retelling of Nevil Shute's novel focuses on two lovers' struggle in World War II Malaysia and in the Australian outback.

Goldschmidt, John, and William Sargent (producers). *Utz*. George Sluizer (director). Viva Pictures, 1992. Available on video. Cast: Brenda Fricker, Armin Mueller-Stahl, and Paul Schofield. Mueller-Stahl is quite good in the title role of this mesmerizing adaptation of Bruce Chatwin's novel.

Graves, John, and Patricia Lovell (producers). *Picnic at Hanging Rock*. Peter Weir (director). Picnic Productions, 1975. Home Vision Cinema. Cast: Dominic Guard, Helen Morse, and Rachel Roberts. An eerie, edgy tale of three schoolgirls and their teacher who climb Australia's Ayers Rock and mysteriously disappear.

Hope, Anthony, Si Litvinoff, and Max L. Raab (producers). *Walkabout*. Nicholas Roeg (director). 20th Century Fox, 1971. Home Vision Cinema. Cast: Jenny Agutter, David Gulpilil, and Luc Roeg. Enigmatic, haunting, dreamlike tale of two white children and an Aboriginal youth adrift in the Australian outback.

Howarth, Jennifer (producer). *On the Black Hill*. Andrew Grieve (director). United Kingdom, 1987. Cast: Mike and Robert Gwilym, Gemma Jones, and Bob Peck.

Schepisi, Fred, and Roy Stevens (producers). *The Chant of Jimmie Blacksmith*. Fred Schepisi (director). Victorian Film Corporation/Australian Film Commission/The Film House, 1978. Cast: Tommy Lewis, Angela Punch, and Freddy Reynolds. Based on Thomas Keneally's novel, this searing indictment of white Australian racism toward Aboriginals still packs a powerful punch.

Stipetic, Lucki (producer). *Cobra Verde*. Werner Herzog (director). Werner Herzog Filmproduktion/ZDF, 1990. Cast: Salvatore Basile, Klaus Kinski, and José Lewgoy. Herzog, a close friend of Bruce Chatwin, directed and adapted this film, which was based on the latter's *The Viceroy of Ouidah*.

Web Sites

Australia: *www.csu.edu.au/australia/tourism.html.*

You can find enlightenment in the sun-shot flatlands of Australia's outback, but shooting the waves at Byron Bay has to be one of the most exhilarating experiences available Down Under. Denise Burch

"Splashes of crimson and

vermilion streak the western sky,

lending further beauty to the

dazzling glass-and-steel columns

of commerce that constitute

Vancouver on the horizon."

2   North America – West

Malcolm Lowry
Paradise Lost in Vancouver

M. R. Carroll

ON A BRILLIANTLY SUNNY Indian summer day, I stand on a scrap of beach on the north shore of Burrard Inlet and look westward. Gleaming in the distance are the office towers of Downtown Vancouver. Directly across the placid deep blue water is Burnaby Mountain and Capitol Hill. To the east, the inlet snakes north as Indian Arm. Behind me is a dense thicket of young pine, birch, and cedar and the lower slopes of Mount Seymour.

Call it Elysium, Eden, Paradise, Valhalla, Utopia, New Atlantis, El Dorado, Walden, Erewhon, Shangri-la, Heaven—its names are legion. People have always searched for ultimate happiness as represented by a mythical or legendary place. Malcolm Lowry, the acclaimed author of *Under the Volcano*, was no different than any of us in his pursuit of the ineffably elusive. What makes him unique is that he was convinced he had found Eden in a little squatter's shack that once stood a stone's throw from where I now bask in the rare sunlight of a West Coast autumn.

With a worldview not unlike that of Dante's, Lowry conceived of a personal *Divine Comedy* that envisioned Mexico as Inferno, New York City as Purgatorio, and the wilderness surrounding his shack as Paradiso. The author saw his own novels, those already written and those he never finished, as part of a daring, ever-changing master work called *The Voyage That Never Ends*. His Mexican book, *Under the Volcano*, incarnated Hell; *Lunar Caustic*, a novella about his unhappy stay in a mental asylum in New York, symbolized Purgatory; and *October Ferry to Gabriola* and "The Forest Path to the Spring," a novel and a long short story that present idyllic meditations on the joys of Canadian nature, conjured up Heaven on Earth. Other works, most of which were published after Lowry's death in England in 1957, fitted into his grand scheme as varying gradations of these three imaginary realms. Eventually Lowry's ambitious design evolved into eight novels, with *Under the Volcano* at the center of the construct.

Had he finished this purposely perpetual project, Lowry might have joined Marcel Proust, James Joyce, and Thomas Mann in the 20th century's pantheon of superliterary genius. Given his fabled predilection for alcohol and erratic behavior, of course, such a feat was never really in the cards. Like Orson Welles, another falling star who dreamed big projects but frequently failed to deliver, Lowry seemed cursed with an inability to complete things. Still, Welles did create *Citizen Kane*, a filmic tour de force for the ages, and Lowry gave us the gift of *Under the Volcano*, a novel so dense with symbolism, allusion, and rippling resonances that the experience of reading it seems to put one in touch with the thrust and parry of universal existence itself.

Born on July 28, 1909, in New Brighton, England, near Liverpool, Clarence Malcolm Lowry was an Englishman who was never comfortable in his native land. Like D. H. and T. E. Lawrence, Somerset Maugham, George Orwell, and Graham Greene, he possessed the soul of an Ancient Mariner. Inspired by the sailing tales of Herman Melville, Jack London, Eugene O'Neill, and Norwegian Nordahl Grieg, Lowry, at 17, took to the sea on a tramp steamer bound for the Far East. Five years later, in 1932, he graduated from Cambridge, then set out on a European Grand Tour. The following year he met his first wife, Jan Gabrial, and published his debut novel, *Ultramarine*, a slender volume that spun his nautical adventures into sophomoric fiction. Already a prodigious drinker and carouser, the young Lowry eventually touched down in New York City, where he was briefly detained in Bellevue Hospital, a harrowing trauma that later engendered *Lunar Caustic*.

Nineteen thirty-six, however, turned out to be one of the most significant years in the young writer's life. That was when he first encountered Mexico, his Inferno, a country that rocked his imagination like no other ever did, a place that nearly killed him, the scene of his final breakup with Jan. Fleeing Mexico, Lowry ended up in Los Angeles, where he quickly met his second wife, Margerie Bonner, the woman who stayed with him for the rest of his life no matter how hard things became, and they did get pretty rough. By the time Lowry and Margerie were married in 1940, they were settled in the first of three shacks they would inhabit on Roche Point in Dollarton, a village east of Vancouver on the north shore of Burrard Inlet. Paradise at last!

In Virgil's *Aeneid*, Eridanus (another name for the actual River Po in Italy) is a stream in the Elysian Fields that flows through a laurel grove, where the blessed dead, particularly poets, end up. The idea of Heaven in Hell no doubt appealed to

Lowry, and he built up his own mythology around what he called Eridanus Inlet (Burrard Inlet) and Enochvilleport (Vancouver). When describing his love for the land he drew strength from in order to write, Lowry could be quite eloquent, as is readily apparent in this passage from the opening of "The Forest Path to the Spring":

> Beyond, going toward the spring, through the trees, range beyond celestial range, crowded the mountains, snow-peaked for most of the year. At dusk they were violet, and frequently they looked on fire, the white fire of the mist. Sometimes in the early mornings, this mist looked like a huge family wash, the property of Titans, hanging out to dry between the folds of their lower hills. At other times all was chaos, and Valkyries of storm-drift drove across them out of the ever reclouding heavens.

Lowry could write equally well about Hell as he could about Heaven, perhaps even better, and with the massively sprawling Shellburn Refinery blighting the land directly across Burrard Inlet from the author's shack, he had more than enough to remind him of modern civilization's ugly side, as he vividly demonstrates in this description of Shell Oil's plant from *October Ferry to Gabriola*:

> But tonight, suddenly as if just now, this same sword-shaped pyre had reappeared, only looking ten times fiercer and taller, so that a fiendish lurid light coruscated from the whole refinery, each of whose cylindrical aluminum tanks reflecting the flambeaux in descending degrees of infernal brilliance, in turn sent those reflections wavering deep within the dark stream, wherein too, when a cat's-paw ruffled the surface, all the reflections in the water dithered together with the image striking down directly from the fiery torch itself, the reflections and the reflected reflections all wriggling and dithering and corkscrewing frenziedly together diminuendo like red-hot slice-bars in a stoker's nightmare. Those luminous digladiations gave at first the impression of taking place in sinister silence but in fact there was a hellish if magnificent din: from the oil-waste pyre came a whishing, whistling, consistent rushing roar, mingling with a noise like rattling giant chains which appeared to come from behind the oil tanks, sounds of machinery, half-submerged in the high lament of huge invisible saws in far sawmills northwestward. While they watched and listened, a coarse cerise light switched on, illuminating in large capitals erected against the grass slope below—someone having omitted to supply the initial S—the word HELL . . .

Before discovering the splendors—and rigors—of life on the wooded shore, Lowry had to endure residence in a number of houses and apartments in

Vancouver, principally on the West Side. Later, in the early 1950s when the winters seemed too harsh, he and Margerie rented various apartments (1359 Davie Street, 1075 Gilford Street, 1058 Nelson Street) in Vancouver's West End, a tightly packed residential area squeezed between Stanley Park and the city's downtown. During these stays, he must have really felt trapped in the jaws of Moloch, not to mention beset by the extra temptation of a lot more beer parlors.

A number of sites scattered around the Vancouver area served as real-life symbols for Lowry's polar extremities of existence. Several of his stories (most notably "The Bravest Boat" in *Hear Us O Lord from Heaven Thy Dwelling Place*) and poems make reference to Stanley Park, one of the largest urban parks in North America. It fascinated Lowry, particularly its wilder sections and Lost Lagoon, and, like Roche Point, it represented a piece of Heaven to him. Two Gulf Islands, Gabriola and Bowen, located in the Strait of Georgia between Vancouver and Vancouver Island, were seen by Lowry as paradisical. Of course, the residents of these islands, and the dozens of others sprinkled throughout the strait, also view their insular habitats in a utopian light, though these days Bowen, the closest island to the mainland (a 20-minute ferry ride), has become something of a bedroom suburb of Vancouver.

As for the flip side of his geographical mythology, Lowry had plenty of

Still a respite for the beleaguered city dweller, Stanley Park's Lost Lagoon, shown here as it appeared in 1927, was one of Malcolm Lowry's favorite haunts. Courtesy of Vancouver Public Library

Underworlds to choose from in the city itself. Unfortunately one of them, the Downtown Eastside, with its nexus at Hastings and Main Streets, is just as hellish today as it was when Lowry knew it. One of the highest concentrations of drug addicts in North America lives here, and many of the neighborhood's crumbling hotels have been turned into flophouses for indigent alcoholics and junkies. Prostitution is a fact of life, AIDS is rampant, and the homeless are myriad. No doubt Lowry sympathized with the damned and the desolate of this area of town, sandwiched between Gastown (where Vancouver got started) and Chinatown (one of the largest in North America). In a verse fragment he wrote, found in *The Collected Poetry of Malcolm Lowry*, he invokes the Malebolge, the name of the sinister barranca, or ravine, in *Under the Volcano*, but links it to Vancouver's skid row. The scrap of poetry captures his disgust with what the good burghers of Enochvilleport preferred to turn a blind eye to:

> Beneath the Malebolge lies Hastings street
> The province of the pimp upon his beat
> Where each in his little world of drugs or crime
> Drifts hopelessly, or hopeful, begs a dime
> Wherewith to purchase half-a-pint of piss
> Although he will be cheated, even in this.
> I hope, although I doubt it, that God knows
> This place where chancres blossom like the rose
> For in each face is such a hard despair
> That nothing like a grief finds entrance there.
> And on this scene from all excuse exempt
> The mountains gaze in absolute contempt.
> Yet this, this is Canada, my friend
> Yours to absolve of ruin, or make an end.

Most of the bars Lowry frequented in Vancouver are long gone, or they've turned into something else. A favorite Lowry watering hole, the Niagara Hotel at 435 West Pender Street, is now a spiffed-up, barless Ramada Inn, although the building is the same one the author knew. In the early 1950s, Lowry got together with another infamous drunk, Dylan Thomas, in the latter's room in the posh Hotel Vancouver at 900 West Georgia Street. You can imagine what they spent most of their time doing. When Lowry and Margerie wintered in the Kenmore Apartments (number 33) at 1075 Gilford Street, they were quite close to the Sylvia Hotel, one of Vancouver's landmarks. The hotel, at 1154 Gilford, is well situated on English Bay, something Lowry would have appreciated, and the bar, then as now, was a popular hangout for writers.

No matter where he drank in Vancouver, however, Lowry was perpetually aggrieved. British Columbia's liquor laws, as in most parts of Canada in the 1940s and 1950s, were remarkably Draconian. Hotels had two entrances, one for single men, the other for "ladies and escorts." Outdoor drinking terraces were nonexistent, alcohol couldn't be sold on Sundays and, in most cases, bars were murky, windowless dungeons hidden from view like smut under plain brown wrappers. In *Under the Volcano*, as in other Lowry works, the drinker's drinker heaped scorn on the provincial denizens of Canada's West Coast "jewel," with particular regard to what passed for pubs: "As for drinking, by the way, that is beset . . . everywhere beset by perhaps favourable difficulties. No bars, only beer parlours so uncomfortable and cold that serve beer so weak no self-respecting drunkard would show his nose in them. You have to drink at home, and when you run short it's too far to get a bottle." In fact, if Lowry wanted a case of beer, he had to (and did) walk several miles from his shack to the Lynnwood Inn at 1515 Barrow Street in North Vancouver, near the present-day Second Narrows Bridge, one of only two bridges that link the North Shore with Vancouver proper.

In June 1944, one of the most cataclysmic events of Lowry's life occurred: his beloved shack burned to the ground along with the manuscript of a novel called *In Ballast to the White Sea*. Thankfully Margerie was able to rescue the manuscript of *Under the Volcano* and dozens of poems, but the other novel was lost forever. Lowry, like Orson Welles, seemed prone to creative disaster. The movie director once lost most of his papers and many masters of his films in a fire in his apartment in Spain; besides losing a novel in a conflagration, Lowry had endured the horror of his only copy of the manuscript of his first novel, *Ultramarine*, being stolen from his publisher, forcing him to rewrite the book.

With the shack gone, Lowry and his wife sought refuge with friends back east in Oakville and Niagara-on-the-Lake, Ontario. Although he wrote most of *Under the Volcano* in his Dollarton cabin, he finished it in central Canada. In early 1945, the Lowrys returned to their Eden and built a third home on the inlet. Soon, though, they were off again; in fact, for the next four years they wandered the world, lingering in Mexico, New Orleans, Haiti, New York City, England, France, and Italy. While visiting New York in February 1947, Lowry finally received the satisfaction of seeing the much-rejected *Under the Volcano* published.

Although Lowry often left his shack by the sea, he always returned, like Odysseus to Ithaca. In January 1949, he and Margerie ended their peregrinations and settled down at Dollarton (with intermittent stays in Vancouver) until the summer of 1954. The land their home was built on was administered by the

District of North Vancouver, which for years had been trying to drive the squatters off and raze the shacks to make way for a proposed park. Originally the area had been home to shipyards and sawmills, and many of these companies' employees had lived in the shacks, a number of which had been slapped together during the Great Depression. After the mills closed and all but one shipyard ceased operations, fishermen and summering Vancouverites (like Lowry) took over the shacks. Then, as each shack became vacant, district bureaucrats made sure it was promptly bulldozed.

For Lowry and Margerie, the casting out from Paradise was regrettably unavoidable. Each winter in the cold-water shack seemed harsher than the last, the wicked minions of Enochvilleport were demanding substantial back income taxes, and the flinty will of the city to the west couldn't be evaded anymore. Worse, irate burghers were harassing them by boat offshore, exclaiming by loudspeaker that "This eyesore has to go!" So the couple packed up their belongings reluctantly, said goodbye to their friends, and headed east to New York City, where they caught a ship to Italy. A year later, in London, England, Lowry, who always drank far more heavily when he was away from his much-loved shack, was committed to a psychiatric hospital after repeated benders and a total breakdown. A few months after that he was released, and he moved to Ripe in Sussex, where he spent the remaining year and a half of his life, trying hard to write, struggling with his inner demons, feuding violently with his wife. The end came after a horrific row with Margerie that caused her to flee their country cottage. Left alone, it appears Lowry kept drinking and then downed a vial of sleeping pills, resulting in his death a few weeks before his 48th birthday, seemingly by drowning in his own vomit.

The coroner ruled the incident "death by misadventure," a vague euphemism that only further clouded the issue. Perhaps that's fitting, though. Lowry was a man whose soul was veiled in a fog of ambiguity. Suicide? Death as a kindness to his wife? Murder by neglect? Ghastly accident? Who knows? One can only conjecture what he might have accomplished if he could have pulled himself together and continued to write. What he did achieve, however, was one great novel, some very good stories and poems, and several unfinished works that hint at the treasures that might have been.

Like the man, Lowry's work is consumed by the clash of opposites and the concept of never-ending circularity. Ebb and flow, departure and return, descent and ascent, sinner and saint, Heaven and Hell are the stuff of his genius, and life. That he died back in the country where he was born, that he believed to the last that one day he would return to his rude shack on the Pacific shore, that new works by him continued to be published long after his death, seems

The view from Hell, or the Shellburn Refinery, in Burnaby, British Columbia, provides a misty eyeful of Malcolm Lowry's Paradise across Burrard Inlet, circa 1940s. Courtesy of Vancouver Public Library

only natural for a man who conceived of a voyage that can never end.

The shacks once inhabited by Lowry and his neighbors are long gone. Shellburn Refinery on the south shore of Burrard Inlet was dismantled years ago. One of the shipyards, McKenzie Barge and Marine Ways, still does business. Roche Point is now part of Cates Park, parts of which are sadly, for me, too domesticated. Today you can view a 50-foot Native war canoe and remnants of the Dollar Sawmill, picnic, buy an ice-cream cone or a rubbery hot dog at a snack bar, watch children and dogs gambol on the pruned grass, or, on the east side of the park, trudge the Malcolm Lowry Walk, which skirts the sites of the author's shacks. Of course, I've chosen the latter.

Canada's West Coast is blessed with spectacular sunsets on clear days and tonight's is truly a light show to remember. Splashes of crimson and vermilion streak the western sky, lending further beauty to the dazzling glass-and-steel-columns of commerce that constitute Vancouver on the horizon. Like the refinery seemingly afire at night in Lowry's day, the skyline of a metropolis that would surely have horrified the writer far more than the overgrown town he knew, could well embody Heaven and Hell in the same breath. Yet, as a cool wind begins to ruffle the purpling water, I find myself glancing east and north again toward what in the gathering gloom appears to be true wilderness. Driven, I hike on, past a trickling creek I imagine to be the almost sacred stream in Lowry's *Walden*-esque "The Forest Path to the Spring." A few stray seagulls swoop along the bruised arm of the sea, and wreaths of mist snake wispy tendrils across the faces of the humped viridian hills before me. I stumble on, finding it harder to see, but not wanting to return to the city just yet, still reaching for something not quite attainable, still searching for what is likely not even definable.

The Writer's Trail

Following in the Footsteps

Destination: Malcolm Lowry may have viewed the Vancouver of the 1940s and 1950s with a jaundiced eye, even though he never ceased to marvel at the natural beauty that surrounded it, but today's cosmopolitan city by the sea has much to recommend it. Despite overwhelming growth that has transformed Vancouver and the adjacent Lower Mainland into a conurbation of nearly two million people, the city's blend of mountains, sea, and forest still reigns supreme. Like their brethren to the south in California, Vancouverites fancy themselves laid-back and casual. Certainly they're not as intense and frenzied as Torontonians or New Yorkers. Weeks of seemingly endless sunshine in the summer are usually the rule, while relentless monsoonlike rain appears equally perpetual in the fall, winter, and spring. Still, it never gets really cold, snow is rare and generally fleeting (though in winter there's plenty to ski on in the nearby mountains), and there's always a coffee bar close at hand.

Location: Tucked into the southwest corner of British Columbia on Canada's West Coast, the Greater Vancouver area is hemmed and stitched by water: the Strait of Georgia to the west, Burrard Inlet in the north, English Bay, False Creek, and the Fraser River in the south. The U.S. border, to the south, is a mere hour's drive from Downtown Vancouver. Coast Mountains, including Black, the Lions, Grouse, and Seymour, rise precipitously above Burrard Inlet. To the east, the Fraser winds through the flats of a valley studded with suburbs and farmland.

Getting There: Many major international airlines fly to Vancouver, including Air India, American, British Airways, Cathay Pacific, Delta, Japan Airlines, KLM, Lufthansa, United and, of course, Air Canada ([604] 688-5515; Web site: *www.aircanada.ca/home.html*). Vancouver International Airport is on Sea Island in Richmond, eight miles south of Downtown Vancouver. Amtrak ([604] 585-4848 or 1-800-872-7245) operates a daily railroad service from Seattle to Vancouver, with connections from the former to other major U.S. cities. VIA Rail (1-800-561-8630) operates train service from Vancouver to Canadian cities in the east. The private service, Rocky Mountaineer ([604] 606-7200 or 1-800-665-7245), has now taken over VIA's Vancouver to Banff/Calgary, Alberta, route, but only runs trains from mid-May to early October. BC Rail ([604] 984-5246 or 1-800-663-8238), the provincially run service, operates rail service from North Vancouver to Squamish, Whistler, Lillooet, 100 Mile House, Williams Lake, Quesnel, and Prince George in the north. Amtrak, VIA, and Rocky Mountaineer operate out of Pacific Central Station in Vancouver at 1150 Station Street, just off Main Street. BC Rail trains depart and arrive from BC Rail Station at 1311 West First Street in North Vancouver. Intercity buses run by Greyhound ([604] 662-3222), Maverick ([604] 662-8051), and Pacific Coach Lines ([604] 662-8074) also operate out of Pacific Central Station. Greyhound links Vancouver to Seattle, other U.S. cities, and eastern Canadian destinations. Pacific Coach connects Vancouver and Victoria, the capital of British Columbia, on Vancouver Island. Maverick operates buses to various B.C. locations, including Nanaimo, Whistler, and Pemberton. You can also reach Vancouver by car ferry, once you're in British Columbia. BC Ferries Corporation (1-888-223-3779) operates numerous routes from Horseshoe Bay, north of Vancouver, and Tsawwassen, south of the city. Ferries link Horseshoe Bay with Nanaimo, Bowen Island, and the Sunshine Coast; ferries from Tsawwassen go to Victoria, Nanaimo, and various Gulf Islands.

Tip: Make sure you bring an umbrella; you'll likely need it at some point no matter what time of the year you visit Vancouver.

Orientation: Greater Vancouver is comprised of West and North Vancouver, the City of

Vancouver, Burnaby, Port Coquitlam, Coquitlam, Surrey, Langley, New Westminster, Richmond, Delta, White Rock, and several other municipalities and communities. One of the first things you'll notice once you're in the City of Vancouver is the number of bridges, which isn't surprising since the city is surrounded by water on three sides. Gastown, Downtown Vancouver, Yaletown (an area of pubs, cafés, and galleries popular with twenty-somethings), the West End, and Stanley Park are on a slender peninsula that curves like a fist northward to West and North Vancouver, across Burrard Inlet. The rest of the city is on a bigger peninsula that stretches from the Fraser Valley farmland in the east to the Strait of Georgia in the west. The West Side, where Malcolm Lowry resided briefly at several locations, includes the neighborhoods of Kitsilano, Point Grey, and Kerrisdale, as well as the extensive campus of the University of British Columbia. Kitsilano features plenty of good restaurants and bars, beaches with great views, and lots of shopping possibilities. On the East Side, close to Gastown, is Chinatown and the Downtown Eastside, the city's poorest neighborhood. Farther east is the Commercial Drive area (sometimes called Little Italy or just the Drive), a lively mix of cafés, restaurants, boutiques, and ethnic groups. Cates Park, where Lowry's three shacks were once located, is in Dollarton in the District of North Vancouver on the north shore of Burrard Inlet, northeast of the City of Vancouver.

Getting Around: Vancouverites who don't rely solely on cars grumble about their public-transit system, and it does have its problems (largely due to not keeping up with the city's spectacular growth), but you can pretty well get to anywhere you want, although expect slow service and crowded buses. From the airport to Downtown Vancouver, you have three options: taxis; shuttle buses, including Vancouver Airporter ([604] 946-8866); and city buses (Coast Mountain BusLink, formerly BC Transit, [604] 521-0400). Airporter's buses leave the airport every 30 minutes, starting at 6:30 a.m., with the last bus departing just after midnight. They make regular stops at most major downtown hotels and at Pacific Central Station. To get by city bus to the center of things, you'll have to take the number 100 and transfer to the number 20 at Granville Street and Seventieth Avenue. Unless you want to spend a lot of time getting to know Vancouver's lumbering buses and trams, you'll probably want to go with one of the other two options. The jewels of Vancouver's public-transit system are SkyTrain and SeaBus. The first is a computerized above- and below-ground rapid-transit train that connects Downtown Vancouver to Burnaby, New Westminster, and Surrey. The city is currently in the process of massively expanding this service, but completion will no doubt take years. SeaBus is a fast passenger-only catamaran service that connects Downtown Vancouver (at Waterfront Station) with North Vancouver. The 15-minute trip is worth it, even if you don't really want to go to North Vancouver, since you'll get a sensational eyeful of Vancouver Harbour and the city's skyline. There are also mini-passenger ferries connecting Granville Island (a must-see blend of shops, markets, restaurants, cafés, theaters, and galleries) to Downtown Vancouver and Kitsilano. To get to Cates Park, you have two options. Take the SeaBus to Lonsdale Quay in North Vancouver, then transfer to bus numbers 229 or 239 to Phibbs Exchange. At Phibbs climb on a number 212 for Deep Cove. Make sure you tell the driver you want to get off at Cates Park. A quicker way might be to take bus number 210 from Downtown Vancouver (Burrard SkyTrain station, Bay 2) to Phibbs Exchange, then transfer to the 212. Of course, you can also rent a car, in which case you'll take the Second Narrows Bridge over to North Vancouver, exit east on the Dollarton Highway, and continue east on the highway until you hit the park.

Literary Sleeps

Hotel Vancouver: Over the years, there have been three Hotel Vancouvers. The current incarnation, one of the quintessentially Canadian château-style railroad hotels with green copper roofs, was opened in 1939, just in time to play host to England's King George VI. Malcolm Lowry first met Canadian poet and novelist Earle Birney here in 1947. Birney became a fast friend and later edited Lowry's poems and *Lunar Caustic*. Not surprisingly, publishers and writers love this place, those who can afford it. If it's out of your budget, merely hanging around in the comfortable bar may do, or you can splurge on an afternoon tea, served daily. 900 West Georgia Street. Tel.: (604)

684-3131 or 1-800-441-1414. Extremely expensive.

Hotel Georgia: Just down the street from Hotel Vancouver, this classy, slightly less expensive alternative was built in the 1930s and has stately rooms that are larger than those in most modern establishments. There's also a lively eatery called the Georgia Street Bar and Grill, with plenty of live music. 801 West Georgia Street. Tel.: (604) 682-5566 or 1-800-663-1111. Expensive.

English Bay Inn: Although small (only five rooms) and pricey, this 1930s bed-and-breakfast is quite genteel and features four-poster beds in each room, a little garden, and a lot of West End charm. 1968 Comox Street. Tel.: (604) 683-8002. Moderate to expensive.

Ramada Inn: In Malcolm Lowry's day, this place was called the Niagara Hotel, and it was one of the writer's favorite spots to get a drink. Newly renovated and reopened as one of the Ramada chain's several inns in the Vancouver area, the hotel doesn't have a beer parlor anymore, but you'll find plenty of those within walking distance. The Ramada people have done a good job of returning the hotel to its former period self, with all the usual modern amenities. 435 West Pender Street. Tel.: (604) 488-1088. Moderate.

West End Guest House: This eight-room Victorian-style bed-and-breakfast was built in 1906 and will make you feel as if you've stepped back in time, particularly since it's only a block from Robson Street, the city's main shopping thoroughfare. 1362 Haro Street. Tel.: (604) 681-2889. Moderate.

Sylvia Hotel: This venerable grand dame of Vancouver hotels opened its doors in 1912, and though it's a bit worn around the edges, it's easily one of the best bargains in the city. Next door to Stanley Park and ensconced on English Bay, the hotel can't be beat for location. The Sylvia's comfy, English-style bar was frequented by Malcolm Lowry when he lived down the street. Book many months ahead! 1154 Gilford Street. Tel.: (604) 681-9321. Inexpensive to moderate.

 Tip: Vancouver isn't as big a city as New York, Chicago, Los Angeles, or Toronto, but it does have more than its share of panhandlers. How you handle them, those deserving of some sympathy and those merely hustling, is up to you, but you'll find them particularly numerous on Granville Street, in Gastown, and in the Commercial Drive area.

Literary Sites

Cates Park: Only two places in the world truly put you in touch with the essence of Malcolm Lowry. Cuernavaca in Mexico is one of them; this is the other. Fittingly, just like the man, Cates and Cuernavaca are polar opposites in atmosphere, ambience, and appearance. You'll find the Malcolm Lowry Walk at the eastern end of the park. There's also a cairn devoted to the author. Except for the shore (minus the shacks), some of the trees, Burrard Inlet itself, and the view (minus Shellburn Refinery, although you can see Chevron's smaller plant farther west), a lot has changed. In some ways, the area is more pristine, with the removal of most of the industry in the immediate vicinity, but a good deal of the park is pretty domesticated and there are a lot more housing developments than there were in Lowry's day (he was already complaining about that trend back in the early 1950s). Dollarton, three miles east of the Second Narrows Bridge, off the Dollarton Highway, in the District of North Vancouver.

Museum of Anthropology: This splendid museum didn't exist when Malcolm Lowry lived in the Vancouver area, but he likely would have made a trek out to it if it had. Simply put, this may well be the most spectacular museum in the city as far as architecture, setting, and collection go. Perched on the Strait of Georgia at the western extremity of the University of British Columbia campus, the grounds of the museum feature a magnificent Haida village and totem poles. Inside the Arthur Erickson–designed glass building, you'll find plenty of West Coast Native poles, masks, and other artifacts, as well as Haida artist Bill Reid's unforgettable sculpture *Raven and the First Men*. Open daily in the summer from 10:00 a.m. to 5:00 p.m., and to 9:00 p.m. on Tuesday; rest of the year, from 11:00 a.m. to 5:00 p.m., but closed Monday. There's an admission charge, but entrance is free on Tuesdays from 5:00 to 9:00 p.m. 393 Northwest Marine Drive. Tel.: (604) 822-5087.

Stanley Park: Vancouver has its share of top-notch museums, but perhaps its real "galleries" are its parks, and Stanley is as close to the soul of the metropolis's inhabitants as anything can get. A 1,000-acre package of Douglas fir, cedar, hemlock, meadows, ponds and lakes, beaches, and various attractions (including an aquarium, restaurants, a children's miniature railroad, and a splendid six-mile seawall promenade), it straddles a peninsula almost completely surrounded by ocean. There are monuments to Scottish poet Robert Burns (near Lost Lagoon) and to Pauline Johnson, the Canadian Mohawk "princess" poet who lived briefly in Vancouver in the early 20th century and penned *Legends of Vancouver*, a collection of West Coast Native tales. Johnson's grave and memorial are near Ferguson Point. Incidentally Lost Lagoon got its name from the title of a poem by Johnson. So far there are no memorials to Malcolm Lowry, but he and his wife loved walking in the park, and you will, too. Don't just stick to the seawall, though; hike among the cathedrals of Douglas fir in the interior.

Vancouver Art Gallery: The permanent collection in the city's chief art gallery is something of a disappointment, and the space, located in what used to be Vancouver's courthouse, doesn't usually attract world-class exhibitions, but its collection of Canadian painter Emily Carr's work is unmatched. Like Malcolm Lowry, Carr was tuned into the West Coast's natural treasures. Her paintings of Native villages, totem poles, coastal scenes, and trees are worth a million words. Open in the summer Monday to Friday from 10:00 a.m. to 6:00 p.m., Thursday to 9:00 p.m., Saturday to 5:00 p.m., and Sunday noon to 5:00 p.m.; closed on Monday and Tuesday from mid-October to Easter weekend. There's an admission price. 750 Hornby Street. Tel.: (604) 662-4719.

Icon Pastimes

Take a stroll along Malcolm Lowry Walk in Cates Park with a copy of *Hear Us O Lord from Heaven Thy Dwelling Place* and a mickey of tequila or Bols gin (or a bottle of mescal, if you can get it) in your pack and soak up the scenery the author loved so much, then drop by the Raven Pub at 1060 Deep Cove Road. There are more than two dozen beers on tap, a great selection of Scotch, good food, and a fireplace. You can bet Lowry would have been a regular if this place had existed in his day. Sit on the Stanley Park seawall, watch the ships go by, and dream of sailing around the world. Motor up to Horseshoe Bay and hop on a ferry to Bowen Island, or to Nanaimo on Vancouver Island. You'll have to go to the latter if you want to get a ferry to Gabriola Island. Relax and reread *October Ferry to Gabriola*; you'll have plenty of time. Part of the true Vancouver experience involves at least one Gulf Island ferry jaunt. Pub-crawling in the West End, Downtown (try the Piccadilly Pub at 620 West Pender Street or the Railway Club at 579 Dunsmuir Street), Yaletown or, if you're courageous, the Downtown Eastside will also put you in the Lowry spirit, particularly if you bring a copy of *Under the Volcano* with you. Stay away from ravines and pariah dogs.

Contacts

City of Vancouver: City Hall, 453 West Twelfth Avenue, Vancouver, B.C. V5Y 1V4 Canada. Tel.: (604) 873-7011. Web site: *www.city.vancouver.bc.ca*.

Tourism British Columbia: 4252 Commerce Circle, Victoria, B.C. V82 4M2 Canada. Tel.: (250) 953-2680, or in Vancouver (604) 435-5622. Web site: *www.travel.bc.ca*.

Tourism Vancouver: 200 Burrard Street in the Waterfront Centre, Plaza Level. Tel.: (604) 683-2000. Web site: *www.tourismvancouver.com.*

In a Literary Mood

Books

Bowker, Gordon. *Pursued by Furies: A Life of Malcolm Lowry.* Toronto: Random House, 1993. Not too many authors get two superb biographies. Bowker's weighty treatment is rich in detail about the man's life and is a joy to read.

Cross, Richard K. *Malcolm Lowry: A Preface to His Fiction.* Chicago: University of Chicago Press, 1980. A good, short introduction to many of the themes in Lowry's work.

Day, Douglas. *Malcolm Lowry: A Biography.* New York: Oxford University Press, 1984. Winner of the National Book Award in the United States, this first major biography of Lowry set the standard for Lowry scholarship. It's still pretty good after all these years (it originally came out in the early 1970s), but the book does favor analysis of Lowry's work over details about his life, and Day can be a little too scathing about some of Lowry's posthumous works.

Grace, Sherrill E. *The Voyage That Never Ends: Malcolm Lowry's Fiction.* Vancouver: University of British Columbia Press, 1982. Grace focuses on the linked nature of Lowry's creative vision and provides some interesting insights into his symbols and allusions.

Lowry, Malcolm. *The Collected Poetry of Malcolm Lowry.* Edited and introduced by Kathleen Scherf. Vancouver: University of British Columbia Press, 1992.

_____. *Dark as the Grave Wherein My Friend Is Laid.* London: Penguin, 1979. A kind of sequel to *Under the Volcano*, only this time the story follows the journey of West Coast Canada novelist Sigbjorn Wilderness to Mexico City, Cuernavaca, and Oaxaca. Cobbled together from reams of manuscript by Margerie Lowry and Douglas Day, Lowry's first biographer, the novel is only a pale shadow of what it might have been. Fascinatingly, Lowry's alter ego, Wilderness, is a writer who has written a novel not unlike *Under the Volcano* and he has come to Mexico to revisit the sites he wrote about. Fiction becomes life becomes fiction in Lowry's personal postmodern perambulation

_____. *Hear Us O Lord from Heaven Thy Dwelling Place.* New York: J. B. Lippincott, 1963. After *Under the Volcano* and *Lunar Caustic*, this collection of long short stories is Lowry's best work. Particularly noteworthy from a Vancouver point of view are "The Forest Path to the Spring" and "The Bravest Boat." Also quite good are "Elephant and Colosseum" (set in Rome) and "Through the Panama" (based on Lowry's late 1940s sea voyage to Europe).

_____. *October Ferry to Gabriola.* New York: World Publishing, 1970. The names of Lowry's protagonists change, but essentially they're always another self of the author. The novel relates the joys and tribulations of Ethan Llewelyn in Canada, especially those he experiences living in a shack near Vancouver with his wife, culminating with a voyage of renewal Llewelyn and his wife undertake to Gabriola Island in the Strait of Georgia. Margerie Lowry, the author's wife, edited her husband's unfinished manuscript. But be prepared: the book has many awkward and infelicitous moments.

_____. *Under the Volcano.* London: Penguin, 1984. As the Second World War is about to break out, Geoffrey Firmin, an alcoholic ex–British consul, wanders through time and bars in Cuernavaca (called Quauhnahuac here), Mexico. His spiritual journey into the dark pit of his soul is harrowing. Penguin is due to bring out a new edition of the novel, originally published in 1947, in March 2000.

Salloum, Sheryl. *Malcolm Lowry: Vancouver Days*. Madeira Park, BC: Harbour Publishing, 1987. Although it's a bit too hodgepodgy and not particularly well organized or designed, this look at sites and people associated with Lowry during his Vancouver years contains many tidbits of information the major biographers failed to notice.

Twigg, Alan. *Vancouver and Its Writers: A Guide to Vancouver's Literary Landmarks*. Madeira Park, BC: Harbour Publishing, 1986. If you want to find out things like where Jack London dallied when he tramped through Vancouver, or how Rudyard Kipling got hornswoggled buying land in the city, this is the book to get. It also has lots of excellent information on the many Canadian writers who make or have made Vancouver their home.

Guidebooks

Wershler, Terri, and Judi Lees. *Vancouver: The Ultimate Guide*. 7th ed. Vancouver: Greystone Books, Douglas & McIntyre, 1999. Of all the guides spawned in Vancouver itself, this much-reprinted one is easily the best.

Wyness, Chris. *Vancouver*. Hawthorn, Australia: Lonely Planet Publications, 1999. As to be expected, lots of publishers have produced guides to Vancouver, but the little Australian travelbook company that grew beats them all. Plenty of color photos, good sidebars on the city's notable features, and all the usual Lonely Planet attention to detail.

Films/Videos

Borman, Moritz, Michael Fitzgerald, Héctor López, and Wieland Schulz-Keil (producers). *Under the Volcano*. John Huston (director). Universal, 1984. MCA Home Video. Cast: Anthony Andrews, Jacqueline Bisset, and Albert Finney. Some novels are practically impossible to capture adequately on film. James Joyce's *Ulysses* is one; Lowry's masterpiece is another, although there's much that's eminently filmic about the book. But Huston does his best, and Finney makes a pretty good Geoffrey Firmin.

Brittain, Donald, and Robert Duncan (producers). *Volcano: An Inquiry into the Life and Death of Malcolm Lowry*. Donald Brittain (director). Documentary. National Film Board of Canada, 1976. Available on video. Richard Burton, who was born to play Geoffrey Firmin in *Under the Volcano*, narrates what is arguably the best documentary ever made about an author. Sadly Burton never got the chance to play the drunken consul, but while he was alive there was talk about it.

Web Sites

Malcolm Lowry: *www.interlog.com/~merlinds/volcano/index.html*. The site features information about Lowry, though it's badly written and not always trustworthy. Still, it does have some interesting photos of Cates Park and Ripe, Sussex, and some great links.

The Beats
Visions of San Francisco

Suzie Rodriguez

FROM THE BEGINNING—when the collection of adobe shacks facing the huge bay was still called Yerba Buena—the literary scene in San Francisco has been dominated by mavericks. Take Richard Henry Dana. After being kicked out of Harvard University for youthful rebelliousness in the mid-1830s, he shipped out as a common sailor aboard a hide-and-tallow buying vessel. His experiences along California's coast and in struggling Yerba Buena, recorded in *Two Years Before the Mast*, made him the city's first important writer.

Over the decades, countless other writer-rebels followed hard on his heels. Some are famous: Mark Twain, Bret Harte, Jack London, Dashiell Hammett, and William Saroyan. Others, although worthy or interesting enough to be remembered, are largely forgotten. Poet, writer, and sometime-actress Ada Clare, an openly unmarried mother in the middle of the 19th century, was considered "the fairest and most accomplished lady ever associated with American journalism" during her San Francisco years. Joaquin Miller's bandit verses were enormously popular. Ina Coolbrith, the country's first poet laureate, encouraged three generations of the city's writers (and introduced London, when a boy, to the world of books). Other forgotten literary nonconformists include Frances Fuller Victor, Ambrose Bierce, Porter Garnett, Yone Noguchi, Mary Austin, George Sterling, Gertrude Atherton, Oscar Lewis . . . The list is endless and impressive.

And that's before we even mention one of the few literary eras ever to become deeply ingrained in America's artistic psyche: the city's 1950s Beat scene. Just whisper the words "San Francisco's North Beach" to anyone with a smattering of literary pretension, and they're bound to respond with a mantra that goes something like this: "KerouacGinsbergBeatBeatsBeatnikshowlontheroadCoolManCool, and dig that craaazy jive!"

In the early 1950s, North Beach (the site of the once-infamous Barbary Coast) was the absolute bedrock of Beat. A quiet, down-at-the-heels, working-class neighborhood, the area, and its cheap rents, attracted young writers and artists disillusioned by the smug conformity of the postwar years. Together—place, time, people—they would produce a few of the decade's Big Bangs: a new and controversial literary style, a far-reaching legal precedent, a nation brimming with seditious beatniks.

Among the many poets who helped create this scene were Gary Snyder, Lawrence Ferlinghetti, Gregory Corso, Kenneth Patchen, Philip Whalen, Kenneth Rexroth, Robert Creeley, Philip Lamantia, Bob Kaufman, William Everson, and Michael McClure. Notable versifiers all, especially Snyder, who would go on to win the 1974 Pulitzer Prize.

However, when most people talk of that faraway time, two other writers inevitably come to mind first. Although both hailed from and usually resided on the East Coast, it's Jack Kerouac and Allen Ginsberg who will forever symbolize North Beach and its Beats.

Kerouac's visits to San Francisco, mostly clustered in the late 1940s and early 1950s, usually didn't last long. In fact, his most legendary stay—at the end of the 1949 cross-country drive with Neal Cassady, which formed the basis of *On the Road*—lasted only a few days. The longest and most significant time he spent in the city was in 1955–56.

At that time the San Francisco Renaissance, encompassing the poets mentioned above and others, was in full bloom. Kerouac stayed wherever and with whomever he could, usually in and around North Beach, near Russian Hill, or across the bay in Berkeley. Despite his frequent rudeness and surly, often drunken behavior, people were drawn to him. And why not? He could be charming, he was talented and intelligent, he was undeniably handsome, he was a strong believer in Buddhism and meditation, and he was open to adventure. Kerouac formed important friend-ships on this visit, particularly with Snyder, whom he strongly admired (and would eventually transform into Japhy Ryder, the hero of *The Dharma Bums*).

Ginsberg—a close friend of Kerouac's since their 1944 introduction in New York City—was living in San Francisco at this time, too. He had recently moved in with Peter Orlovsky, the man who would be his partner for many decades. He had also quit his job and decided to write poetry full-time. Unfortunately he was suffering from a massive writer's block. Kerouac tried to help by teaching him meditation and Buddhist theory, but it didn't do much good.

However, one day in early August 1955, quite miraculously, the writer's

The original caption for this photograph, penned by Allen Ginsberg himself, says it all: "Bob Donlin (Rob Donnelly, Kerouac's *Desolation Angels*), Neal Cassady, myself, painter Robert LaVigne, poet Larry Ferlinghetti, in front of City Lights Bookshop, Broadway and Columbus, North Beach, San Francisco, 1955. Donlin worked seasonally as a Las Vegas waiter, Neal looks good in T-shirt, *Howl* first printing hadn't arrived from England yet, Peter Orlovsky held camera in the street, we were just hanging around." Courtesy of Allen Ginsberg estate and Fahey/Klein Gallery, Los Angeles

block lifted. Ginsberg sat down in his edge-of-the-Beach apartment, started pecking at the typewriter, and produced in a single sitting the long poem that would alter mid-century American literature: *Howl*.

The poem was first introduced to the world in San Francisco on the night of October 13, 1955, a date most historians consider to be the defining moment in Beat chronology. The event was a poetry reading held in a converted auto-repair shop known as the Six Gallery. Notices had been put up around town, and more than 100 hipsters had gathered that evening (including Cassady, who arrived in his railroad brakeman's uniform; Kerouac; and poet/publisher/book-store owner Ferlinghetti). In his book *The Birth of the Beat Generation*, Steven Watson states that a tangible air of excitement filled the room, "for it was the first time the scattered contingents of San Francisco's poetry intelligentsia-bohemia had come together." Kenneth Rexroth emceed, and among the other poets reading were Lamantia, McClure, and Whalen.

At the beginning of the evening, Kerouac collected money for wine. The readings were delayed while he made a liquor-store run, but he soon returned with three gallon jugs of cheap California burgundy. The wine began making the rounds in the audience and the readings got under way.

It wasn't until 11:00 p.m. that skinny, bookish Ginsberg stood at the dais. Only a few of those present—Kerouac, Snyder, Ferlinghetti, and Whalen—had read his poem. Nobody else in the audience had any idea of what was to come. Ginsberg later admitted that he'd had quite a bit of wine and was feeling no pain as he glanced around the room. Nervous, a little shy, he spoke softly at first, allowing the galvanizing opening lines of *Howl* to work their particular magic: "I saw the best minds of my generation destroyed by madness, starving hysterical naked,/dragging themselves through the negro streets at dawn looking for an angry fix . . ."

Increasingly confident thanks to the crowd's enthusiastic reception, he spoke louder and began swaying rhythmically. At the end of each line, Kerouac thumped on a gallon jug, shouting "Go!" and "Yeah!" The audience joined in. "Everybody was yelling 'Go! Go! Go!' (like a jam session)," Kerouac wrote later in *The Dharma Bums*. Cassady was so ecstatic that he couldn't stop grinning. Many in the audience were in tears, including the stately Rexroth. As Ginsberg finished the last lines, a huge roar went up. A new poetic star had given voice to an entire generation of rebels.

These days, when nothing seems shocking, it's hard to grasp just how groundbreaking this poem really was. Using language that most Americans considered obscene, Ginsberg, in essence, turned the concept of decency upside down. It wasn't him or his homosexual actions or his language that was obscene, he seemed to say, but the modern world with its atom bombs and insane hatreds, its poverty and mechanization.

In *Memoirs of a Beatnik*, the poet Diane Di Prima writes movingly about her discovery of the poem shortly after its 1956 publication. She was leading a bohemian, poverty-stricken existence in New York City when a friend brought a copy to her apartment. Di Prima was so jolted by the first few lines that, wanting to be alone, she walked over to the Sixtieth Street pier, sat down, and finished the poem. "I knew," she wrote years later, "that this Allen Ginsberg, whoever he was, had broken ground for all of us. . . . We had come of age. . . . I made my way back to the house and to supper, and we read *Howl* together. I read it aloud to everyone. A new era had begun."

The story of *Howl* doesn't end there, of course. The poem would soon be published by Ferlinghetti's City Lights Press (*Howl and Other Poems* sold 50,000 copies in the first year). When the second edition was confiscated by a U.S. Customs agent in 1957, Ferlinghetti was arrested for selling obscene material. The San Francisco U.S. district attorney eventually declined to initiate proceedings, which so irritated the city's police that *they* arrested Ferlinghetti on the same charge. This time the matter went to trial. Ferlinghetti was defended by the American

Still the mecca for all things Beat, Lawrence Ferlinghetti's City Lights Bookstore is truly one of the great retail repositories of books in the world. Let's just say it's a bit like having F. Scott Fitzgerald running a bookshop in Paris with an emphasis on Lost Generation writers. Lawrence Ferlinghetti

Civil Liberties Union; *Howl's* merits were testified to by leading poets, critics, and editors; and the presiding judge ruled the material wasn't obscene, setting a strong legal precedent that would be used in the next decade to allow publication of D. H. Lawrence's *Lady Chatterley's Lover,* Henry Miller's *Tropic of Cancer,* and other books. Today City Lights continues to publish *Howl.* The small vest-pocket-size book is in its 55th edition, and 835,000 copies have been printed.

In mid-1956 Kerouac left San Francisco, returning to the East Coast. *On the Road* was published the next year, garnering excellent reviews from the *New York Times* and many other publications. Even reviewers who weren't sure what to think helped sell the book with their provocative words. "With his barbaric yawp of a book," commented *Time's* critic, "Kerouac commands attention as a kind of literary James Dean. The story is set in the late 1940s, told in the first person by Sal Paradise, a budding writer given to ecstasies about America, hot jazz, the meaning of life, and marijuana." Almost immediately *On the Road* shot into the bestseller lists' top 10.

The publicity over Kerouac's novel and Ginsberg's poem focused national attention on San Francisco, with its population of young poets and writers. The Beach became synonymous with the Beats. Young hipsters wanted to be like

When you're sipping an espresso at Caffe Trieste in North Beach, you can almost hear the beat of a bongo and the hip rap of Allen Ginsberg's ghost. Eric Miller

Kerouac's characters, the ones who were "mad to live, mad to talk, mad to be saved, desirous of everything at the same time, the ones who never yawn or say a commonplace thing but burn, burn, burn like fabulous yellow roman candles." They flocked to North Beach to do their burning. Soon poetry readings, little magazines, coffee houses, the sound of bongo drums, and the scent of marijuana dominated the scene.

The nickname *beatniks*, bestowed by *San Francisco Chronicle* columnist Herb Caen, caught on and went nationwide. Beatniks were suddenly in, and nowhere more so than in their spectacular North Beach backdrop. Just as middle-class tourists thronged Haight-Ashbury in the late 1960s to ogle the hippies, so they jammed the 1950s Beach to observe the beatniks at play. The area became a major gawk stop. Suburban kids in sunglasses carried bongos and hogged the sidewalks on weekends; sightseeing buses jammed the narrow streets; and squares from Dullsville ambled around, clutching beatnik vocabulary guides ("chick: a young beatnik woman, usually wears black").

By that time, though, Kerouac, Ginsberg, and most of the others—the real Beats, the ones who wouldn't be caught dead using the word *beatnik*—had moved on, dispersing to New York, Morocco, and Mexico. They left behind something vitally important, however: a legend that continues to inspire the crazy jive in a rebel's soul. They left behind a real gone beat, a bongo joy. If you visit San Francisco—and use a touch of imagination—you can hear it still.

The Writer's Trail

Following in the Footsteps

Destination: Founded as a presidio and mission by the Spanish in 1776, San Francisco has long been the number-one tourist choice in the United States. Perhaps that has something to do with its rakehell beauty and astonishing charm, its perch on high hills overlooking a large, protected bay. Then, too, it might be due to the city's world-class, cutting-edge cuisine, or to major attractions such as Golden Gate Park, Pier 39, Fisherman's Wharf, and the Golden Gate Bridge, not to mention top-notch music, theater, opera, and dance performances and those cable cars that climb halfway to the stars. One thing is clear, though: anyone who visits this city can't wait to return.

Location: San Francisco is on the West Coast of the United States in northern California on the tip of a 30-mile-long peninsula between the Pacific Ocean and San Francisco Bay.

Getting There: Every major domestic airline and most international carriers service San Francisco. San Francisco International Airport is 14 miles south of the city's center. The Bay Area has two other airports: Oakland International on the east side of the Bay and San Jose International at the southern end of the Bay. All three airports service domestic flights, but San Francisco International is where you're likely to arrive, though some Mexican and Canadian flights use the other two airports. Minibus shuttles and airport buses are good, inexpensive ways to get from San Francisco International to downtown, but you can also take SamTrans buses to the nearest Bay Area Rapid Transit (BART) station or to the main bus terminal, and there is a free shuttle to the nearest CalTrain station, with connections to the city center. Numerous intercity buses connect San Francisco with Los Angeles, Lake Tahoe, Portland, and Seattle. If you're arriving by long-distance Greyhound or Green Tortoise buses, you'll find yourself at Transbay Bus Terminal at 425 Mission Street at First Street, two blocks south of Market Street. You can get to San Francisco by train from just about any major U.S. city, with connections to many Canadian destinations, if you're a real train lover with a hankering for long trips. Amtrak's relatively new Bay Area terminal is at Jack London Square over in Oakland, but a free shuttle-bus service will take you to San Francisco's CalTrain Station at Fourth and Townsend Streets in SoMa (South of Market district) or to the Ferry Building on the Embarcadero.

Orientation: The part of San Francisco you're likely to be most interested in is pretty compact: Chinatown, North Beach, Civic Center, Nob Hill, Russian Hill, Union Square, the Financial District, and Fisherman's Wharf are crammed between Van Ness Avenue, Market Street, and the Embarcadero. SoMa, Mission, and Castro are south of Market Street. West of Van Ness are Marina, Pacific Heights, Japantown, and Haight-Ashbury. Farther west, toward the Pacific Ocean, are Golden Gate Park, the Presidio, and Lincoln Park. North Beach is tucked in between Russian Hill, the Financial District, and the Bay, with Coit Tower visible from many vantage points.

Tip: San Francisco is one of the safest big cities in the United States, but there are certain areas one should avoid at night, especially if you're alone. These are the Tenderloin, Western Addition, Market Street and SoMa, Hunters Point, and some city parks, particularly Mission Dolores and Buena Vista.

Getting Around: You don't really want to drive around in the heart of San Francisco. If you stick to North Beach, you won't need to; almost all of the places with Beat associations listed in **Literary Sites** are within walking distance of one another. That said, all major rental-car agencies (Hertz, Avis, National, Budget) have a presence at San Francisco International Airport and in numerous locations in the city. The cost of a rental car usually runs from $40 to $80 per day, although frequent specials at this destination can bring the price down. A trip to San Francisco, though, wouldn't be complete without at least one ride on a cable car; not much beats the thrill of hurtling down Russian Hill toward Fisherman's Wharf in one of them. The city has an excellent public-transit system. The Municipal Transit Agency (Muni) operates more than 100 bus and streetcar lines as well as the few remaining cable-car runs. Muni information is available from the Visitor Information Center ([415] 391-2000) in Hallidie Plaza at Market and Powell Streets or at City Hall Information ([415] 554-7111) at 400 Van Ness Avenue. Bay Area Rapid Transit, or BART ([415] 788-2278), is a subway system that links San Francisco with the East Bay (Oakland, Berkeley, and farther out). You can transfer from BART to Muni, but at an additional charge. San Francisco, like other major U.S. port cities, once had whole fleets of ferryboats. Today, though, if you love ferries, you can still get your fill. Fisherman's Wharf is the place to take Red & White ferries to Alcatraz Island, Angel Island, and Sausalito. From the Ferry Building on the Embarcadero, you can hop on a Blue & Gold boat to Jack London Square in Oakland, where you'll find the Jack London Museum, a cabin the author inhabited in Canada's Yukon, and Heinold's Last Chance Saloon, which dates back more than a century.

Literary Sleeps

There are no places where the Beats lived or slept that are now hotels, but here is a range of good lodgings, some of which have literary connections.

Sheraton Palace Hotel: The original Palace Hotel opened for business in the Financial District in 1875 but was destroyed in the fire that followed the 1906 earthquake. The current building (much renovated and expanded over the years) debuted in 1909. Oscar Wilde and Rudyard Kipling made the old Palace their home when in San Francisco, as did magnates J. P. Morgan, John D. Rockefeller, and Andrew Carnegie; Presidents Ulysses S. Grant, Theodore and Franklin Roosevelt, William Taft, William McKinley, Woodrow Wilson, and Warren Harding; General William Tecumseh Sherman; and actresses Sarah Bernhardt, Lillie Langtry, and Lillian Russell. Harding actually died in the hotel. Today the gigantic pile's Garden Court still gives one a sense of Gilded Age elegance. 2 New Montgomery Street. Tel.: 1-800-325-3535 or (415) 392-8600. Extremely expensive.

Westin St. Francis Hotel: Conveniently located on Union Square in the heart of downtown, the elegant St. Francis is a member of Historic Hotels of America. Opened in 1904 just before the big quake, the hotel's guests have included Queen Elizabeth II, Mother Teresa, and General Douglas MacArthur. Afternoon tea at the St. Francis has been a tradition for decades. 335 Powell Street. Tel.: 1-800-228-3000 or (415) 397-7000. Expensive to extremely expensive.

Hotel Bohème: In the heart of North Beach, this cozy, European-style hotel has photos of the Beats gracing its walls and will be happy to direct you to local poetry readings. Rooms are well done, with bistro tables and chairs, antique armoires, TVs with remotes, and telephones with modem jacks. 444 Columbus Avenue. Tel.: (415) 433-9111. Moderate.

Grant Plaza Hotel: It's a little worn around the edges, but the rooms aren't too tiny; they have telephones, TVs, and attached bathrooms; the price will be kind to your pocketbook; and you're right in the thick of Chinatown and not too far from North Beach. Amazingly, unless you sleep in the daytime, a room right on Chinese banner–festooned Grant Avenue, the main thoroughfare in Chinatown, is surprisingly noise-free. As added bonuses, the hotel is only steps away from the California Street cable car and the Chinatown gateway. 465 Grant Avenue. Tel.: 1-800-472-6899 or (415) 434-3883. Inexpensive.

San Remo Hotel: As the only budget-priced hotel in North Beach, this place might well put you in the Beat mood (the name alone conjures up the bar in New York City where Beat writers hung out). Built in 1906, the hotel has 62 rooms, all with spiffy bathrooms with enchanting Victorian fixtures. Each room has antique or would-be antique furniture. Drawbacks include no TVs or telephones, and the hotel hasn't got a restaurant. 2237 Mason Street. Tel.: (415) 776-8688. Inexpensive.

Tip: To avoid long lineups and crowds, especially in the summer, visit San Francisco's major attractions (Alcatraz, Fisherman's Wharf, cable cars) as early in the morning as you can, leaving Bay cruises, the Golden Gate Bridge, Golden Gate Park, and museums such as the California Palace of the Legion of Honor (where some scenes in Alfred Hitchcock's *Vertigo* were shot) and the Museum of Modern Art for the afternoon.

Literary Sites

Nearly a half century later, the presence of the Beats and of the beatnik era they wrought is ingrained in the North Beach legend. As you stroll along narrow Grant Avenue or take in the vista down Columbus Avenue, that time is easily brought to mind. The catalyst might be tangible—a glimpse of Lawrence Ferlinghetti in his City Lights Bookstore, for instance. Or it could be ethereal: the scent of roasting coffee, a heightened breeze spinning off the water. But usually no alchemic agent is necessary because, even today, tucked between the expensive shops and voguish restaurants, it's easy to find traces of that long-gone bohemia. If you want to retrace the footsteps of Beats and beatniks, a good place to start is at the corner of Greenwich Street and Grant Avenue.

Bread and Wine Mission: A book-lined meeting place for local poets and artists, the Mission hosted lively Sunday dinners. An influential literary magazine, *Beatitude*, was published here on an old mimeograph machine. 510 Greenwich Street.

The Place: Already a bohemian hangout in the 1940s, by the next decade The Place was hosting a weekly anything-goes Dada Night. In the late 1950s, this evolved into Blabbermouth Night, where anybody could sound off about politics or read poetry aloud. Today it's a design studio. Look closely at the top of the ground-floor window and you'll see a giant plaster dog peering at you. Dada lives! 1546 Grant Avenue.

Co-Existence Bagel Shop: It's hard to imagine, now that the building has been modernized in classic ugly-video-store style, but this place was one of the great beatnik hangouts. It offered something for everybody: a casual meeting place, a center for local gossip, beer, coffee, sandwiches—oh, yeah, and bagels. A young Richard Brautigan was a regular, and poet Bob Kaufman wrote *Bagel Shop Jazz* in its honor. 1398 Grant Avenue.

The Coffee Gallery: First known as Miss Smith's Tea Room, the Coffee Gallery lasted until 1980. During the 1950s, it was one of the top places to hear poetry read to live jazz. The walls were covered with works by local artists. You can still enjoy an evening here; as today's lively Lost & Found Saloon, the joint offers live music most nights. 1353 Grant Avenue.

Gino & Carlo's: The bar here was a big Beat favorite, and the restaurant was popular, too. It's still in business, serving good Italian food at modest prices. The walls hold many photos from the 1950s. 548 Green Street.

The Jazz Cellar: The Cellar was without doubt the most famous of all the Beat jazz/poetry places. It cost a quarter on Wednesday nights to hear Lawrence Ferlinghetti, Kenneth Patchen, Kenneth Rexroth, and others read poetry to the accompaniment of the Cellar Jazz Quartet. Many of these performances were recorded and can now be found on CD. Jack Kerouac, drunk and unpleasant, was eighty-sixed from here at least once. Unfortunately the site is now occupied by a newish and very ugly building. 576 Green Street.

Fugazi Hall: The Poets' Follies were held here, as were poetry readings. These days it's called Club Fugazi and it's home to *Beach Blanket Babylon*, a wonderful, only-in-San Francisco theatrical review that's a must for any tourist (or, for that matter, any resident!). 678 Green Street.

Caffe Trieste: In business since 1954, the Trieste is, strictly speaking, the only remaining coffee house from the Beat days. Almost without exception every Beat poet, writer, and artist hung out here. The interior decor hasn't changed much, and on Saturday afternoons you can enjoy live Italian arias. 601 Vallejo Street.

Vesuvio: This bar/café, founded in 1949, was the Beat era's most popular hangout. Until recently a sign hung to the right of the front door proudly listing the famous writers thrown out at one time or another, including Jack Kerouac and Gregory Corso. 255 Columbus Avenue at Jack Kerouac Alley.

City Lights Bookstore: Opened in June 1953, City Lights was the first all-paperback bookstore in the United States. It's been described by owner Lawrence Ferlinghetti as being in the "anarchist, civil libertarian, antiauthoritarian tradition." In the beginning, the store's profits supported a pop-culture magazine, *City Lights*, which soon transformed into a small publishing company. There are more than 100 City Lights books in print today. Ferlinghetti is often in the store. 261 Columbus Avenue.

Specs Museum Café: This truly original bar and museum dates back decades and was a favorite drinking spot for many writers (William Saroyan hung out here during his San Francisco years). The "museum" aspect derives from the thousands of artifacts—some valuable, some not—hanging from the walls and ceilings, or preserved under glass. Henri Lenoir, a bartender at Specs after World War II, ended up moving across the street in 1949 to open Vesuvio. The nascent Beat clientele moved with him. 12 William Saroyan Place.

hungry i: In the 1950s, this site (the building you see is new) was one of the country's most happening clubs, attracting performers such as Woody Allen, Barbra Streisand, and Bill Cosby. Lenny Bruce's arrest for obscenity was made at the hungry i, and a Beat opera, *The Pizza Pusher*, debuted here. (You may notice another hungry i near the corner of Broadway and Columbus Avenue; it has no relationship to the original.) 599 Jackson Street.

Allen Ginsberg Residence: The poet lived in this Victorian building in 1955 while writing *Howl*. 1010 Montgomery Street.

Six Gallery: It's surprising, I know, but this important site isn't in North Beach. It's in the Marina district (an enjoyable two-mile walk from the Beach's heart). Today it's a store called Silkroute, which sells tribal rugs and kilims, pottery, and other items. The interior is handsomely done, and it's not difficult to imagine the room filled with hipsters swigging wine from a bottle, their shouts of approval providing an almost musical backdrop to a poet's words. 3119 Fillmore Street.

Icon Pastimes

If you're old enough and so inclined, hoist a cheap glass of red wine—a favorite of Jack Kerouac's—at Specs or Vesuvio. You'll be honoring a long, writerly tradition by doing so (just don't hoist so much that you get thrown out, à la Kerouac). Read poetry over an espresso at Caffe Trieste. Spend an hour or so browsing the Beat section at City Lights, buying a copy of Ginsberg's *Howl and Other Poems* on your way out. Eat dinner at Gino & Carlo's and then take in a performance of *Beach Blanket Babylon* in the old Fugazi Hall, where the Poets' Follies were once held. You could also take the North Beach Tour sponsored by the all-volunteer City Guides ([415] 557-4266). Walking at a leisurely rate, you'll learn the area's history, starting with the Gold Rush/Barbary

Coast days, through the bohemian era at the turn of the 20th century, and finishing with the glory years of the beatniks. Tours are held each Saturday at 10:00 a.m. and meet on the steps of Saints Peter and Paul Church (where Joe DiMaggio and Marilyn Monroe were photographed after their marriage), across from Washington Square. No need for advance reservations. The tour is free, but your donations help support City Guides.

Contacts

San Francisco Convention and Visitors Bureau: 201 Third Street, San Francisco, California 94103-3185 U.S. Tel.: (415) 974-6900. Fax: (415) 227-2668. Web site: *www.sfvisitor.org.*

In a Literary Mood

Books

Charters, Ann, ed. *The Portable Beat Reader.* New York: Penguin, 1992. Over 600 pages, Charters's book is a compilation of works from all the major poets and writers of the Beat period. It's a good addition to anyone's literary collection.

Di Prima, Diane. *Memoirs of a Beatnik.* New York: Penguin Putnam, 1998. Erotic, enlightening, sometimes irritating but never less than entertaining, this is one of the most startling books—one of the few by a woman—to emerge from the Beat era.

Ferlinghetti, Lawrence, and Nancy J. Peters. *Literary San Francisco.* San Francisco and New York: City Lights Press/Harper & Row, 1980. This ultimate overview of San Francisco's illustrious literary history begins with legends from the Costanoan Native people and runs straight through to the late 1970s. The section on Allen Ginsberg's *Howl,* written by the very man put on trial for selling it, is particularly fascinating.

Ginsberg, Allen. *Howl and Other Poems.* San Francisco: City Lights Press, 1991. The ringmaster of Beat's seminal book still has the ability to thrill new generations. The umpteenth printing has an introduction by William Carlos Williams.

Kerouac, Jack. *The Dharma Bums.* New York: Penguin, 1991. Originally published in 1959, this book by the always-autobiographical Kerouac is the one most influenced by his time in San Francisco. Many of its characters are thinly disguised real-life figures, most notably his close friend, Pulitzer Prize–winning poet Gary Snyder.

_____. *On the Road.* New York: Penguin, 1991. First published in 1957, the Bible of Beat is still fresh after all these years.

Nicosia, Gerald. *Memory Babe: A Critical Biography of Jack Kerouac.* New York: Penguin, 1986. There are numerous biographies of Kerouac, but this one is by far the best. Nicosia presents an unflinching portrait of the troubled Beat and serves up an incisive appreciation of his work.

Peabody, Richard, ed. *A Different Beat: Writings by Women of the Beat Generation.* New York: Serpent's Tail, 1997. The Beats numbered many female writers in their ranks who have been unjustly overshadowed by their more famous male contemporaries. This book, which tries to right the situation, features work by 26 women, including Jan Kerouac, Joan Haverty Kerouac, Eileen Kaufman, Diane Di Prima, Ruth Weiss, and many others.

Richards, Rand. *Historic San Francisco: A Concise History and Guide.* San Francisco: Heritage House Publishers, 1995. A wonderful complement to *Literary San Francisco,* this profusely illustrated book is a great companion on a walking tour of the city's neighborhoods.

Watson, Steven. *The Birth of the Beat Generation.* New York: Pantheon, 1995. A fun, readable, fast-paced look at pivotal members of the Beat Generation, particularly Jack Kerouac, Allen Ginsberg, Neal Cassady, and William Burroughs. A long section takes place in San Francisco. One of the great joys of this book is its many sidebars. Neatly placed in very wide margins, they don't detract from your reading of the main content, and they're filled with fascinating facts about the people, era, and vocabulary.

Wolfe, Tom. *The Electric Kool-Aid Acid Test.* New York: Bantam Doubleday Dell, 1999. Although this classic, which debuted in 1969, is about Ken Kesey and his Merry Prankster band, it presents one of the best-ever portraits of Neal Cassady. More than 20 years after his road trip with Jack Kerouac, Cassady was still driving. This time he piloted the Pranksters' bus, *Further*, on its own inimitable cross-country trip.

Guidebooks

Bosley, Deborah. *San Francisco: The Rough Guide.* 4th ed. London: Rough Guides, 1998.

Emerson, Connie. *The Cheapskate's Guide to San Francisco.* Secaucus, NJ: Carol Publishing Group, 1997. The title says it all. If you're seeking bargains in the City by the Bay, this fun-to-read book will help you find them.

San Francisco. 2nd ed. London: Michelin Travel Publications, 1999. If you've used a Michelin green guide before, you're probably as great a fan of them as I am. These slender, no-nonsense volumes tell you what you want to know about the sights, they weigh hardly anything, and they're inordinately intelligent.

Wurman, Richard Saul. *San Francisco Access.* 8th ed. New York: Access Press, 1999. Chockablock with informative capsule descriptions of all the great sites, restaurants, cafés, bars, hotels, and shops in the city, plus numerous fascinating sidebars.

Films/Videos

Aronson, Jerry (producer and director). *The Life and Times of Allen Ginsberg.* Documentary. First Run Features, 1993. Available on video. Joan Baez, William Burroughs, Ken Kesey, Timothy Leary, Abbie Hoffman, and Jack Kerouac all contribute insights into the Bard of Beat.

Axelrod, David, Edward R. Pressman, and others (producers). *Heart Beat.* John Byrum (director). Further Productions/Orion Pictures, 1980. Warner Home Video. Cast: John Heard, Nick Nolte, and Sissy Spacek. There is a terrific film to be made about the three-corner relationship of Neal Cassady (Nolte), Carolyn Cassady (Spacek), and Jack Kerouac (Heard), but this muddled movie isn't it. Ray Sharkey plays a character who's supposed to be Allen Ginsberg, but who's inexplicably called Ira here.

Felver, Christopher (producer and director). *The Coney Island of Lawrence Ferlinghetti.* Documentary. Mystic Fire Video, 1996. Gregory Corso, Allen Ginsberg, Kenneth Rexroth, and Gary Snyder talk about Beat impresario Ferlinghetti.

Freed, Arthur (producer). *The Subterraneans.* Ranald MacDougall (director). MGM, 1960. Cast: Leslie Caron, Roddy McDowall, and George Peppard. Based on Jack Kerouac's novel of the same name, this film is a true curiosity. Kerouac was paid $15,000 for the rights, and MGM set out to make a big-budget CinemaScope color movie about the Beats. Try twisting your mind around

Peppard and McDowall as Kerouac characters. The film does have some terrific cameos by jazz greats Art Pepper, Carmen McRae, Gerry Mulligan, and Art Farmer. Rumors continue to swirl about the possibility of film versions of *Desolation Angels* and *On the Road*, but to date this is still the only movie made from a Kerouac book.

Hitchcock, Alfred, and Herbert Coleman (producers). *Vertigo*. Alfred Hitchcock (director). Paramount, 1958. MCA Home Video. Cast: Barbara Bel Geddes, Kim Novak, and James Stewart. There are dozens of films—*The Barbary Coast, San Francisco, The Maltese Falcon, Psyche-Out, Bullitt, Dirty Harry, The Conversation, Basic Instinct*, to name a few—that have San Francisco as a backdrop, but few use the city as well as Hitchcock's masterpiece does.

Web Sites

Beat Generation: *www.charm.net/~brooklyn*; *www.geocities.com/~terrylyoung*. The last site, called *Jack Kerouac's San Francisco Blue Neon Alley*, is an excellent repository of all things Beat, with special emphasis on Kerouac. The links will get you almost everything online about the Beat Generation.

Neal Cassady: *www.halcyon.com/colinp/cassadyl.htm*. A printed, annotated version of Cassady rapping is available here.

Allen Ginsberg: *www.buffnet.net/~deadbeat/ginsberg*; *www.ginzy.com*; *www.naropa.edu/ginsberg.html*; *www.english.upenn.edu/~afilreis/50s/ginsberg-fbi.html*. The first three sites are memorial pages devoted to *Howl*'s creator, who died in 1997. The last site is the poet's FBI file online.

Jack Kerouac: *www.geocities.com/Hollywood/Boulevard/6713/kerouac.htm*; *www.levity.com/corduroy/kerouac.htm*. Sites that offer Kerouac singing and reciting, interviews with the author, and links to other Kerouac and Beat sites.

D. H. Lawrence
Coal Miner's Son in New Mexico

Nancy Wigston

DAVID HERBERT LAWRENCE was a writer who broke all the rules—especially about sex. This coal miner's son from Nottinghamshire in England spent much of his adult life in search of a private utopia. In 1922 Lawrence and his wife, Frieda, found their Eden in Taos, New Mexico, a small town situated on a high plateau ringed by the Sangre de Cristo Mountains, cut by the deep gorge of the Rio Grande. When Lawrence wrote home from Taos to his niece in England, he was euphoric. Here was "beauty, absolute beauty, any hour of the day." Taos had changed him forever. Always restless, Lawrence ended his days in the south of France, where he died at 44 of tuberculosis in the village of Vence.

Taos, 7,000 feet above sea level, looks as if it's modeled out of earth-colored clay; even the fast-food places feature the Southwestern adobe look. No high rises blight the landscape. The effect, combined with clarity of light, skies of cerulean, and looming mountain ranges in the distance, is quite surreal. And it's here that you'll find D. H. Lawrence enshrined in the most unlikely places. Taos Plaza, a fortified square erected by order of Spanish governors after the 1680 Pueblo Native uprising, anchors the town. (Pueblo is a generic term for some 25 New Mexico Native American tribes that include the Hopi, Zuñi, and Taos.) At one corner is the hotel La Fonda de Taos. Dating from 1937, it seems newly built for a western movie. You wouldn't be surprised to glimpse *Gunsmoke's* Miss Kitty—or her ghost—waving to you from an upper floor.

Outside La Fonda a somewhat prurient sign beckons the stranger: "D. H. Lawrence, Author, *Lady Chatterley's Lover*. This is the only showing of the writer's controversial paintings since his exhibition was permanently banned by Scotland Yard when the show opened at the Warren Galleries, London, 1929."

Banned paintings? Scotland Yard? Lady Chatterley? In sunny New Mexico? Step inside. A hall of curiosities awaits: jewel-bedecked matador suits in glass cases, an old-fashioned slot machine, pictures by many and varied artists, Pueblo blankets, red leather chairs, carved wooden ceiling beams. At the back, for a $3 fee, you'll discover a marvelous array of paintings by England's most famous banned author. The hotel's longtime owner, Saki Karavas, purchased them from Frieda Lawrence's estate. The price was $50,000 for the lot; another interested buyer was rumored to be the Aga Khan, who had seen the original London show.

Lawrence was a brilliant writer, but not a brilliant artist. The pictures, painted while he and Frieda were living in Italy, celebrate his private mythology—himself as a bearded Pan, the blond, ample Frieda (née von Richthofen and cousin of Germany's World War I air ace, the Red Baron) as Earth Mother/Amazon. The writer was angry when his paintings were called obscene. But he could hardly have been surprised. His challenges to straitlaced England had a long history, from the suppression of *The Rainbow*, his second novel, to his difficulties finding a publisher for *Women in Love* on the grounds it was too hot to handle. (The latter book was first published privately by Thomas Seltzer in the United States in 1920.) His final novel, the notorious *Lady Chatterley's Lover*, was banned for 30 years after his death. When the 1960 Lady Chatterley Trial overturned the ban, a new era in freedom of expression dawned. Lawrence's last blast at his repressed homeland sold more than three million copies and helped usher in the sexual revolution of the 1960s.

The paintings, their content mild by current standards, are banned to this day from British soil. Periodically stories surface—in such august newspapers as the *Sunday Times*—that England wants them back. Too late. In the still quiet of this surprising art gallery, you can see what Lawrence stood for, and what his books say better. Send the paintings back to England? "No! No! No! No!" you can almost hear Lawrence rage, using the same negative he scrawled furiously over a manuscript sent him by the coolly rational Bertrand Russell during their brief friendship. So here his art remains.

By running off with Frieda, Lawrence had demonstrated his skill for scandal as early as 1912. Blond, buxom, and bored by her marriage to Lawrence's tutor, Ernest Weekley, at Nottingham University, the mother of three had enjoyed many affairs while holidaying in Germany, long before the tall, handsome Lawrence appeared on her doorstep, early for an appointment. While England was at war, the couple were overheard singing German songs with friends in their cottage in Cornwall—Lawrence was known to be antiwar—spiking local rumors that they were enemy spies. After they were formally ordered to move away from the vulnerable English coast, Lawrence's outrage against his native land only increased. But the couple's passports were seized, and they were stranded.

Lawrence had been fantasizing since 1914 about an island utopia he called Rananim, inspired by a Hebrew song an artist friend used to sing. Those invited to join included Bertrand Russell and Aldous Huxley, as well as numerous other writers and friends. Rananim may only have existed in Lawrence's mind, but Taos was the closest he came to finding his Paradise on Earth. In his last invitation to his London friends to join him in Paradise, it was to New Mexico that he urged them to come. An eccentric artist, the Honorable Dorothy Brett, daughter of Viscount Esher, impulsively responded. Enchanted with everything she saw, Brett ended her days in Taos, aged 94. Lawrence spent less than two years in New Mexico between 1922 and 1925, yet it is Taos, of all the places he touched, that nearly captured his untamed spirit.

"I think New Mexico was the greatest experience from the outside world that I have ever had," Lawrence writes in the essay "New Mexico," collected in *Phoenix*. "The moment I saw the brilliant, proud morning shine high up over the deserts of Santa Fe, something stood still in my soul, and I started to attend." Driving Frieda and Lawrence from Santa Fe to Taos in September 1922 were Mabel Dodge Sterne and Tony Luhan, her lover, a Native from Taos Pueblo who would become her fourth husband.

Mabel had assiduously wooed the famous author. She had read *Sons and Lovers*, his novel about a son's struggle with his powerful mother, as well as his anti-Freudian rant *Psychoanalysis and the Unconscious*. In Italy Lawrence had received her long, scrolled letter of invitation, enclosing various "magic" substances, charms from Pueblo rituals, and a necklace for Frieda. Lawrence was the perfect candidate to write about *her* New Mexico, dreamed Mabel. He would "formulate it all into a magnificent creation."

A wealthy culture maven from Buffalo, the dark-haired, youthful-looking Mabel—at 43 she was exactly Frieda's age—had previously run salons in Florence and New York City. She had "discovered" Taos in 1917 and was completely won over by Pueblo life, which she saw as a cure for the ills of modern life. Besides the 700-year-old Taos Pueblo, which to the newcomer's eye resembled a series of Cubist squares, Taos had been home to the Spanish of the Southwest. The town's art colony dates back to 1898. That year painters Bert Phillips and Ernest Blumenschein broke a wagon wheel on their trek through New Mexico, and decided to stay; Taos has been a home to artists ever since.

When the Lawrences arrived at the train station in Lamy, New Mexico, they had been roaming for four years. What Lawrence called their "savage pilgrimage"

San Francisco de Asis Church, popularly known as Ranchos de Taos because of its location, was one of Georgia O'Keeffe's favorite subjects to paint, as it has been for countless artists. Nancy Wigston

had taken them from Italy to Ceylon, Australia, New Zealand, Tahiti, and finally to Taos via San Francisco. Lawrence was one among many cultural icons the tireless Mabel seduced with her tales of this wild, unspoiled land. Actress Greta Garbo, conductor Leopold Stokowski, photographer Ansel Adams, playwright Thornton Wilder, painter Georgia O'Keeffe, and many other celebrities and artists fell into Mabel's orbit and benefited from her largesse. And Lawrence wasn't the only one who found her overbearing; writer Thomas Wolfe stayed exactly one day before heading out of town again.

Mabel and Tony had built a beautiful home, the Big House, on 12 acres at the edge of town. Cozy yet grand, the place had wood-beamed ceilings, fire-places called kivas, and a mural by Pueblo artist Awa Tsireh. Its 17 rooms quickly became a hub for entertaining friends and guests. Today the Mabel Dodge Luhan House is an upscale bed-and-breakfast, popular for writing and yoga retreats, with a conference center on the grounds. The house seems much as it was in Mabel and Tony's time: roomy, comfortable, with delicious baking smells coming from a big old-fashioned kitchen. An upstairs bathroom still sports the bright designs Lawrence painted on the windows after he looked out one morning and, shocked, realized anyone could be gazing in on him. Earlier he had scold-ed Mabel for sunbathing while wearing only a burnoose and moccasins.

Lawrence's books may have initiated an era of looser sexual mores, but he could be puritanical.

Although Mabel put the Lawrences up in a specially built house on her property and arranged Pueblo dances for him and Frieda, their writing partnership never bore fruit. Instead, relations grew frosty. A woman with her own agenda, Mabel discovered that Lawrence couldn't be bossed. And Frieda, no matter how tempestuous her marriage was, wouldn't cede control of her artistic husband. If Lawrence was made edgy by Mabel, he was baffled by the strong, silent, illiterate Tony Luhan. As he candidly wrote to novelist E. M. Forster about the Natives and their culture, "I haven't got the hang of them yet." While exploring an American reality he had only ever imagined, Lawrence wrote a letter to the *New York Times* at Mabel's behest, defending Native American rights to their land and traditions, which were threatened by Washington.

Lawrence's Taos sojourn resulted in a burst of creativity: the poems "Eagle in New Mexico" and "Mountain Lion," the short story "The Princess," *The Plumed Serpent* (his 1926 Mexican novel), and *Mornings in Mexico*, a travel book dedicated to Mabel. In two of his most famous works from this time, the novella *St. Mawr* and the story "The Woman Who Rode Away," a Mabel-like figure gets a starring, if not flattering, role. Mabel later said that Lawrence thought "he had finished me up" in "The Woman Who Rode Away," the tale of a woman who offers her heart—quite literally—to the Natives. Rather than portraying an artistic, powerful woman who chose to find her soul among the indigenous people of the Southwest—the way Mabel saw herself—Lawrence draws a portrait of a nameless woman who escapes her conventional marriage to join the Natives, where she is eventually sacrificed in a drug-addled state. But the woman may stand for Lawrence's hatred of the feminine in his own character—this, after all, is fiction. In reality Mabel and her friends were very alert and fought to preserve the land and improve the quality of life of the Pueblo. They helped defeat the Bursum Bill, which would have broken up the reservations and allowed commercial exploitation of Native lands.

Perhaps no writer's life was so marked by personal dustups as Lawrence's. He followed his own creed, as he outlined in a letter: "My great religion is a belief in the blood, the flesh, as being wiser than the intellect." Typically he fought, then made up with his friends. One of Lawrence's less feisty friendships was with Aldous Huxley, nine years younger, a writer whose Oxford-educated, scientific mind roamed just as freely as did that of the miner's son. Lawrence wasn't offended by Huxley's thinly veiled portrait of him as the preachy "gas-bag" Mark Rampion in *Point Counter Point* (1928). Huxley and his Belgian wife, Maria, comforted Lawrence and Frieda as he lay dying in Vence. Huxley even paid for his friend's burial and tried to help his widow with her uncertain finances. The Huxleys later visited Frieda in Taos, where she lived happily until her death in 1956.

On their first visit, Frieda and Lawrence soon moved away from Mabel's immediate reach, renting two cabins on Del Monte Ranch outside town. Lawrence proudly outfitted himself in western gear: cowboy boots and hat, sheepskin coat, riding breeches. Two young Danish artists, Knud Merrild and Kai Götzsche, joined them, helping with the heavy work and designing book jackets for Lawrence's poetry and fiction. During that first cold winter, there was a shortage of water for bathing, and the Danes, in their Ford Model T, would drive the Lawrences 20 miles into Manby Hot Springs. When they were unable to get into town, everyone would rub themselves down with snow.

Early on the red-bearded Lawrence had startled the artistic colony in New Mexico with his unpretentious domestic skills. When staying in Santa Fe with poet Witter Bynner, he astonished his host by getting up early, washing the supper dishes, clearing things away, and preparing everyone's breakfast. Ranch life kept him busy building or improving his digs, milking cows, fixing roast beef and Yorkshire pudding, baking breads and cakes. During his last stay, Lawrence made his own adobe oven in which to bake bread. Having been taught to ride by Tony Luhan, Lawrence enjoyed getting about on horseback. One morning ride during his last May in Taos took him high into the mountains to the Pueblo ceremonial cave at Arroyo Seco. The cave, hidden by a waterfall, appears in "The Woman Who Rode Away."

D. H. Lawrence's Dandelion Wine

Saucepan of water
Half tin of dandelions

Boil briskly for an hour or one and a half hours. Strain and put in one heaped cupful of sugar. When just pleasantly warm, crumble in a yeast cake, stir up, and leave in a warm place for three or four hours. Strain bottle. Cork TIGHT. Keep warmish.

Today, 10 miles north of town, at the end of four and half miles of dirt road, the visitor comes to a sign announcing the D. H. Lawrence Ranch. Now owned by the University of New Mexico, the property, dubbed Kiowa Ranch by Lawrence, is situated in 160 acres of pine forest. Originally Mabel Luhan tried to give the ranch to Lawrence, but he disdained owning anything and so she deeded the place to Frieda in exchange for the manuscript of *Sons and Lovers.* No doubt Lawrence would approve of the ranch's contemporary atmosphere of benign neglect; there is no visitors' center, no guides, postcards, tea towels, or refrigerator magnets. The air is pure, the views spectacular: mountain ranges stretch southward all the way to Albuquerque, 150 miles distant. There are blue skies overhead, and the delicious scent of tall pine woods drifts on the wind.

The house where the Lawrences lived remains almost as it was a half century ago. Unfortunately it isn't open to visitors. Here Lawrence felt all his burdens—his money worries, his constant, long-denied illness—soar away. "In the magnificent fierce morning of New Mexico one sprang awake, a new part of the soul woke up suddenly, and the old world gave way to the new," he writes in "New Mexico." Here, at Kiowa, breathing the air that Lawrence breathed, you feel in your gut his knowledge of nature's gods, and imagine that you, too, are free—as he briefly was—of life's travails.

That this thin, tubercular English genius could find happiness on a New Mexico ranch says much about Lawrence the man. John Middleton Murry (who with his wife, Katherine Mansfield, were the originals of *Women in Love*'s doomed lovers) had serendipitously called Lawrence "the outlaw of modern English literature." That phrase explains what Lawrence was doing in New Mexico or, for that matter, in Australia, Sicily, or any of the dozens of places he and Frieda visited. What better location for a literary outlaw than the American West? Taos has seen its share of outlaws—even its artists' colony was composed mostly of runaways from the cultural congestion of the north. A century earlier, the town was home to Kit Carson, the most famous frontiersman and scout of the Southwest (another notorious figure of the Wild West, Billy the Kid, made southern New Mexico his stomping grounds). Colorfully embroidered accounts of Carson's life made him a star of the tabloidlike penny dreadfuls of his day. Today, in Taos, you can still visit the home he built for his family.

The walk to the Lawrence Memorial from the house at Kiowa Ranch literally takes your breath away. At 8,000 feet above sea level, the sturdy white chapel has a stunning location, with a view across the wooded valley to the mountains. The simple structure was the work of Angelo Ravagli, the Italian army officer who became Frieda's third husband. Crowning the top is a phoenix, symbol of Lawrence's indomitable spirit. Inside is a small altar where Lawrence's ashes are mixed with cement. This was Frieda's doing, after the rumor reached her that Mabel Luhan and Dorothy Brett were planning to steal the ashes and scatter them over the desert. In September 1935, Frieda arranged a sunset ceremony, with Pueblo dancing and drumming, to honor Lawrence in a corner of the

D. H. and Frieda Lawrence (center) enjoy the company of friends in Taos during happier times. Courtesy of Spud
Johnson Collection, Harwood Museum/University of New Mexico Archives

earth he had loved.

The whitewashed building on the knoll has become a sacred site for Lawrence
fans, as Frieda, a wise and stubborn woman, knew it would. The altar is littered
with stones, notes ("Thank you for giving me the essence of sex"), and handwritten poems praising Lawrence and the dawn. Names written in the visitors'
book reflect Lawrence's undiminished appeal. Tourists from Switzerland to Japan,
on their own Lawrencian pilgrimages, have made the trek here, although some
question the building's downmarket charm. Dorothy Brett hated it, calling
Ravagli's building "a mausoleum looking like a station toilet." Maria Huxley,
visiting with Aldous in 1937, more kindly termed it "a childish little chapel,"
but praised Frieda's generous hospitality. "Surely you could have done better than
this, Frieda!" writes one English visitor 60 years later. Outside the chapel is Frieda's
own grave, not the simple wooden cross she asked for, but a more elaborate
tomb decorated with a European-style enameled photograph. Ravagli didn't
want people to think he was cheap, and for this we can be grateful: Frieda grins
in the photo, involving all of us in the enormous drama that was her life.

Descending the slope to the Lawrences' ranch house, you can peer in the
windows and see the typewriter Brett used to type Lawrence's handwritten
manuscripts, and a hat and coat the author left on his last visit. Reclining on a

rickety bench nearby and gazing up into the branches of an enormous pine tree, you can enjoy the exact view Georgia O'Keeffe painted several times. "Here," Lawrence once wrote, "on this little ranch under the Rocky Mountains, a big pine tree rises like a guardian spirit in front of the cabin where we live." Living here, Lawrence felt in harmony with the world.

The day my husband and I visit Kiowa Ranch, the only other tourists are a California couple in an RV who have just returned from enjoying several evenings at the Santa Fe Opera. When a caretaker arrives in his red pickup, I hurry over to ask some questions. The man, who wants to remain nameless, remembers Frieda well. Obviously he reveres her. "Living with Lawrence was like living with the devil, was what she said," he tells me. Twice. That Lawrence had many flaws as a husband is undeniable. His and Frieda's union could be violent even in public; they frequently shocked onlookers, but they endured.

One thing is clear: this wild and empty place is still haunted by this vivid, memorable couple, whose union has been called a mismatch made in heaven. As I gaze around, the ghostly voices of literature's most tumultuous marriage fade into silence. Here Lawrence, Frieda at his side, responded to the spirit of the land, as only he could. He once described the many mornings when he stood in "the fierce, proud silence of the Rockies, on their foothills, to look far over the desert to the blue mountains away in Arizona, blue as chalcedony, with the sage-brush desert sweeping grey-blue in between, dotted with cube-crystals of houses, the vast amphitheatre of lofty, indomitable desert, sweeping round to the ponderous Sangre de Cristo mountains on the east, and coming up flush at the pine-dotted foot-hills of the Rockies! What splendour! Only the tawny eagle could really sail out into the splendour of it all." Overhead, a solitary American eagle arcs gracefully toward the distant mountains as I ponder Lawrence's heartfelt words.

The Writer's Trail

Following in the Footsteps

Destination: Commenting on his first impression of Taos after his arrival in 1922, D. H. Lawrence wrote: "I think the skyline of Taos the most beautiful of all I have seen in my travels round the world." High praise indeed, considering all the places Lawrence saw during his short lifetime. To many the drive from Santa Fe to Taos is spectacular beyond words, particularly the 20 miles or so of road that corkscrews along the Rio Grande canyon on its way up to the broad plateau, where you get your first glimpse of Taos Mountain. At the base of the mountain is Taos Pueblo, built by the indigenous people of the area centuries before the Spanish settled in Santa Fe. Big blue skies, invigoratingly clean, dry air, and a human-size town with deep artistic roots make Taos a place you'll want to linger at for some time. Who knows? You might even decide to settle down for a while, just as Lawrence, Georgia O'Keeffe, Mabel Dodge Luhan, Ansel Adams, and western scout Kit Carson did.

Location: Seventy miles north of Santa Fe in northern New Mexico, Taos is on the Rio Grande, nestled between the Carson and Santa Fe National Forests and surrounded by the Sangre de Cristo Mountains, with 13,161-foot Wheeler Peak just to the northeast of the town.

Getting There: Taos has an airport, but only for private planes. If you're flying into New Mexico, you'll have to go to Albuquerque, which has the nearest major-airline access. American, America West, Continental, Delta, TWA, United, Southwest, and USAir all fly into New Mexico's capital. Once you're at Albuquerque International Airport, you're best bet is to rent a car. All the usual agencies (Budget, Avis, Hertz, National, Thrifty) are represented at the airport. Greyhound/Trailways and Texas, New Mexico & Oklahoma Coaches (TNMO) provide regular bus service to Santa Fe and Taos. The Albuquerque bus station is on Silver Avenue between First and Second Streets. Shuttlejack ([505] 243-3244) offers daily runs from Albuquerque International to Santa Fe, but unfortunately doesn't go to Taos. Amtrak (1-800-872-7245) operates the *Southwest Chief* daily between Chicago and Los Angeles, with a stopover in Albuquerque. Amtrak's station in the New Mexican capital is at First Street and Silver Avenue, but if you stay on the train and get off at Lamy, Lamy Shuttle Service ([505] 982-8829) will take you farther north to Santa Fe. Taos has no railroad service.

Tip: Don't forget that Taos is nearly a mile and a half above sea level. If you find yourself getting short of breath, take it easy and acclimatize yourself. If you have a heart condition, check with your physician to see if traveling in high altitudes is something you should avoid.

Orientation: With only about 5,000 people, the town of Taos is pretty compact. Taos Plaza is the heart of the place. From here Kit Carson Road runs east, intersecting with Paseo del Pueblo, the north-south thoroughfare. These are Taos's two major streets. Several of the town's more than 70 art galleries, as well as Kit Carson's Home, are found on Kit Carson Road. Bent Street, between Camino de la Placita and Paseo del Pueblo and north of Kit Carson Road, also has numerous art galleries. The Plaza itself features a few art galleries as well as some of Taos's better restaurants and hotels, although you'll also find a forest of T-shirt and souvenir shops there. A number of interesting sites are outside town, including Taos Pueblo, Mabel Dodge Luhan House, Rio Grande Gorge Bridge, D. H. Lawrence Ranch and Memorial, and Ranchos de Taos Church.

Getting Around: Since a lot of the places in Taos you'll want to see are outside town (particularly the D. H. Lawrence Ranch and Memorial), you should really have a car to get around. In Taos itself you can easily do most of your sightseeing on foot, rent a bicycle, or call a cab (check with your hotel). There is no municipal bus system.

Literary Sleeps

Mabel Dodge Luhan House: Originally a 200-year-old adobe, Mabel Dodge Luhan's hacienda was massively renovated and enlarged by the literary patroness, complete with adobe archways, vigas (Southwest-style rafters), *latillas* (wooden slats), flagstone patios, and the gates from the original San Francisco de Asis Church in Ranchos de Taos. The list of celebrities that Mabel attracted to her home on the fringe of Taos is truly impressive. Besides D. H. and Frieda Lawrence and Georgia O'Keeffe, Willa Cather, Aldous Huxley, Robinson Jeffers, Ansel Adams, and Carl Jung made stops here. Jung once lectured on the outdoor patio. After Mabel died in 1962, actor Dennis Hopper bought the place and stayed in it while filming *Easy Rider*. Now a bed-and-breakfast that frequently hosts cultural seminars, the home features sumptuous rooms named after Mabel, Tony Luhan (her final husband), O'Keeffe, Cather, Adams, Jeffers, and Spud Johnson. Some guest rooms have shared baths. 240 Morada Lane. Tel.: (505) 751-9686 or 1-800-846-2235 (within the United States). E-mail: *mabel@taos.newmex.com*. Web site: *www.unink.com/mabel*. Moderate to expensive.

Taos Inn: Sections of this hotel date back to the 1600s, but the whole place was substantially renovated in the Southwest style in the 1980s. Near the heart of town, the inn has rooms with kivas (Pueblo-style wood-burning fireplaces) and all the usual amenities of a top-notch hotel. Just off the lobby is the Adobe Bar, a popular watering hole for local artists and writers. 125 Paseo del Pueblo Norte. Tel.: 1-800-826-7466 or (505) 758-2233. Moderate.

La Fonda de Taos: Built in the 1930s, this is the hotel where you'll find the locked side room containing D. H. Lawrence's erotic paintings, the ones that were banned in England in 1929. The fee to see them is $3. As for the somewhat small 24 rooms in the establishment, you might find them a little musty with age, but that just adds to the ambience of the place. The lobby is lined with old paintings and newspaper clippings. South Taos Plaza. Tel.: (505) 758-2211 or 1-800-833-2211 (within the United States). Inexpensive.

Laughing Horse Inn: Spud Johnson, who worked as Mabel Dodge Luhan's secretary, used this century-old adobe, now a hotel, as a base for his *Laughing Horse Press*, a literary and satirical journal. The inn is on the outskirts of town under some shade trees on the banks of the Rio Pueblo. D. H. Lawrence once stayed here with Johnson, and so did Georgia O'Keeffe, Gertrude Stein, and Alice B. Toklas. Poet Witter Bynner, Johnson's lover, was also on hand a good deal of the time. Today the place is pretty eccentric, with dark, small rooms that contain loft or bunk beds, though a few rooms have regular beds. Most rooms don't have private bathrooms. However, there is a central hot tub and music and video libraries. 729 Paseo del Pueblo Norte. Tel.: (505) 758-8350. Inexpensive.

 Tip: Visiting Taos during the early fall is actually a good time to go if you want to avoid the crowds of tourists in the summer and the hordes of skiers in the winter. Spring, too, is a pretty good bet, even though you can expect some rain. Still, with more than 300 days of sunshine yearly, northern New Mexico only experiences a handful of truly rainy days.

Literary Sites

D. H. Lawrence Ranch and Memorial: Off State Road 522, 10 miles north of Taos, the Lawrences' former ranch is on a four-and-a-half-mile dirt road that branches eastward off the highway just before the village of Cristobal. The memorial is at the end of a crooked walkway that leads up from the ranch buildings. Lawrence's ashes were mixed into the cement of the shrine's altar, and Frieda is buried just outside the memorial. The ranch itself serves as a scholarly retreat and is owned by the University of New Mexico. Admission to the memorial is free, but the ranch buildings are closed to the public. Open daily from 8:00 a.m. to 5:00 p.m. Tel.: (505) 776-2245.

Kit Carson Home: A native of Kentucky, frontiersman, scout, hunter, soldier, and Indian fighter Kit Carson is synonymous with northern New Mexico. Carson came to Taos in 1826 and once said: "No man who has seen the women, heard the bells, or smelled the piñon smoke of Taos will ever be able to leave." It was certainly true of him; he lived off and on in the town for 42 years until his death in 1868. In 1843 he bought this 12-room adobe, now a museum, as a wedding present for his wife, Josefa. Three of the rooms in the house are furnished in a manner similar to Carson's era; other rooms feature gun exhibits and mountain-man lore. Admission fee. Open daily from 8:00 a.m. to 6:00 p.m. in summer; 9:00 a.m. to 5:00 p.m. in winter. 113 East Kit Carson Road. Tel.: (505) 758-4741.

Ranchos de Taos Church: Actually called San Francisco de Asis, this adobe church was built in 1730 and has been painted by many artists over the years, including Georgia O'Keeffe. Donation requested. Open Monday to Saturday from 9:00 a.m. to 4:00 p.m. St. Francis Plaza in Ranchos de Taos, off U.S. Highway 68, four miles south of Taos. Tel.: (505) 758-2754.

Taos Pueblo: If you only have time to see one thing in northern New Mexico, this should probably be it. Taos Pueblo, a U.S. national historic landmark and a UNESCO World Heritage Site, is easily one of the most significant man-made creations in the American West. Established 700 years ago, the still-populated Native village consists of two five-storied brown structures made of mud and straw that rise on either side of the Rio Pueblo, which divides the settlement's plaza. Tiwa-speaking Natives bake bread in outdoor ovens, stage festivals and dances devoted to the turtle, deer, buffalo, and corn, and go about their daily business. Visitors must obey the rules respecting traditions, including no picture-taking on festival days. There is a parking fee, and camera and video permits are necessary. Open April to November daily from 8:00 a.m. to 5:30 p.m.; December to March daily from 8:30 a.m. to 4:30 p.m. Closed for one month in late winter. Two miles north of Taos and a couple of miles east of Paseo del Pueblo Norte (State Highway 68). Tel.: (505) 758-9593.

 Tip: Every year New Mexico ranks among the worst three states in automobile deaths per capita in the United States. Driving the roads here can be a hair-raising adventure just given the topography, but some say the state's drivers are particularly impatient and that they frequently run red lights and fail to put on their turn signals. Driving defensively is always a good idea; here it may well save your life.

Icon Pastimes

Besides being a literary center, Taos is also a mecca for artists. Cruise the town's many galleries and shops, where you'll find Pueblo handicrafts, Old West memorabilia, Southwest antiques, and the work of local painters and sculptors. Eat a Southwestern meal (chicken tostadas, buffalo roast chimichangas, chalupas, tamales, tortilla-wrapped rellenos) in one of the numerous fine restaurants. Browse the various bookstores for out-of-print books about Pueblo life and the Old West. You might even find a copy of Frieda Lawrence's hard-to-find autobiography. For a real thrill, head out to the Rio Grande Gorge Bridge west of town and prepare yourself for a massive dose of vertigo. The bridge is 650 feet above the seemingly thin trickle of the river.

 ## Contacts

Taos Chamber of Commerce: Taos County Chamber of Commerce, P.O. Drawer 1, Taos, New Mexico 87571 U.S. Tel.: 1-800-732-8267 or (505) 758-3873. E-mail: *info@taoschamber.com*. Web site: *www.taoschamber.com* or *www.taosguide.com*.

In a Literary Mood

Books

Burgess, Anthony. *Flame into Being: The Life and Work of D. H. Lawrence.* London: Heinemann, 1985. An idiosyncratic appreciation of one inspired author by another. You may not always agree with Burgess's cogent, acerbic comments but you will look at Lawrence with fresh eyes.

Byrne, Janet. *A Genius for Living: The Life of Frieda Lawrence.* New York: HarperCollins, 1995. A measure of the increased interest in the wives of famous male writers, this biography treats Frieda in her own right. Byrne gives equal time to Frieda's sojourns in New York City and Taos.

Jackson, Rosie. *Frieda Lawrence.* London: Pandora, 1994. A look at the mythology surrounding Frieda, with a bonus reprinting of the strong-willed woman's autobiography *Not I, but the Wind.* Also available in a recent (1999) paperback version through Rivers Oram Press.

Lawrence, D. H. *The Plumed Serpent.* New York: Vintage, 1992. A Mexican Indian general (Don Cipriano Viedma), an Irish widow (Kate Leslie—a thinly disguised Frieda), a Spanish Mexican politician (Don Ramón Carrasco), and a cult devoted to Quetzalcoatl, the Aztecs' plumed serpent god, combine amid violent blood sacrifices and a revolutionary uprising to present what is perhaps Lawrence's most overtly politico-religious novel.

_____. *Sons and Lovers.* New York: New American Library, 1989. Always autobiographical, Lawrence is particularly so here in the saga of a young Nottinghamshireman and his tortured relationship with his overbearing mother.

_____. *St. Mawr and the Man Who Died.* New York: Random House, 1987. In the novella *St. Mawr,* Lawrence paints a powerful picture of a woman named Lou Witt, aka Mabel Dodge Luhan, who destroys every man she encounters, though secretly she wishes to be dominated by a male. Mabel's last husband, Tony Luhan, makes an unflattering appearance as the Native American Geronimo Trujillo, whom Lou calls Phoenix. Part of the story is set in a landscape not unlike that of Lawrence's Taos ranch.

_____. *The Woman Who Rode Away and Other Stories.* New York: Penguin, 1997. Not content with one savage portrait of Mabel Dodge Luhan in *St. Mawr,* Lawrence provides another fictional portrayal of her in the title story of this collection, which concerns an American woman who becomes embroiled in ancient Mexican Indian customs and religion that result in human sacrifice—her own!

_____. *Women in Love.* New York: Signet, 1995. Some deem this novel Lawrence's best. The tale takes up the story of sisters Ursula and Gudrun Brangwen, introduced in the author's earlier novel, *The Rainbow.* Ostensibly it's a torrid exploration of the relationships Ursula and Gudrun have with, respectively, Rupert Birkin and Gerald Crich, two English Midlands men who also feel an attraction for each other. However, there's a great deal of Lawrence's own life and loves embedded in the novel.

Lawrence, Frieda. *Not I, but the Wind.* London: Heinemann, 1934. Frieda's autobiography is hard to come by on its own, though you may find it in a library or a secondhand bookstore.

Maddox, Brenda. *D. H. Lawrence: The Story of a Marriage.* New York: W. W. Norton, 1996. Maddox provides an excellent view of the Lawrences' marriage, giving a full portrait of Frieda and restoring her importance in her husband's life in the same way she did for Nora Joyce in *Nora: The Real Life of Molly Bloom.*

Meyers, Jeffrey. *D. H. Lawrence: A Biography.* New York: Alfred A. Knopf, 1990. An evenhanded account of Lawrence's life and writing.

Robinson, Roxana. *Georgia O'Keeffe: A Life.* New York: Harper & Row, 1989. Since O'Keeffe's death in 1986, there have been a lot of books about her, but this is still the authoritative biography.

Rudnick, Lois Palken. *Mabel Dodge Luhan: New Woman, New Worlds.* Albuquerque: University of New Mexico Press, 1995. The life of the woman at the center of the Taos literary and artistic culture, and the only woman who truly inspired D. H. Lawrence to plan murder.

Sagar, Keith. *The Life of D. H. Lawrence.* New York: Pantheon, 1980. Includes plates of some of Lawrence's idiosyncratic paintings. Sagar also published *The Art of D. H. Lawrence* (Cambridge: Cambridge University Press, 1966), a more thorough study of the writer's artistic oeuvre.

Guidebooks

Harbert, Nancy. *New Mexico.* 3rd ed. Oakland, CA: Fodor's Travel Publications, 1998. Featuring photographs by Michael Freeman, this thoughtful guide has well-chosen excerpts from letters that D. H. Lawrence wrote from New Mexico.

Metzger, Stephen. *New Mexico Handbook.* 4th ed. Chico, CA: Moon Publications, 1997. Some people think Moon guides are a poor man's Lonely Planet, but this overview of New Mexico isn't bad. The Taos section could be a bit more detailed, though.

Santa Fe/Taos/Albuquerque Access. 4th ed. New York: Access Press, 1999. As always, Access provides informative, color-coded capsule descriptions of sights, restaurants, bars, shops, hotels, and museums arranged by neighborhood. The well-conceived sidebars on Georgia O'Keeffe, New Mexico architecture, Hispanic and Native arts and crafts, Pueblo life, and Southwestern cuisine add further insight.

Films/Videos

Baird, Roy, Larry Kramer, and Martin Rosen (producers). *Women in Love.* Ken Russell (director). United Artists/Brandywine Productions, 1969. MGM/UA Home Video. Cast: Alan Bates, Glenda Jackson, and Oliver Reed. Possibly the usually over-the-top Ken Russell's best film, this adaptation of D. H. Lawrence's novel is particularly memorable for Jackson's Oscar-winning performance as Gudrun Brangwen. Two scenes stand out and express the sexual energy and tension in Lawrence's work: Bates as Rupert Birkin peeling a fig, and Bates and Reed (as Gerald Crich) engaging in a bit of nude wrestling.

Dimsey, Russ (producer). *Kangaroo.* Tim Burstall (director). Naked Country Productions, 1986. Uni Distribution (video). Cast: Judy Davis, Colin Friels, and John Walton. Unlike most critics, Anthony Burgess deems D. H. Lawrence's novel *Kangaroo* as one of his best. However, this muddled film version of the writer's Australian opus won't give you that impression.

Golan, Menahem, Yoram Globus, André Djaoui, and Christopher Pearce (producers). *Lady Chatterley's Lover.* Just Jaeckin (director). Cine-Source, 1981. Cast: Shane Briant, Nicholas Clay, and Sylvia Kristel. Snigger, snigger. What can you expect when the director and star (Kristel) of the soft-core porn *Emmanuelle* series team up and take on D. H. Lawrence's erotic novel? Ken Russell took a whack at filming the book for TV in 1992 (Joely Richardson plays Lady Chatterley), with unfortunate results, and there's also a 1955 French film starring Danielle Darrieux as Lady C. But it's the porn industry that's taken poor Lawrence's novel to heart, with titles such as *Young Lady*

Chatterley (plus a sequel), *Lady Chatterley's Passions* (and two sequels), *Fanny Hill Meets Lady Chatterley*, *Lady Chatterley in Tokyo*, and *The Loves of Lady Chatterley*.

Harper, Kenneth (producer). *The Virgin and the Gypsy*. Christopher Miles (director). U.K., 1970. Cast: Honor Blackman, Franco Nero, and Joanna Shimkus. A priest's daughter (Shimkus) falls for a Gypsy (Nero) and all hell breaks loose. Director Miles tries hard to breathe life into his telling of D. H. Lawrence's novella but falls short, though the period atmosphere makes the movie more bearable.

Miles, Christopher, and Andrew Donally (producers). *Priest of Love*. Christopher Miles (director). U.K., 1981. Cast: Ava Gardner, Ian McKellen, and Janet Suzman. Based on Harry Moore's popular D. H. Lawrence biography of the same title, this film focuses on the author's last years. The cast delivers pretty good performances, with McKellen as Lawrence and Suzman as Frieda. Gardner sinks her hammy teeth into Mabel Dodge Luhan with gusto. And the rest of the New Mexico gang—Dorothy Brett, Tony Luhan, and the Huxleys—are also portrayed. John Gielgud, Helen Mirren, and Sarah Miles pop up in minor roles.

Mills, John, and Earl St. John (producers). *The Rocking Horse Winner*. Anthony Pelissier (director). Rank Organization/Two Cities Films, 1949. Cast: John Howard Davies, Valerie Hobson, and John Mills. D. H. Lawrence's superb story about a boy with a knack for picking horse-race winners is brilliantly realized in what is easily one of the best celluloid versions of a Lawrence work. Remade twice (1982, 1997) as a short.

Russell, Ken, Dan Ireland, and William J. Quigley (producers). *The Rainbow*. Ken Russell (director). Vestron Pictures, 1989. Cast: Sammi Davis, Amanda Donohoe, and Glenda Jackson. After Russell's success with *Women in Love*, it was inevitable that he would eventually get around to D. H. Lawrence's earlier novel about the Brangwen family. The director actually controls his excessive tendencies, but the film still misfires, though Donohoe is delicious as the woman who takes Davis (young Ursula Brangwen) under her wing sexually, and it's interesting to see Jackson play Mother Brangwen this time.

Wald, Jerry, and Tom Morahan (producers). *Sons and Lovers*. Jack Cardiff (director). 20th Century Fox, 1960. Cast: Wendy Hiller, Trevor Howard, and Dean Stockwell. An Oscar winner for cinematography, this version of D. H. Lawrence's autobiographical story of a tortured mother-son-father triangle may well be the best celluloid adaptation of the writer's work. Stockwell as Paul Morel and Hiller as his domineering mother crackle, while Howard does his usual fine work as the beleaguered coal-mining father.

Web Sites

D. H. Lawrence: *http://home.earthlink.net/~rudedog2/dhlgrove.htm*; *http://ourworld.com-puserve.com/homepages/nigel_h/dhl.htm*; *www.utexas.edu/research.dhlr*. The first site, put together by an amateur Lawrence lover, has lots of excerpts from his work. There are also good links to other Lawrence sites. The second site provides a tour by pictures of buildings associated with Lawrence in Eastwood, Nottinghamshire, his birthplace. At the last site you'll find *The D. H. Lawrence Review*, a journal.

Georgia O'Keeffe: *http://artcyclopedia.com/artists/okeeffe_georgia.html*. A great site that lists all the O'Keeffe artwork online. The home page for this electronic encyclopedia will link you up with the online art of more than 6,000 artists.

Garrison Keillor and Sinclair Lewis
Prairie Days in Minnesota

Elaine Glusac

WILL KENNICOTT DELIGHTS in Gopher Prairie life. "Nothing like an hour on a duck-pass to make you relish your victuals," he says, driving along novelist Sinclair Lewis's fictional Main Street, oblivious to his despairing wife, Carol, "unheroic heroine in a drama insanely undramatic."

Two generations post-Kennicott, Florian Krebsback of Lake Wobegon relishes his 20-year-old 1966 Chevy, with only 42,000 miles on it. "It may be odd that a man should be so proud of having not gone far, but not so odd in this town," writes village chronicler Garrison Keillor.

My own drive into central Minnesota's unlikely literary hotbed—home to fictional towns Gopher Prairie and Lake Wobegon—featured duck blinds and old Chevys as well as grazing Holsteins, horizon-spiking silos, and field-plowing farmers. The Interstate 94 billboard welcomed me to Stearns County: You're in Dairy Country Now!

You betcha, as they say in these parts. But judge not those parts by their placid lakes, their sturdy stands of corn and oak, or even their amiable advertisements. Authors Lewis and Keillor both scratched this rich Minnesota topsoil and exposed the manners and morals of small-town life rooted in pettiness, complacency and, humanely, hilarity.

If genius springs from the most surprising places, this is Unlikely, U.S.A. Unassuming Sauk Centre, 90 minutes north of Minneapolis by car, incubated budding writer Sinclair Lewis who penned a tellingly titled high-school essay, "The Long Arm of the Small Town." By 1920 that arm grabbed the world's attention with the novel *Main Street*. Ten years later he won the Nobel Prize for literature, becoming the first American to do so.

Similar terrain inspired Minnesotan Keillor, who used the central region of the state as a model for his 1985 small-town biography *Lake Wobegon Days* and weekly village updates on his syndicated National Public Radio show *A Prairie Home Companion.*

It's Keillor's renown in the area that lures me to cow country this late-spring day. If his celebrated dreamers, grudge-holding farmers, and feuding Lutherans bear any real-life animosity toward their ridiculer, they don't show it. Instead they celebrate his fictional realm in the Lake Wobegon Regional Trail, a 28-mile paved cycling route stringing together five rural towns from Sauk Centre to Albany where "all the men are strong, all the women are good-looking and all the children are above average," to quote from *A Prairie Home Companion.* Which proves that for all the talk of "Minnesota nice"—the smiles and nods, the pleases and thank-yous—the locals have a great sense of humor. Or, as the authors might assert, a huge blind spot. Sauk Centre resident Joyce Lyng sees a literary link directly from Lewis to Keillor. "They're both sarcastic when you start to think of it," she says.

Lyng is the town's Lewis expert, a docent at both the Sinclair Lewis Interpretive Center and the Sinclair Lewis Boyhood Home across town. A widowed farmer, she took up the post after raising pigs, cattle, chicken, and four children. She promptly read *Main Street* and got on with the business of Lewis locally. "What I got out of it is he was telling people to do something with their lives besides playing cards and gossiping," she tells me.

Lewis would have liked Lyng. Son of a stern country doctor, he grew up in Sauk Centre not long after it was wrested from Native Americans. He was a shy kid, fond of long walks and few friends. He left for college—Ohio's Oberlin and then Yale—in 1902, but took with him vivid impressions of home, calling it "a good time, a good place and a good preparation for life."

In *Main Street*, his "unheroic heroine" Carol Kennicott views Gopher Prairie for the first time as the young, idealistic wife of Dr. Will Kennicott:

> She saw that Gopher Prairie was merely an enlargement of all the hamlets which they had been passing. Only to the eyes of Kennicott was it exceptional. The huddled low wooden houses broke the plains scarcely more than would a hazel thicket. The fields swept up to it, past it. It was unprotected and unpro-tecting; there was no dignity in it nor any hope of greatness. Only the tall red grain-elevator and a few tinny church-steeples rose from the mass. It was a frontier camp. It was not a place to live in, not possibly, not conceivably.

Immediately upon the book's publication, the good place turned its frontier back on him. But, sensing a good thing, locals embraced him and his fame a mere two years later. Eventually his childhood home was made a historical museum on the redubbed Sinclair Lewis Avenue. It intersects, one-block away, with the resanctioned Original Main Street.

Visiting Lewis's former home, fellow Nobel laureate Pearl Buck described it as "somber, comfortable, middle class . . . where a fiery and important spirit came from." The antique-filled clapboard re-creates Lewis's youth as he might have eaten Sunday dinner or visited his father's study or sacked out on the narrow little bed under the eaves. "I could only see him bursting out of those walls and that town, loving it so much he hated it," said Buck.

Lyng envisions a more carefree Lewis here: "I suppose he slid down that banister like most boys."

Before quitting town, Lewis worked at the Palmer House Hotel, a grand landmark at the corner of Lewis and Main that still functions as a way station for travelers and diners. Although it's prettied up for contemporary tastes with comfortable lobby couches and botanical prints, old photos on the wall attest to the hotel Lewis would have known and written about—an austere setting arranged like a cavernous waiting room.

Sinclair Lewis's Sinful Christmas Cookies

In John Koblas's book Sinclair Lewis: Home at Last, *the following is described as Lewis's favorite Christmas cookie recipe.*

1/2 lb. of butter
1/2 cup of finely chopped almonds
2 eggs
1 shot glass of bourbon
2 cups of sugar
2 tablespoons of Droste's cocoa (or any cocoa if unavailable)
2 cups of flour

Make sure you mix the ingredients together well, otherwise several of the cookies will have a very strong taste. Refrigerate mixture overnight. Roll out thin on a floured board and cut with a cookie cutter, or just drop little balls on a well-greased cookie sheet. Bake for eight to 10 minutes in a 375-degree oven.

If you can smell the cookies cooking, they are done.

More intimate details about Lewis's life emerge at the Interpretive Center's museum. Journalist Dorothy Thompson, his wife at the time, thought he was joking when he told her he had won the Nobel Prize. "How nice for you," she apparently said. "I've got the order of the garter!" His last companion, Ida Compton, donated some of Lewis's belongings, an odd collection of Japanese paintings, Wedgwood plates, a chess set, a cigarette lighter, and a kaleidoscope.

Lewis died in 1951, alone, in Rome, Italy. His cremation urn resides, glass-encased, at the museum, though his ashes are interred beneath a modest head-stone in the local cemetery. It's a peaceful, pine-shaded, untrafficked place, only about a mile from Main Street, a surprising resting place for a lifelong embittered Sauk Centre expatriate.

Today's Main Street is lined with knickknack shops, a 1950s vintage movie theater, and a bakery. The 1885 First National Bank building now inventories Christmas nativity dioramas in its basement vault. Midday the town is hot and shadeless and hard, something Carol Kennicott would have despised, and Will Kennicott embraced.

If this isn't exactly Lake Wobegon, it's similar. Keillor describes his fictional town's main thoroughfare thus: "It's a wide street; the early Yankee promoters thought they would need it wide to handle the crush of traffic." Which never arrives to endanger Florian Krebsback's pristine Chevy. Or my secondhand

You can't get more Smalltown, U.S.A., than the intersection of Original Main Street and Sinclair Lewis Avenue in Sauk Centre, Minnesota, birthplace of Sinclair Lewis. Elaine Glusac

You won't have much trouble with hills biking the Lake Wobegon Regional Trail. Here the trail passes by Charlie's Café (seen in the background) in Freeport, Minnesota. Charlie's is often touted as the model for Garrison Keillor's Chatterbox Café. Elaine Glusac

Schwinn as I pedal off to the field-splicing route through Wobegon country, past cattle herds and creeks, cornfields and duck ponds. This is prairie all right, I think, recalling the Wobegon motto: "'Sumus quod sumus.' We are what we are." Lake Wobegon itself, wrote Keillor, is a Native American name for either "'Here we are!'" or 'we sat all day in the rain waiting for [you].'"

"I have only seen about six and a half miles of it," Keillor told a crowd attending the bike trail's opening in 1998, "but I saw it on a bicycle that has no low gear, and a bicycle that has a flat tire, and riding into a northwesterly wind, so I feel I paid the price for the little bit of it I've seen."

"Oh, yeah," says Stearns County park technician Peter Theismann of the trail's dedication. "He came up and made fun of us and we all laughed."

Keillor's photo and a copy of *Lake Wobegon Days* occupy a corner of the large plate-glass window fronting Charlie's Café in Freeport, "dairy center of the world." A habitué of the diner known to eavesdrop, Keillor reputedly modeled Wobegon's Chatterbox Café on Charlie's, whose neon-yellow paint and numerous highway billboards prove it is keen to compete with the likes of McDonald's. I stop in for a famed chocolate milk shake, a more famed gooey caramel roll, and a legendary sugar high, hoping to catch some Wobegon gossip myself.

Three farmers in John Deere caps seated at the counter use few but exacting words to rehash President Clinton's impeachment. "[Congress] spent all that time to find out he flirted," says one. The other two nod and sip their coffees.

"Most men wear their belts low here," I read in the first chapter of Keillor's *Lake Wobegon Days* while slurping my shake, "there being so many outstanding bellies, some big enough to have names of their own and be formally introduced. Those men don't suck them in or hide them in loose shirts; they let them hang free, they pat them, they stroke them as they stand around and talk. How could a man be so vain as to ignore this old friend who's been with him at the great moments of his life?"

The remaining trail towns—Melrose, Avon, and Albany—are so Wobegon-esque I feel I've entered the story's architecture, plotted with awkward grain elevators, grand old churches, Red Wing shoe stores, and antique shops selling cast-off cast-iron pans and 40-year-old lightbulbs. I search for a high point, a tourist's zenith, some spectacular thrill. But there's nary a hill in the gentle road. Just prairie. And its people. *Sumus quod sumus.*

Buckling up for the car ride back to Minneapolis, I tune into that week's edition of *A Prairie Home Companion*. Keillor is extolling spring in Wobegon. "It's the week when the bachelor farmers take off their long underwear and lean them up against the house," he says. "After a few rains, they melt."

The Writer's Trail

Following in the Footsteps

Destination: What can you say about a state that elected an ex-wrestler as governor? Plenty. The lonely passions of small-town prairie dwellers may not instantly reveal themselves to outsiders visiting central Minnesota, a pastoral region of cornfields where cows frequently outnumber people, but the welcome is genuinely friendly and the pace comfortingly slow.

Location: Minnesota is bordered by Manitoba and Ontario, Canada, in the north; Lake Superior and Wisconsin in the east; Iowa in the south; and North and South Dakota in the west. Minneapolis is on the west bank of the Mississippi River; St. Paul, the state's capital, is on the east bank. The Twin Cities are in southeast Minnesota. Sauk Centre and the Lake Wobegon region are 108 miles northwest of Minneapolis via Interstate 94, where northern Minnesota lake country meets central Midwestern dairy land.

Getting There: Nine commercial U.S. airlines—including Northwest (1-800-225-2525) and American (1-800-433-7300)—fly from major American cities to Minneapolis/St. Paul, which will be your jump-off point for Garrison Keillor/Sinclair Lewis country. The major car-rental agencies (Avis [1-800-331-1212], Hertz [1-800-654-3131], et cetera) are represented at Minneapolis/St. Paul International Airport, which is eight and a half miles from downtown St. Paul. You can also get to the Twin Cities by long-distance Greyhound bus. The Greyhound terminal in St. Paul is at Seventh and St. Peter Streets. Minneapolis/St. Paul is a stop on Amtrak's Chicago-Seattle run. The Twin Cities Amtrak Depot is at 730 Transfer Road in St. Paul's Midway area, 10 minutes from the capital's downtown.

Orientation: Of course, you can rent a car as soon as you touch down at the Twin Cities' airport and head out for Wobegon country, but you might want to freshen up before you hit the road. There are a number of reasons to stay a night or two in St. Paul, particularly at the St. Paul Hotel (see **Literary Sleeps**). First and foremost, from a literary point of view, the state capital is the birthplace of F. Scott Fitzgerald, another great American writer, and there are a number of places in the city associated with him (see **Literary Sites**). Second, St. Paul has some pretty good museums and art galleries, a charming, revitalized Mississippi riverfront, a great many stately Victorian mansions, and a lively performing-arts scene.

Tip: When you go to Minnesota, be prepared to chitchat. Locally such social intercourse is termed "Minnesota nice" and includes the please-and-thank-you-style politeness rapidly diminishing elsewhere in the United States.

Getting Around: If you do tarry a while in St. Paul, you can easily walk to most central sights. If you want to get farther afield and haven't rented a car, there are, of course, municipal buses and taxis. But you'll probably want that rental car if you decide to check out Minneapolis or the colossal Mall of America in nearby Bloomington. Unbelievably the mall, a monument to mega-consumerism, attracts more tourists than Disney World, the Grand Canyon, and Graceland combined. Each of the five towns on the 28-mile-long Lake Wobegon Regional Trail—Sauk Centre, Melrose, Freeport, Albany, Avon—are small enough to take in on foot. To bike between them, rent cycles from A-OK Sauk Centre Rental (967 Main Street, [320] 352-2700). A good map will take car drivers over rural routes connecting the towns, though not as directly as the bike trail.

Literary Sleeps

St. Paul Hotel: A Historic Hotel of America, this establishment opened for business in 1910 and would have been a familiar sight to F. Scott Fitzgerald. Today the hotel is still one of the poshest in the Midwest and is close to many of the major attractions in the state capital. 350 Market Street, St. Paul. Tel.: 1-800-292-9292 or (651) 292-9292. Fax: (651) 228-9506. Moderate.

Palmer House Hotel: Built in 1901 and recently restored, the hotel retains much of its turn-of-the-century appeal. Sinclair Lewis once worked here as a night clerk. The hotel maintains a restaurant and pub. Near the hotel is Main Street Drug; Lewis's father ran his medical practice on the second floor of this building. 228 Original Main Street, Sauk Centre. Tel.: (320) 352-3431. Inexpensive to moderate.

AmericInn: Not much from a literary standpoint here, but it's a clean motel option if you want to save money. 1230 Timberlane Drive (southeast corner of I-94 and U.S. 71), Sauk Centre. Tel.: (320) 352-2800. Inexpensive.

Literary Sites

Charlie's Café: Garrison Keillor is a regular at this Freeport hangout. Reputedly it's the model for the author's fictional Chatterbox Café. Open daily 6:00 a.m. to 10:00 p.m. Tel.: (320) 836-2105.

F. Scott Fitzgerald Sites: Fitzgerald spent a fair bit of his youth in the Minnesota capital. There's a statue of him outside the Landmark Center (formerly the Federal Court Building) at 75 West Fifth Street. The center was once the scene of some of the FBI's most famous gangland trials. Criminals who made an appearance here included Ma Barker's gang, Alvin "Creepy" Karpis, Baby Face Nelson, John Dillinger, and Machine Gun Kelly. During the 1920s and 1930s, St. Paul was a magnet for urban desperadoes. Today the center is devoted to culture, but the courtrooms are still there and gangster tours are available, as they are in the nearby Wabasha Street Caves, once the site of a notorious nightclub patronized by St. Paul's flashy mobsters. The Fitzgerald Theater, erected in 1910, is the oldest surviving stage facility in St. Paul. Located at 10 East Exchange Street, it's the place where Garrison Keillor's radio show *A Prairie Home Companion* is broadcast live. The magnificent theater was originally called the Schubert; Fitzgerald would have been quite familiar with it. For tickets to or information about Keillor's show, call (651) 290-1221, or check out the Fitzgerald's Web site at *www.fitzgeraldtheater.org*. Summit Street, with its stately Victorian homes, was the swankiest St. Paul address in Fitzgerald's day, and it still is. The author was born in a rented apartment just off Summit at 481 Laurel Avenue; eventually his family moved to 599 Summit (now a national historic landmark), and that's where he rewrote his first novel *This Side of Paradise*. The James J. Hill House, once the biggest mansion in the Midwest, is also on Summit. It's now a museum. Hill was a 19th-century railroad baron with whom Fitzgerald was obviously fascinated. The tycoon's name pops up frequently in the writer's fiction, and he's also one of the models for Dan Cody, Jay Gatsby's wealthy patron in *The Great Gatsby*.

Sinclair Lewis Boyhood Home: Built in 1880 and now restored to its turn-of-the-century interior glory, the home contains, among other memorabilia, the rolltop desk of Lewis's doctor father. Legend has it that young Sinclair's father made his son bury amputated human limbs in the house's backyard. The ladies' literature readings that Lewis writes about in *Main Street* were actually held by the author's stepmother in the Lewis parlor. Open Memorial Day (last Monday in May) through Labor Day (first Monday in September) Monday to Saturday 9:30 a.m. to 5:00 p.m., Sunday 10:30 a.m. to 5:00 p.m. October to Memorial Day by appointment. 810 Sinclair Lewis Avenue, Sauk Centre. Tel.: (320) 352-5201.

Sinclair Lewis Grave Site: Lewis's gravestone is three rows in from the main gate and 26 stones to the left. Greenwood Cemetery at Sinclair Lewis Avenue and County Road 17.

Sinclair Lewis Interpretive Center: The center features a display called the "Birth of a Novel," which shows the various stages one of Lewis's books went through to become a reality. The museum also contains old photos and a history of Sauk Centre, Lewis's writing desk, the author's diplomas from high school and Yale University, his death certificate, and various other odds and ends from his life. Open Memorial Day through Labor Day Monday to Friday 8:30 a.m. to 5:00 p.m., Saturday and Sunday 9:00 a.m. to 5:00 p.m.; winter Monday to Friday 8:30 a.m. to 4:30 p.m. Interstate 94 and U.S. Highway 71, Sauk Centre. Tel.: (320) 352-5201.

> **Tip:** Fans of children's writer Laura Ingalls Wilder (*Little House on the Prairie*) might want to make a side trip to Walnut Grove in southwestern Minnesota. There you'll find a museum devoted to her, as well as the site of that famous little house.

Icon Pastimes

After touring the F. Scott Fitzgerald sites in St. Paul, take a walk along the city's reborn riverfront, get aboard a paddlewheeler for a cruise on the Mississippi River, search out the haunts of the town's old-time gangsters, or see a live broadcast of Garrison Keillor's *A Prairie Home Companion* at the Fitzgerald Theater. If you're in Sauk Centre in October, catch the annual Sinclair Lewis Writers Conference. If you're in the town around mid-July, you'll have a chance to attend Sinclair Lewis Days, the municipality's annual fair.

Contacts

Minnesota Office of Tourism: 121 Seventh Place East, Suite 500, St. Paul, Minnesota 55101. Tel: 1-800-657-3700. Web site: *www.exploreminnesota.com*.

Sauk Centre Chamber of Commerce: P.O. Box 222, Sauk Centre, Minnesota 56378. Tel.: (320) 352-5201. Web site: *www.saukcentre.com*.

Stearns County Parks: 455 Twenty-eighth Avenue South, Waite Park, Minnesota 56387. Tel.: (320) 255-6172.

In a Literary Mood

Books

Dregni, Michael, ed. *Minnesota Days*. Stillwater, MN: Voyageur Press, 1999. This colorful assemblage of writing, photography, and artwork focusing on Minnesota history and culture features contributions by Sinclair Lewis, Garrison Keillor, F. Scott Fitzgerald, Laura Ingalls Wilder, and many other Minnesotans.

Keillor, Garrison. *Lake Wobegon Days*. New York: Penguin, 1995. Although he had been retailing Wobegon stories for years on his public radio show *A Prairie Home Companion*, this book truly propelled Keillor to national fame. The author, employing his trademark wryness, recounts his youth in the fictional central Minnesota town where German Catholics feud with Norwegian Lutherans.

_____. *Wobegon Boy*. New York: Penguin, 1998. Keillor revisits Wobegon's Mist County 10 years after his smash success, *Lake Wobegon Days*. Here the autobiographical narrator is the manager of a college radio station in upstate New York who, when he's not fulminating against the modern world or caught up in humorous memories of his Midwest Norwegian origins, is embroiled in a touching love affair with a female historian. Less successful than his earlier book, the novel seems a little shopworn in its devices.

Lewis, Sinclair. *Arrowsmith*. New York: Signet, 1998. In this stirring tale of a dedicated young research doctor, Martin Arrowsmith, who is perpetually tempted to sell out, Lewis practically introduced a new character to the mainstream novel: the conflicted scientist. This edition has an added bonus of an introduction by novelist E. L. Doctorow.

_____. *Babbitt*. New York: Bantam, 1998. Published two years after *Main Street* in 1922, this novel solidified Lewis's reputation as a hard-hitting critic of middle-class America, here embodied by the book's protagonist, archconformist George Babbitt, a real-estate agent whose name has been enshrined in the dictionary as synonymous with unthinking adherence to conventionality.

_____. *Dodsworth*. New York: Signet, 1995. Released a year before Lewis won the Nobel Prize in 1930, this novel likely helped him cinch the award. The author returns to George Babbitt's fictional town of Zenith in the American Midwest to tell the story of Sam Dodsworth, a successful automobile manufacturer who sells his business and retires to Europe, where he and his wife, Fran, undergo numerous traumatic experiences. Call it Midwest Gauche meets Old World Snobbery.

_____. *Elmer Gantry*. New York: Signet, 1982. Here Lewis takes on evangelical religion in a blistering saga of a seemingly conscienceless preacher with the gift of gab and a dearth of morals. When it was originally published in 1927, *Elmer Gantry* enraged just about every religious denomination in America, which is probably why it still rings a note of familiarity today.

_____. *Main Street*. New York: Signet, 1998. Lewis's bestselling account of Midwestern small-town hypocrisy and the troubled lives of Dr. Will Kennicott and his wife, Carol, still stings more than eight decades after its original publication.

Meyers, Jeffrey. *Scott Fitzgerald: A Biography*. New York: HarperCollins, 1994. There are plenty of Fitzgerald biographies, but Meyers, as he did with the lives of Katherine Mansfield, Wyndham Lewis, Ernest Hemingway, D. H. Lawrence, Joseph Conrad, and Edgar Allan Poe, provides a highly readable, sympathetic, yet critical portrait. Like all accounts of the doomed Fitzgerald's life, Meyers's book pays scant attention to the writer's early days in St. Paul. Still, he does provide some interesting insights about this period.

Schorer, Mark. *Sinclair Lewis: An American Life*. New York: McGraw-Hill, 1961. Apparently Richard Lingeman, the executive editor of *The Nation*, is working on a new major biography of Lewis, but at the moment this classic rendering is the only definitive narrative of the author's life. Impressive in his research and detail as he is, Schorer still gives the reader the impression that he profoundly dislikes his subject. A fresh approach is long overdue.

Guidebooks

Nettleton, Pamela Hill. *Minneapolis/St. Paul Access*. New York: Access Press, 1998. Once again Access delivers a sprightly, savvy metropolitan guide, supplying everything you need to know about hotels, restaurants, cafés, bars, shops, museums, and assorted sights in an attractive, easy-to-follow package.

Shepard, John G. *Minnesota: Off the Beaten Track*. Saybrook, CT: Globe Pequot Press, 1999. There aren't many good guides to Minnesota, but this one does have some merit, though it lacks the kind of detail Lonely Planet devotes to its travel books. Still, Sauk Centre and Wobegon country do make an appearance.

Films/Videos

Beaumont, Harry (director). *Main Street*. No producer credited. Warner Bros., 1923. Cast: Noah Beery,

Monte Blue, and Florence Vidor. Amazingly Sinclair Lewis's great novel has only been filmed once—silently.

Bischoff, Samuel (producer). *Babbitt.* William Keighley (director). Warner Bros./First National Productions, 1934. Cast: Claire Dodd, Guy Kibbee, and Aline MacMahon. Not surprisingly, given the swaggering Kibbee in the title role, this movie doesn't have much in common with Sinclair Lewis's novel. The self-inflated business types in the film come across more as cartoons rather than full-blown characters. Pity.

Goldwyn, Samuel (producer). *Arrowsmith.* John Ford (director). Howard Productions, 1931. HBO Video. Cast: Richard Bennett, Ronald Colman, and Helen Hayes. John Ford does Sinclair Lewis! Having a great director take on a great book should be a plus, but a muddled script and unfocused direction hamstring the story. The first is surprising, since the screenwriter was Sidney Howard, who scripted the excellent film version of *Dodsworth.* Still, Colman as the good Dr. Arrowsmith and Hayes as his wife have some fine moments.

Goldwyn, Samuel, and Merritt Hulburd (producers). *Dodsworth.* William Wyler (director). Samuel Goldwyn Company, 1936. HBO Video. Cast: Ruth Chatterton, Walter Huston, and Paul Lukas. With the exception of *Elmer Gantry*, this is by far the best screen adaptation of a Sinclair Lewis novel. Huston is outstanding as the title character. More than 60 years later, director Wyler's gem continues to shine as a masterful translation of novel into celluloid.

Smith, Bernard (producer). *Elmer Gantry.* Richard Brooks (director). United Artists, 1960. MGA/UA Home Video. Cast: Arthur Kennedy, Burt Lancaster, and Jean Simmons. Lancaster, as Gantry, won an Oscar for his performance, and it's easy to see why. The actor burns up the screen so effectively as the magnetically monstrous preacher that he simply becomes the character for all time.

Web Sites

Garrison Keillor: *www.phc.mpr.org.* This is the site for Keillor's *A Prairie Home Companion* radio show on Minnesota Public Radio.

Sinclair Lewis: *www.ilstu.edu/~separry/lewis.html*; *www.saukherald.com/lewis/default.html.* The first site belongs to the Sinclair Lewis Society, located at Illinois State University's English department. It features a Lewis newsletter, bibliographies, a chronology, a biography, and great links. The second site is hosted by the *Sauk Centre Herald* and has a number of articles about Lewis in relation to his hometown.

"What would be regarded as

strange and bizarre behavior in

another city is not only tolerated

in the Big Easy, but cherished."

Tennessee Williams
Streetcar Named New Orleans

Marda Burton

"THEY TOLD ME to take a streetcar named Desire, transfer to one called Cemeteries, and ride six blocks and get off at Elysian Fields," Blanche DuBois says in Tennessee Williams's play *A Streetcar Named Desire*. With that loaded metaphor the lady from Laurel is introduced to the world.

Williams, who was born in Columbus, Mississippi, conjured up the most famous of his vast gallery of doomed heroines while immersed in the provocative and pungent resonances of the Vieux Carré (Old Square or French Quarter), a square-mile anachronism that casts such a net of illusion over its willing victims that even visitors are compelled to drop their inhibitions like so many unwieldy packages. What would be regarded as strange and bizarre behavior in another city is not only tolerated in the Big Easy, but cherished. In London they say if two people stand on a corner, a queue forms. In New Orleans's French Quarter, a parade starts.

The pace is Southern slow, but the pulse is quick. That rare sense of the unexpected lies in wait around every twist of the street. Stories hover in every bar and behind every walled courtyard. The exotic architecture and misty, sultry air evoke rich imaginings. Even the foods sound sensual: mirliton, cushaw, Creole tomatoes, okra, grits, chicory and roux, gumbo, and étouffée. The entire city suggests a character whose eccentricities demand center stage—dramatic, blowsy, and overblown, a self-conscious cliché of itself yet very real. It's irresistible to all but the most cynical of hearts, and certainly those impressionable creatures called writers can't withstand its summons. Not surprisingly, countless literary greats have embraced New Orleans as either a sometime sweetheart or a lifetime muse.

Besides Williams, a number of other famous, now-departed writers haunt the literary landscape, among them Washington Irving, Lafcadio Hearn, Walt Whitman, Mark Twain, Kate Chopin, Oscar Wilde, O. Henry, Sherwood Anderson, Carl Sandburg, Sinclair Lewis, Thornton Wilder, Erskine Caldwell, John Dos Passos, F. Scott Fitzgerald, Katherine Anne Porter, William Faulkner, Frances Parkinson Keyes, Truman Capote, Lillian Hellman, and Walker Percy. Even Ernest Hemingway (who haunted the dime shooting galleries on Canal Street), John Steinbeck, Anita Loos, and Gertrude Stein reportedly dropped in to match wits with resident writers. Like Paris in those heady days, the French Quarter was a literary mecca. Today New Orleans nurtures the creativity of Richard Ford, Andrei Codrescu, Anne Rice, Shirley Ann Grau, and many other talented writers, none of whom seem intimidated by icons of the past.

Having writerly aspirations myself—not to mention having lived my entire life in Blanche and Stella's hometown of Laurel, Mississippi—I felt fated to seek my own literary future in the French Quarter. Hoping to follow in the spiritual footsteps of the city's literati, I was sure its characters, conversations, and settings would fill notebooks of creative musings that could be put to good use in my own great American novel. That years of another kind of writing life in Laurel were obligatory before I left Mississippi didn't deter me from my goal. Wasn't it a mistress of Louis XVI who said, "We buy our wisdom with our youth"?

Like Blanche, I left Laurel behind and arrived in New Orleans with nothing more than a suitcase full of clothes and a romantic ideal. Early the next morning, reality rudely intruded upon romanticism. Traveling by motorcar, not by train as Blanche did, I realized my New Orleans experience would be uniquely my own when my vehicle was callously yanked out of the way of a street-cleaning machine by a city tow truck. It cost me $90 and a load of hayseed to get it back. Welcome to the real New Orleans. But in the French Quarter feet easily replace cars; everything necessary for life and its enjoyment is just a stroll away. Eventually, when my automobile collected $1,000 worth of parking tickets and a dead battery, I sold it without a qualm and went to find a streetcar named Desire.

Instead I found a bus named Desire. The old Desire streetcar stands permanently parked in front of the Old Mint Museum at Esplanade Avenue and Decatur Street, its loop through the French Quarter having been demolished long ago.

But grand red streetcars (*never* say trolleys) clang up and down the riverfront, and the same olive-green antiques still trundle along St. Charles Avenue past Lee Circle through the tree-canopied Garden District. In one of the city's countless ironies, the old Canal streetcar line is now being rebuilt at great cost but won't venture into the Vieux Carré's narrow streets.

I also found that Williams took literary liberties for the sake of metaphor. The directions he gave Blanche wouldn't have led to 632 (Williams's own house

Tennessee Williams once said that going to mass at New Orleans's St. Louis Cathedral was like going to the theater. Dating back to 1794, the impressive French Quarter structure is the oldest cathedral in the United States. Marda Burton

number on St. Peter Street) Elysian Fields Avenue, which is not technically in the French Quarter anymore, but in Faubourg Marigny; nor could she have heard the bells of St. Louis Cathedral from so far away. But that's nitpicking. While you can't follow in Blanche's exact footsteps, it's almost impossible not to track those of literary lions, especially her creator's.

In the same way that George Washington seems to have slept in every town in New England, Tennessee Williams appears to have partied with his friends—a favorite Quarter pastime—in every bar and restaurant in the Vieux Carré. He lived in a great number of French Quarter domiciles, from $4-a-week rooms in his early, destitute days to his last New Orleans home, a fine town house at 1014 Dumaine Street. During my own peripatetic apartment moves, I lived for a time at 431 Royal Street, once a small hotel where Williams rented a $4-a-week room when he first arrived in the city; later he moved to a garret at 722 Toulouse Street, where he paid $10 a month.

While people dine out on stories about Williams, who returned to New Orleans year after year until his death in 1983, tales about other writers—famous or otherwise—also come out of the woodwork. Ask almost any bartender if he or she knows any writers, then just lean back and listen. Or sit on a bench in Jackson Square and watch as potential or past book characters parade by. Mimes, musicians, street artists, acrobats, palmists, and tarot readers are every-where, and often the people watching them are just as colorful. The scene is pure theater, as both conscious and unconscious eccentricities provide a fascinating feast for the imagination. Early on I staked my claim to one of the little tables half on the banquette (Quarterspeak for *sidewalk*) and half in an open doorway of the Napoleon House at the corner of St. Louis and Chartres (pronounce it *Charters*, please) Streets. Because my garret apartment was upstairs, I didn't have far to go. At this musty old literary hangout, classical music blares forth (purists grieved when the old gramophone with scratched records was retired in favor of a CD player), and witty, intellectual repartee seems to go on at every table.

Common sense says that rather than the philosophy of Jean-Paul Sartre or Albert Camus or the latest book review in the *New York Times*, most patrons are probably chatting about ordinary things. Or they could be debating the relative merits of an in-house muffuletta as opposed to one from Central Grocery over on Decatur Street—a subject good for at least a half hour's discourse. (A muffuletta is a huge, heavenly Italian sandwich; I always choose the Napoleon House version because the restaurant heats it up until the cheese melts.)

Eventually my Napoleon House habit gave way to the habit of eating regular-ly. Writing on a computer in an office, while not as picturesque, was more efficient and hence more productive than sitting in a beatup bar writing in a beatup notebook. Likewise, my romantic but airless garret was sacrificed to fiendishly hot New Orleans summers. Now I live in a pricey "maisonette" with central air-conditioning and my own brick-walled patio.

Lately, with my old notebook rescued from premature burial on a sagging bookshelf, I began returning to the Napoleon House. It is exactly as before, just as though I had never left, except for more tourists to usurp my table. Classical music still plays, table service is still ostentatiously slow, and passing buggy drivers still spiel tales of the failed conspiracy to spirit away the imprisoned Napoleon

Forty-six days before Easter, every year, New Orleans explodes with Mardi Gras, the biggest, loudest, most colorful bash in the United States. Marda Burton

to Nouvelle Orleans, where he would reside in this very house.

I'm not sure, but maybe the tables have turned, so to speak. Could it be that sitting in a beatup bar writing in a beatup notebook, while less efficient, is more productive than writing on a computer in an office? I'll find out soon enough when this manuscript—and a fledgling novel—put that question to the test. Often now I sit and watch Blanche or Anne Rice's Lestat amble by the Napoleon House, grazing my way through a muffuletta washed down with a Dixie beer and desultorily trying to identify Mozart or Haydn on the sound system. At such times the past hovers so tangibly I can almost feel its breath, and words begin to flow as if from some past life.

In fact, leading a literary life in the French Quarter is almost too easy. It's too easy to talk about writing instead of doing it, too easy for writers (and readers) to get together and party, too easy to take in a Tennessee Williams or a Robert Harling play at Le Petit Théâtre du Vieux Carré, the oldest continuously operating community theater in the United States. It's too easy to spend valuable days of writing time at one of the two major literary festivals put on each year in the Quarter. It's too easy to dine out not only on great food, but on great stories. In short, it's too easy to neglect your work.

So, take it from me, if you plan to come here to write, be careful. Pack a suitcase full of discipline, because New Orleans is no friend to the Protestant work ethic. In her own beguiling way, she'll offer up every temptation to procrastinate, and she'll whisper in your writer's ear, "But, dawlin', it's research."

Walker Percy lived in self-imposed exile in Covington, across Lake Pontchartrain from the city, for just this reason. The late National Book Award winner often said he was too distracted by the city, that he needed a less-stimulating environment in which to write. In essays and interviews, Percy called New Orleans the only "foreign" city in the United States. He considered Covington a border where the Latin, Mediterranean, Catholic culture and the WASP South came together, and found the clash of the two very conducive to writing.

There's also the vibrant African-American culture that produced jazz and continues to turn out world-famous musicians as well as a form of Haitian voodoo that melds with Catholicism. To catch more than a hint of Percy's reasoning, just pick up a *Times-Picayune*, the city's daily newspaper. Sports-page headlines scream "St. Augustine Bashes St. Aloysius." The local professional football team is named the Saints. Mardi Gras is more popular than Easter or Christmas, and the day after the huge city-wide bacchanal, most celebrants quit drinking for the day and go around with ashes on their foreheads. Precisely the sort of place that draws writers like a magnet.

Writer Andrei Codrescu, a resident of Chartres Street, fully appreciates the more bizarre aspects of the French Quarter. Besides reading his commentary on PBS and bringing out book-length works as fast as they drop from his pen, he writes short essays for *Gambit*, a free newspaper out each Monday. Often he can be found mining material at Molly's At The Market on Decatur Street, his favorite hangout, and he enjoys lunching at an outdoor table at the Pirate's Alley Café behind St. Louis Cathedral.

The yellow town house next door is every visiting writer's first stop: Faulkner House Books (624 Pirate's Alley)—where William Faulkner lived and wrote his first novel *Soldier's Pay* in 1925—now the home of Joe and Rosemary DeSalvo, who live above the bookshop in four exquisitely restored floors filled with books and antiques. The DeSalvos were among those who spearheaded the late-1980s renaissance of the Quarter's literary legacy by originating the late-September Faulkner birthday celebration and writers conference in 1990. Rosemary edits the *Double Dealer Redux*, successor to the literary magazine of the 1920s that published pieces by Anderson, Faulkner, Hemingway, and others. Joe chairs the national Pirate's Alley Faulkner Awards, always presented on the big birthday weekend.

The Tennessee Williams/New Orleans Literary Festival and Writers Conference, held in March, began in 1987 with about 500 people. Now as many as 8,000 readers, authors, and wannabes flock to Le Petit Théâtre, the Historic New Orleans Collection at 533 Royal Street, and other venues around the Quarter for a long weekend of plays, lectures, literary panels, music, and food. Both the Williams and Faulkner events feature, but aren't limited to, their respective honorees.

When he's not holed up in Montana, Maine, or Paris, Richard Ford can be spotted at the bookshop schmoozing with Joe. I remember walking by Ford's house on Bourbon Street in 1996 after his prize-winning novel *Independence Day* was published. Something wonderfully fragrant was blooming in his garden, perhaps sweet olive or wisteria. "What's that smelling so sweet?" I asked my companion. He quickly shot back, "That's the Pulitzer Prize."

To follow literary ghosts, begin in Jackson Square at St. Louis Cathedral where, in 1882, Oscar Wilde was driven in a carriage by General P. G. T. Beauregard. In the park, rearing high above the pigeons and winos, rides Andrew Jackson, the hero of the Battle of New Orleans in 1815. Faulkner was fascinated by the statue's combination of stasis and motion; everyone is spellbound by the wacky scene below. The square is described in the writings of Twain, Whitman, O. Henry, and many others. Lillian Hellman hid here when she ran away from her uptown home, as described in *An Unfinished Woman*. It's easy to picture the strange Lafcadio Hearn stalking the square, gathering vignettes for newspaper articles in the 1870s. He eventually left for Japan, where he spent the rest of his life, but is remembered for writing "It is better to live here in sackcloth and ashes than to own the entire state of Ohio."

In the Pontalba Apartments beside the square (540B on St. Peter Street), Sherwood Anderson and his wife, Elizabeth, lived and entertained local and visiting writers for several years in the 1920s. Faulkner also stayed here in early 1925 in the Andersons' extra room. (When he first came to New Orleans, Anderson lived on the third floor at 708 Royal Street, and also bought a house at 715 Governor Nicholls Street in which he never lived.) Across the street, Café du Monde is today's version of the old Morning Call, a coffee shop popular with the literary set. The beignets and chicory coffee are still legendary.

Steamboats once tied up on the river in front of Jackson Square, disgorging passengers such as Twain and Washington Irving. O. Henry's favorite restaurant was Madame Begue's, once upstairs over Tujague's on the corner of Decatur and Madison Streets. Stroll up Madison to 536, the former Lyle Saxon residence where John Steinbeck married his second wife, Gwen, in 1943. Take a look at the courtyard at La Marquise (625 Chartres Street), where Faulkner, Anderson, and "Aunt" Rose Arnold, formerly a Storyville madam, frequently took afternoon "tea" under the chinaberry tree. Anita Loos recalled a time when Faulkner was curled up underneath a table fast asleep.

On the St. Peter Street corner of Jackson Square stands Le Petit Théâtre du Vieux Carré, where Sinclair Lewis appeared in a 1940 production of *Shadow and Substance*. Off and on from December 1924 to 1926, Faulkner lived upstairs at both the Häagen-Dazs Ice Cream Shop across the street behind the cathedral (621 St. Peter Street; a drawing on the wall commemorates the building's literary connections) and the Faulkner Bookshop around the corner. From their vantage point, Faulkner and his artist friend William Spratling, with whom he shared the attic apartment at 621 St. Peter in 1926, shot passersby with BBs. In their "high-spirited" game, priests and nuns won the most points.

At age 27, Faulkner came to New Orleans as a mediocre poet and left as a competent novelist, taking Anderson's advice to "go home and write about what you know." During his New Orleans sojourn, he wrote *Soldier's Pay* and *Mosquitoes*. When the latter was accepted for publication, he threw a dinner party at Galatoire's with the advance, inviting several people whom he had satirized in the book.

At 722 Toulouse Street, Tennessee Williams's landlady, the irascible Mrs. Anderson, poured a bucket of boiling water through her kitchen floor, which was directly over the first-floor studio where a local photographer was throwing a loud party. Williams put another landlady at that same address, the suspicious Mrs. Louise Wire, who slept on a cot in the hall, into his play *Vieux Carré* and the short story "Angel in the Alcove." During those days (1939 to 1941), the French Quarter was mostly a cheap and congenial slum, not the relatively upscale neighborhood it has since become. Williams also lived at 708 Toulouse Street, at 711 Orleans Street, and at 538 Royal Street, across from what was formerly a well-known gay bar, the St. James. He lived at 632 St. Peter Street in 1946–47 while working on *A Streetcar Named Desire*.

In 1945 Truman Capote moved back to New Orleans, took up residence at 811 Royal Street, and wrote many short stories and part of the novel *Other Voices, Other Rooms*. He was born Truman Steckfus Persons at Touro Infirmary and lived for a time at 1801 Robert Street in uptown New Orleans, but always said he was conceived at the Monteleone Hotel (214 Royal Street). The hotel has been declared a literary landmark for its association over the years with many famous writers.

Around the corner, at 209 Bourbon Street, sandwiched between a sex shop and a "gentleman's club," stands a bastion of old-line gentility and literary prominence—Galatoire's Restaurant. Patronized and written about by numerous authors, the old restaurant has opened a bar and upstairs rooms to accommodate the overflow that used to form a long, convivial line outside—distinguished by being the only place New Orleanians would ever stand in line.

In April 1882, Mark Twain dined at Antoine's (713 St. Louis Street), and Faulkner was honored there after he won the Nobel Prize for literature in 1949.

Gertrude Stein and Evelyn Waugh were among hundreds of celebrity diners during the past century. I was lucky enough to be one of the 16 invited guests for the 50th anniversary re-creation of Frances Parkinson Keyes's *Dinner at Antoine's*.

For informal literary eats, you can sample a Lucky Dog from one of the weenie carts immortalized in John Kennedy Toole's *A Confederacy of Dunces*. The tragic author lived his entire life here, and committed suicide at age 31 on a nearby beach in Biloxi, Mississippi. After his death, his mother prevailed upon Walker Percy to read her son's rejected novel, a comic and surreal vision of New Orleans in 1962. It was published by Louisiana State University Press to great acclaim and won a posthumous Pulitzer Prize in 1981. A statue of the book's main character, the slovenly Ignatius J. Reilly, stands in front of the Chateau Sonesta Hotel at 819 Canal Street, back then the city's traditional meeting place "under the clock" at D. H. Holmes Department Store. The famous clock can be found in the Clock Bar inside the hotel.

The other boundary of the French Quarter, Esplanade Avenue, has found literary fame, as well. Kate Chopin's Edna Pontellier and husband resided there in a Creole mansion in *The Awakening*, and in 1924 John Dos Passos secluded himself at number 510 to work on *Manhattan Transfer*. Bourbon Street landmarks include number 516 where Lafcadio Hearn resided in 1879, and number 623, once rented by Thornton Wilder and now owned by politician and author Lindy Boggs.

You can do this literary exploring all by yourself, or you can have even more fun in the company of Dr. Kenneth Holditch, a noted historian whose Heritage Tours are witty and anecdotal. Since he's the city's preeminent authority on Williams, Faulkner, Toole, Ford, Rice, and others, you'll soon find out where all the bodies are buried. If you're lucky, and if he's so inclined that day, Dr. Holditch might end his tour at Galatoire's sitting at his favorite table by the right front window—appropriately called the Tennessee Williams table.

Then call to mind the words a man named Charles Dudley Warner wrote back in 1887, no doubt while idling in some ancient bar or bistro: "I suppose we are all wrongly made up and have a fallen nature; else why is it that the most thrifty and neat and orderly city only wins our approval, and perhaps gratifies us intellectually, and such a thriftless, battered and stained, and lazy old place as the French Quarter of New Orleans takes our hearts?"

The Writer's Trail

Following in the Footsteps

Destination: Since its founding by the French in 1718, New Orleans has become a gumbo of so many cultures layered so closely that it is a true American melting pot. Its days and nights are flavored by distinctive customs and celebrations that welcome all comers. Nowhere is this more evident than in the small, densely packed French Quarter, historically a sympathetic haven for artists, musicians, writers, and bohemians from everywhere. While the present state of the French Quarter's evolution leans heavily toward tourism—and the street hustlers, vagrants, and tacky T-shirt shops are always with us—the old place still retains more than enough decaying elegance and local oddities to celebrate, albeit somewhat self-consciously, its own exoticism.

Location: Situated in southeast Louisiana, New Orleans is almost an island. The mighty Mississippi River sweeps past the city in a huge curve (hence the name Crescent City), and to the north lies Lake Pontchartrain. Built on the first high ground upriver from the Gulf of Mexico, much of the city is below sea level. Consequently cemeteries are aboveground and huge levees and pumping systems are needed to protect the city from flooding.

Tip: The Mississippi River twists so much as it goes past the city that nobody can ever determine north, south, east, or west—locals included. So don't bother asking about north and south when you're trying to find something in the French Quarter; use toward Canal Street/away from Canal Street and toward the river/away from the river.

Getting There: New Orleans can be reached by automobile, by riverboat, by train, or by plane. Drivers follow Interstate 10 and take Vieux Carré exits into the French Quarter. Overnight excursion riverboats such as the *Mississippi Queen*, the *American Queen*, and the *Delta Queen* dock at the waterfront's Robin Street Wharf. The Delta Queen Steamboat Company can be reached by phone at 1-800-543-1949 or (504) 586-0631. A new deluxe river barge/cruiser also makes excursions to and from various port cities. You can call RiverBarge Excursion Lines at (504) 365-0022 or check out its Web site at *www.riverbarge.com*. Amtrak (1-800-872-7245) serves New Orleans, going north (Chicago and New York), east (Miami), and west (Los Angeles). Trains arrive and depart from Union Terminal on Loyola Avenue between South Rampart and Girod Streets in the Central Business District. Long-distance intercity Greyhound buses also use Union Terminal. All major U.S. airlines serve New Orleans; international carriers include British Airways, Air Canada (direct service from Toronto), AeroMexico, and LACSA. New Orleans International Airport is a mere four feet above sea level in suburban Kenner, 11 miles west of downtown New Orleans.

Tip: While the natives are exceedingly friendly and will go out of their way to assist visitors, don't forget that New Orleans has been mining tourism for almost three centuries and there has always been a guy who will bet you a buck that "I can tell you where you got your shoes." So be street-smart. Hold on to your wallet, take cabs late at night, and remember, you got your shoes on Bourbon Street.

Orientation: Most major sites in New Orleans are located in or near the 90-square-block French Quarter, all within walking distance of one another. The Quarter is bordered by Faubourg Marigny, Treme (the former site of the city's fabled Storyville red-light district), the Central Business District/Riverfront area and, of course, the Mississippi River.

Tip: In the daytime, you should move slowly and leave enough energy for your New Orleans nights.

Getting Around: Operating 24 hours a day, airport shuttle vans go to individual hotels; the ride takes 30 to 45 minutes, depending on the traffic. Ticket desks and pickup are on the lower level of the airport terminal near the baggage-claim area. Frequent airport-downtown express buses, departing from the west side of the terminal's upper level, run from 5:30 a.m. to 11:30 p.m. New Orleans, especially in the French Quarter, is one of the few cities in the United States in which an automobile is a liability. If you're driving, the best thing to do is park your car at your hotel or in a lot and walk or take taxis wherever you want to go. Stick with United, Yellow, Bell, or White Fleet cabs. In the French Quarter and the Central Business District, walking is the best option, but take cabs late at night and never walk on dark streets where there are no pedestrians. City buses are somewhat undependable and streetcars don't run frequently at night. Several bus companies— Gray Line ([504] 587-0861) and New Orleans Tours ([504] 592-0560), for example—do city, swamp, and plantation touring. On your own, the St. Charles streetcar provides a wonderful uptown mansion tour. The Riverfront streetcar line skirts the Mississippi River from the lower French Quarter to the Warehouse District. One of the city's best sightseeing bargains is the $4 VisiTour Pass for a day of unlimited rides; $8 for three days. The pass is a real bargain because you'll probably want to hop on and off the streetcars several times during your visit. For experiencing the French Quarter, shoe leather is best but everybody succumbs at least once to those surreys and cabrioles lined up with their flower-festooned nags and raffish drivers. Go to the head of the line and announce your intentions. When a carriage is full, it will roll slowly through the Quarter, holding up traffic for a half hour. Your driver narrates his own special spiel, not always true, but certainly entertaining. The cost is set at $8 per person in a surrey, and $40 for one to four persons in a carriage. Paddlewheelers (try New Orleans Paddlewheelers [504] 524-0814 or New Orleans Steamboat Company [504] 586-8777) churn up and down the Mississippi, offering prime sightseeing, music, and meals. As to be expected, New Orleans is a mecca for the specialty tour. Save Our Cemeteries ([504] 525-3377) provides organized walking tours of historic city graveyards to help fund maintenance and preservation projects. And all sorts of other tours on various themes can be taken: literary (see **Literary Sites**), music (Cradle of Jazz Tours, [504] 282-3583), film (Film Site Tours, [504] 861-8158), architecture (Preservation Resource Center of New Orleans, [504] 581-7032), antiques (Let's Go Antiquing, [504] 899-3027), and voodoo (Historic New Orleans Walking Tours, [504] 947-2120).

Literary Sleeps

Hotel Maison de Ville: In room 9, adjacent to the picture-book courtyard of this 16-room historic hotel, Tennessee Williams is said to have completed *Cat on a Hot Tin Roof.* These were his favorite digs during periodic visits to the city before purchasing his own French Quarter town house. Old-fashioned rooms on the small side are beautifully furnished with period reproductions. Next door is one of the city's best (and tiniest) restaurants, the Bistro at Maison de Ville, known for its exquisite wines. Nearby, on Dauphine Street, the hotel operates seven pretty Audubon Cottages, where celebrities like to hide away. Here you'll find peace and seclusion and a swimming pool. Noted 19th-century naturalist John James Audubon once lived in cottage 1. Both places serve complimentary continental breakfast in your room. 727 Toulouse Street. Tel.: 1-800-634-1600 or (504) 561-5858. Web site: *www.maisondeville.com.* Extremely expensive.

Omni Royal Orleans Hotel: This is the site of the old St. Louis Hotel, where slaves were auctioned on the second floor and a horse might be encountered on a balcony. The present establishment, which features all the usual luxury amenities, has a great location, with terrific views from its rooftop bar and pool. The Rib Room is a favorite hangout of tycoons and state and local politicians. 621 St. Louis Street. Tel.: 1-800-843-6664 or (504) 529-5333. Expensive to extremely expensive.

Soniat House: A very special French Quarter hideaway favored by the rich and famous, including bestselling authors, this fully restored 1830s town house has more than 30 elegant rooms and suites that feature European and American antiques, oriental rugs, and deluxe baths. The Soniat's courtyard is resplendent with flowers, a fountain, and a fishpond. 1133 Chartres Street. Tel.: 1-800-544-8808 or (504) 522-0570. Expensive to extremely expensive.

Windsor Court Hotel: Besides actors, this British-style beauty hosts literary lions and the annual winners of the Pirate's Alley Faulkner Awards, tomorrow's icons of literature. Just across Canal Street and very accessible to the French Quarter, the hotel boasts the best restaurant in town, the Grill Room, and services fine enough to earn the 1998 Best Hotel in the World award from *Condé Nast Traveler.* So it's not surprising that its guests have included Princess Anne, Margaret Thatcher, Rod Stewart, Kevin Costner, Kathleen Turner, and Julia Child. 300 Gravier Street. Tel.: 1-800-262-2662 or (504) 523-6000. Expensive to extremely expensive.

Hotel Monteleone: Many writers have made this old favorite their headquarters, among them William Faulkner and Truman Capote. In fact, Capote was fond of saying he was conceived here. Recently the hotel was marked with a plaque commemorating its literary significance. Very writer-friendly, the Monteleone is often the setting for literary conferences. 214 Royal Street. Tel.: 1-800-535-9595 or (504) 523-3341. Moderate.

Le Richelieu: A great bar, a big pool, 86 spacious rooms, easy self-parking, a friendly staff, and reasonable rates make this place, located in the quiet residential end of the French Quarter, immensely popular. Writers, such as the late Lillian Hellman, loved its seclusion and neighborhood flavor; Paul McCartney once rented a suite for more than two months while cutting an album. 1234 Chartres Street. Tel.: 1-800-5359653 or (504) 529-2492. Moderate.

Literary Sites

A walking tour of the French Quarter with Dr. Kenneth Holditch is the best way to see literary sites. The fee is $20 per person, with a minimum of three persons in a group. Heritage Tours, P.O. Box 70495, New Orleans, Louisiana 70172 U.S. Tel.: (504) 949-9805. Fax: (504) 948-7821.

Antoine's: Established in 1840, this venerable eatery is New Orleans's oldest continuous restaurant. Over the years, just about everyone famous has eaten here, including the Duke and Duchess of Windsor, Cecil B. DeMille, and Mick Jagger, not to mention writers Mark Twain, Gertrude Stein, Evelyn Waugh, and William Faulkner. Try the oysters Foch, originally created here. Make sure you have plenty of cash or a good credit limit. 713 St. Louis Street. Tel.: (504) 581-4422.

Beauregard–Keyes House and Garden: Erected in 1826 for a rich auctioneer, this Greek Revival raised cottage was the home of Confederate General P. G. T. Beauregard after the Civil War. In the 1940s, novelist Frances Parkinson Keyes, author of *Dinner at Antoine's,* lived here. Open for touring. 1113 Chartres Street. Tel.: (504) 523-7257.

Brevard–Mmahat House: Merchant Albert Brevard had this handsome mansion built for himself in 1857. Now vampire-novel specialist Anne Rice calls it home. The author used the house as the setting for her bestselling *The Witching Hour.* 1239 First Street in the Garden District.

Galatoire's: Upper-crust New Orleanians have been coming to this Parisian-style bistro for years, and the restaurant has always been a favorite haunt of writers, including William Faulkner. Order the famous lamb chops béarnaise or the broiled pompano topped with lump crabmeat. Be prepared for crowds; reservations are accepted. 209 Bourbon Street. Tel.: (504) 525-2021.

George Washington Cable House: Nineteenth-century novelist George Washington Cable played host to Mark Twain here many times. The 1874 raised cottage is now a private residence. 1313 Eighth Street in the Garden District.

Lafitte's Blacksmith Shop: Legend has it that this late-18th-century cottage, now a bar, was once a front for the smuggling activities of brother pirates Jean and Pierre Lafitte. One of the earliest examples of brick-between-posts Creole houses in the city, Lafitte's has never been a blacksmith shop. As for the pirate connection, who knows? One thing is certain, though: Tennessee Williams used to be a regular. 941 Bourbon Street. Tel.: (504) 523-0066.

Napoleon House: Dating back to 1797, this world-class bar and restaurant has atmosphere with a capital *A.* Two centuries' worth of writers and other notables have sat by the open French doors and watched the passing Quarter parade. You can, too, while noshing on muffuletta, one of the eatery's specialties. 500 Chartres Street. Tel.: (504) 524-9752.

Le Petit Théâtre du Vieux Carré: The oldest continuously operating community theater in the United States got its start in 1916 elsewhere in New Orleans, then moved into this faithful 1922 reproduction of the 18th-century house that once stood here. The theater company usually offers a selection of six musicals and plays from September through June. 616 St. Peter Street. (504) 522-2081.

Icon Pastimes

You can't take a streetcar named Desire anymore, but you can hop on red streetcars up and down the Mississippi waterfront or step aboard green St. Charles Avenue cars, part of the oldest continuously operating street railway system in the world. Since 1835 the St. Charles streetcars have trundled from Canal Street in the Central Business District, through the Garden District and the Uptown/University area, to Palmer Park in Carrollton. Originally they were steam-powered; now they're electric. Mardi Gras, 46 days before Easter, is the city's most fabled occasion for drinking, eating, and listening to music, and then there's the world-famous Jazz Fest, held on the last weekend in April and the first weekend in May. But you can indulge in such pastimes year-round. New Orleans is the birthplace of jazz, and there are plenty of clubs where you'll find everything from Dixieland and ragtime to bebop and funk. And if jazz isn't your thing, try zydeco, Cajun, blues, classical, gospel, or plain old rock and roll. As for restaurants, the selection is mouth-watering. After all, famous chef Emeril Lagasse owns three establishments in the city (NOLA, Emeril's, Delmonico), and superstar Cajun Paul Prudhomme cooks up a storm at K-Paul's Louisiana Kitchen. And that's just the beginning.

Contacts

Louisiana Office of Tourism: Attention: Inquiry Department, P.O. Box 94291, LOT, Baton Rouge, Louisiana 70804-9291 U.S. Tel.: 1-800-334-8626 or (504) 342-8119.

New Orleans Metropolitan Convention and Visitors Bureau: 1520 Sugar Bowl Drive. Tel.: (504) 566-5003 or 1-800-672-6124. Fax: (504) 566-0506. Web site: *neworleanscvb.com.*

Pirate's Alley Faulkner Society: 624 Pirate's Alley, New Orleans, Louisiana 70116 U.S. Tel.: (504) 524-2940. Fax: (504) 522-9725. Web site: *www.wordsandmusic.org.*

Tennessee Williams/New Orleans Literary Festival and Writers Conference: 225 Baronne Street, 17th floor, New Orleans, Louisiana 70130 U.S. Tel.: (504) 581-1144. Fax: (504) 529-2430. Web site: *www.tennesseewilliams.net.*

In a Literary Mood

Books

Faulkner, William. *New Orleans Sketches.* New York: Random House, 1968. A series of short pieces done by Faulkner for the *Times-Picayune* when he lived in New Orleans in 1925–26.

Kennedy, Richard S., ed. *Literary New Orleans: Essays in Meditation.* Baton Rouge: Louisiana State University Press, 1992. Scholarly takes on various New Orleans authors.

_____. *Literary New Orleans in the Modern Age.* Baton Rouge: Louisiana State University Press, 1998.

Leverich, Lyle. *Tom: The Unknown Tennessee Williams.* New York: W. W. Norton, 1997. An artful and detailed account of the playwright's early life.

Long, Judy, ed. *Literary New Orleans.* Athens, GA: Hill Street Press, 1999. An anthology of writing by just about every author who has lived in or passed through New Orleans.

Spoto, Donald. *The Kindness of Strangers: The Life of Tennessee Williams.* New York: Da Capo Press, 1997. The first complete critical biography of the playwright.

Williams, Tennessee. *Memoirs.* Garden City, NY: Doubleday, 1975.

_____. *A Streetcar Named Desire.* New York: New Directions, 1989. Torrid passion and painful memories ignite sparks in the lower depths of the Vieux Carré

_____. *The Theater of Tennessee Williams 8.* New York: New Directions, 1991. Part of a series that collects Williams's complete plays, this volume includes *Cat on a Hot Tin Roof, Orpheus Descending,* and *Suddenly, Last Summer.* The latter is rooted in New Orleans, circa 1930s.

_____. *Vieux Carré.* New York: New Directions, 1979. Late in life, Williams returned to the setting of his earlier success in *A Streetcar Named Desire,* but to less effect.

Guidebooks

Bultman, Bethany Ewald. *New Orleans.* New York: Compass American Guides, 1998. Inside scoop in spicy prose with literary excerpts from famous New Orleans authors.

Larson, Susan. *The Booklover's Guide to New Orleans.* Baton Rouge: Louisiana State University Press, 1999. Writers share their favorite places with readers.

Leblanc, Guy. *Frommer's Irreverent Guide to New Orleans.* New York: Frommer, 1998. A fun, honest look at New Orleans's good and not-so-good aspects.

Saxon, Lyle, ed. *The WPA Guide to New Orleans.* New York: Pantheon, 1983. Reprint of an old and very good guidebook. It's worth reading, even if things have changed a lot in the decades since this book was first published.

Snow, Constance, and Kenneth Snow. *Access New Orleans.* 4th ed. New York: Access Press, 1999. Informative sidebars (voodoo, Mardi Gras, jazz, walking tours, cuisine, crayfish, and others), an easy-to-follow format, and incisive information about city sites and attractions are all packaged together in the inimitable Access style.

Taylor, James, and Alan Graham. *New Orleans on the Half Shell: A Native's Guide to the Crescent City.* New Orleans: Pelican Press, 1996. Sassy, offbeat coverage, with an emphasis on budget travel.

Films/Videos

Feldman, Charles K. (producer). *A Streetcar Named Desire.* Elia Kazan (director). Warner Bros., 1951. Warner Home Video. Cast: Marlon Brando, Kim Hunter, and Vivien Leigh. Many versions of this classic Williams French Quarter play have made it to celluloid and TV, but they have a tough act to follow when it comes to Brando as Stanley and Leigh as Blanche.

Rasky, Harry (producer and director). *Tennessee Williams: A Portrait in Laughter and Lamentation.* Documentary. Canada, 1986. Filmed in New Orleans and elsewhere, this is an excellent look at Williams's art and life, with great interviews with the playwright. However, it's difficult to track down unless you're lucky enough to catch it on television.

Spiegel, Sam (producer). *Suddenly, Last Summer.* Joseph L. Mankiewicz (director). Columbia Pictures/Horizon Films, 1959. Columbia Tristar Home Video. Cast: Montgomery Clift, Katharine Hepburn, and Elizabeth Taylor. Lobotomy, cannibalism, a quintessential Williams Southern dragon lady (Hepburn), and over-the-top Grand Guignol—who could ask for more? The 1992 British TV version with Maggie Smith, Rob Lowe, and Natasha Richardson also packs a punch, especially since its director didn't have to worry about censors.

Web Sites

Tennessee Williams: *www.olemiss.edu/depts/english/ms-writers/dir/williams_tennessee/index.html.* The University of Mississippi English department's compendium of information on Williams includes bibliographies, photographs, and some other good links.

Margaret Mitchell and Tom Wolfe
Scarlett and the Right Stuff in Atlanta

Kathryn Means

TWO WRITERS—one long dead, the other very much alive—have made a considerable impact on Atlanta, Georgia, with flamboyance and flair. One, Margaret Mitchell, is practically an institution in the city of her birth; the other, Tom Wolfe, is a newcomer who, with his second novel, *A Man in Full*, has made the New South's capital his own. Mitchell, in her only novel, *Gone with the Wind*, limned an indelible portrait of a South already long vanished in her own time; Wolfe, New Journalism's irreverent scourge and the popularizer of phrases like "the right stuff" and "radical chic," has recently blazed a vision of late-20th-century Atlanta that looms next to *Gone with the Wind* like the skyscrapers that crowd Mitchell's former home on Peachtree Street. But it is Mitchell who first made the city a major character in fiction.

On a lightly cluttered bedside table in a tiny, cramped apartment in Midtown Atlanta sits a framed snapshot of a little girl with a dimple in a her chin, copper curls, electric-blue eyes, and cupid-bow lips. Her name is Peggy Mitchell. As she matured, her hair darkened but her beauty and a childlike zest for life remained long after she became known around the world as Margaret Mitchell, author of *Gone with the Wind*, the bestselling novel of all time.

From her fiery imagination sprang the green-eyed, raven-haired temptress Scarlett O'Hara, the most captivating and complex heroine in modern fiction. Much of the novel was written on a secondhand Remington portable typewriter in a cramped alcove of this Peachtree Street apartment irreverently referred to by Mitchell as "the Dump." After leaving her parents' white-columned mansion, she called everywhere she lived a dump.

Mitchell's ability to propel readers into the world she wrote about was masterful. She did exhaustive research, selecting from her material the precise details that make us smell the bloom of magnolias or the stench of battle, hear the song of a mockingbird or the cry of a dying baby, feel the pain of unrequited love (Scarlett's for Ashley; Rhett's for Scarlett) and the joy of a soldier returning from battle. It took her 10 years of struggle to write her epic masterpiece of love and war, perhaps because she started with the last chapter and worked backward.

In many ways, Peggy Mitchell *was* Scarlett O'Hara. Like her fictional character, she was a Southern belle from a well-to-do family who refused to be demur and decorous except when it played to her advantage. Full of charm and vitality, she collected admirers and a racy reputation that filled up space in newspaper gossip columns and caused her grandmother to disown her. A debutante, she was blackballed by the Atlanta Junior League partly because she scandalized city society at a charity ball when she danced the wildly sensuous Apache Dance with a handsome student from the Georgia Institute of Technology.

Like Scarlett, she was willful, capricious, manipulative, flirtatious, and head-strong. If these had been Mitchell's only attributes, it's doubtful the novel she wrote would have won a Pulitzer Prize, or that the 1939 movie based on her book would have been an Oscar-winning, timeless classic. Mitchell endowed her fictional heroine with her own strength, courage, and willpower. Armed with such virtues, Scarlett was able to wrest her beloved Tara from the destruction of the Civil War, while her father and others of his class gave in to poverty and devastation. Mitchell may have inherited these personality traits from her grandmother, Annie Fitzgerald Stephens, a strong-willed, independent, and shrewd businesswoman.

The serial drama of Mitchell's private life at times matched that of her heroine. Plagued by accidents, illness, and depression, she was battered and victimized by her first husband, Berrien "Red" Upshaw, a handsome, high-testosterone alcoholic bootlegger. This led to the first divorce in the history of her Irish Catholic family. She was rescued from her tendency to be dissolute and self-destructive by John Marsh, her second husband, who adored her. He became her confidant and motivator, and also happened to be a fastidious editor. After the publication of her novel and the purchase of the movie rights by David O. Selznick, Mitchell became a very wealthy woman, philanthropist, and reluctant celebrity who craved privacy. Were she living today, TV talk shows would be vying with one another to sign her up for a tell-all appearance.

Mitchell was born on November 8, 1900, only 36 years after Atlanta was burned

The old and the new—the Crescent Avenue view of the Margaret Mitchell House on Peachtree Street, which Mitchell snidely dubbed "the Dump." Courtesy of Margaret Mitchell House and Museum

to the ground by Union General William T. Sherman's army on its infamous March to the Sea. Stories of the war, referred to by Mitchell's relatives as the War of Northern Aggression, were still very much alive in the memories of the men and women who survived it. Their personal anecdotes fascinated young Peggy, who was an attentive listener. On one occasion, according to Civil War historian and tour guide Peter Bonner, she was riding her pony through the countryside with grizzled old veterans who disagreed on a particular detail of the Battle of Jonesboro so vehemently that they dismounted and started a fistfight. While another young girl might have fled, Peggy hovered nearby and absorbed every word.

To separate fact from legend and to understand how a spoiled, undisciplined debutante could write such a sweeping, powerful novel, it is best to begin the journey in Jonesboro, 22 miles south of Atlanta in Clayton County. Mitchell's great-grandfather, Philip Fitzgerald, was an Irish immigrant who became the richest planter in the county before the Civil War, amassing a 2,300-acre cotton plantation.

The future author spent her girlhood summers at the plantation known to the family as Rural Home. It was here that she listened to her great aunts, Sis and Mamie Fitzgerald, tell stories of how the Old South struggled unsuccessfully to preserve its way of life. She heard how the churches were turned into hospitals where the women nursed the wounded and the walls ran red with the blood of Confederate soldiers.

The modern siege of Atlanta is the parade of tourists looking for Tara, Scarlett O'Hara's mansion. It is the most sought-after *nonexistent* tourist attraction in Georgia. The name was actually taken from the Hill of Tara in Ireland. Mitchell often said it was her grandparents' plantation home she imagined when writing about Tara. With her talent for embellishing the truth, she took the liberty of setting the comfortable, sprawling house back from the road on the crest of a hill, but she didn't turn it into a mansion. That was accomplished by set designers at Selznick International Pictures, who added the pretentious Greek Revival columns. The Tara depicted in the movie was an opulent facade built on a studio lot in California. The rooms were constructed separately on sound stages, as was the practice in 1930s Hollywood.

Mitchell's characters are composites of people she knew, heard of, or read about. She did, however, admit that Melanie Wilkes was inspired by Mattie Holliday, her third cousin from Jonesboro, and Prissy was based on a housekeeper at a nearby plantation. Before she became a nun, Holliday had the misfortune to fall in love with her first cousin, John Henry Holliday. According to the strict rules of the Catholic Church, they weren't permitted to marry. Mattie joined a convent where she took the name Sister Melanie, and John Henry moved west to become Doc Holliday, friend of the legendary American lawman Wyatt Earp.

Aside from the summers she spent in Jonesboro, Margaret Mitchell lived most of her life on and around Peachtree Street. She met her death in August 1949, a few months before her 49th birthday, after being struck by a speeding car driven by an off-duty taxi driver at the intersection of Peachtree and Twelfth Streets. Her grave can be visited in Oakland Cemetery, across from Atlanta's picturesquely named Cabbagetown.

When Tom Wolfe's *A Man in Full* hit the bestseller lists in November 1998, after being named a finalist for the National Book Award in fiction, a chorus of Yankee book reviewers screeched, "Atlanta has been burned again!" If so, the conflagration was immediately extinguished by a black-tie brigade of Atlanta's top-tier real-estate developers, bankers, and assorted socialites, the same people allegedly burned in his blockbuster satire. Almost to a man—and certainly to the literary ladies-who-lunch—Atlantans agreed that the author didn't hide among them as a Wolfe in sheep's clothing despite his penchant for white suits. Like a modern Honoré de Balzac, Emile Zola, or Charles Dickens, Wolfe observes, listens, and records wherever he goes. He was introduced around Atlanta and given an insider's view of the entire state of Georgia by, among others, a prominent real-estate developer and his high-profile wife.

Wolfe's main character, Charlie Croker, *the* Man in Full, is a good-ol'-boy real-estate developer with a staggering load of debt and a trophy wife half his age. Atlantans agree he is a fictional composite of several likely models, but no one has taken offense.

Like the book, Atlanta is a sprawling work of late 20th-century art. Happily for the literary traveler, the doorstopper morality tale is also a multilayered, Wolfeian travelogue of skyscrapers, sports stadiums, shopping malls, and residential neighborhoods of the boomtown-in-progress that Atlanta has been since it started sprucing up to host the 1996 Olympics.

In one long section of Wolfe's novel, the fictional, blue-blooded African-American mayor takes an upper-middle-class black lawyer on a tour of the city from ultrawealthy Buckhead to black-dominated Sweet Auburn. His purpose is to graph-ically illustrate a narrative that brings home some truths about the racial mixture of a city where blacks hold the political power and whites control the money.

Croker is a former Georgia Tech football hero with a bum knee. As his testos-terone level plunges from macho to wimp, his buildings become more phallic—tall

Heady times: the successful author of *Gone with the Wind* poses with her Remington. Mitchell eventually found her newfound fame quite daunting. Courtesy of Atlanta Historical Society

and sheathed. By the time he reaches 60, he's developed Croker Concourse, a grandiose tower hemorrhaging cash.

Croker lacks the lady-killer looks of Rhett Butler, but like the blockade runner in Margaret Mitchell's *Gone with the Wind*, this freewheeling real-estate baron has a moral compass that quivers dangerously as greed overtakes ethics. His trophy wife, Sabrena, is the Scarlett O'Hara of the 1990s—drop-dead gorgeous, sexy, manipulative. She lacks Scarlett's redeeming courage, but perhaps that's because she has to survive her husband's bankruptcy, not the Civil War.

Like false clues in a treasure hunt, Wolfe throws in a few fictional landmarks to make it tricky when you follow his trail. Don't, for example, try to find Croker Concourse, even though Wolfe locates it in the "sylvan spaciousness" of Cherokee County. Unfortunately for Croker, Cherokee County turns out to be a little too far from the center of Atlanta to attract tenants.

Croker's plantation, Turpmtine (slang for *turpentine*), is also an imaginary place, though it's based on several South Georgia plantations Wolfe visited. During the media tour to promote his book, Wolfe said these plantations, maintained at enormous expense and used only a few months of the year during quail-hunting season, were the most egregious example of conspicuous consumption he had ever seen. Remember, we're talking about a man who examined the excesses of Wall Street traders in a previous novel, *The Bonfire of the Vanities*, and doesn't live—or dress—too shabbily himself.

Until his bankers put the squeeze on Croker during a merciless "workout" session, he is the king of conspicuous consumption. He makes fun of the Old Money crowd by reminding them during quail-hunting safaris to Turpmtine that he started life as a poor boy "below the gnat line." Wolfe, who was born in Richmond, Virginia, in 1931, has a perfect grasp of the Southern idiom and puts it to good use in Croker's Southern-fried drawl.

After he's stripped of his wealth, Croker gives up riches for religion. The slave to money, power, and sex adopts the Stoicism of Epictetus, a Roman slave who lived in the second century. Ironically—and everything Wolfe writes is full of irony—Croker becomes a television evangelist and gets rich all over again.

A Man in Full has fueled interest in the ancient ethic that advocates reason over passion and has confirmed, once again, Wolfe's status as the foremost chronicler of the contemporary zeitgeist. Atlanta, as it seeks to become the New International City, is not the only place on Earth where rich and poor alike hunger for a code of conduct that will make sense of their lives at the dawn of a new millennium.

Margaret Mitchell would likely have a hard time recognizing today's ultramodern Atlanta, though her onetime home, the Dump, still stands along with other city landmarks—the State Capitol, the Candler and Flatiron Buildings, City Hall—amid the glittering "Crocker" towers of Downtown and Midtown. With a certain irony that Tom Wolfe must appreciate, technology, in a sense, killed Mitchell. Still, we shouldn't forget that *Gone with the Wind* isn't really a wistful vision of the Old South seen through rose-colored glasses; it's about how that society was swept away by war and Reconstruction. The film version might smack of nostalgia, but the novel itself doesn't take such a simplistic view. An early Mitchell booster, historian Henry Steele Commager, noted just that in a review when he wrote: "It is one of the virtues of Miss Mitchell's book that she presents the myth without being taken in by it or asking us to accept it, and that she makes clear the reasons for both its vitality and its ultimate demise."

After all, let's face it. Scarlett did have the right stuff.

The Writer's Trail

Following in the Footsteps

Destination: Fans of *Gone with the Wind* who fly into Atlanta expecting to see white-columned mansions at the end of the runway will instead find themselves in a thriving, fast-paced, sky-scraper city crisscrossed by three interstate highways. Atlanta undertook a major facelift in preparation for the 1996 Olympics and continues to be the entertainment and cultural center of the South, with more than 18 million visitors each year. Major attractions include the sports facilities—Turner Field (baseball's Braves), Georgia Dome (football's Falcons), Philips Arena (ice hockey's Thrashers and basketball's Hawks)—and other sites such as the CNN Center, the Georgia State Capitol, the World of Coca-Cola, Woodruff Arts Center, High Museum of Art, Carter Presidential Center, Martin Luther King Jr. National Historic Site and, since its official opening in 1997, the Margaret Mitchell House and Museum. However, the aura of the Old South depicted in Mitchell's epic novel has been kept alive in nearby towns such as Jonesboro and Marietta.

Location: Nicknamed the City Without Limits, Atlanta is located in northwest Georgia on the flanks of the Appalachian foothills of the United States. To the north of Georgia is Tennessee and North Carolina, while South Carolina and the Atlantic Ocean border the east, Florida the south, and Alabama the west. Interstates 20, 75/85, and 285 are major arteries into Atlanta, which is within a two-hour flight of 80 percent of the U.S. population.

Getting There: Atlanta's Hartsfield International Airport is serviced by all major domestic and international airlines, including Atlanta-based Delta Air Lines (1-800-221-1212). The airport is located 12 miles south of Downtown Atlanta. MARTA (Metropolitan Atlanta Rapid Transit Authority—[404] 848-4711) operates an integrated network of rail cars and buses from the airport. Shuttle buses, taxis, vans, and rental cars are also available. Amtrak (1688 Peachtree Street; tel.: 1-800-872-7245) operates a daily train, the *Crescent*, from and to New York City, with stops in Philadelphia, Washington, D.C., Baltimore, Charlotte, and Greenville. The *Crescent* continues on from Atlanta to New Orleans. Greyhound (232 Forsyth Street; tel.: 1-800-231-2222) connects Atlanta by bus with most major U.S. cities.

Tip: More than 50 streets in Atlanta bear the name Peachtree. Twelve of them are in blue-stocking Buckhead. So get to know your Peachtrees and arm yourself with a good city map.

Orientation: Margaret Mitchell House and Museum is located in the heart of Midtown Atlanta at 990 Peachtree Street, adjacent to the Midtown MARTA Station and just three blocks from I-75/85. Historic Jonesboro is located 22 miles south of Atlanta in Clayton County. Marietta, home to five National Register Historic Districts and over 150 antebellum and Victorian homes, is located on the northwest fringe of metropolitan Atlanta in Cobb County.

Getting Around: Renting a car is the easiest way to follow the *Gone with the Wind* trail from the Margaret Mitchell House in Midtown Atlanta to Jonesboro and Marietta. Just remember that Atlanta's large commuter population can cause major traffic jams at peak travel times. Scenic secondary routes may be preferred to major highways. Express bus service is available Monday through Saturday from MARTA ([404] 848-4711) stations in Buckhead, Midtown, and Downtown to Cobb County. To check bus schedules, call Cobb Community Transit at (770) 427-4444. To get around Atlanta, MARTA, through its network of buses and rapid-rail trains, will get you to most places, though the best way, again, is to rent a car, or take taxis if your budget allows for it.

Literary Sleeps

Ansley Inn: Located in posh Ansley Park, this hotel is within walking distance of the High Museum of Art and other sites mentioned in Tom Wolfe's *A Man in Full*. 253 Fifteenth Street. Tel.: (404) 872-9000. Expensive.

Georgian Terrace: Margaret Mitchell scandalized Atlanta society with the risqué Apache Dance she performed in this hotel's elegant ballroom during a charity gala. The Georgian is where she interviewed Rudolph Valentino for the *Atlanta Journal* and handed over the manuscript of *Gone with the Wind* to Harold Latham, a vice president of Macmillan Publishing. Clark Gable, Vivien Leigh, and other *GWTW* stars stayed here when the movie premiered at Loew's Grand Theater in December 1939. Local legend says that opera star Enrico Caruso sometimes serenaded passersby from his room's balcony. 659 Peachtree Street. Tel.: 1-800-437-4824 or (404) 897-9116. Expensive.

Inn Scarlett's Footsteps: This antebellum bed-and-breakfast boasts big-city amenities, old-fashioned comfort, and a large private collection of *Gone with the Wind* memorabilia. Bedrooms are named in memory of the novel's characters. Each room has a private bath. In Concord, midway between I-75 and I-85, just south of Atlanta. Tel.: (770) 884-9012. Web site: *www.gwtw.com*. Moderate.

Marietta Conference Center and Resort: There's no direct connection to Margaret Mitchell here, but this 200-room resort situated on 123 acres is a pleasant place to stay, exercise, play golf, and dine while following Mitchell's trail. Next door is an antebellum landmark, Brumby Hall and Gardens, a restored 1851 home that was the residence of the dean of the Georgia Military Institute. 500 Powder Springs Street, Marietta. Tel.: (770) 427-2500. Web site: *www.mariettaresort.com*. Moderate to expensive.

Tip: The Atlanta Preservation Center ([404] 876-2041) offers 10 walking tours of historic city areas for $5 each. Especially worthwhile are tours of Sweet Auburn, Martin Luther King Jr.'s old stomping grounds, and Druid Hills, the genteel neighborhood where *Driving Miss Daisy* was filmed.

Literary Sites

Atlanta-Fulton Public Library: Located across the street from Margaret Mitchell Square, the library has a permanent exhibit of Mitchell memorabilia on the first floor. The author did much of her research in the old Carnegie Library, which was razed in 1977 to make room for the present building. 1 Margaret Mitchell Square. MARTA: Peachtree Center.

Della-Manta Apartments: Margaret Mitchell spent the last 10 years of her life in apartment 3 in this 1917 American Renaissance building in Ansley Park. Unfortunately the flat is privately owned and not open to the public. The manuscript of *Gone with the Wind* was burned in the boiler room by Mitchell's secretary following the instructions of the author's husband. 1268 Piedmont Avenue.

1401 Peachtree Street: A plaque marks the site of the Mitchell family home that was destroyed at her request after her brother Stephens Mitchell, an Atlanta attorney, moved out in 1952.

Georgia-Pacific Center: A skyscraper that symbolizes the New South looms over the site of the old Loew's Grand Theater where *Gone with the Wind* premiered on December 15, 1939. The theater burned in 1979. Fire destroyed several sites associated with Margaret Mitchell. Three of her early homes burned in the great fire of 1917. The Margaret Mitchell House, though not the apartment where she lived, was torched by arsonists twice before it opened in 1997. 133 Peachtree Center.

Grady Memorial Hospital: During her debutante years, Mitchell did charity work at this hospital in the clinic for blacks and the poor. After she became wealthy from royalties and film rights, Mitchell funded emergency clinics at Grady. She nursed friends, relatives, and household help at beside and was taken to Grady Memorial the night she was struck by a speeding automobile. It was here that she died on August 16, 1949, five days after her accident. 80 Butler Street.

Margaret Mitchell House and Museum: Mitchell wrote the majority of her Pulitzer Prize–winning novel in a small apartment located in this restored turn-of-the-century, three-story Tudor Revival mansion listed on the National Register of Historic Places. The building was known as Crescent Apartments when Mitchell and her husband, John Marsh, lived here from 1925 to 1932. Group tours and special-event rentals daily by appointment only. Open every day 9:00 a.m. to 4:00 p.m. Closed Thanksgiving, Christmas Eve and Day, and New Year's Day. Adults $7, seniors/students $6, children under five free. 990 Peachtree Street. Tel.: (404) 249-7012.

Margaret Mitchell Square: Bounded by Peachtree and Forsyth Streets and Carnegie Way, this memorial to the famous author contains a fountain, an inscription, and a sculpture.

Oakland Cemetery: Mitchell is buried beside her husband, John Marsh, in this historic cemetery, located on 88 acres in Downtown Atlanta. Open daily 8:00 a.m. to 6:00 p.m. (until 7:00 p.m. during Daylight Saving Time). 248 Oakland Avenue at Memorial Drive. MARTA: King Memorial Station. Tel.: (404) 688-2107.

Seventeenth Street at West Peachtree Street: Margaret Mitchell completed *Gone with the Wind* in the Russell Apartments, which once stood on this site. Mitchell and her husband lived here from 1932 to 1939.

Ashley Oaks Mansion: This restored 1879 mansion recalls the romance of the Old South. It's open for tours, weddings, receptions, and special events. 144 College Street, Jonesboro. Tel.: (770) 478-8986.

Road to Tara Museum: Located in the restored Jonesboro Train Depot, the museum has a collection of books and film memorabilia associated with *Gone with the Wind*. There's a gift shop adjacent. Open Monday to Saturday 10:00 a.m. to 3:00 p.m. 102 North Main Street, Jonesboro. Tel.: (770) 210-1017.

Stately Oaks: Nineteenth-century costumed guides provide tours of this 1839 Greek Revival mansion that once sat on 404 acres. The home played an important role in Civil War history. Open Monday to Friday (most Saturdays) 10:30 a.m. to 3:30 p.m. Group tours available on request. Adults $5, seniors $4.50, children (three to 12) $3.00. 100 Carriage Lane at Jodeco Road, Jonesboro. Tel.: (770) 473-0197. Web site: *www.gwtw-jonesboro.org*.

Marietta Museum of History: Located on the second floor of the historic Kennesaw House on Marietta Square, the museum portrays the rich history of the area from the early days of the Cherokee to the present. Daniel O. Cox, executive director, historian, and collector, seems to have stepped out of the pages of Confederate history. Open Tuesday to Saturday 11:00 a.m. to 4:00 p.m. 1 Depot Street, Suite 200, Marietta. Tel.: (770) 528-0431.

Icon Pastimes

When you're in Margaret Mitchell country, you might want to take Gone with the Wind: The Tour, conducted by Jonesboro historian Peter Bonner, who focuses on the true tales behind the world's best-loved story of the Old South. Tours are given from the Jonesboro Train Depot daily at 1:00 p.m. or by appointment. Rates are $15 per person; group discounts are available. For more information, call (770) 477-8864. Mitchell loved to dance and party, especially during her debutante years. Unfortunately for fans attempting to duplicate her madcap adventures, most of the parties she attended were held in private homes and clubs. Few of her haunts, including her parents' spacious home on Peachtree Street, still exist. One notable exception is the exclusive Piedmont Driving Club, which Mitchell frequented all her life. The author once lived across the street from the club, and around four o'clock every afternoon made a visit to it carrying a mason jar in a paper bag. She returned with a jarful of champagne cocktails, according to some reports, and martinis, according to others. She also went to parties at the Capitol City Club, now an upscale businessmen's club. As for Tom Wolfe, the best way to link Atlanta and *A Man in Full* is to let the author's fictional mayor of the city, Wesley Dobbs Jordan, show you around town as he does with his friend and old fraternity brother Roger White II, an Atlanta attorney called in to represent a black athlete accused of raping the daughter of a prominent white man. Their driving tour begins at City Hall in Downtown Atlanta and continues on to Buckhead, where some of the city's finest mansions are located. Along the way, they pass through Sweet Auburn, once the heart of black Atlanta. Martin Luther King Jr.'s former home at 501 Auburn Avenue is found here; the King memorial, the Center for Nonviolent Social Change (449 Auburn Avenue), is in the next block. When the mayor and his friend reach Ponce de Leon Avenue, he notes that this is the dividing line between white Atlanta in the north and black Atlanta in the south. As they proceed, the land rises, reminding us that we are in the foothills of the southernmost range of the Blue Ridge Mountains. The mayor—and you—are now in Buckhead. Continuing north along Ponce de Leon, the car skirts 180-acre Piedmont Park on the right. At Fourteenth Street a white fence with stone pillars leads to the exclusive Piedmont Driving Club. When the mayor reaches the top of Piedmont Hill, he turns left onto Peachtree Street, then right onto West Paces Ferry Road, where the Tullie Smith House, a pre–Civil War working farm, and the 1928 Italianate Swan House are spotted. As the mayor crosses the intersection of West Paces Ferry and Habersham Road, the Governor's Mansion comes into view. The car then turns right onto Tuxedo Road, where some of Atlanta's most luxurious homes, with their quoins, groins, pilasters, curves, and cornices, are hidden in the trees. Inman Armholster, the novel's fictional pillar of Atlanta society whose daughter was allegedly raped by the black football star, lives in an Italian Baroque palazzo on Tuxedo Road. If you take the mayor's tour, your trip back downtown will bring you past the geometrically shaped High Museum of Art, the 11-block-long Peachtree Center (a canyon of skyscrapers), the angular limestone CNN Center, the Georgia World Congress Center, the Georgia Dome, Centennial Olympic Park, and Atlanta University Center.

Contacts

Atlanta Convention and Visitors Bureau: 233 Peachtree Street NE, Suite 100, Atlanta, Georgia 30303 U.S. Tel.: 1-800-ATLANTA or (404) 521-6600. Fax: (404) 577-3293. Web site: *www.acvb.com* or *www.ci.atlanta.ga.us* (City of Atlanta site).

Clayton County Convention and Visitors Bureau: 104 North Main Street, Jonesboro, Georgia 30236 U.S. Tel.: (770) 478-4800.

Georgia Department of Industry, Trade and Tourism: 285 Peachtree Center Avenue NE. Marcus Two Tower, Suite 1000 and 1100, Atlanta, Georgia 30303-1230 U.S. Tel.: (404) 656-3545. Fax: (404) 656-3567. Web site: *www.georgia.org.*

Marietta Welcome Center and Visitors Bureau: 4 Depot Street, Marietta, Georgia 30060 U.S. Tel.: (770) 429-1115.

In a Literary Mood

Books

Bridges, Herb, and Terryl C. Boodman. Gone with the Wind: *The Definitive Illustrated History of the Book, the Movie, and the Legend.* New York: Simon & Schuster, 1989. Lavishly illustrated, this behind-the-scenes book was produced as a tie-in to Turner Entertainment's *Gone with the Wind* 50th Anniversary Celebration.

Farr, Finis. *Margaret Mitchell of Atlanta: The Author of* Gone with the Wind. New York: Morrow, 1965. Authorized by Mitchell's only sibling, Stephens Mitchell, an Atlanta attorney, this biography tends to idealize its subject but is generally the starting point for those interested in learning more about the author's life.

Harmetz, Aljean. *On the Road to Tara: The Making of* Gone with the Wind. New York: Harry N. Abrams, 1996. Lucid and witty, this is the story of the making of the Academy Award–winning classic.

Mitchell, Margaret. *Gone with the Wind.* New York: Simon & Schuster, 1996. This 60th anniversary edition of the Pulitzer Prize–winning classic boasts an introduction by James A. Michener and a preface by Pat Conroy.

_____. *Lost Laysen.* Edited by Debra Freer. New York: Scribner, 1996. This novella was written by Mitchell when she was 16, but wasn't discovered until many years after her death.

Pyron, Darden Asbury. *Southern Daughter: The Life of Margaret Mitchell.* New York: Oxford University Press, 1991.

Walker, Marianne. *Margaret Mitchell and John Marsh: The Love Story Behind* Gone with the Wind. Atlanta: Peachtree Publishers, 1993. Carefully researched and full of previously unpublished material from letters and personal interviews, this is an account of the complex, intertwined lives of the 24-year marriage between the celebrated writer and her lesser-known husband and editor.

Wolfe, Tom. *The Bonfire of the Vanities.* New York: Farrar, Straus & Giroux, 1987. New Journalism's attack dog takes on Manhattan's stockbroker scions in one of the top-10 bestselling novels of the 1980s.

_____. *A Man in Full.* New York: Farrar, Straus & Giroux, 1998. After taking on Wall Street, Wolfe turns his sights on Atlanta's New South 1990s real-estate barons.

_____. *The Right Stuff.* New York: Farrar, Straus & Giroux, 1979. Wolfe's comprehensive, sometimes irreverent history of America's manned-space-flight program won the American Book Award for general nonfiction.

Guidebooks

Goldman, David, and Pam Perry. *Insiders' Guide to Metro Atlanta.* 2nd ed. Manteo, SC: Insiders' Publications, 1996.

Kurtz, Wilbur George. *Historic Atlanta: A Brief Story of Atlanta and Its Landmarks.* Cherokee Publishing, 1999.

Lee, Mary. *Frommer's Atlanta.* 6th ed. New York: Macmillan Travel, 1999.

Thalimer, Carol, and Dan Thalimer. *Quick Escapes Atlanta.* Old Saybrook, CT: Globe Pequot Press, 1998.

Films/Videos

Brubaker, James, Robert Chartoff, and Irwin Winkler (producers). *The Right Stuff.* Philip Kaufman (director). Warner Bros., 1983. Warner Home Video. Cast: Scott Glenn, Ed Harris, and Sam Shepard.

The heroic film version of Wolfe's saga of America's manned launch into outer space captures all of his book's impressive sweep as well as the very human side of the test pilots and astronauts who risked their lives.

De Palma, Brian, Fred C. Caruso, Monica Goldstein, Peter Guber, and John Peters (producers). *The Bonfire of the Vanities.* Brian De Palma (director). Warner Bros., 1990. Warner Home Video. Cast: Melanie Griffith, Tom Hanks, and Bruce Willis. One of the all-time bombs of movie history, which is a pity, since Wolfe wrote a damn good novel that deserved better. Still, one experiences a certain fascination in watching the disastrous flop unfold.

Selznick, David O. (producer). *Gone with the Wind.* Victor Fleming (director). MGM/Selznick International Pictures, 1939. MGM/UA Home Video. Cast: Clark Gable, Vivien Leigh, and Hattie McDaniel. What can you say about a film that received 13 Academy Award nominations and won eight Oscars? Simply one of the most popular movies of all time.

Web Sites

Gone with the Wind (Book): *www.gwtwbooks.com.* An online resource for *GWTW* book collectors.

Gone with the Wind (Movie): *www.lib.utexas.edu/Libs/HRC.* The Selznick Archives, including the Oscar the producer won for *GWTW*, are housed in the Harry Ransom Humanities Research Center at the University of Texas at Austin.

Margaret Mitchell: *www.franklymydear.com.* A virtual tour of the Margaret Mitchell House.

Tom Wolfe: *www.tomwolfe.com.* Farrar, Straus & Giroux's site for the author of *A Man in Full.*

Ayn Rand
Top of the World in New York

Eric Miller

As THE 21-YEAR-OLD Ayn Rand prepared to sail to New York City in 1926, a cousin said to her, "When they ask you in America, tell them that Russia is a huge cemetery and we are all dying slowly." New York was nothing but lights on the horizon to Rand then, but she would sit through silent films several times just to get a glimpse of it. To the aspiring writer leaving a country to which she would never return, the tower-studded silhouette of New York represented the philosophy that made the motor of the world move.

It was dark when her boat docked in New York Harbor. Catching a glimpse of the Woolworth Building, then the tallest skyscraper in the world, Rand supposedly commented, "The Finger of God," although she later denied saying it.

However, as reported by someone else in the film *Ayn Rand: A Sense of Life*, Rand says about her arrival: "It was dark then. It was kind of early evening. I think about seven o'clock or so. And seeing the first lighted skyscrapers—it was snowing very faintly, and I think I began to cry because I remember feeling the snowflakes and the tears sort of together."

It's hard to describe what a city like New York represented to someone from a country like Russia, with all of its repression and historical baggage. A city like New York, despite it's flaws, was not a phenomenon known in Rand's native land, or anywhere else in the world for that matter. New York was what life was about: a purposeful pursuit, a place where achievement abounded. "New York is activity and activity is life," says Dr. Harry Binswanger, a longtime Rand associate and editor of *The Ayn Rand Lexicon,* when I talk to him in New York by telephone. "That's what Ayn Rand would say."

New York was not only a place different in appearance, but it represented a different way of thinking as well as another philosophy. To Rand, the skyscrapers of New York weren't built out of steel, stone, bricks, and mortar; they were erected out of adherence to individualism, the only moral philosophy the planet had ever known.

The foundation stones of New York weren't like those in Russian or even European cities. The first foundation of America's premier metropolis was the philosophy of Aristotle. The skyline of New York grew out of a recognition that *A* is *A,* that the mind and the body are one entity and that each human being has a right to exist, not for God, king, or country, but for his or her own sake.

"America is the land of the uncommon man," Rand wrote in the periodical *Plain Talk* in 1947, "the land where man is free to develop his genius." New York is the capital of a place where such thought prevails, where uncommon people prosper. As a result, New York is the financial capital of the world.

"If you ask me to name the proudest distinction of Americans, I would choose the fact that they were the people who created the phrase 'to make money,'" Rand states in her novel *Atlas Shrugged*. Before that, she notes, wealth had been a static quantity to be seized, begged, inherited, shared, looted, or obtained as a favor. "Americans were the first to understand that wealth has to be created," she insists. And with wealth coming from its only moral source, production, a city like no other was created.

New York symbolized what Rand idealized in her novels—man as a creator—and the city fostered invention and ingenuity. Looking toward a corrupt world, the New York skyline stood against the Atlantic as a proud achievement boasting of what could happen when men played their proper role. New York showcased the magnificence of the Empire State Building, the George Washington Bridge, and the RCA Building, structures that surpassed anything ever built.

"I like to see man standing at the foot of a skyscraper," newspaper magnate Gail Wynand says in Rand's first major novel, *The Fountainhead*. "It makes him no bigger than an ant—isn't that the correct bromide for the occasion? The Goddamn fools! It's man who made it—the whole incredible mass of stone and steel. It doesn't dwarf him, it makes him greater than the structure. It reveals his true dimensions to the world."

Wynand then adds, "I would give the greatest sunset in the world for one sight of New York's skyline. The sky over New York and the will of man made visible. What other religion do we need? I feel that if a war came to threaten this, I would throw myself into space, over the city, and protect these buildings with my body."

Rand lived in New York for most of her life. Although she lived in Los Angeles twice, once shortly after arriving in America and once while the big-screen

Somehow the Empire State Building, long since surpassed as the world's tallest skyscraper, still epitomizes New York's thrusting, hubristic nature, not to mention Ayn Rand's vision of Manhattan as the motor of the world. Hoyen Tsang

version of *The Fountainhead* was being produced, New York was the only city that could be home for her.

There were other cities that would grow to rival New York—Chicago and Los Angeles, for example. But Chicago grew from New York capital and Los Angeles could never measure up. "Chicago was always a second city," Binswanger notes. "In New York, the whole area from Wall Street to the Cloisters is one solid man-made environment." And in Los Angeles, the people were less the doers, creators, and achievers than the schemers and others who just wanted to be famous. "In New York, people seemed happy with their work and weren't waiting for the weekend," Binswanger maintains. At one point, Binswanger moved to Los Angeles himself, and he recalls that Rand told him her opinion of him went up significantly when he moved back to New York.

Rand's time away from New York wasn't easy for her. "I miss New York in a strange way, with a homesickness I've never felt before for any place on earth," she told her editor Archibald Ogden in 1943. "I'm in love with New York, and I don't mean I love it, but I mean I am in love with it." Rand once recalled that her husband, Frank O'Connor, told her that she was in love with the New York she had built, not the real city. "That's true," she had agreed. "I feel the most unbearable, wistful, romantic tenderness for it—and everybody in it."

Dr. Leonard Peikoff, Rand's legal and intellectual heir, says in *Ayn Rand: A Sense of Life* that "New York represented, to her, the pinnacle of human achievement in physical terms. It wasn't about acquiring philosophy. It was acquiring ideas and science and then remaking the earth accordingly." Rand and the builders of New York re-created the world accordingly.

"I trust that no one will tell me that men such as I write about don't exist," Rand wrote in a letter that appeared as a note to *Atlas Shrugged*. "That this book has been written and published is my proof that they do." She might have also said that New York, too, was proof that they do.

In the 1970s, a period now known as New York's "darkest hour," Binswanger says that it appeared as if the city were going downhill. "I said to her, 'Why don't you move?'" he recalls. "She looked at me sternly and said, 'I'll go down with New York.'"

"In passing," Binswanger recalls, "Ayn referred to New York as the center of the center of the universe." If the center of the universe were to go dark, as it seemed it would in the 1970s, the world might be coming to a point in which the creative "prime movers," as she called them, might just not want to live. "Now in our age, collectivism, the rule of the second-hander and second-rater, the ancient monster, has broken loose and is running amuck," Rand states in *The Fountainhead*.

Binswanger remembers that Rand told him New York was the intellectual capital of the country because it was its publishing and financial capital, as well. "You stand in the midst of the greatest achievements of the greatest productive civilization and you wonder why it's crumbling around you, while you're damning its life-blood—money," she writes in *Atlas Shrugged*, seeming to explain what would go wrong with the financial capital of the world. "You look upon money as the savages did before you, and wonder why the jungle is creeping back to the edge of your cities."

Defending the legacy of men like railroad builder and steamship operator Cornelius Vanderbilt, whose statue stands in front of the bold and sure Grand Central Terminal on Forty-second Street, opposite fashionable Park Avenue, she might have been writing to the people of New York when she expressed, in *Atlas Shrugged*, that "Now the looters' credo has brought you to regard your proudest achievements as a hallmark of shame, your prosperity as guilt, your greatest men, the industrialists, as blackguards, and your magnificent factories as the product and property of muscular labor, the labor of whip-driven slaves, like the pyramids of Egypt."

The buildings of New York were so unlike the pyramids in Egypt or the Great Wall in China because they weren't built by forced labor; they were created through trade by great men, those who made the motor of the world move.

The buildings, the people, and the energy of New York would serve as inspiration for *The Fountainhead* and *Atlas Shrugged*, which are fictional works about the ideal man and what would happen if he went on strike. Later, in books such as *The Virtue of Selfishness*, *Capitalism: The Unknown Ideal*, and *For the New Intellectual*, Rand used nonfiction to expound her philosophy.

Many New York sites have either direct or philosophical connections to Ayn Rand. Although she set both of her major works in New York, most of the specific locations and characters were imaginary. But New York was where she imagined them, and they are likely her perfections of real-life places and people.

A statue that stands across from New York's Saint Patrick's Cathedral depicts Atlas holding the weight of the world on his shoulders. *Atlas Shrugged*'s title, of course, invokes the name of the mythological ancient Greek Titan. "If you saw Atlas, the giant who holds the world on his shoulders, if you saw that he stood, blood running down his chest, his knees buckling, his arms trembling but still trying to hold the world aloft with the last of his strength, and the greater his effort the heavier the world bore down upon his shoulders—what would you tell him to do?" Rand asks in the novel. "To shrug," she answers.

Grand Central Terminal also has some significance to Rand. *Atlas Shrugged* depicts a fictional railroad known as the Taggart Transcontinental, which is handed down in the family from its creator Nathaniel Taggart to an incompetent heir, James, and is kept going only through the capabilities and effort of James's sister, Dagny. The real-life stories of railroads and railroad families like the Vanderbilts have similar tales to tell of men who accomplished great feats that their sons couldn't live up to.

If New York is the center of the universe, where people coming from all corners of the globe meet, then the four-sided clock inside Grand Central must be the center of New York. It is this center where Rand went in the 1970s to be photographed for a *Look* magazine shoot when it seemed as if a film or miniseries of *Atlas Shrugged* would be made. Other photographs of Rand were taken in front of the New York Stock Exchange, and with her husband atop the RCA Building, looking over the city she loved.

Many of the commercial sites important to Rand are gone, including Schrafft's Restaurant, where she got the idea for the dynamiting climax in *The Fountainhead*. After a visit to the Bellemore Cafeteria, she walked up Park Avenue from Twenty-eighth Street to Thirty-sixth Street and finalized a way to prove her ethics, the root of the concept *value* in the concept *life*. "It is only the concept of 'Life' that makes the concept of 'Value' possible," she writes in *Atlas Shrugged*. "It is only to a living entity that things can be good or evil."

Her favorite restaurant was the Russian Tea Room on West Fifty-seventh Street. Another frequented eatery was La Maison Japonaise at East Thirty-ninth Street and Lexington Avenue, but it has moved just around the corner from where it was when she went there.

Rand liked the architecture of the old blue-green McGraw-Hill Building (now the home of Group Health Insurance) on West Forty-second Street between Eighth and Ninth Avenues; today the office tower is showing its age. *The Ayn Rand Letter* had its editorial headquarters at 183 Madison Avenue (near East Thirty-fourth Street), and the nearby Empire State Building was home for *The Objectivist Newsletter* for a couple of years. So Thirty-fourth Street was important to Rand. When she and her husband moved back to New York from Los Angeles in 1951, driving cross-country, they sang together, to the tune of "Tipperary": "It's a long way to Thirty-fourth Street . . ."

Rand lived in the Bromley, located at the northeast corner of Thirty-fifth Street and Lexington Avenue from 1940 to 1943, and finished writing *The Fountainhead* there. Thirty-six East Thirty-sixth Street was her address from 1951 to 1965. There she finished *Atlas Shrugged*, began *The Objectivist*, and published *The Virtue of Selfishness*. It was also in this apartment that a group of like minds (including Alan Greenspan, chairman of the Federal Reserve), known affectionately as "the collective," gathered to read the manuscript of *Atlas Shrugged*

It's hard to believe today that New Yorkers almost let Grand Central Terminal be demolished, as the old Pennsylvania Station had been. The main concourse of the grand old lady never fails to thrill. Hoyen Tsang

as the pages were written. Rand's last home, from 1965 to her death from heart failure on March 6, 1982, was at 120 East Thirty-fourth Street.

If Rand had lived to see New York today, Binswanger says she would be quite happy with it. The sun that was setting on the city in the late 1970s has risen again, and today the city is as safe, dynamic, and alive as it has ever been.

At the end of Rand's time in New York, buildings like Grand Central Terminal were threatened with demolition, but today they stand as a more permanent part of the city. In the late 1970s, Times Square was dirty, deteriorating, and unsafe. Today it has been reclaimed. "This is the best time I've ever seen in New York," Binswanger says, telling me he can see at least seven new buildings from his Manhattan window.

"In a fundamental sense, stillness is the antithesis of life," Rand writes in *Atlas Shrugged*. "Life can be kept in existence only by a constant process of self-sustaining action. The goal of that action, the ultimate value which, to be kept, must be gained through its every movement, is the organism's life."

New York has the most potential for change and innovation because it is the crossroads of the world where innumerable races and ethnicities of varying educational and philosophical backgrounds come together to, as Rand would say, move the world.

It's said that some people in New York spend most of their lives in their co-ops and apartments, rarely venturing out to see a show or shop on Fifth Avenue. It's enough to be where the heart of the world beats a few floors below. It's enough to live on an island with a harbor graced by a magnificent statue of a lady called liberty that assures them hope is great, that the game is fair, and that the little, congested, condensed bit of real estate called Manhattan is a place where men and women aren't subservient to anything but their own wills and abilities. For some it's enough to just be in the city of life.

The Writer's Trail

Following in the Footsteps

Destination: New York boasts a variety of landscapes: the concrete-and-glass canyons of Manhattan; the sylvan joys of Central Park; the broad expanse of one of the world's most magnificent harbors; the ethnic "towns" of Queens cheek by jowl with the bird sanctuaries of Jamaica Bay; the bombed-out, blasted look of parts of the Bronx; the still-genteel riverside neighborhood of Brooklyn Heights; and the woodsy suburbanism of Staten Island. However, for Ayn Rand pilgrims, as well as for most tourists, 13-mile-long Manhattan Island is the real New York, specifically its lower half.

Location: Situated on the East Coast of the United States between Philadelphia and Boston, America's premier city is squeezed between New Jersey on the west and the Atlantic Ocean on the south and east.

Getting There: All major airlines service New York City, which is also accessible by Amtrak, New Jersey Transit, the Long Island Railroad, and various bus lines. For information on buses, call Port Authority Bus Terminal at (212) 502-2500. For information on trains, call Grand Central Terminal at (212) 630-6401, or Penn Station at (212) 768-1818.

Tip: You may want to plan your trip from the airport to Manhattan in advance by calling a transportation provider—New York Airport Services (JFK, LaGuardia): (718) 706-9658; Olympia Trails (Newark): (908) 354-3330. AirLink (Newark): 1-800-772-2222 (within New Jersey), (973) 762-5100 (elsewhere).

Orientation: Although there are five boroughs that make up New York, the city's major sites, such as the Empire State Building, Grand Central Terminal, the Chrysler Building, the United Nations, the Statue of Liberty, Central Park, the Museum of Modern Art, the Metropolitan Museum of Art, the World Trade Center, Radio City Music Hall, and a host of other places too numerous to list, are located on or near Manhattan Island, with the chief exception of Ayn Rand's grave, which is in Valhalla, New York.

Tip: New York is perhaps the most diverse and dynamic city on Earth. Whoever you are, you can become a New Yorker as soon as you get off the train, plane, or bus. Don't be surprised if someone asks you for directions.

Getting Around: Driving a car in New York is frustrating and costly, so consider using the city's extensive public-transit system, which includes everything from subways and ferries to trams, trains, and buses that connect every place from New Haven, Connecticut, to Philadelphia, Pennsylvania. Ferry rides can be a cheap and lasting experience. The Staten Island run ([718] 815-2628) will give you a breathtaking ride in New York Harbor for pocket change for a return trip. You pay when you leave Manhattan. Ferries depart from South Ferry Terminal (top of Battery Park) every half hour. Other ferry companies are Express Navigation (1-800-BOAT-RIDE) for New Jersey–Manhattan ferries and New York Waterway (1-800-533-3779) for ferries and water shuttles from New Jersey and Queens (including a LaGuardia shuttle) to Manhattan. You can also get ferries to Ellis Island and the Statue of Liberty from Battery Park. For information on subways and buses, call MTA New York City Transit at (718) 330-1234. Rail information can be had from Amtrak (1-800-872-7245). For information on Roosevelt Island trams, contact Roosevelt Island Operating Corporation ([212] 832-4540).

Tip: When it comes to taxis in New York, everyone seems to have a bit of wisdom to impart. Perhaps the best advice is to surrender yourself to the experience. You can expect to meet crazy cabbies, you can bet you will go very fast (or very slow if the traffic is snarled, which it is most of the time), and you can count on getting real close and personal with a quintessential New Yorker, who may or may not speak English.

Literary Sleeps

New York City has a vast array of hotels, hostels, and bed-and-breakfasts, almost none of which are cheap. Since Ayn Rand lived in the city, there really aren't any hotels associated with her, but there are plenty of lodgings with literary connections.

Plaza Hotel: Ayn Rand never stayed here, but one of her heroes, architect Frank Lloyd Wright, loved this still-luxurious grand hotel. Marlene Dietrich lived here. F. Scott and Zelda Fitzgerald stayed here (a key scene in *The Great Gatsby* takes place in the Plaza). Cary Grant's character in the Alfred Hitchcock film *North by Northwest* dashed through. Neil Simon set a play here. Truman Capote staged his famous Black and White Ball here in 1966. Great bars, great restaurants (Trader Vic's, Edwardian Room, Palm Court), and great rooms. The last isn't surprising, since the same architect (Henry J. Hardenbergh) who did the Dakota (where John Lennon was murdered) also created this masterpiece. 768 Fifth Avenue. Tel.: (212) 759-3000. Extremely expensive.

Algonquin Hotel: As far as writers go, the only ones you'll likely encounter here will be ghosts, but you couldn't ask for better spooks. Back in the 1920s and 1930s, this is where the Round Table met. The circle of literary lights included Dorothy Parker, Robert Benchley, Alexander Woollcott, and George S. Kaufman. In later days, Sylvia Plath stayed here. Pop into the hotel, have a vodkatini in the tiny, low-lit Blue Room and make a silent toast to Parker and company, or rub elbows with the gents in the Oak Room, the hotel's legendary, clubby drinking spot. 59 West Forty-fourth Street. Tel.: (212) 840-6800. Expensive.

Chelsea Hotel: Well, it's not the bargain it was in the 1970s and early 1980s, but then how many hotels can say they were once patronized by O. Henry, Mark Twain, Thomas Wolfe, Dylan Thomas, Brendan Behan, Tennessee Williams, James T. Farrell, Mary McCarthy, Arthur Miller, Vladimir Nabokov, William Burroughs, and Clifford Irving (of Howard Hughes memoir hoax infamy), to name only a very few? And then there was Sex Pistol Sid Vicious, who murdered his girlfriend, Nancy Spungen, here 20 years ago. Some rooms still have the fabled high ceilings and spaciousness that hark back to a former era, but renovations over the years have removed much of the once-upon-a-time splendor of the place, and you might encounter a cockroach or two. Keep an eye out for ghosts, and who knows? You might spot the Jack Kerouac of the 21st century. 222 West Twenty-third Street. Tel.: (212) 243-3700. Moderate.

Washington Square Hotel: Think Henry James if you stay here. The location is terrific—right in Greenwich Village and near SoHo—but you might find the rooms a bit spartan. 103 Waverly Place. Tel.: (212) 777-9515. Moderate.

Carlton Arms: In the early 1990s, this became what the Chelsea was many years ago. The Carlton is particularly popular with artists, but you'll probably find more than a few down-at-the-heels writers here, too. Each room has been transformed into environments by different artists from around the world. The rooms are pretty basic, but you can't beat the price or the location (in Grammercy Park). 160 East Twenty-fifth Street. Tel.: (212) 679-0680. Inexpensive.

Literary Sites

Chumley's: This former speakeasy has some of the richest literary associations of any bar in

Manhattan. John Dos Passos, Ring Lardner, and John Steinbeck drank here on a regular basis. So did Edna St. Vincent Millay. 86 Bedford Street. Tel.: (212) 675-4449.

Four Seasons: Elegance and élan, with a dusting of sophistication, highlight this restaurant's two dining areas: the lavish Pool Room and the Grill Room, where moguls, megabuck novelists, and media tycoons have permanently reserved tables. If Ayn Rand had gotten out more, she would have loved this place, though the prices are drop-dead frightening. 99 East Fifty-second Street. Tel.: (212) 754-9494.

McSorley's Old Ale House: Ayn Rand probably wouldn't have been caught dead in this place, but it is one of the oldest taverns in New York City and dates back to the 1850s. (Fraunces Tavern at Pearl and Broad Streets is even older; it began life in 1763.) The 19th-century painter John Sloan painted it; Abraham Lincoln, Theodore and Franklin Roosevelt, and John F. Kennedy patronized it; and a lot of writers have dropped by to hoist a few pub-brewed creamy ales and kick the sawdust on the floor. Today New York University students hobnob with tourists, but the saloon still has ambience. 15 East Seventh Street. Tel.: (212) 473-9148.

Oyster Bar: It's doubtful Ayn Rand ever paid a visit to this venerable Big Apple establishment, but just about everybody else in New York has. Actually, they all seem to be in the place simultaneously. It's raucous, rude, cavernous, in-your-face—let's just say quintessential Manhattan. As a bonus, it's located in the nether regions of Grand Central Terminal, and Rand did have a great deal of affection for that marvelous old pile. The seafood—including chowders, lobsters, clams, and oysters—can be terrific or so-so, and the mob scene has to be seen to be believed. Grand Central Terminal, at East Forty-second Street, lower level. Tel.: (212) 490-6650.

Russian Tea Room: Ayn Rand had a soft spot for this eatery where you can actually get Russian food (albeit a bit mediocre) in a sumptuous Czarist setting. The Tea Room is still a popular meeting spot for showbiz types. 150 West Fifty-seventh Street. Tel.: (212) 974-2111

White Horse: Remember the photograph of Dylan Thomas bellied up to the bar and looking straight into the camera, his small hands wrapped around a beer stein? Well, it was taken here, a saloon he held court at in the 1950s. The bar was also once favored by Norman Mailer and his cronies. 567 Hudson Street. Tel.: (212) 243-9260.

Icon Pastimes

Ayn Rand liked to talk about ideas, to play Scrabble, and to collect stamps, but she didn't have a lot of free time. Writing was her life. According to Dr. Harry Binswanger, once, when she was on a deadline to finish *The Fountainhead*, she worked for 30 hours straight, with no sleep, interrupting her writing only to eat. Later, he says, when she was writing *Atlas Shrugged*, which took 12 years, she didn't leave her apartment for an entire month.

Contacts

New York Convention and Visitors Bureau Information Center: 810 Seventh Avenue. Tel.: (212) 484-1222. Web site: *www.nycvisit.com.*

In a Literary Mood

Books

Berliner, Michael S., ed. *Letters of Ayn Rand.* New York: Dutton, 1995.

Binswanger, Harry. *The Biological Basis of Teleological Concepts.* Los Angeles: Ayn Rand Institute Press, 1990.

Branden, Barbara. *The Passion of Ayn Rand.* Garden City, NY: Doubleday, 1986. Still the only full-length biography of Rand.

Burrows, Edwin G., and Mike Wallace. *Gotham: A History of New York City to 1898.* This first volume of the best history of New York you're ever likely to read won the Pulitzer Prize. New York: Oxford University Press, 1999.

Edmiston, Susan, and Linda D. Cirino. *Literary New York: A History and Guide.* Boston: Houghton Mifflin, 1976.

Harriman, David, ed. *Journals of Ayn Rand.* New York: Dutton, 1997.

Paxton, Michael. *Ayn Rand: A Sense of Life.* Layton, UT: Gibbs-Smith, 1998. The companion book to the Oscar-nominated documentary film of the same name.

Peikoff, Leonard. *Objectivism: The Philosophy of Ayn Rand.* New York: Dutton, 1991. A primer for Rand's Objectivism, which holds that humans are rational, self-interested, and committed to individualism.

Rand, Ayn. *Anthem.* New York: Dutton, 1995. A short novel, originally published in 1938, that depicts the dilemma of an individual faced with an oppressive, totalitarian society.

_____. *Atlas Shrugged.* New York: Signet, 1996. John Galt, another version of *The Fountainhead*'s Howard Roark, sets out to stop the "motor of the world" in his bid to supplant altruism with self-determination. Along the way, he rubs up against Dagny Taggart, the head of a transcontinental railroad hamstrung by massive bureaucratic pressures and restrictions.

_____. *Capitalism: The Unknown Ideal.* New York: New American Library, 1984.

_____. *For the New Intellectual: The Philosophy of Ayn Rand.* New York: New American Library, 1984.

_____. *The Fountainhead.* New York: Signet, 1996. Brilliant architect Howard Roark refuses to compromise his genius, a stubbornness that launches him into a violent battle with conventionality and plunges him into a tempestuous love affair with a beautiful woman who attempts to subvert his will. Rand's 1943 novel set the course for her evolving Objectivism.

_____. *The Virtue of Selfishness: A New Concept of Egoism.* New York: New American Library, 1989.

_____. *We the Living.* New York: New American Library, 1996. Rand's first novel, originally published in 1936, is a semiautobiographical portrayal of the Russian Revolution and its impact on three people—Kira, Andrei, and Leo—who insist on the right to live their lives as they see fit. Here Rand presents her initial thoughts on the struggle of the individual against the state.

Sante, Luc. *Low Life: Lures and Snares of Old New York.* New York: Vintage, 1992. A delicious jaunt through the saloons, opium dens, bohemian cafés, dives, brothels, and slums of a New York that has mostly vanished but which still lives on in all of our imaginations.

Guidebooks

Access New York City. 8th ed. New York: HarperCollins, 1998. Probably the best all-round guide there is on the Big Apple.

Fodor's 2000 New York City. New York: Fodor's Travel, 1999.

Wright, Carol Von Pressentin. *Blue Guide New York.* 2nd ed. New York: W. W. Norton, 1991. As always, Blue Guide serves up a rich cornucopia of information, history, and lore about landmarks, museums, and must-see sites.

Films/Videos

Blanke, Henry (producer). *The Fountainhead.* King Vidor (director). First National Pictures/Warner Bros., 1949. MGM/UA Video. Cast: Gary Cooper, Raymond Massey, and Patricia Neal. Ayn Rand wrote the screenplay, but the movie is portentous and plodding.

Holzer Erika, and Henry Mark Holzer (producers). *We the Living (Noi Vivi).* Goffredo Alessandrini (director). Scalera Films, 1942. Available on video. Cast: Rossano Brazzi, Fosco Giachetti, and Alida Valli. Based on Rand's first novel, this curious film was actually made during Mussolini's reign in Italy. When the censors wised up to the antiauthoritarian nature of the script, however, they quickly banned the movie.

Paxton, Michael, Jeff Britting, and Ellen Raphael (producers). *Ayn Rand: A Sense of Life.* Michael Paxton (director). Documentary. AG Media Corporation/Copasetic, 1997. Strand Releasing Home Video.

Siegel, Sol C., and Joseph Sistrom (producers). *The Night of January 16th.* William Clemens (director). Paramount, 1941. Cast: Donald Douglas, Ellen Drew, and Robert Preston. Soapy treatment of Ayn Rand's hit Broadway mystery.

Web Sites

Objectivism: *net-www.objectivism.net.*

Leonard Peikoff: *www.alshow.com.*

Ayn Rand: *www.aynrand.org*; *www.hypermall.com/cgi-bin/rand-quotes.pl.* The first site is the Ayn Rand Institute's, while the second is called the Ayn Rand Quote Generator.

Mark Twain

Connecticut Southerner in Yankee Land

Jennifer Huget

BLUE AUTUMN SKY frames the corbeled chimneys and multicolored slate roof tiles of the big brick house before me. A breeze rustles vibrant tree leaves overhanging the building's third-floor porch—the "Texas Deck." I close my eyes and think I smell cigar smoke wafting from inside. For a moment, it feels as if it's 1878, and Mark Twain is living right here in this house.

Well, it's not, and he's not, but being at Hartford, Connecticut's Mark Twain House puts me as close to the real Twain as I'm likely to get at the turn of *this century*.

The technology-smitten Victorians were big on time-travel stories. Six years before England's H. G. Wells published *The Time Machine*, America's Mark Twain had penned *A Connecticut Yankee in King Arthur's Court*, his own time-warp tome, in which the author's alter ego, Hank Morgan, gets hit on the head while working at Hartford's Colt gun factory. When he awakens, he finds himself in sixth-century England, and the ensuing clash of cultures provides fodder for some of Twain's most telling and sharp-witted insights into 19th-century American life.

It is in the spirit of Hank Morgan that I approach Twain's ornate mansion, the home he built for his family in 1874 and in which he lived for the 17 happiest and most productive years of his life. Within these painted-brick walls, Twain—or Samuel Langhorne Clemens—raised three daughters; wrote *The Adventures of Tom Sawyer*, *The Adventures of Huckleberry Finn*, *Connecticut Yankee*, and other books; made and lost fortunes; and lived the ultimate upper-class Victorian life. In making my pilgrimage to Hartford, I hope both to brush up on the facts of Twain's life and to immerse myself in the spirit of the 19th century.

I want to be transported. I want Mark Twain House to be my own personal time machine.

When Sam Clemens built his house on the western edge of what was then one of America's most prosperous cities, it was really like moving to the country. The family kept horses, cows, and other animals on the property, which included a river that ran behind the house and a meadow in which the girls played. Today the house, which now, as always, stands just yards away from Farmington Avenue, has lost all vestiges of rural life. The avenue, currently a major city thoroughfare, buzzes and blasts with traffic noise. There are no horses or cows, just lots of pigeons and squirrels. The river has long since been buried (in the late 1960s) by the Army Corps of Engineers, and where once there were meadows and other attractive houses, now there are apartment buildings and a high school. To its credit, though, the museum that occupies and operates Mark Twain House has worked to reclaim as much of the original landscape as possible, re-creating a lovely green space around the home. And I should be thankful: half a century ago the house's very existence was imperiled when developers threatened to demolish it.

Still, if much has changed here, much has also remained the same. And for an authentic Twain experience, you've simply *got* to come to Hartford, to the place where, given the option to live anywhere in the world, Huck Finn's creator chose to settle and spend his best years.

Twain and his lovely, intelligent, and wealthy wife, Olivia, commissioned architects Edward Tuckerman Potter and Alfred H. Thorpe to build a 19-room mansion in what is now called the Picturesque Gothic style. As it was built, onlookers would gather on the lawn to gawk, and a local newspaper called the structure "one of the oddest looking buildings in the State ever designed for a dwelling, if not in the whole country." Towered and turreted, festooned with porches and balconies, and decorated with rows of bricks painted black and vermilion, Twain's house is, like Twain himself, exuberant.

Since my goal is to transport myself to a different era, I start early in the morning so I won't be distracted by the din of rush-hour traffic. I stand on the front lawn, which Twain's house shares with the modest, more utilitarian home of Harriet Beecher Stowe, stationing myself near the wisteria bush that tangles the porch rail under the porte cochere, where the Clemens family's guests dismounted their carriages and entered the house's main hall. I stroll up to the ombra, the covered porch on which the family dined on summer evenings and where, after dinner, neighborhood parents played whist while their children frolicked on the lawn. I walk over to the carriage house where Twain once set up an office, hoping to boost his productivity by escaping household distractions.

The Clemens family on the porch of their Hartford house in happier times before deaths and financial setbacks soured the mood of America's greatest humorist. Courtesy of Mark Twain Memorial, Hartford

(At this writing, the carriage house is being restored, its office spaces converted back to replicas of the original horse stalls and haylofts.)

In the morning quiet, it's easy to imagine Twain choosing this pastoral spot as his home base. Upon his first visit to Hartford, he wrote: "Of all the beautiful towns it has been my fortune to see this is the chief. . . . You do not know what beauty is if you have not been here." The neighborhood he selected, called Nook Farm because it was nestled in the nook of that now-buried Park River, was home to a colony of thinkers, writers, and do-gooders, all of them wealthy enough to build fashionable homes on good-size, unspoiled lots. In addition to Stowe, who was about 63 (and *Uncle Tom's Cabin* 22) years old when the Clemens family moved in, neighbors included the Gillettes, whose son William grew up to be an actor best-known for his signature portrayal of Sherlock Holmes. Also in residence at Nook Farm was Charles Dudley Warner, editor of the *Hartford Courant*. Twain tried to buy into the *Courant* before he moved to town, but his petition was denied. (The publishers later grew eager to bring Twain onboard, but by that time his other commitments prevented his doing so.) Still, he and

Warner became fast friends and even collaborated on the novel whose title was to become the Victorian era's most enduring epithet: *The Gilded Age*. After visiting Nook Farm, the novelist, editor, and Twain cohort William Dean Howells wrote that "There was constant running in and out of friendly houses where the lively hosts and guests called one another by their Christian names or nicknames, and no such vain ceremony as knocking or ringing at doors. . . ."

Having arrived at seven, I have to wait a while to go inside the house. I might have brought a picnic breakfast to enjoy on the lawn. Instead I visit local hangout Mo's Midtown on Whitney Street for a memorable stack of pancakes and a good cup of coffee. Then I venture across to Stowe's house and take in her Victorian gardens. It would be a good idea to bring a book: I would recommend *The Adventures of Huckleberry Finn*, which Twain wrote right here (the author once wrote of Hartford: "I never saw anyplace where morality and huckleberries flourish as they do here"), or perhaps Justin Kaplan's masterful, Pulitzer Prize–winning biography *Mr. Clemens and Mark Twain*. At nine o'clock, I walk around to the rear of the building and buy my tour ticket.

The best—and the worst—thing about the museum is the guided tour. At 45 to 60 minutes for $9, it's a bargain. Groups are limited to an intimate 15 or fewer visitors. The guides are well informed, well trained, and engaging, and they are knowledgeable enough to answer almost any question thrown at them. Every guide devises his own version of the basic tour, thus avoiding the "canned" routine. Visitors see almost every room and are allowed to enter most, and the guides offer plenty of information about Twain.

The downside is that the guided tour is the *only* way folks can experience Twain's house. And some of us would really enjoy being allowed to linger in silence, evoking Twain's presence in our own ways. A tour guide's spiel, no matter how fully researched and skillfully presented, isn't fuel for the old-time machine.

But, of course, the museum can't let people wander unguarded through this precious and irreplaceable treasure. So I do the next best thing: I lag behind the group as much as my guide will allow. As we are led from room to room, I bring up the rear and find I have a few moments nearly alone here and there.

Our inevitable guide tells us that Twain's wife, whom he called "Livy," typically called him "Youth." That pet name, Twain wrote, was "gently satirical but also affectionate. I had certain mental and material peculiarities and customs proper to a much younger person than I was." As I step inside the front hall, just as the Clemenses' visitors did more than a century ago, I marvel at the startlingly beautiful stencil work designed and executed by Louis Comfort Tiffany and Associated Artists. In the front hall and up the winding walnut staircase, the walls appear to be decorated with mother-of-pearl inlay, which would have sparkled in the gas- and firelight of a century ago.

The first floor was the setting for the family's public life. There is the drawing room and dining room in which the Clemenses entertained (at least twice a week) and the cozy library with its imposing mantelpiece (which is among the many original Clemens-family artifacts that have made their way back to the house through purchase, donation, or happenstance), where Twain read aloud from his works-in-progress while Olivia listened with an ear toward editing. Extending from the library is a lush, plant-filled, circular conservatory and, beyond that, a guest room whose bathroom features the Clemenses' original copper showerhead, a novel luxury in those days. Its head measures some eight inches across.

Upstairs, on the second floor, is the room in which Twain's mother-in-law stayed during her frequent visits. Next to that is the Clemens girls' schoolroom, whose masculine features hint at the fact that the room was designed to serve as Twain's study. It turned out to be too close to the girls' nursery (on the left) and the mother-in-law's room (on the right) and was soon abandoned to its new purpose. On the other side of the staircase, in the Clemenses' master bedroom, stands the Venetian carved walnut bed that the couple purchased in Europe. When they got it home, they put their pillows at the bottom so they could enjoy looking at the carved headboard as they lay in bed. On each of the bed's four posts is a cherub, one of which the Clemenses' daughters were sometimes allowed to remove and play with as a baby doll.

In a small sitting room connecting the master bedroom to the eldest daughter's room, I take a close look at the framed photograph of a young boy that sits on a corner bookshelf. This is the first Clemens child, the couple's only son, Langdon, who died of diphtheria at 22 months. Would the world have been different if Twain's son had been allowed to live to adulthood? There's a time-travel story *I'd* like to write.

All of these artifacts give clear glimpses into Twain's life, and no other Twain-related experience can hold a candle to them as far as authenticity goes. But the transcendent moment is yet to come. The guide leads us up that last set of stairs to the third floor. At the top of the staircase is a small room once occupied by butler George Griffin, who Twain said showed up one day to wash windows and never left. He was Twain's buddy and laughed at all his jokes for 18 years.

Then, at last, we come to the billiards room. This is the spot Twain settled on as his office, and there *is* a desk (one that really belonged to the author) at the back of the room. But the icons stenciled on the ceiling and etched into two marble windows suggest the room's more common functions: instead of quill

Having your own billiards room is one of the perks of literary fame. Mark Twain found the game a great way to relax. Courtesy of Mark Twain Memorial, Hartford

pens and ink pots, these are images of pipes, steins, and billiards cues. Here Twain was free to smoke his 22 cigars each day, to have a swig of whiskey, to play a game of billiards when the mood struck (and apparently it struck often). Here he could curse without offending his wife and children. Here was where Mark Twain was most fully Mark Twain.

Happily here, too, is where the best opportunity for quiet reflection occurs. It's the end of the tour, and the guide lets us mill about one end of the room for a bit. Here's where my time machine finally gets cranking. While my tour mates are asking their last questions, I take a moment to step back and imagine Twain hunched over his desk, a cigar clamped between his teeth, scribbling the words that would become the great American novel. Here, at the top of Twain's world, I can almost smell those Old Fish cigars and whiskey, gaslight and wood smoke. I can almost hear Twain's three daughters romp in the nursery below, almost see George Griffin guffawing at his boss's jokes. And here, far from the traffic noise and the jarring sights of late-20th-century Hartford, I feel Twain walking among us, see him shaking his head, marveling at mankind's unceasing folly—and wondering where he could get himself a gadget like my tape recorder.

The Writer's Trail

Following in the Footsteps

Destination: Hartford, Connecticut, is known as the Insurance Capital of the world and, to be sure, there are lots of insurance companies. But there are also many more arts and entertainment offerings than you would expect in a small city (population 145,000), and the area is rich in historical treasures, particularly those related to the Victorian era, such as Elizabeth Park with its antique rose gardens. Still, it is customary for residents to bemoan their neither-here-nor-there position halfway between Boston and New York City. Hartford was America's most prosperous city during Mark Twain's time; today it is among the nation's poorest. But don't be daunted: many rewards await the patient and perceptive traveler.

Location: Connecticut is situated in New England and is bordered by New York on the west, Massachusetts on the north, Rhode Island on the east, and the Atlantic Ocean on the south. Hartford, the capital of Connecticut, is located just north of the state's center at the intersection of Interstates 84 and 91 on the Connecticut River. The city is about a two-and-a-half-hour drive from New York City and about two hours from Boston.

Getting There: Bradley International Airport at Windsor Locks, about 12 miles from Hartford, is served on a daily basis by more than 20 airlines, including American, Delta, TWA, and United. Metro North (New Haven Line, [212] 532-4900) carries rail passengers between New York City's Grand Central Terminal and New Haven, with connecting service from Stamford to New Canaan, South Norwalk to Danbury, and Bridgeport to Waterbury. Metro North also offers special excursion and sightseeing packages with round-trip rail service from New York City. Amtrak (1-800-872-7245) operates rail service between New York City's Penn Station and Boston, with stops along the shore. It also links, at New Haven, with service to Hartford. Regularly scheduled interstate bus services are provided for most points in Connecticut, including Hartford, by Greyhound (1-800-231-2222), Bonanza Bus Lines ([212] 564-8484), and Peter Pan Bus Lines (1-800-343-9999).

Tip: While you're in the area, take some time to explore the Connecticut River Valley. You'll find lots of pleasant little towns dating from the U.S. colonial period, plenty of antique stores, scenic drives, some decent restaurants, and more than one curious local museum.

Orientation: None of the places listed in **Literary Sites** is more than a two-hour drive from Hartford, and all are easily accessible from major highways. Redding is about an hour west of Hartford, Bridgeport about an hour south, Collinsville/Canton a half-hour northwest, and Simsbury 20 minutes northwest.

Getting Around: CT Transit ([860] 525-9181) provides bus services for Hartford and 28 surrounding towns. Still, you really should rent a car to travel around Connecticut. All the usual major agencies (Budget, Avis, Hertz, Enterprise) do business at Hartford's airport.

Literary Sleeps

Avon Old Farms Inn: Avon and its historic inn are located just "over the mountain," in local parlance. The inn is about 20 minutes from downtown Hartford. 279 Avon Mountain Road (Routes 10 and 44, I-84 Exit 39). Tel.: (860) 677-1651. Expensive

Goodwin Hotel: Connecticut's only real old-style grand hotel first opened for business in 1881, so it dates back to Mark Twain's era and he undoubtedly knew it. Today the hotel's dark red classical facade appears puny amid the nearby ultramodern Civic Center. 1 Haynes Street. Tel.: 1-800-922-5006.

Moderate to expensive.

Sheraton–Hartford Hotel: If there's no room at the Goodwin Hotel, you might consider this place. It's the largest hotel in Hartford and is connected to the Civic Center by an enclosed bridge. 315 Trumbull Street. Tel.: (860) 728-5151. Moderate.

Nutmeg Bed & Breakfast: A sort of one-stop shopping service that can match you with a bed-and-breakfast that meets your needs. Tel.: 1-800-727-7592. Rates vary.

 Tip: Plan to spend time in the Mark Twain House gift shop which, in addition to T-shirts, trinkets, reading-related paraphernalia, and Victorian gift items, carries one of the best selections anywhere of books by and about Twain.

Literary Sites

Asylum Hill Congregational Church: Mark Twain called it the "Church of the Holy Speculators," but it's the one he and his family attended. The Reverend Joseph Twichell, who presided there in Twain's time, was the author's closest friend. Services are at 5:00 p.m. Saturday and 9:30 a.m. Sunday during the summer; 5:00 p.m. Saturday and 9:00 a.m. and 10:15 a.m. Sunday during the rest of the year. The Clemens family pew is marked with a plaque. 814 Asylum Avenue, Hartford. Tel.: (860) 525-5696

Barnum Museum: Built in 1893, the museum pays tribute to Connecticut's other flamboyant Victorian, P. T. Barnum, who lived in Bridgeport. Here you'll see artifacts belonging to and otherwise related to General Tom Thumb, Jenny Lind, and other Barnum protégés, along with a miniature hand-carved five-ring circus layout as big as your living and dining rooms combined. Open Tuesday to Saturday 10:00 a.m. to 4:30 p.m., Sunday noon to 4:30 p.m. Adults $5, seniors $4, children (four to 18) $3, children under four free. 820 Main Street, Bridgeport. Tel.: (203) 331-9881.

Colt Factory Building: Recognizable from Interstates 84 and 91 for its blue onion-shaped, star-studded dome, the factory is the site of Mark Twain hero Hank Morgan's famous time-warping blow to the head in *A Connecticut Yankee at King Arthur's Court.* Now home to artists and their studios, the building also features the David Glass dessert factory, where Mr. Glass produces and sells his world-famous designer cheesecakes and other dense delights. Down the hall is the funky Blue Onion Tortilla Deli. Open Monday to Friday from 9:00 a.m. to 5:00 p.m. 140 Huyshope Avenue, Hartford. Tel.: (860) 525-0345.

Elizabeth Park Rose Gardens: The first municipal rose garden in the country features greenhouses, nature walks, perennials, and rock gardens. Peak bloom: late June. Pond House has a snack bar, lounge, and auditorium. There is another entrance located on Walbridge Road in West Hartford. Open daily from dawn to dusk; greenhouses daily (except holidays) 10:00 a.m. to 4:00 p.m. Admission free. Prospect Avenue, Hartford (I-84, Exit 44). Tel.: (860) 722-6514 or (860) 242-0017.

Gillette Castle State Park: Believe it or not, this park features a full-scale medieval castle built in 1919 by the actor William Gillette, who is best known for creating the stage role of Sherlock Holmes. Gillette, who grew up in Nook Farm, joined Mark Twain's family in amateur theatricals and games of charades and called those early experiences key to his choice of career. Due to renovations, the castle itself will be closed to the public until Memorial Day weekend of 2000. The park surrounding the castle remains open to the public. Memorial Day to Labor Day, Friday to Sunday 10:00 a.m. to 5:00 p.m. Adults $4, children (six to 11) $2, under 5 free. 67 River Road, East Haddam. Tel.: (860) 526-2336.

Harriet Beecher Stowe House: Right across the lawn from Mark Twain's house, Mrs. Stowe's soft-spoken home is an emblem of Victorian domestic life. Tours available. Open Monday to

Saturday 9:30 a.m. to 4:00 p.m.; Sunday noon to 4:00 p.m. Closed Monday Memorial Day to Columbus Day. Closed major holidays. Adults $6.50, seniors $6, children (six to 16) $2.75. 71 Forest Street, Hartford. Tel.: (860) 525-9317.

Heublein Tower/Talcott Mountain State Park: The tower atop Talcott Mountain, with its glorious view of the Farmington Valley, was the destination of Mark Twain's and the Reverend Joseph Twichell's frequent hikes. They would leave Nook Farm and walk the 7.5 miles to the mountain, talking all the way. Twain recalled in his *Autobiography* that the pair often carried along a manuscript of his bawdy story *1601* and read it aloud, laughing themselves silly. Modern travelers would do best to drive to the site and hike 1.5 miles from the parking area up to the tower and picnic area. Open April to August Thursday to Sunday 10:00 a.m. to 5:00 p.m.; September to October daily 10:00 a.m. to 5:00 p.m. Route 185, Simsbury. Tel.: (860) 242-1158.

The Jumping Frog: This bookstore, which takes its name from one of Mark Twain's most celebrated stories, specializes in secondhand and rare editions of books by and about the author. It also pays homage to Harriet Beecher Stowe, and owner Bill McBride says he sometimes, though rarely, comes across books by Hartford's other two notable writers, the poets Lydia Sigourney and Wallace Stevens. 585 Prospect Avenue, West Hartford (three traffic lights west of Mark Twain House). Tel.: (860) 523-1622.

Mark Twain House: Built in 1874, this impressive orange-and-black-brick Victorian home is where Twain gave birth to some of his most famous creations, including Tom Sawyer and Huck Finn. Last tour at 4:00 p.m. Open Memorial Day to October 15 and December Monday to Saturday 9:30 p.m. to 5:00 p.m.; Sunday noon to 5:00 p.m. Closed Tuesday January to May and October 16 to November. Open Monday holidays but closed New Year's Day, Easter, Thanksgiving, Christmas Day, and Boxing Day. Adults $9, seniors $8, children (six to 12) $5, under six free. 351 Farmington Avenue, Hartford. Tel.: (860) 493-6411.

Noah Webster House and Museum: If you like words and dictionaries, here is the American mecca. This 18th-century farmhouse was the noted lexicographer's birthplace. Today it contains Webster memorabilia and period furnishings along with temporary exhibitions. Call for opening times. Admission $5. 227 South Main Street, West Hartford. Tel.: (860) 521-5362.

Redding Library: Nearly 300 books from Mark Twain's personal library are found here, including the one (Thomas Hardy's *Jude the Obscure*) he was reputedly reading when he died. The library also has some Twain letters. Redding was the site of Twain's final home, which has since burned down. His youngest daughter, Jean, died there. Twain founded the library in 1908, two years before his own death, with books from his private collection. I-84 West to Exit 5, then Route 53 south for 10 miles to the library. Tel.: (203) 938-2545.

State Capitol: This so-ugly-it's-beautiful gold-domed Victorian building (built in 1879) still serves as the state capitol, and a recent restoration has brought its manifold virtues to light. Among the edifice's highlights is a statue of Connecticut's official state hero, Nathan Hale, created by Karl Gerhardt. Mark Twain was Gerhardt's patron, whisking the struggling sculptor from his Pratt & Whitney job and sending him to Europe to study his art. One-hour tours of this architectural marvel are free and begin in the neighboring Legislative Office Building. Call for admission and tour times. Closed state holidays. 210 Capitol Avenue, Hartford. Tel.: (860) 240-0222.

Icon Pastimes

Little remains of Mark Twain's Hartford. You can't, for instance, eat at any of the restaurants he might have frequented. But you can retrace the steps of his beloved trips to Talcott Mountain (see **Literary Sites**), and you can always curl up on his lawn with a good book. Or get yourself a cigar, sit back, and read a copy of the *Hartford Courant*. Then again, you could contact Huck Finn

Adventures (9 Gemstone Drive [860] 693-0385), one of the few area businesses to take its name from something associated with Mark Twain. It's located in nearby Collinsville and offers a variety of water adventures, including a boat ride that takes you on an underground tour of Hartford's buried Park River. Collinsville—a section of the town of Canton—is about a half hour's drive north-west of Hartford. The town has a handful of decent antiques stores, making it worth the trip. The three-hour boat ride costs $45 for adults and $35 for kids, though it's not appropriate for children younger than 10. If you decide to become a subterranean Huck Finn on a make-believe Mississippi River, make sure you book well in advance. In Hartford itself you'll find a helpful organization called the Hartford Guides (101 Pearl Street, [860] 522-0855), a roving band of uniformed goodwill ambassadors who provide services ranging from concierge-like tips about tourist attractions to emergency first aid—and everything in between.

Contacts

Connecticut Office of Tourism: Department of Economic and Community Development, 505 Hudson Street, Hartford, Connecticut 06106 U.S. Tel.: 1-800-282-6863 or (860) 270-8081. Web site: *www.tourism.state.ct.us.*

Greater Hartford Convention and Visitors Bureau: One Civic Center, Hartford, Connecticut 06103 U.S. Tel.: 1-800-446-7811 or (860) 728-6789. Web site: *www.enjoyhartford.com.*

Greater Hartford Tourism District: 234 Murphy Road, Hartford, Connecticut 06114 U.S. Tel.: 1-800-793-4480 or (860) 244-8181. Web site: *www.grhartfordcvb.com.*

In a Literary Mood

Books

Kaplan, Justin. *Mr. Clemens and Mark Twain: A Biography.* New York: Simon & Schuster, 1966. This Pulitzer Prize winner establishes the dichotomy between Sam Clemens's personal life and Mark Twain's public persona. It focuses on the author's adult years—as opposed to his childhood—and is a great companion for a trip to Hartford.

Stowe, Harriet Beecher. *Uncle Tom's Cabin.* New York: HarperCollins, 1987. Abraham Lincoln called this the book that started the Civil War. Despite its political and social agenda, it's a great story with compelling characters.

Twain, Mark. *The Adventures of Huckleberry Finn.* New York: Fawcett, 1997. Ernest Hemingway said that modern American literature began with this book. This is the edition to get, since it features an introduction by Twain biographer Justin Kaplan and reprints the illustrations from the original edition.

_____. *The Adventures of Tom Sawyer.* New York: Oxford University Press, 1992. Twain's ever-popular tale of a mischievous boy is pretty simple compared to its more complex companion, *Huckleberry Finn,* but it's one of Twain's most lighthearted books. In later years, trying to recapture some of the optimism and simplicity of an earlier day, and perhaps to recoup some of his lost fortune, Twain wrote two short sequels, *Tom Sawyer, Detective* and *Tom Sawyer Abroad.* But the magic was gone.

_____. *The Autobiography of Mark Twain.* Edited by Charles Neider. New York: HarperPerennial, 1990. While Twain's own account of his life can't be relied upon for accuracy, it is characteristically colorful and makes a great read.

_____. *A Connecticut Yankee in King Arthur's Court.* New York: Bantam, 1994. Twain's time-travel tale in which the 19th century meets the sixth with hilarious results.

_____. *Selected Shorter Writings of Mark Twain*. Edited by Walter Blair. Boston: Houghton Mifflin, 1962. This well-chosen sampling ("The Notorious Jumping Frog of Calaveras County," "The Babies," "The Facts Concerning the Recent Carnival of Crime in Connecticut," "The Private History of a Campaign That Failed," etc.) of Twain's shorter pieces includes his three scathing indictments of what he called "the damned human race." Twain wrote "The Man That Corrupted Hadleyburg," "To the Person Sitting in Darkness," and "The Mysterious Stranger" in his twilight years after deaths in his family and financial disaster. The bitter pessimism is like a slap in the face.

_____. *1601*. New York: Oxford University Press, 1996. Twain's bawdy tale, set in Elizabethan England, puts Queen Elizabeth, William Shakespeare, and others around the hearth, entertaining each other with naughty stories.

Guidebooks

Ritchie, David, and Deborah Ritchie. *Connecticut: Off the Beaten Path*. 3rd ed. Old Saybrook, CT: Globe Pequot Press, 1998.

Films/Videos

Butler, David (director). *A Connecticut Yankee in King Arthur's Court*. Fox Film Corporation, 1931. Fox Video. Cast: William Farnum, Maureen O'Sullivan, and Will Rogers. Myrna Loy plays Morgan le Fay, Rogers is Hank, the Connecticut Yankee, and Farnum is King Arthur in what is still arguably the best adaptation of Twain's novel, though the scriptwriters bent the plot to suit Rogers's comic persona. Lots of contemporary wisecracking. In 1949 Bing Crosby took on the role of the Yankee in a musical version of the book, almost making the Rogers incarnation seem like utter faithfulness to Twain's great comic novel.

Lasky, Jesse L. (producer). *The Adventures of Mark Twain*. Irving Rapper (director). Warner Bros., 1944. Warner Home Video. Cast: John Carradine, Fredric March, and Alexis Smith. March does a wonderful job of bringing Twain to life in this entertaining biopic, which takes the usual Hollywood liberties with a famous person's history. Smith plays Twain's wife, Olivia.

Mankiewicz, Joseph L. (producer). *The Adventures of Huckleberry Finn*. Richard Thorpe (director). MGM, 1939. MGM/UA Home Video. Cast: William Frawley, Rex Ingram, and Mickey Rooney. Rooney doesn't seem to be the right kid to play Huck (he'd have been better as Tom Sawyer), but this version of Twain's best novel still holds up pretty well, even though the book has been made into numerous film and television adaptations. The MGM remake in 1960 is also good. Directed by Michael Curtiz, it stars unknown Eddie Hodges as Huck and an excellent Archie Moore as Jim, with Tony Randall costarring.

Selznick, David O. (producer). *The Adventures of Tom Sawyer*. Norman Taurog (director). Selznick International Pictures, 1938. Anchor Bay Video. Cast: Walter Brennan, Tommy Kelly, and Jackie Moran. As with *Huckleberry Finn*, Hollywood has never tired of making movies about Tom, and television has carried on the tradition. However, this version is still the best. Too much slapstick perhaps, but the famous Injun Joe cave sequence has never been done better. Kelly plays Tom; Moran brings Huck to life.

Web Sites

Mark Twain: *www.hartnet.org/~twain*; *http://marktwain.miningco.com/arts/marktwain*. The first site is the Mark Twain House home page. It includes background information about Twain, his home, the museum, and upcoming events. The second site has lots of information about Twain and links to the many other Twain locations on the Net.

Elizabeth Smart
Poetry and Passion in Ottawa

Marilyn Carson

IN THE JOURNALS AND FICTION of Elizabeth Smart, we encounter the Ottawa that stands behind the Ottawa of today. For someone like myself who grew up in Canada's capital, it's comparable to being told the family secrets or overhearing a conversation in the next room. It suddenly comes together; you understand. "Oh," you say to yourself, "so that's why I never knew that."

When I read Smart, the presence of another time is as palpable as when I gaze at old family albums where snapshots are held in place with black triangles against black paper: the photos appear to blur at the edges and I can smell the crisp, cold air and feel the shiver of those who stand wrapped in black lamb fur coats with fox-fur collars. It is another time, but somehow not so far away. Smart awakens memories carefully packed in the trunks of childhood. It's the hats-and-gloves Ottawa, stockings with seams, streetcars, the Honeydew Café, trains puffing with steam and champing at the bit right across from the Chateau Laurier Hotel, where one could always stop for high tea.

Elizabeth Smart was born in Ottawa on December 27, 1913. Her father was a self-made man who became a successful patent lawyer, and her mother was an admired Ottawa hostess. They weren't among the city's most prominent families, but their house was a gathering place for the up-and-coming in all fields. One of their friends describes the Smarts as creating "an oasis in a cultural desert." Familiar faces on these occasions were the Pearsons (Lester was later to be prime minister of Canada in the 1960s); Frank Scott, the poet, and his wife; Graham Spry, who helped found the Canadian Broadcasting Corporation; and many other civil servants, diplomats, artists, and writers. Smart attended Elmwood School where many of the privileged sent their children. She recalled it as a pretentious, snobbish place where she was taught "the honouh of the mothah countrih." The experience left her with the desire to sever Canada from the British Empire.

One can't help but reflect that these feelings were inextricably bound up with the difficult and intense relationship she had with her own mother. All her life she struggled to understand the mother/child bond, and even late in her life she was heard crying out in her sleep for her mother.

Throughout Smart's childhood, her family moved from one well-kept, genteel neighborhood to another. From the time of her parents' marriage until her father, Russell Smart, died, they lived at nine different addresses, finally settling in Rockcliffe Village, Ottawa's most prestigious area. Smart was presented at Rideau Hall; danced at the Chateau Laurier; skied at Camp Fortune in Quebec's Gatineau Hills; and generally enjoyed the elegant social life available in the Ottawa region at that time.

Even though it is much larger and far more sophisticated, today's Ottawa is not so different on the surface from the city Smart grew up in. Rockcliffe is more magnificent and exclusive than ever. The British influence lingers in the Parliament Buildings, while the Changing of the Guard offers tourists a theatrical theme-park vision of the traditional links with the "mothah countrih." One can motor along elegant Sussex Drive and drop in at the governor general's residence, visit the garden there (Smart loved gardens), or wander through Byward Market which, despite determined efforts to ruin it, retains a great deal of its flowers-and-vegetables charm.

Of course, Ottawa has developed since Smart's day. The city has some splendid new facilities: architectural gems such as the National Arts Centre and the National Gallery, and across the Ottawa River in Hull, Quebec, the Museum of Civilization. Smart would have liked the fact that Ottawa's city art gallery is housed in a defunct jail, and she would have applauded the capital's wonderful variety of festivals, such as the Spring Tulip Festival in May and the Winterlude Festival in February, which features many events on the Rideau Canal, reputed to be the longest skating rink in the world. In July Ottawa has notable festivals of chamber music and jazz, and the city also boasts two excellent symphony orchestras, a reasonably proficient opera company, and many venues for rock, blues, and light entertainment. Its array of restaurants would have astounded Smart, and the city has added, on its outskirts, two major sports palaces, one for its National Hockey League team (the Senators) and the other for its Triple A baseball club (the Lynx). There is even a large gambling casino in Hull.

Smart would have cheered the passion in Ottawa for gardening, and would surely have noted that, even in the middle of the city's Siberian winter, when the Rideau Canal is crowded with skaters and ablaze with lights, it resembles a scene out of a Hans Christian Andersen fairy tale.

Winter is an inescapable fact in what may be the coldest and snowiest capital in the world. Here, along the Rideau Canal Driveway circa early 20th century, one finds a typical street scene that wouldn't look out of place in the early 21st century. City of Ottawa Archives

Ottawa remains a very easy city to escape from. A few minutes' drive in any direction and one is in the countryside. The National Capital Commission, the official body responsible for monitoring change in the cityscape, has left the Ottawa River undeveloped and has maintained the cottage minimalism of former Prime Minister William Lyon Mackenzie King's summer estate on Kingsmere Lake in Quebec.

A short drive north of Ottawa, Kingsmere Lake is high in the beautifully wooded Gatineau Hills. The longtime prime minister rescued large blocks of stone from demolished Ottawa mansions to create a classic 18th-century Gothic "ruin." Here he used to hold conversations with the spirits, including that of his mother, whom he obsessively loved. King held office between 1921 and 1948 (although not continuously) and was therefore a fixed background to Smart's world. His Herridge Cottage, which sits beside the ruins, still exists and is a must visit for anyone who wishes to get a sense of the atmosphere of the time. The whole estate has a haunting, wistful air, as though it once offered a passage to another time and place; it is like a porthole to eternity whose key has somehow been lost.

In 1920 the Smart family bought a cottage at Kingsmere Lake right next to Herridge Cottage. The Smarts named theirs The Barge because its shape suggested the hull of a ship. Smart attributes her spiritual salvation to the Kingsmere experience and to the contact with the natural world that it brought. It was here that a tempestuous, ill-behaved child became a young woman deeply and passionately in touch with nature. Like the poet William Wordsworth, Smart had a mystical relationship with the hills, woods, flowers, and trees, and these provided a lifelong inspiration for her writing. She noted once that "the woods where I wandered ecstatically, on the eastern fringe of the Laurentian mountains, made of hard huge beautiful very very old rocks of the pre-Cambrian shield, offered the true the blushful happiness."

Such images of joy in nature abound in Smart's writing. What is most compelling are those passages where she catches the dark, secretive moments, times when a presence is felt and something Pan-like is revealed. Smart first articulated her vision of nature when she was 14 in a story entitled "The Birth of a Genius." In this little piece, she creates the feeling of a cool, damp, dark place where a child is sitting on a mushroom stump. The boy is being told a secret, and Smart ends her story with: "When a genius is born he is just like any other baby. But his real birth is when he is lifted up through the musical air of the Mushroom Forest." One apprehends here her sense of a sacred place where body and spirit are unified.

Smart wrote *By Grand Central Station I Sat Down and Wept*, one of the great prose poems of English literature. In her introduction to Smart's greatest work, the novelist Brigid Brophy writes: "I doubt if there are more than half a dozen masterpieces of poetic prose in the world. One of them, I am convinced, is Elizabeth Smart's . . ."

An exquisite dissection of the female heart, *By Grand Central Station*, with Maria Callas–like beauty, renders the anguish of love through the voice of an angel. The book is as much about poetry, the power of language, as it is about love. In fact, the two are so fused that it is impossible to separate them. Smart has taken the great tradition of Western literature, the canon some have characterized as bearing the voices of dead white males, and transmuted this hierarchical tradition into her own lyrical Song of Songs. There isn't a page in her novel that doesn't reverberate with the cadence and rhythms of the great writers of the past. It is almost a shock to encounter so freshly the biblical Psalms, the Greek myths, the works of William Shakespeare, the poetry of T. S. Eliot, and so much else, so magically blended and androgynously transformed.

Despite its brilliance, *By Grand Central Station* didn't have a propitious beginning. Originally published in 1945, it wasn't an overwhelming critical success. The anonymous reviewer in the *Times Literary Supplement* wrote that "Miss Smart has considerable skill in expression and a gift for poetical phrase which is occasionally arresting; but her heroine's self-absorption is so intense that it produces a revulsion of feeling in the reader and leaves the impression that the author has wasted a great deal of poignancy on a trivial and undeserving subject." Still, the *Sunday Times* praised the book, and Cyril Connolly, with some reservations, gave her a favorable review in his influential magazine *Horizon*.

The really devastating response to the book, however, came from Smart's mother, Louie. She burned her personal copy of her daughter's masterpiece and dropped in at an Ottawa department store to buy the six copies they stocked, which she also burned. Not content with these incinerations, she called in favors from her political friends, probably including Mackenzie King, and had the book banned in Canada.

One can surely forgive Louie Smart for not recognizing the literary merits of her daughter's work, but it is hard to believe that she remained so callously indifferent to the pain and suffering so vividly expressed there. Mrs. Smart complained to Jane, Elizabeth's sister, about the "erotomania" of the book, but her vituperation had more to do with the fact that she felt personally insulted by her daughter's meager references to her in the text. And with the excessive response of the unbridled narcissist, she read the few lines referring to her as a searing indictment of her mothering. Louie's reaction couldn't have been more hostile if her daughter had written *Mommie Dearest*.

By Grand Central Station tells the story of a young woman's love affair with a married man, who subsequently returns to his wife. The young woman is pregnant with the man's child, and the novel ends with the woman waiting for her lover at New York City's Grand Central Station. The novel, in fact, is based on true events (Smart's enduring affair with the poet George Barker) and was written from the author's journal notes from that period in her life.

On the surface, the book's structure is simple. It is divided into 10 chapters and the story unfolds as the protagonist travels from California through the Midwest to New York, with a major stop, Ottawa, in between. The outer journey on the road is the narrative thread that advances the inner journey. Tension is kept high, and there is an intensity of longing that rivals the mystic's yearning for Christ. As Shakespeare has it, journeys are meant to end in lovers' meetings, and here one can't help feeling that, from the feminine perspective at least, Smart has redefined the nature of tragedy and comedy. Tragedy occurs when journeys don't end in lovers' meetings!

Although it only appears briefly in two sections halfway through the book, Ottawa is a powerful presence in the text, both as a symbol of hope and promise and as a place of despair. Smart writes: "Asking no one's forgiveness for sins I refuse to recognize, why do I cry then to be returning homeward through a land I love as a lover?" In the two Ottawa sections, we encounter Smart as daughter of Ottawa and as daughter of her parents. In her powerful evocation of the natural beauty that surrounds her city of birth, we glimpse the elemental forces that awakened her poetic vision as a child:

> But the old gold of the October trees, the stunted cedars, the horizons, the chilly gullies with their red willow whips, intoxicate me and confirm belief in what I have done, claiming me like an indisputable mother saying Whether or No, Whether or No, my darling. The great rocks rise up to insist on belief, since they remain though Babylon is fallen, being moulded, but never conquered, by time pouring from eternity.

An enduring image of the city for any visitor fortunate enough to arrive in Ottawa in October is the great, colorful tapestry of the Gatineau Hills rising behind the city. The oranges, reds, and yellows of the autumn trees almost appear to be on fire, and at twilight the city is warmed with a blazing, burnished glow. Smart grew up passionately loving these hills, for here was the birthplace of her artistic soul, the place where she first felt deeply connected with nature.

Today the paintings of the great Canadian landscape artists—the Group of Seven, Emily Carr, and others—are almost a commonplace image of the North. We take them for granted, so intrinsically have they become a part of our defining heritage, so completely have they formed our seeing. The visitor who is unfamiliar with these paintings should certainly go to Ottawa's National Gallery of Canada and spend some time with them. To some people who know these icons of massive mountains, windswept pines, wild coasts, primeval forests, and perpetual muskeg all too well, they have become visual clichés, but nevertheless they did represent a new way of seeing the Canadian landscape.

It is hard to believe that at one time such works were castigated as nonart because they didn't follow the standards laid out by the British or Canadian academies. The Group of Seven painters were responding to the sublimity and mystery of the Canadian wilderness, and a similar epiphany took hold of Smart. But another connection between Smart and Canadian visual art is worth mentioning. Stored in the National Gallery's drawing collection and not often seen is the work of Henry Jackson, brother of A.Y. Jackson, one of the most prominent of the Group of Seven painters. For nearly 30 years, beginning in 1930, Henry Jackson painted mushrooms, always with meticulous execution. Like Smart, he may have been drawn to their chthonic "otherness." Smart writes: "A mushroom seems more mysterious than Cézanne's apples. Because their bodies are underground (female sexuality hidden)."

Sexuality was never a thing apart for Smart. She recognized the same passion for connectedness in the work of D. H. Lawrence. When Smart was a young woman, her parents arranged for her to be a traveling companion to a Mrs. Watts, who had organized the Country Women's Institutes in England and who was taking her message of female solidarity around the British Commonwealth. Accommodating herself to this righteous, self-important, opinionated woman could not have been easy for Smart. She records a very amusing conversation in her diary in which the woman chastises her when she appears at lunch carrying Lawrence's novel *Lady Chatterley's Lover.* "I think it's perfectly disgusting to want to read a book my country won't allow!" declared the righteous Mrs. Watts. Smart, as a paid companion, couldn't reply, but her own intuitive sense of profound artistic expression comes through in her diary notes: "How people can contaminate things! She almost made it unclean for me. But no. There it was and I was swept on its great tide."

While this fragment of conversation highlights the primness of life among the middle-class genteel set in Smart's era and exemplifies their fear of both art and nature, Smart's response serves to remind us what a courageous act it was for her to return home pregnant with a married man's child. In *By Grand Central Station,* the Ottawa arrival is poignantly prepared for as the heroine reflects on the deeper, more gracious values of the familiar Canadian world she is approaching, contrasting it to the America she has just left:

> Coming from California, which is oblivious of regret, approaching November
> whips me with the passion of the dying year. And after the greed already harden-
> ing part of the American face into stone. . . . And over the fading wooden houses
> I sense the reminiscences of the [Canadian] pioneers' passion, and the determi-
> nation of early statesmen who were mild but individual, and able to allude to
> Shakespeare while discussing politics under the elms. No great neon face has
> been superimposed over their minor but memorable history. Nor has the blood
> of the early settlers, spilt in feud and heroism, yet been bottled by a Coca-Cola
> firm and sold as ten-cent tradition.

Smart echoes, I think, a sentiment cherished by many Canadians. Elizabeth, the narrator, however, is judged by her city and found wanting—by her parents, above all: "'Love? Stuff and nonsense!' my mother would say. 'It's loyalty and decency and common standards of behaviour that count . . .'" As for her father, Smart writes in the novel: "But from my father I had hoped for more." Then she has him ask her, "Aren't you just a little obsessed about this thing?"

It's here in the center of *By Grand Central Station* that Smart most clearly articulates her vision of love in all its nuances. Due to the hovering, ominous presence of war, a sense of apocalypse pervades these pages, and as a drum roll of voices shout the commonsense shibboleths of the time, one quiet voice affirms the eternal truth that "Love is as strong as death."

Throughout her life, Smart never wavered from what she perceived to be the deep truths of human existence. "How I have come to hate the words *good taste* and *fastidiousness*," she wrote in her diary. This sense of alienation from the prevailing canons of good taste and decorum would haunt the author all her life. Both as a young woman seeking to express her own truths in her novel, and as an old woman returning to Canada at the end of her life, Smart was the odd woman out. While in Canada in 1983, she wrote to George Barker, the English poet who is the original of the betraying lover in *By Grand Central Station*:

> Remember:
> Seventy is sweeter
> than seven and twenty
> when we met and & didn't miss.
> So I send you a kiss
> for Feb 26th
> from far far far away
> where—topsy-turvy
> incomprehensible place,
> drinking & thinking
> are mad words
> not to be done in public.

Smart's eternal verities were love, art, and nature. Vulnerable and resilient, she lived her life experiencing great joy and sorrow, and fully expressing her own nature. She had four children with the man she loved but could never marry; she struggled to write while raising her children on her own; she lived generously, sharing what she had with others; and she continued to garden and write passionately until she died, in England, on March 4, 1983.

At the memorial service, Smart's son, Sebastian, read the poem that his mother, age 12, had copied from the works of 17th-century English poet Henry Vaughan into the first page of her journal and which she later pinned on the wall of her treasured cabin, The Pulley, the writing retreat she built in the Gatineau Hills when she was a young girl:

> Then bless thy secret growth, nor catch
> At noise, but thrive unseen and dumb;

A good deal of Ottawa's social life swirled between the Chateau Laurier Hotel, on the left, circa 1930, and the railroad station (now a conference center). Elizabeth Smart knew both of these city landmarks well. City of Ottawa Archives

> Keep clean, bear fruit, earn life and watch,
> Till the white winged reapers come.

Will the visitor to Ottawa find passion in Elizabeth Smart's city? Perhaps, perhaps not. The capital's Chamber of Commerce recommends Ottawa as the perfect place for a family vacation. Indeed it is—and there's nothing wrong with that. Ottawa remains clean, safe, and well laid out. It is full of diverse treasures and gives manifold opportunities for excursions to delightful places by land or water. In Ottawa there are no shadows, no bohemian side streets. Here, everything seems to declare itself publicly, if no longer so unambiguously, for the "mothah countrih."

Nevertheless, it was in a very similar Ottawa that Smart learned to approach life as a pilgrim and not as a tourist. She believed that life at its best embraced, as she put it, both the "gutter and the Ritz." And her work is a passionate reminder that life is most fully lived when one chooses to follow, at any cost, the truth of the heart.

The Writer's Trail

Following in the Footsteps

Destination: The Ottawa urban region has a population of more than a million, yet it is nonindustrial and the surrounding green space is easily accessed. Back in the mid-19th century, the city, then little more than a frontier logging town, was known as Westminster in the Wilderness. A great deal has changed since then, but winters are still harsh and bitterly cold. Summers, however, are hot and generally sunny. While Ottawans are not likely to throw their arms around you in welcome, they are polite and helpful to tourists. Both French and English are widely spoken.

Location: The capital of Canada is located in northeastern Ontario at the junction of the Ottawa and Rideau Rivers. The Ottawa River serves as the border between Quebec and Ontario.

Getting There: Air Canada ([613] 736-6689 or 1-800-361-5373), American Airlines (1-800-433-7300), Northwest Airlines (1-800-225-2525), and USAir (1-800-432-9768), as well as a number of regional airlines, fly in and out of Ottawa's Macdonald-Cartier International Airport, which is 11 miles from downtown. Access is especially easy by air from Toronto, but there are also direct flights from Chicago and New York City. VIA Rail ([613] 244-8289 or 1-800-361-5390) links Ottawa with major centers across Canada (with connections to Amtrak in Niagara Falls, New York). The city's train station is located at 200 Tremblay Road in the southeastern end of town, about three miles from Parliament Hill. Voyageur Colonial Bus Lines ([613] 238-5900) and other bus companies have frequent service to Montreal and Toronto, with connections from there to numerous destinations in Canada and the United States. The bus station is at 265 Catherine Street.

 Tip: Just across from the Parliament Buildings at 90 Wellington Street, you'll find Capital Infocentre ([613] 239-5000), which can provide you with everything you'll want to know about the Ottawa region, an area bristling with museums, including the National Gallery of Canada, the Canadian Museum of Civilization, the Canadian Museum of Nature, and the Canadian Museum of Contemporary Photography.

Orientation: The Rideau Canal divides Ottawa into Upper and Lower Town. The Gothic-inspired Parliament Buildings are the high point in Upper Town; Sussex Drive, where the National Gallery of Canada and the prime minister's residence are found, is in Lower Town. The road follows the curving west bank of the Ottawa River all the way out to Rockcliffe Village. Hull, across the Ottawa River in Quebec, is joined to Ottawa by five bridges. Just north of Hull is Gatineau National Park, where Kingsmere Lake, a 30-minute drive from downtown Ottawa, is found.

Getting Around: There are two major public-transport systems in the National Capital Region—OC Transpo ([613] 741-4390), serving Ottawa-Carleton, and Société de transport de l'Outaouais ([819] 770-3242), which provides service on the Quebec side of the Ottawa River. However, if you aren't driving your own car, you'll enjoy your visit to Ottawa a great deal more if you rent a vehicle or book a tour. Parties of one to seven can book a personally tailored trip with an Elizabeth Smart—or any other—theme with Pegasus Excursion ([613] 731-1030). For scenic cruises, an excellent way of seeing Ottawa and environs, try Paul's Boat Tours ([613] 225-6781). Booths are located near the Chateau Laurier Hotel.

Literary Sleeps

Chateau Laurier Hotel: This 425-room railroad hotel is one of the most famous inns in Canada.

In Elizabeth Smart's day, the main train station (the building, now the Government Conference Centre, still stands) was opposite the front door. If a room here is too rich for your bank account, drop in and have tea or a cocktail at Zoe's Lounge. Smart often visited the hotel, which has been a social focal point since it was erected in 1912. 1 Rideau Street. Tel.: (613) 241-1414 or 1-800-441-1414. Moderate to extremely expensive.

Auberge McGee's Inn: This comfortable Victorian home was once owned by John J. McGee, half brother of Thomas D'Arcy McGee, a famous Canadian orator, writer, and politician who was assassinated in Ottawa in 1867. The inn is situated in Sandy Hill, a residential area not far from downtown, on a street lined with similar 19th-century homes. 185 Daly Avenue. Tel.: (613) 237-6089. Moderate to expensive.

Albert House Inn: This lovely Victorian guesthouse is within walking distance of all downtown attractions. Elizabeth Smart may well have visited here when the house belonged to one of Ottawa's first chief architects. 478 Albert Street. Tel.: (613) 236-4479 or 1-800-267-1982. Inexpensive to moderate.

Lord Elgin Hotel: Built in 1941 and renovated in 1991, the Lord Elgin, which has the look of a grand hotel, is a cheaper alternative to the Chateau Laurier. Located diagonally across Confederation Square from the Chateau, it, too, is conveniently situated near the Parliament Buildings, the National Arts Centre, and Byward Market. For decades, the hotel's Connaught Restaurant was a familiar meeting place for Ottawans. 100 Elgin Street. Tel.: (613) 235-3333 or 1-800-267-4298. Inexpensive to moderate.

Literary Sites

National Archives of Canada: Videos, films, television programs, photo exhibits, letters, and maps documenting Canada's literary and cultural history are found here. So, too, are Elizabeth Smart's papers, although you'll need special permission to inspect original documents. Tours are available. 395 Wellington Street. Tel.: (613) 995-5138.

Parliament Buildings: Rising grandly from the limestone bluff known as Parliament Hill on the Ottawa River, these three venerable Gothic-style edifices opened for the nation's business in 1867. The present structures, except for the Library of Parliament, had to be rebuilt after a devastating fire in 1916. The buildings have been undergoing restoration for the past few years. The Centre Block, where all the action is, contains Canada's Senate and House of Commons. Thrusting sublimely skyward in the middle of the Centre Block is the Peace Tower, which features a war memorial and a 53-bell carillon. Outside the Centre Block, on the lawn, the Changing of the Guard takes place daily from late June to late August, weather permitting. North of the Centre Block, but attached to it, is the Library of Parliament. The other two buildings in front and on other side of the Centre Block are the East and West Blocks. The latter isn't open to the public; the former has four historic rooms associated with 19th-century governors general; Canada's first prime minister, Sir John A. Macdonald; and Sir Georges Etienne Cartier, one of the Fathers of Confederation. The Privy Council Chamber is also here. For all Ottawans, past and present, the Parliament Buildings are such familiar sights that they have practically become part of the geology in the same way the Ottawa and Rideau Rivers and the Gatineau Hills have. Don't miss the half-hour Sound and Light Show, which focuses on Canada's history. Parliament Hill. Tel.: (613) 992-4793 or (613) 996-0896.

Tip: Try to avoid tours of the Parliament Buildings immediately after the Changing of the Guard, the busiest time.

Rideau Hall: As the official residence of Canada's governor general (the sovereign of England's representative and Canada's titular head of state) since 1865, this grand pile has been an integral part of the Ottawa social scene for more than a century. Built in 1830, the mansion has a ballroom, a skating rink, and a cricket pitch. 1 Sussex Drive. Tel.: (613) 998-7113.

William Lyon Mackenzie King Estate: There are fine views of the Ottawa Valley from various points along the way to former Prime Minister William Lyon Mackenzie King's estate on Kingsmere Lake in Quebec's Gatineau Hills. To get there, take the Chaudière Bridge across the Ottawa River to Hull, exiting west onto Boulevard Taché. Then follow the boulevard along the river until you see signs for the Gatineau Promenade, which will take you northward through Gatineau National Park to Kingsmere. A walk on the 568-acre grounds will be a treat for nature lovers. You may even meet a ghost or two amid the ruins at twilight! King's estate actually contains a number of residences that he used at different times. By the lake, there's a small cottage that was expanded over the years. Moorside, a much larger summerhouse, with formal gardens and a grand entrance, was used for entertaining when King was prime minister. From Moorside, trails lead off to the Gothic folly created by Canada's onetime leader. In Moorside you'll find a museum (free admission) and a tearoom; the former is open from Victoria Day in May until Canadian Thanksgiving Day in October. A third house, the Farm, was King's winter residence. Today it's the official home of Canada's Speaker of the House of Commons. It's not open to the public. There are no convenient motels in Gatineau Park. An additional destination might include Chelsea, Quebec, a chic hamlet Elizabeth Smart often visited, only minutes away from Kingsmere. For further information about Kingsmere or park activities, call the Gatineau Park Visitor Centre ([819] 827-2020) in Chelsea.

Icon Pastimes

Drive, hike, or canoe in Gatineau National Park in Quebec, as Elizabeth Smart often did (or cross-country ski in the winter). The park features low-rise hills and numerous small lakes. Visit some of Ottawa's wonderful gardens. Rideau Hall, the residence of the governor general, has 88 acres of lawns, gardens, and woods right on the edge of Rockcliffe Village, where the Smart family lived. In west Ottawa, the historic walled garden at Maple Lawn (529 Richmond Road) is open year-round. The city's Experimental Farm ([613] 991-3044) also has a splendid set of gardens. To get there, drive south on Queen Elizabeth Drive from Laurier Avenue and Elgin Street and look for the traffic circle, around which the various parts of the Experimental Farm cluster. Make sure you also visit the Rockcliffe Rockeries, near Acacia Avenue, where the Smart family lived for a while. Take Sussex Drive from downtown; at the governor general's residence the street becomes Rockcliffe Drive. The views along the Ottawa River are marvelous. Watch for signs where the road divides, indicating the Rockeries.

 ## Contacts

Ottawa Tourism and Convention Authority: 130 Albert Street, Suite 1800, Ottawa, Ontario K1P 5G4 Canada. Tel.: (613) 237-6822. Web sites: *www.tourottawa.org* or *www.ottawa.touch.com.*

In a Literary Mood

Books

Gwyn, Sandra. *The Private Capital: Ambition and Love in the Age of Macdonald and Laurier.* Toronto: McClelland & Stewart, 1984. Although this book actually deals with the world Elizabeth Smart's parents knew, it still gives a pretty good picture of the social world the author grew up in.

Smart, Elizabeth. *The Assumption of the Rogues and Rascals.* London: Paladin, 1991. Smart's second short novel, originally published in 1978, is hard to find but worth the effort if you're interested in the author, although it doesn't really measure up to the brilliant *By Grand Central Station.*

_____. *By Grand Central Station I Sat Down and Wept.* London: Flamingo, 1992. Smart only wrote two novels, and this one, her major literary achievement, is more of a prose poem, but it's one of the literary touchstones of the century. Few writers have written so poignantly about love found and lost.

_____. *In the Meantime.* Ottawa: Deneau, 1984. A useful collection of Smart's poetry and prose. Also see the author's two volumes of poetry, *A Bonus* (1977) and *Eleven Poems* (1982).

_____. *Necessary Secrets: The Journals of Elizabeth Smart.* Edited and introduced by Alice Van Wart. Toronto: Deneau, 1986. This first volume of Smart's diaries provides fascinating glimpses into her mind.

_____. *On the Side of the Angels: The Second Volume of the Journals of Elizabeth Smart.* Edited and introduced by Alice Van Wart. London: HarperCollins, 1994.

Sullivan, Rosemary. *By Heart: Elizabeth Smart, a Life.* Toronto: Viking, 1991. Objective yet sensitive, Sullivan's fine biography, like the diaries listed above, is indispensable for anyone who wants to understand Smart and her world.

Guidebooks

Brado, Edward. *Brado's Guide to Ottawa: A Cultural and Historical Companion.* Kingston, ON: Quarry Press, 1991. This guide may be hard to find, but it's well worth hunting for in libraries and secondhand bookstores.

Fletcher, Katharine. *Capital Walks: Walking Tours of Ottawa.* Toronto: McClelland & Stewart, 1993. A neighborhood-by-neighborhood jaunt among Ottawa's historic and architecturally interesting buildings that is just the kind of book Elizabeth Smart would have loved.

Martin, Carol, and Kevin Burns. *Ottawa: A Colourguide.* Halifax, NS: Formac Publishing, 1997. It's a little skimpy and a bit too photo-happy, but this is still one of the better single guides devoted to Canada's capital.

Web Sites

Ottawa: *www.ottawaregion.com.* Virtually an electronic guide to Ottawa, this site gives updated information on all aspects of visiting the capital.

"For the first time, I see pink flamingos picking their way through the green swamp; they remind me of the women of Havana strutting delicately, yet with purpose, across the 16th-century Plaza de Armas."

Ernest Hemingway
To Have and Have Not in Cuba

Victoria Brooks

THE CAYO IS ATTACHED to the mainland by a narrow yellow tongue lined with weeds and wild grasses. The tongue or Pedraplen, post–Ernest Hemingway, is Fidel Castro's work—17 miles of landfill severing and bridging a daiquiri-frothed sea. The road continues, slicing a man-made swath through mangroves. For the first time, I see pink flamingos picking their way through the green swamp; they remind me of the women of Havana strutting delicately, yet with purpose, across the 16th-century Plaza de Armas. They, too, are birds fishing for their next meal. Clouds of mosquitoes hover, a smoky stain over the shallow green of the water. The salmon-hued bodies and long necks of the flamingos arch and crane, thrusting wavering pink mirror images across the marsh. It seems like a mirage, a hallucination, then the birds spread their wings and it becomes a spectacle hot and sultry like Cuba.

By the mid-1930s, 20 years before he was awarded the Nobel Prize for literature, before his years in Cuba, Ernest Hemingway had made a considerable literary reputation for himself, one illuminated both by his lifestyle and by his larger-than-life presence. His spare, terse prose had been cultivated as a newspaper correspondent, the short sentences finely honed and tightly packed. His emotional suitability for drama was sharpened, too, through unrequited love, the specter of three wars, a difficult childhood (his mother dressed him as a girl) and, when he was 27, his father's suicide. It was when Hemingway became the breadwinner in the family that he nicknamed himself Papa.

Hemingway lived hard, played hard, and wrote hard, bringing a new energy and style to American literature. His method suited America, as did his persona: both embodied the nation's physical brashness and honesty. Already a cult figure in the mid-1930s due to the success of his first novel, *The Sun Also Rises* (1926), Hemingway was the voice of the Lost Generation that roamed Europe aimlessly, disillusioned by the empty aftermath that inevitably follows war.

The Sun Also Rises, with its romantic disenchantment punctuated by splendid heroics, the running of the bulls in Pamplona, and nonchalant banter, was so close to the mood of the period that Hemingway's catchphrase, "Have a drink!" was taken up by youth in Paris, New York City, and even the backwaters of middle America. Everywhere, bright young men emulated Hemingway's heroes, using understatements, talking tough. The novel, based on the author's own wanderings with first wife Hadley Richardson and their friends, was a thinly camouflaged version of people and events that really took place. This would be the course of all his writing.

A Farewell to Arms (1929), his second novel, drew on his experiences as an ambulance driver in World War I, ensuring his reputation as the most powerful chronicler of war America had ever seen. Hemingway was not just a literary influence: each city, town, or country that he brought to life with his carefully chosen words attained instant and permanent star status. But only Cuba, he admitted, attracted him so strongly that he wanted to "stay here forever."

Ernest Miller Hemingway was 33 when he discovered the voluptuous delights of 1932 Havana and the marlin that run like sleek blue torpedoes past Cayo Coco and Cayo Guillermo. These exquisite little islands float like dreams in the blue-green velvet warmth of the Gulf Stream. It is easy to picture Papa here, running naked down the long, pale ribbon of beach, taut muscles visible under tanned skin, his immense feet stamping deep prints into the floury white sand. His hair and mustache are stiff with salt from the sea and from a day of marlin fishing. The darkly handsome author is solid and masculine. He carries his weight, nearly 200 pounds, like an athlete, and although his height is five feet 11 inches, he appears to be taller. His body, toned by boxing and the rigors of deep-sea fishing, is the shade of 10-year-old Havana Club rum.

The *Pilar*, his 38-foot custom-built motor launch, floats alone on an ethereal horizon. White clouds puff languidly by, like tendrils of smoke from his last cheroot. The Gulf Stream is so utterly transparent that the *Pilar's* anchor seems to ripple, a dark cross under the phosphorescent sea. On the beach, the famous Royal portable typewriter awaits Hemingway's touch, the black keys made even darker by the partial shade of a coconut palm.

America's favorite literary son, the heavy drinker, the avid sportsman, the fearless hunter, the constant womanizer, the immensely talented writer whose lyrical prose cut to the core, made Cuba his own, particularly in the pages of his posthumously published novel *Islands in the Stream* (1970). Cayo Coco and Cayo Guillermo are not only Hemingway's landscape, they are his story: the artist living on an island in the Gulf Stream in the 1930s; the deep-sea fishing, his passion; and the hunt for Nazi U-boats in the translucent waters. More to the point, it was in Cuba that he was to write some of his greatest works and spend most of his last 22 years.

When Hemingway wasn't on his habitual rounds of traveling, deep-sea fishing in Cuba and the Bahamas, hunting big game in Africa, or a sporting sojourn in Europe (Spain for the bullfighting, Switzerland for the skiing), he used his home in seedy, unpretentious Key West, Florida, as his writing base from 1929 to 1939. His clapboard house, now a museum, was courtesy of his second wife, the spoiled socialite Pauline Pfeiffer. In 1927 Hemingway married Pfeiffer and converted to Catholicism. A few months before the first of many separations that began in 1932, he left Pauline and their newborn son, Gregory, in Key West and headed for Havana on one of his frequent marlin-fishing trips. At the Hotel Ambos Mundos, he resumed his relationship with 22-year-old Jane Mason. Mrs. M., as she was called, was the wife of Grant Mason—heir to a fortune, part owner of Cubana de Aviación, and a founder and manager of Pan American Airways. Mrs. M., a strawberry-blond, was stunning in every sense.

The Masons were ensconced in the extravagant and decadent lifestyle that Havana and some Third World cities such as Tangier offered. The golden spoon of Spanish and later, American, interests in sugar-rich Cuba hadn't become tarnished yet. Havana was a lifestyle "on a rumba," Hemingway's own phrase for what we used to call "a bender" and youth now call "a rave." It was the dissolute, madcap life that F. Scott Fitzgerald captured in his novels. Hemingway was later to use Mrs. Mason as a model for Helène Bradley, the bottled platinum-blond vixen in his novel *To Have and Have Not* (1937). This violent story of rumrunners smuggling human contraband between Key West and Cuba during Prohibition also details the revolution that overthrew Cuba's tyrannical Machado regime. The 1944 film version of *To Have and Have Not* catapulted new star Lauren Bacall to fame. While filming, Bacall and Humphrey Bogart, her costar, became lovers and went on to become Hollywood's most romantic married couple.

The scene of Papa's and the lovely Mrs. M.'s illicit lovers' tryst was the Hotel Ambos Mundos in the heart of Havana's shabbily sensual La Habana Vieja district.

The stunning Spanish architecture in this historic area resonates with the spirit of the *habaneros* and still seems haunted by Hemingway's specter, although he hasn't walked these streets for nearly 40 years. It was in the midst of this still infinitely physical quarter that Papa was destined to live and work, on and off, for the next five years. The daring Mrs. Mason is reputed to have climbed five floors up the outside of the hotel, through the transom of Hemingway's window, and into his shaded room for a sexual rumba, Havana-style, in Papa's *doble* bed. One daiquiri-swishing evening years later, Hemingway posed this frank question: "What's a man supposed to do when a beautiful woman comes in and he's lying there with a big stiff?"

I arrive in Havana on a hot Sunday in early February and, like Hemingway, head straight for the corner of Calles Obispo and Mercaderes, where the 52-room 1920s Hotel Ambos Mundos still stands. On the sun-splashed intersection, Cubans of both sexes linger, waiting for tourists to chat with, sell a cigar or a factory tour to, or just stroll beside. A mulatto poses, flaunting her physical attributes the way a tropical bird does to attract a mate. Displaying herself against a streetlight like a cliché, she has one bare elbow crooked close to her tiny spandex-covered waist, while her middle and index fingers, elongated and painted, embrace an ebony holder, the burning ember of its cigarillo as hot as she is. Her bare coffee-colored legs stretch to her stop sign of red shorts, one rounded hip thrust saucily, an obvious invitation for wolf whistles. Then a 1948 Buick, its surfaces thick with innumerable coats of barracuda-gray house paint, sidles up to the stone curb, and I'm reminded again of Hemingway, whose own Buick, except for the color, was this very same model.

I insist on a room in the northeast corner of the fifth floor of the Hotel Ambos Mundos, as close as possible to room 511, birthplace of *For Whom the Bell Tolls* (1940), Hemingway's novel of the Spanish Civil War. Between Hemingway's time and mine, the Ambos Mundos functioned as a state hotel for teachers, but it has been recently renovated for tourism.

The young male desk clerk's officious attitude, like Castro's wagging finger, reminds me that this *is* a Communist country and passports must be shown, forms filled out, and bills paid in advance. That done, I ride in the ornate metal cage of the original elevator to what used to be Papa's room, and am delighted to discover that it is just the way he left it.

My room is next door, with the same northern view over red roof tiles of colonial buildings to Havana Bay. As Hemingway described the view, "The rooms on the northeast corner of the Ambos Mundos in Havana look out, to the north, over the old cathedral, the entrance to the harbor, and to the sea, and to the east to Casablanca peninsula, the roofs of all the houses in-between and the

A familiar sight in 1950s Havana: Ernest Hemingway hoisting a few drinks with friends. Courtesy of John F. Kennedy Library

width of the harbor."

Papa's day in the small hotel room often began with a parched throat brought on by a large quota of Papa Dobles, the double-shot frozen daiquiri invented for him at El Floridita. Legend has it that he once drank 16 of them in a single evening.

My room, like Papa's, is small, but the ceiling soars and the double louvered doors open wide onto a facade balcony. Through the pale pink and whitewashed pillars of the balcony, I can see the ruins of Morro Castle and a small strip of blue Caribbean. I hear the emotional strains of *son* music and later the laughter of Creole children backed by the drawl of a freighter's horn. Below, the 16th-century street is under siege by renovators, courtesy of the World Heritage Fund.

La Habana Vieja's subtle odor drifts up to me on the sea's breath. It has swallowed the many kisses of lovers, swallowed the ageless tale of the old fisherman who sits stoically or shares stories with his stubble-faced cronies on the worn wall of the Malecón, Havana's beautiful oceanfront thoroughfare not so far from where I stand. The tangy aroma is a long drink of Russian diesel, Havana cigars, *jineteras*, and perfume, the dust of old rubble, and the choke of new concrete.

Ernest Hemingway's Finca Vigía, now the Museo Hemingway, is a time capsule of his life there. Eerily, when you look in through the house's windows, it's as if Papa never left. Victoria Brooks

The stately columned Spanish palaces lining the Malecón rub noble shoulders. Once the most exclusive and elegant of addresses, the seafront is now a boarded and bitter remnant of a lost era. The narrow two- and three-story structures teem with lonely residents who loiter, jobless, bored, and hungry on rococo balconies that peel *pastillas* of sunburned paint. Empty-eyed, they gaze across the sea toward Miami, where many of their countrymen have gone to escape the economic disaster that plagues them. The Malecón, I remember from a previous visit, is veiled with the sea spray of human tears. Now, looking upward on my hotel balcony, I watch a vulture turn on serrated wing, and somewhere nearby piano music does a Cuban crescendo. Next to me is Papa's balcony, the shutters thrown wide.

When she could bear no more of the small, gloomy hotel room, second wife Pauline Pfeiffer abandoned Papa's double bed for Key West. Third wife Martha Gellhorn, a talented journalist of a more practical bent than her predecessor, perused the classified ads in Havana's newspaper for a solution. She rented Finca Vigía (Lookout Farm) in nearby San Francisco de Paula, a 45-minute drive from the fishing village of Cojímar, where Papa kept the *Pilar*, and nine miles from Havana and the Floridita, his favorite bar.

Hemingway first met the feisty Gellhorn in 1936 at Sloppy Joe's, a bar in Key West. Papa accompanied Joe Russell, the bar's owner, on his rum–running forays during Prohibition, drawing from these experiences when he wrote *To Have and Have Not*. Russell also opened the now-defunct Sloppy Joe's in Havana. A year after Gellhorn and Hemingway met, they became lovers while covering the Spanish Civil War. The blond, attractive Gellhorn, on assignment for *Collier's*, was one of the first female war correspondents.

In 1940, after his divorce from Pfeiffer was official, Hemingway and "Marty" wed, staying on at the Finca. Gellhorn soon grew tired of the writer's refuge she herself had discovered for Papa. Back in Europe, World War II raged, and she wanted to cover it. Hemingway, now a familiar fixture in Havana, decided to further the war effort from Cuba with his own heroic scheme.

At Finca Vigía today there is a document that reads:

18 May 1943

To Whom It May Concern:

While engaged in specimen fishing for the American Museum of Natural History, Sr. Ernest Hemingway, on his motor boat PILAR, is making some experiments with radio apparatus which experiments are known to this *Agregado Naval*, and are known to be *arreglado* [arranged] and not subversive in any way.

Hayne D. Boyden
Colonel, U.S. Marine Corps
Agregado Naval de los Estados Unidos, Embajada Americana

This informal authorization, written for Papa's use if the Nazis captured him (an escape hatch of dubious merit), was given to him by the American naval attaché. The U.S. navy issued Hemingway radio direction finders, hand grenades, .50-caliber machine guns, a bazooka, and extra rations of liquor, all for use aboard the *Pilar* while engaged in antisubmarine activities off Cuba's coast. Papa's personal mission was to capture a Nazi submarine with the *Pilar* (now tarted up as a Q-boat but disguised as a fishing vessel), take prisoners, and seize secret codes.

Hemingway never sank or disabled a submarine in the two years the *Pilar* patrolled Cuba's coastal waters, but he and his nine men, including Gregorio Fuentes (at the wheel) and a couple of jai alai players (chosen for their ability to throw grenades down hatchways), sighted one German sub. It got away, though. They also consumed great quantities of raw crabs with lemons. Fuentes,

Gregorio Fuentes, Ernest Hemingway's Old Man, resplendent with fat Cuban cigar. Courtesy of Restaurante La Terraza, Cojímar, Cuba

Hemingway's loyal captain of the *Pilar* from 1938 on, was the model for Antonio in *Islands in the Stream*.

Just before embarking on his hunt for U-boats, Papa began a short-lived spy ring he called the Crook Factory. Its secret mission was to infiltrate pro-Nazi organizations in Havana and report traitors to the American embassy. Hemingway, code name Agent 08, financed the project and held covert meetings at the Finca. He recruited during his pleasurable rounds at Havana's bars and the Basque Club. His agents were fisherman, drinking pals, lottery salesmen, a man of the cloth who brought knowledge of machine guns from the war in Spain, an American ambassador, and two intelligence officers—friends with antifascist leanings.

Papa relished playing chief until he tired of the role, then turned his attention to submarine hunting. To Hemingway's latter-day detractors, both efforts smacked of James Wormold and his bumbling, fictitious spy ring in Graham Greene's *Our Man in Havana*. Hemingway was ridiculed as naive and romantic, a playboy who chased submarines off Cuba's coast on a whim. Papa called the *Pilar*'s covert operation "Friendless" after one of his cats.

In late 1943, Gellhorn left Papa and Havana for the battlefields of World War II. She dismissed Hemingway's Secret Service–style contribution to the war effort as a thinly veiled ploy to fish and get extra gasoline rations in wartime.

Gellhorn was replaced in 1946 by Hemingway's fourth and final wife, Mary Welsh, a correspondent for *Time*. Unlike his first three wives, "Miss Mary," as he called her, would remain constant in his heart, just as Finca Vigía and the *Pilar* would.

It was on the grounds of the Finca that one of Hemingway's favorite guests, the beautiful actress Ava Gardner, swam naked on a late September afternoon. While the curvy actress swam, Papa banned his 11 servants (including two Chinese cooks) from the second-floor windows. He alone stood and watched the actress do her paces in the square blue swimming pool surrounded by African orchids.

Gardner is now only a delicious memory, and the pool is empty, but the *Pilar*, Hemingway's beloved boat, sits dry-docked on a wooden throne built on the writer's tennis court. September, the best game-fishing month, brought an endless swarm of friends—bullfighters, Hollywood stars, prizefighters, soldiers, and artists—who came to fish with him in the Gulf Stream and to drink Papa Dobles. Now tourists wander the spacious and shady grounds where Papa bred fighting cocks and dogs.

Hemingway finished *For Whom the Bell Tolls* at the Finca and went on to write *Across the River and into the Trees* (1950), his masterpiece *The Old Man and the Sea* (1952), and *A Moveable Feast* (1964). Papa wrote the drafts in pencil, usually standing up. *The Old Man and the Sea*, a profound story of the struggle between a huge blue marlin and Santiago, a determined old fisherman down on his luck, was set in Cojímar, where Hemingway kept the *Pilar.* The story, inspired by Gregorio Fuentes, helped earn Papa the 1954 Nobel Prize for literature. He dedicated the prize to Nuestra Señora de la Caridad, the virgin patron saint of Cuba's only basilica in nearby Santiago de Cuba.

Now the Museo Hemingway, Finca Vigía was given to the Cuban people by Papa's widow, Mary Welsh. The one-story Spanish Colonial house is painted a ghostly white. After paying the $3 entrance fee, I wander around the edge of the house, peering through the large wood–framed windows. What I see is pure Hemingway: a hunter's palace, a sportsman's abode, a writer's haven. It is a place of dead things and guns, exactly as he left it.

Except for the kitchen, a cat cemetery, and the cellar, all the rooms are visible through the windows. No one is allowed in to disturb Papa's things: his glasses with the round metal frames, his collection of Nazi daggers, his guns, his fishing rods, his photographs and trophies. The hunting trophies take center stage; a maned lion from his first African safari in 1934 languishes on the tiled floor, its long incisors yellowed in death, its golden coat backed by red felt. A leopard, thick, soft fur the marbled color of my faux tortoiseshell sunglasses, is a souvenir taken by Papa from Kenya's Kimana Swamp in 1953. The taxidermist has artfully shaped the luckless leopard's jaws into a perpetual snarl. Sports magazines and books are strewn on desks and tables. The spines of some 8,000 volumes crowd the floor-to-ceiling bookshelves in a vertical litany of color and type. A wooden stepladder stands ready to access the highest shelves. Two lion skulls watch from a camel-skin bench.

I amble around to the shady side of the house. The cool stone floor I stand on is dappled in the late-afternoon shade of a giant ceiba tree. Papa stood on a lesser kudu rug when he wrote. His bedroom would stay comfortably cool. Now it is neat except for the mail, strewn Hemingway-fashion on his bed. An old issue of *Spectator* and a magazine called *Sports Afield* lie ready for his bedtime reading. A Royal typewriter waits on a polished wood shelf. An hour earlier at the Hotel Ambos Mundos, I saw a young hotel maid in European cap and apron dust a glass case that holds a similar typewriter. One of them must be a replica, but which one?

Around a corner, the dining-room table is laid with white linen. Good china, silver, and crystal are set for Papa's dinner guests. In the living room, next to his chintz-covered and flounced easy chair, is an elbow-height table bar covered with liquor bottles and clean glasses. Hemingway drank while he read, usually in the afternoon. Posters of bullfights and matadors, oils of bulls by Paul Klee and Joan Miró, and a white chalk bull sculpted by Pablo Picasso decorate the walls. More animal hides, kudu and water buffalo, hang beside African trophy heads, dead

The Old Lion and the Young Dictator: When the revolution in Cuba was new, Ernest Hemingway and Fidel Castro were friends. Courtesy of El Floridita

eyes staring at me. Their bestial mouths gape, yet are perpetually silent. Through the large, clean panes of the Finca's windows, I have a portal on Hemingway's sporty, some say bloodthirsty, soul. Graham Greene once commented dryly, "Don't know how a writer could write surrounded by so many dead animal heads."

Hemingway's incredibly massive size 11 shoes wait beside his bed. They look bigger than life, bigger than any man could possibly fill. On Mary Welsh's last trip to Havana in 1977, she said, "Everything is just where we left it in 1960. But the house is nothing without Ernest." I, too, feel his absence.

It is late afternoon in La Habana Vieja, and the sun has stoked the heat to savage intensity on the stone streets outside. In my dim room next to Hemingway's at the Hotel Ambos Mundos, the rhythm of a rumba shakes its Havana hips like maracas through my open window. It is useless to ignore its call. "Have a drink," I say aloud, Papa-style, and prepare to hit the Floridita for a frothed green sea in a glass.

I take the hotel's gray marble staircase down five flights. My hand slides along the smooth, worn wrought-iron balustrade. In my imagination, it's still

Although worn and battered, Havana's Spanish Colonial buildings still have a certain nobility and panache that contribute to an ambience rich with possibilities. Victoria Brooks

warm from Papa's large hand. The strains of "Unforgettable You" waft with old-fashioned sweetness from the hotel's public room.

Strolling the short nine blocks up Calle Obispo toward the Plazuela de Albear and another of Papa's shrines, I get hotter and thirstier by the minute. My feet move progressively quicker past a café fragrant with the smell of freshly ground Cuban coffee, past Creole babies, children, and women of all colors, past a museum fronted by a rusted-out Russian Lada. A pedicab, its leather seats shiny with wear, careers around a corner, the muscles in the driver's legs moving like thick snakes under the thin covering of his skin. My feet dodge potholes swimming with construction rubble, a dead cockroach belly-up, cigar ends and wrappers, and unlucky lottery tickets. A small dog yaps from behind an ironclad window, two small children tug at my dress, their mouths open with need—for a dollar, maybe just a kind word. I walk straight up Obispo, shaded from the sun by the tall, yellowed buildings. I am hot on Hemingway's trail and I want a Papa Doble.

A Cuban resplendent in red tuxedo and bow tie greets me at the Floridita. He opens the door with a flourish, and I take my place at the long, dark mahogany bar. The room is as cool as crushed ice. I note the "golden frieze and episcopal drapes" that Gabriel García Márquez describes in his introduction to Norberto Fuentes's book *Hemingway in Cuba*. "There," Márquez writes, "the daiquiri cocktail was created, a happy combination of the diaphanous rum of the island, crushed ice and lemon juice."

I order my first Papa Doble under Hemingway's watchful eye. His bronze bust hangs above me, smiling and carefree. The drink, sans sugar, is capped with froth like Mount Kilimanjaro's snow-covered peak. The liquid glides down my throat. It is the green of the Gulf Stream; it is as heady as the thought of Ava Gardner in Papa's pool. I feel expansive. Although the Papa Doble costs me $6.50, I order a second. It, too, slips down my throat. I am now on my third. It is delicious. I could catch a marlin by his slippery, silvery tail. I am drunk, proud to be on a rumba.

Papa Doble

4 oz. of Havana Club rum, or another good Cuban rum if unavailable

2 tsp. fresh grapefruit juice

1 tsp. grenadine

Juice of lime

Crushed ice

Shake well, but don't strain.

Old photographs of Hemingway stare at me from the walls: Papa with Gary Cooper, Papa with Errol Flynn, Papa with Spencer Tracy, Papa with his wives, Papa with the circus's Ringling brothers, Papa with Castro. I read the sign across the bar: La Cuna del Daiquiri. I float in the liquid embrace of the daiquiri. To me, the cool of the Floridita's air-conditioning is a breeze swept from the sweet curve of Havana Bay. There are no windows in this elegant red room. Nothing exists outside the Floridita's Hemingway-covered walls. My thoughts are as clear as the ice that my good friend Constante has deftly shaken into my Papa-size glass.

I am seized by a thought: maybe Hemingway didn't kill himself with a 12-gauge double-barreled shotgun blast in Ketchum, Idaho, in July 1961. Maybe he's waiting to return to his typewriter in the room next to mine at the Ambos Mundos, or to his writing desk covered with papers at the Finca Vigía. Maybe, like the daring Mrs. M., I'll climb through the transom of Papa's window after dark for a hot and sweaty sexual rumba, Havana-style.

Feeling flushed, I turn my head slowly and marvel at Hemingway's own leather-topped bar stool sectioned off by a polished brass chain. Then, startled, I think I see Papa—a little older than in his photos on the wall behind the bar.

A little paunchier, too. I squint through the smoky darkness, my eyes crossing with effort. But, no, of course it isn't Hemingway. It's a look-alike, a German tourist with a white mustache and beard come to pay homage to the legend.

I look around again and notice another Papa, round-faced and mustachioed à la Hemingway. He's wearing the white guayabera I could have sworn hung in Papa's bedroom closet at the Finca. This one looks exactly like the darkly handsome young author (before the neatly trimmed beard, before the gray of age) photographed behind the wooden wheel of the *Pilar*, tanned face shadowed by a long-billed fishing cap. I detect a South African accent and stretch to hear his conversation from across the room, but I needn't strain. I hear him cry Papa's famous incantation in a brazen voice: "Have a drink!" Then I understand. Hemingway is still an influence, still alive in the imagination of the entire world. And these look-alikes, these Papa *dobles* who emulate the author's style and flock to his stool at the famous Floridita are my proof.

So now I know. And there is nothing to do but order my fourth Papa Doble, put my head down on the long, cool bar and, in my rummy stupor, visualize running naked down a sandy beach, my huge size 11 footprints leaving imprints as deep as ditches in the glittering sand. Across a short expanse of water, my trusty blue-eyed Captain Gregorio Fuentes waits silently, patiently, at the *Pilar*'s wheel, the iridescent wake from the boat running behind like the pale green froth of my drink . . .

The Writer's Trail

Following in the Footsteps

Destination: Cuba sits in a time warp. You may fall in love with it. You will definitely never forget it. Marvel at 16th-century buildings and the gleaming 1950s American cars that roam Havana like lumbering dinosaurs. Russian automotive relics compete with Americana in a twist of irony. Havana is exquisitely rich in architecture, the arts, and history, but it is much more; it is a heartfelt treat and an eye-opener. Cuba's compelling and wonderful people are in a state of economic depression, but their suffering is cloaked by an innate zest for life and never-ending hope. You may very well go home saying, "End the U.S. embargo. The Cuban people are just that—*people*. They are not the enemy."

Tip: U.S. citizens need a license to engage in any transactions related to Cuba, but tourist and business travel aren't licensable, even through a third party such as other Caribbean nations, Mexico, or Canada. That said, thousands of Americans skirt the law every year by entering Cuba illegally through different countries. These days U.S. citizens can also visit Cuba as "fully hosted" travelers under special arrangements with tour operators. Packages, direct flights, and individual travel arrangements can be booked from Canada, Jamaica, the Bahamas, Mexico, and Europe. Call the Cuba Tourist Office ([416] 362-0700 in Canada) for travel information and the names of travel agents who will book for you, or contact Cubatur at 156 Calle 23, Vedado, Havana, Cuba (tel.: [53-7] 32-4521).

Location: Cuba is the largest of the Caribbean Sea's islands and is situated only 90 miles south of Key West, Florida, across the Straits of Florida.

Getting There: José Martí International Airport is 15 miles southwest of downtown Havana. Cubana de Aviación ([514] 871-1222 in Canada) flies to Havana from major cities in Europe, Mexico, Central America, South America, the Caribbean, and Canada. Air Jamaica (1-800-523-5585 or *www.airjamaica.com*) has flights from some major North American cities to Montego Bay, Jamaica, with connections to Havana. Air Canada ([416] 925-2311 or *www.aircanada.ca*), Air Transat (1-877-872-6728 in Canada or *www.airtransat.com*), and Canada 3000 (1-888-241-1997 in Canada or *www.canada3000.com*) have charter flights from Canada. Aeroméxico ([52-5] 207-6311) and Mexicana de Aviación ([52-5] 325-0990) offer regular flights from Mexico City to Havana. Trans-Caribbean Air has daily flights from Havana to Cayo Largo and Cayo Coco, sometimes with a stop in Varadero. There is no contact number, so you have to book and pay for your flight at Trans-Caribbean's booth in Havana's airport or at a tourist agency in Cuba. It is sometimes possible to book flights through the tour desk or concierge at your hotel. It is a 25-minute taxi ride from Cayo Coco's small airport to Cayo Guillermo.

Tip: The U.S. embargo and the demise of Communist Russia have made Cuba a needy place. Bring gifts of shampoo and soap and light foodstuffs for adults. Crayons, pens, and fruit bars are welcome gifts for children. These small offerings will make you a friend of the Cuban people. Bring American cash even if your credit cards aren't American. Many restaurants and shops claim to accept some non-U.S. credit cards but make the ordeal so lengthy that it's not worthwhile. At the time of writing, no credit cards issued in the United States are accepted in Cuba. American Express, no matter where issued, is also unacceptable.

Orientation: Havana spreads out on both sides of Bahía de la Habana, due south of Florida. Ernest Hemingway's trail starts in old Havana (La Habana Vieja) at the Hotel Ambos Mundos (corner of Calles Obispo and Mercaderes), his first digs. A walk southwest down Calle Obispo takes you to the Floridita, Papa's favorite hangout and the place where he got his special daiquiri, the Papa

Doble. A short block northwest of the Hotel Ambos Mundos is the beautiful Plaza de la Catedral where La Bodeguita del Medio (207 Calle Empedrado), Papa's preferred place for a *mojito* (rum mint julep), is located. Here you'll find Hemingway's supposed scrawl on the graffiti-covered walls: *"Mi mojito en La Bodeguita, mi daiquiri en El Floridita."* Before you have a drink there, though, catch a metered cab to Finca Vigía, Papa's home for 22 years. It's now a historical site dedicated to his memory.

Getting Around: Use metered cabs for short excursions around and outside Havana, or have your hotel rent a car and driver for you. Illegal taxis, some relics of the American-backed past—1950s Chevys, Packards, Buicks, and Fords—are available for a spin (with driver) down the oceanfront Malecón or around Havana. Be warned that many leak carbon monoxide, making for an uncomfortable ride. Car-rental agencies will supply self-drive cars. These are expensive and only worthwhile if you're leaving Havana. Cars can be rented at desks in the lobbies of major hotels. There is public bus and train service in Cuba, but you'll find traveling this way frustrating and difficult, particularly when it comes to buses. Public transit in Havana itself is to be avoided at all costs.

Literary Sleeps

Parque Central: This modern 281-room hotel has a good location and a gorgeous rooftop pool. Neptuno e/Prado y Zulueta, La Habana Vieja. Tel.: (53-7) 66-6627. Fax: (53-7) 66-6630. Expensive.

Hotel Ambos Mundos: With an excellent location on Calle Obispo, Papa's favorite street in the heart of fascinating old Havana, this hotel has plenty of charm and convenience. Ask for a room with a view of Havana's harbor. Be warned that if you take the room beside Papa's 511, there may be constant comings and goings. Rooms are comfortable enough, but you may want to ask the maid to remove the plastic mattress pad. 153 Calle Obispo, La Habana Vieja. Tel.: (53-7) 61-4860. Fax: (53-7) 33-8697. Moderate.

Hotel Plaza: Built in 1909, this 188-room establishment has plenty of atmosphere (two parrots flying around the lobby, for instance) and Spanish decor. The exquisite rooftop terrace has superb views of Havana harbor and the old city. El Floridita, Hemingway's favorite bar, is only steps away. 267 Calle Agramonte, La Habana Vieja. Tel.: (53-7) 33-8583. Inexpensive to moderate.

Cayo Coco, Cayo Guillermo: There were no hotels on these tiny cays during the Ernest Hemingway years. Now the islands are dotted with large all-inclusive hotels for the package tourist. The Hotel Cayo Coco is an expensive, rambling complex of 23 two- and three-story faux colonial buildings erected in 1993. On Cayo Guillermo, try the pricey Villa Cojímar. Although these modern hotels certainly give no feeling of Hemingway, the ocean still gleams, the long sand beaches are still magnificent, and the mangrove swamps still teem with pink flamingos. If the natural setting doesn't satisfy your longing for things Hemingway, rent your own motor launch and call it the *Pilar*.

Literary Sites

Bar Dos Hermanos: Once a haunt of Ernest Hemingway, this bar is now largely left to locals. For a few months in 1930, poet Federico García Lorca made Dos Hermanos his favorite hangout. Plenty of tasty food and a salty air make this one of the best bars in Havana. 304 Calle San Pedro (at Calle Sol near Muelle Luz on the waterfront).

La Bodeguita del Medio: Along with Ernest Hemingway's purported scrawl on the wall of this busy rustic bar and restaurant, you'll find the autographs of Salvador Allende, Fidel Castro, Harry Belafonte, and Nat "King" Cole. To get in the Hemingway mood, order a *mojito*. 207 Calle Empedrado, La Habana Vieja.

El Floridita: Immortalized by Ernest Hemingway's *Islands in the Stream*, this bar is a great place to hang out. Order a Papa Doble in the elegant room and listen to the musicians play. Drinks are expensive but worth it. Take a look at the Hemingway bust, his bar stool, and the photographs on the walls. Be warned: you'll be rubbing elbows with a lot of fellow tourists. 557 Calle Obispo, La Habana Vieja.

El Pacífico: Ernest Hemingway patronized this restaurant when he was in the mood for Chinese food. Havana's Chinatown, once a haven for prostitution and opium dens, is now a commercial district. The restaurant is located on the top floor. 518 Calle San Nicolás (at Calle Cuchillo), Barrio Chino, Centro Habana.

Marina Hemingway: This modern harbor and self-contained village on the western edge of Havana doesn't really suggest Ernest Hemingway, but there is a fountain dedicated to him and a disco called Papa's. You can rent boats for fishing excursions or book through an agent. The Ernest Hemingway International Marlin Fishing Tournament is held here in May. Tel.: (53-7) 33-1831 or (53-7) 33-1150.

Museo Ernest Hemingway: The contents of Finca Vigía, Ernest Hemingway's home for 22 years, are frozen in time. In 1961 the house was given to the Cuban state by arrangement in Hemingway's will. Open Monday to Saturday 9:00 a.m. to 4:00 p.m. and Sunday 9:00 a.m. to noon. Have your hotel call before you go. The museum may be closed on rainy days. Admission is approximately $3 per person. Located in San Francisco de Paula, nine miles southeast of Havana on the Carretera Central, a 20-minute taxi ride from La Habana Vieja. Tel.: (53-7) 91-0809.

Icon Pastimes

Take a look at Ernest Hemingway's room at the Hotel Ambos Mundos, then wander down Calle Obispo before hitting El Floridita for a night "on a rumba." Or drive out to Cojímar, the fishing village where Hemingway kept his boat, the *Pilar*. The town is also the home of Gregorio Fuentes, Hemingway's model for the fisherman in *The Old Man and the Sea*. A lunch of fish soup and paella at Restaurante La Terraza (on the main street), is a must. It was Hemingway's favorite meal. Ask here about Fuentes. To get to this fishing village, take the exit marked Cojímar, 14 miles east of Havana, on the six-lane Via Monumental. Another spot the Hemingway fan will want to visit is Bacuranao, a tiny beach east of Cojímar. This is where Hemingway often berthed the *Pilar*. It's also the setting of a violent scene in *To Have and Have Not*, the one in which Harry Morgan throttles Mr. Sing's throat "until it cracked." A little farther on, 16 miles east of Havana, is Marina Tarará, where the Old Man and the Sea Fishing Tournament takes place every July.

Contacts

Center for Cuban Studies: Offers current literature and information on Cuba. Ask for a copy of *Cuba Update*, a bimonthly magazine about life in today's Cuba. 124 West Twenty-third Street, New York, New York 10011 U.S. Tel.: (212) 242-0559.

Cuban Interests Section: For information on Cuban entry requirements, U.S. citizens should write to 2630 Sixteenth Street NW, Washington, D.C. 20009 U.S. Tel.: (202) 797-8518.

Cuba Tourist Office: 55 Queen Street East, Suite 705, Toronto, Ontario M5C 1R6 Canada. Tel.: (416) 362-0700.

Havanatur: 7 Calle 2, e/1 y 3, Miramar, Municipo Playa, Havana, Cuba. Tel.: (53-7) 33-2273.

In a Literary Mood

Books

Brian, Denis. *The True Gen: An Intimate Portrait of Hemingway by Those Who Knew Him*. New York: Grove Press, 1988. The author interviews everyone who knew Hemingway well, including his other biographers. A fascinating read.

Burgess, Anthony. *Ernest Hemingway and His World*. London: Thames & Hudson, 1999. Excellent insights into Hemingway's life and writing.

Fuentes, Norberto. *Hemingway in Cuba*. Introduction by Gabriel García Márquez. Edited by Larry Alson. Translated by Consuelo E. Corwin. Secaucus, NJ: Lyle Stuart Inc., 1984. Everything you'll want to know about Hemingway's Cuba can be found here. A treasure!

Hemingway, Ernest. *Ernest Hemingway Reads Ernest Hemingway*. New York: HarperCollins, 1990. An audiocassette that features Hemingway reading his Nobel Prize acceptance speech and selections from some of his lesser-known works. If you rent a car in Cuba with a cassette deck, take this along.

_____. *Islands in the Stream*. New York: Scribner, 1997. Published posthumously in 1970, this autobiographical novel of high adventure in the 1930s and 1940s in and around Cuba's Cayo Coco and Cayo Guillermo is perfect reading material while taking in the sun on one of the islands' terrific beaches.

_____. *To Have and Have Not*. New York: Scribner, 1996. Dramatic, tough, and tender portrait of Harry Morgan, a man forced to run human contraband, then rum, between Key West and Cuba during 1930s Prohibition. Hemingway took a chance in this novel by using multiple narrators, as if he were trying to emulate William Faulkner's style. The experiment failed, but the book does have many memorable moments.

_____. *The Old Man and the Sea*. New York: Scribner, 1999. The simple but powerful Pulitzer Prize–winning novel about a fisherman and his struggle with a huge marlin displays Hemingway's talent at its very best.

Hemingway, Mary Welsh. *How It Was*. New York: Ballantine, 1977. Welsh was married to Hemingway for the last 15 years of his life. This is her story and his.

Hotchner, A. E. *Papa Hemingway: A Personal Memoir*. London: Weidenfeld & Nicolson, 1966. Vivid portrayal written by one of Hemingway's close friends and admirers.

Meyers, Jeffrey. *Hemingway: A Biography*. New York: Harper & Row, 1985. In a field crowded with biographies, this one is certainly a good place to start.

Samuelson, Arnold. *With Hemingway: A Year in Key West and Cuba*. Toronto: Random House Canada, 1984. Twenty-two-year-old farm boy Samuelson hitchhiked to Hemingway's Key West home in the hopes of meeting the author and learning about writing. He stayed with Papa for a year, accompanying him on numerous fishing trips to Cuba.

Guidebooks

Baker, Christopher P. *Cuba Handbook*. Chico, CA: Moon Publications Inc., 1997. Written lovingly by award-winning author Christopher P. Baker, this is the most comprehensive guide available on

Cuba. Baker takes a sensitive, honest, and unbiased approach to the country's fascinating history and America's role in Cuba.

Fodor's Cuba. 2nd ed. New York: Fodor's Travel Publications, Inc., 1998.

Stanley, David. *Cuba.* Hawthorn, Australia: Lonely Planet Publications, 1997. Not bad, but second-best to Moon's guide.

Films/Videos

Bart, Peter, and Max Palevsky (producers). *Islands in the Stream.* Franklin J. Schaffner (director). Paramount, 1977. Paramount Video. Cast: David Hemmings, Gilbert Roland, and George C. Scott. Scott puts in a decent performance as sculptor Thomas Hudson, a Hemingway alter ego, but the film runs out of steam in the final third.

Guila, Ricardo (producer). *Hello Hemingway.* Fernando Pérez (director). Documentary. Instituto Cubano del Arte e Industrias Cinematográficos (ICAIC) & Metro, 1991.

Hayward, Leland (producer). *The Old Man and the Sea.* John Sturges (director). Warner Bros., 1958. Warner Home Video. Cast: Harry Bellaver, Felipe Pazos, and Spencer Tracy. Hollywood icon Tracy tries his best to bring Hemingway's sea parable to life, but the story reads far better on the page than on film. Remade in 1990 as a TV movie with Anthony Quinn.

Wald, Jerry (producer). *The Breaking Point.* Michael Curtiz (director). Warner Bros., 1950. Cast: John Garfield, Patricia Neal, and Phyllis Thaxter. Hollywood loved refilming *To Have and Have Not.* After this version, it was done again as *The Gun Runners* in 1958, starring Audie Murphy and Eddie Albert. *The Breaking Point,* however, is the best, and most faithful, celluloid rendition of Hemingway's book. The film may even be better than the novel. Garfield turns in a searing, gritty performance as Harry Morgan. Once again, the setting has been changed—this time to California and Mexico after the Second World War—but the spirit of the book, and most of the plot, are intact.

Warner, Jack L. (producer). *To Have and Have Not.* Howard Hawks (director). Warner Bros., 1944. Warner Home Video. Cast: Lauren Bacall, Humphrey Bogart, and Walter Brennan. Believe it or not, William Faulkner had a hand in the screenplay, but there's practically nothing remaining of what he wrote, or of Hemingway's novel, in the final script. Bogart and Bacall redo Casablanca in Second World War Martinique, complete with French Resistance types and Nazis. Cuba and Key West? Forget it. The film made a star of Bacall, though.

Web Sites

Cuba: *www.greatestscapes.com; www.lonelyplanet.com; www.moon.com; http://travel.state.gov/tips_caribbean.html; www.unipr.it/~davide/cuba/HomePage.html.*

Ernest Hemingway: *www.hemingwayhome.com; www.hemingway.org.* The first site belongs to the Ernest Hemingway Home and Museum in Key West, Florida. The second site is the home page of the Ernest Hemingway Foundation, situated in his childhood home in Oak Park, Illinois. It features a virtual tour of his birthplace house, lots of information on the author, and excellent links.

Ian Fleming and Noël Coward
Seduced by Jamaica

Victoria Brooks

JAMAICA CALLED in her siren's voice and whispered in my ear, her breath as soft and sweet as a trade wind: "Write about that golden era of famous writers. Take a trip down the authors' trail into my star-studded past. Begin in the Second World War when Commander Ian Fleming of Britain's Royal Navy first saw me and fell hard for my charms."

At that time, Fleming wasn't a famous writer yet. In fact, he still hadn't put pencil to bond. The darkly handsome naval-intelligence officer arrived in Kingston, Jamaica, in the middle of the war for an Anglo-American conference during a perilous moment when Britain was worried about Nazi U-boats in Caribbean waters. (It is interesting to note that British intelligence put a high value on Fleming's tertiary education in languages at German and Swiss universities.)

Fleming must have taken time out from his important job to dream because, like others seduced by Jamaica, he knew from the very beginning that he had to own a piece of it. Not long after his fateful first visit, he bought property on the island's northeast coast in an area called Oracabessa (a Spanish name that means "Golden Head"). Eventually he contracted a builder to erect a house, and in January 1946, after retiring from navy intelligence, he arrived to claim his fiefdom.

Fleming originally purchased about 15 acres—which sits on a bluff overlooking the turquoise sea—then added another 15 later. Some of this land was acquired from Blanche Blackwell, famous beauty, socialite, landowner, and mother of well-known modern-day hotelier and entrepreneur Chris Blackwell. Of Island Outpost fame, Blanche's son was also the founder of Island Records, as well as Bob Marley's producer, financier, and promoter. Rumor has it that the dashing Fleming had a love affair with the ravishing, fascinating Blanche.

The creator of James Bond dubbed his new house Goldeneye—derived, depending on who you consult, from the name of the Allied defense plan for Gibraltar, the title of Carson McCullers's novel *Reflections in a Golden Eye*, or simply from a print of a goldeneye duck that Fleming liked—and wrote his bestselling spy series there; many of the books' scenes and plot details were rooted in the Jamaican landscape that surrounded him. Fleming got the name for his suave hero from the author of his Bible, *Birds of the West Indies*, by James Bond. The British espionage writer referred to this guide as one of his "Jamaican links." Later, when he met the bird-loving Mr. Bond and his wife, he apologized to them for lifting the name. Fleming reported that the couple kindly commented that it helped them clear customs when they traveled.

Like other writers who have holed up in a beautiful spot that awakens their creative spirit, Fleming felt indebted to Jamaica—so much so that he once asked, "Would these books have been born if I hadn't been living in the gorgeous vacuum of a Jamaican holiday? I doubt it."

At Goldeneye, Fleming began and finished *Casino Royale*, the first Bond novel, as well as the 12 stylish thrillers that followed. While in residence at his simple house on the north shore, Fleming also wrote his first major article, a mood piece that extolled the virtues of Jamaica. The piece, entitled "Where Shall John Go? Jamaica," was published in *Horizon* magazine in 1947. In it Fleming recommended a visit to Rose Hall Great House, eight miles east of Montego Bay, and a simultaneous read of Jamaican novelist Herbert George DeLisser's *The White Witch of Rose Hall*. DeLisser's Gothic tale of sadism and slaves, set in the 1850s, is based on the true story of Annie Palmer, a woman who murdered her three husbands in the Great House bed and treated her slaves with imaginative and sexually inspired cruelty. The Great House, built in 1780, has been perfectly restored, including the original bed where Palmer is said to have—black widow–style—made love to and then disposed of her husbands.

DeLisser's potboiler, however, wasn't the first Gothic bodice ripper to tout Jamaica as exotica for writers. As early as the late-18th-century, British novelist and plantation owner Matthew "Monk" Lewis set his bestseller *The Monk* in ever-sensual Jamaica. Later, Jean Rhys, the Dominican writer, used Jamaica as the setting for her novel *Wide Sargasso Sea*, although she had never set foot on the island. Rhys took her inspiration from Charlotte Brontë's *Jane Eyre* to devise a prequel to that classic, using Rochester's ill-starred Creole wife as her protagonist to tell the tragic story of a Jamaican woman who is too passionate for her British husband, is treated with disdain, goes mad, and is later locked up by that husband because her West Indies–style passion is misunderstood. The movie

For James Bond fans, the desk at Goldeneye where Ian Fleming wrote all the 007 novels has special signifi-cance. Victoria Brooks

based on the novel was beautifully filmed in the lush Blue Mountains of Jamaica. (When novelists, filmmakers, and magazines need a tropical setting that exudes sensuality, Jamaica is often the choice.)

During the 1940s and 1950s, Fleming invited his friends and wealthy Jamaicans to Goldeneye, which became well-known on the cocktail circuit of high-flying movie stars, writers, and famous faces. At Goldeneye, friends honeymooned, stricken cronies regained their strength, and celebrities—such as Cecil Beaton, Truman Capote, Graham Greene, Evelyn Waugh, and Noël Coward—drank cocktails, slept them off, and then wrote and painted.

Fleming and Coward had known each other during the war (Coward put on charity concerts for troops in South Africa). The inexhaustible Coward was one of the most consummate actors of his time, and brilliantly used his own plays (*Private Lives, Design for Living*) as vehicles for his acting ability. When his plays fell out of favor with the public, Coward became a movie director. When his public tired of that, he started a one-man Las Vegas show. A man-about-town and bon vivant, Coward also set fashion trends. When he was photographed in pajamas and silk dressing gown, the whole world copied him and began receiving visitors in night attire. When not charming the world with his talents, he escaped for three months every year to Jamaica.

Coward's fascination with Jamaica began, as it did with Fleming, during the war when he made a brief visit. In 1948 the playwright rented Goldeneye from Fleming for £50 (about $200 then) a week. The multitalented songwriter and raconteur had received poor notices from critics for the American revival of his cycle of one-act plays, *Tonight at 8:30*, and when it closed, he and his companion, Graham Payn, were happy to seek refuge in an island paradise.

Coward and Payn sailed to Jamaica from New York City in five days. On arrival, a boyish, teasing friendship and good-natured rivalry over Jamaica began between Coward and Fleming. During his visit, Coward celebrated Goldeneye with a song that complained about the airless rooms and the hardness of Fleming's furniture, ending the ditty with: "That I was strangely happy in your house/In fact I'm very fond of it." Sardonically he referred to his host's home as "Golden Eye, Nose and Throat" because it reminded him of a hospital.

Fleming, too, enjoyed the sparring and wrote about the outcome of Coward's first visit in the introduction to the now out-of-print book *Ian Fleming Introduces Jamaica*: "He [Coward] then went off, and, as close to me as he could get, built a house (what am I saying—four houses) and—to hell with the charms of Bermuda and Switzerland!—comes here every year."

During his lengthy stay at Goldeneye in 1948, Coward, with his constant companion Payn at his side, searched the island for "an idyllic bolt-hole to return to when life becomes too frustrating." Under star-shot evening skies, the two would discuss over drinks the possibility of "building a shack somewhere isolated on the island." In the daytime, they would hunt for suitable property. Finally they found their place to build a "shack" five miles east of Goldeneye and Oracabessa near Port Maria. Located on a hill, the property tumbles to the sea and is set against the vivid aquamarine of the Blue Mountains. Coward immediately purchased the property for a song, had a local architect draw up plans for a two-story villa and two guest cottages, and named his "idyllic bolt-hole" Blue Harbour, after its picturesque view of Port Maria.

But Blue Harbour was just the beginning of Coward's "until death do we part" love affair with Jamaica. A mere two weeks after purchasing their first property, Coward and Payn were out exploring and painting when they stumbled on a second piece of land. The 360-degree view from the property was intoxicatingly spectacular, and the two men spent the evening sitting in the grass drinking a thermos of ice-cold dry martinis and watching fireflies flit across Jamaica's night sky. The four-acre plot, 1,000 feet above Blue Harbour, was called Look Out by the locals, as it had been used as such 300 years earlier by the pirate Henry Morgan. Coward bought Look Out with the idea of building himself a writing retreat as soon as he had enough cash. Already he had named it Firefly. But it wasn't until his successful 1956 stint in Las Vegas that he had the money to build what he called his "dream home."

Coward's Firefly acreage, like some of Fleming's Goldeneye property, was sold to him by the wealthy Blackwell family. The prolific Coward went on to write 50 more plays and 300 songs, many of them penned at Blue Harbour and Firefly, almost next door to the socially affable Fleming.

When Coward joined Fleming on the Jamaican landscape, an even bigger round of entertaining began that included avid martini-drinking James Bond–style while watching the Jamaican sun, a brilliant golden ball, drop below the silvery surface of the sea.

Dinner parties were casually served outdoors and sometimes included callaloo soup (made with greens, onions, and crabmeat) and dessert in the manner of Alice B. Toklas: sprinkled liberally with finely ground Jamaican spices, including the local cannabis, or ganja. An unnamed source—we shall say only that she is a Dame—who attended the rounds of parties given in those grand days said, "My grandchildren can't hold a candle to me when it comes to the sheer quantities of ganja ingested in the name of fun."

Famous friends whom Coward entertained at Blue Harbour and Firefly included Sean Connery, Katharine Hepburn, Errol Flynn (who had his own piece of Jamaica at Navy Island, close to Port Antonio), Sophia Loren, Joan Collins, Elizabeth Taylor, Sir Winston Churchill, and even Britain's Queen Mother.

Shaken Not Stirred: Round Hill Recipe for a Martini in the Style of Bond and Coward

2 1/2 oz. gin
1/4 oz. dry vermouth
2 cocktail olives
Twist of lime

Pour gin and dry vermouth into a cocktail-mixing glass. Add three cubes of ice and shake.
Pour into a rock-crystal glass over ice. Add olives and a twist of lime.
Use less vermouth for an extra-dry martini.

In 1954 Coward was putting the finishing touches on his musical adaptation of Oscar Wilde's *Lady Windermere's Fan*. At the same time, a young Jamaican entrepreneur, John Pringle, was planning his own creative endeavor: a cottage colony to appeal to those on the social register. Pringle dreamed of building an exclusive club on a prime oceanfront property near Montego Bay. It would be rented and owned by the crème de la crème of society, both American and English. Pringle, desperate to find the right takers for his colony project, realized that Coward was the draw he needed. He offered the playwright a cottage for the price of a Jamaican dance-hall song. The rent would be one shilling a year.

Not wanting to take advantage of Pringle, Coward bought his "leased cottage" at contract price. To help launch the cottage colony, Coward issued opening invitations to prominent friends and promised to entertain with songs at midnight. It was a stroke of genius; Round Hill and its socialite weekenders became the focus of cover stories in glossy magazines across the United States and Europe. A 1954 issue of *Holiday* magazine featured Mrs. William Paley (the wife of the CBS television magnate, and a woman often cited as the best-dressed in the world) on the cover. Inside, photographs show socialites and movie stars (including Clark Gable looking decidedly wolfish with a woman on each arm) posing happily by their villas and pools and at the perfect little bay that Round Hill patrons still enjoy today. The text of the *Holiday* article attempted to explain the Round Hill phenomenon: "The smallness of the cabins make the wealthy feel refreshingly economical. This is a response to both the tax laws and the airplane by making the best of both—by buying a lovely and rather small house on a tropical fringe of the airplane's orbit."

Coward's modern, comfortable cottage became a convenient stopover for his glamorous friends on the way to play at Blue Harbour. (Coward, tired of the constant round of entertaining, fled to the quiet sanctuary of Firefly when it was completed in 1956, leaving Blue Harbour to his guests.) At Firefly Coward's studio was built to be inaccessible to his admirers. Eventually he sold his Round Hill cottage for a profit, insisting it was the first time he made money from an investment. Even without the charming Coward's presence, though, Round Hill had its own celebrity status.

In March 1973, Sir Noël Pierce Coward died of a heart attack in the shower stall of his tiny bathroom at Firefly. He was 74. Three years earlier, he had been honored with a knighthood for services in the arts. Today Firefly stands just as it did during Coward's lifetime. Some of his clothes—Hawaiian short-sleeved shirts, for example—hang unwrinkled in his bedroom closet, and an unfinished painting sits ready for his brush. Coward's vivid oils adorn violet walls; his art speaks of both Jamaica and his homosexuality: black male nudes gambol and

Famous guests, such as the young Sean Connery, dropped in on Noël Coward frequently when he was staying at one of his Jamaican homes. Courtesy of Blue Harbour

strut on the island's sunny beaches. Posters of his famous plays—*Private Lives, Blithe Spirit, Hay Fever*—are displayed proudly. A tour guide at the house informs visitors about the playwright's island life in a soft, lilting Jamaican accent.

Coward's Blue Harbour also stands much the way he left it. Casual and shabbily rustic, it still complements the natural beauty of the surrounding landscape that so charmed the charmer. The yard is alive with tropical fragrance, hummingbirds flicker between brilliant scarlet hibiscus and banana palms, the light of ships twinkle in the distant night, and all is soft and serene in Coward's once-private Jamaican playground. His two-bedroom house and the guest cottages below are modestly comfortable, as they would have been in the playwright's grand days. The buildings are old-fashioned, certainly not luxurious or opulent.

My husband, Guy, and I spent a night at Blue Harbour, which anyone can do. We slept in Coward's double wooden sleigh bed, the mattress so lumpy and hard that it could only have been his. On the master's outdoor dining patio, we ate delicious jerk chicken and Jamaican rice and peas. And as Coward used to describe it, we got "drunk on the altitude" under Jamaica's heavenly evening roof, the noise of a martini shaker in the kitchen sounding like maracas.

In the morning, we examined black-and-white photographs of the famous, both male and female, on the sun-bleached walls of the old wooden house's interior. We gazed with interest at the original shots of Coward's distinguished playmates posing happily behind glass, and noted a particularly wonderful picture of Coward himself in his trademark silk smoking jacket. Oddly, as far as we could tell, there were no pictures of Coward's longtime companion, Graham Payn.

We spent many idyllic hours in the house's pool, perched over the lovely bay. Fortunately the staff had just filled the pool with seawater. On a prior visit, the water had been an indescribably filthy ganja-green, certainly not suitable for Coward and his crowd, nor, we felt, for us. Coward built the pool in 1953 after his friends, the Douglas Vaughans of Brimmer Hall, Port Maria, showed him a home movie they had taken while enjoying the playwright's hospitality. The film showed a dolphin being devoured by a dozen sharks (one over 12 feet long) in an enclosed section of Blue Harbour's beach. (The beach no longer exists, and the rocky outcroppings that remain make entering the water a difficult task.) Coward believed that the reef protecting his man-made swimming beach kept out big fish. Sometime later, when he was reminded of the gruesome movie, he remarked, "It is comforting to reflect that I have built a pool."

An American has purchased Blue Harbour from Payn and runs it as a guesthouse. It gets few visitors, and although the bed badly needs a new mattress, a stay at the house makes for an interesting experience.

Ian Fleming's cherished Goldeneye also remains, but not in the ramshackle, yet authentic, state of Coward's Blue Harbour. Nor is it frozen in time like Firefly, which is now a national museum. The exterior of Fleming's wood-and-stone home hasn't changed, but the unmistakable hand of progress has obviously been at work. Goldeneye is in the capable possession of Blanche Blackwell's son, Chris, who has revamped the interior, added limestone cottages with wooden shutters to the property, and built a man-made island.

The scion of Island Outpost entertains renowned singers and composers, such as Quincy Jones, U2's Bono, Harry Belafonte, Jimmy Buffett, Marianne Faithfull, Rita Marley, and Tom Waits. And famous actors mingle with the musical set, just as they would have during the golden era of Fleming and Coward. But now it isn't the dashing Errol Flynn sipping martinis at Goldeneye; today the latest Bond, Pierce Brosnan, might be found on the patio with Blackwell, who also rents the resort's secluded cottages to the traveling elite. Further inspection of the estate reveals trees planted by River Phoenix, Jim Carrey, Martha Stewart, and Naomi Campbell, among others.

Remembering that Fleming both loved and valued Blanche Blackwell, as he did his beautiful muse, Jamaica, it is fitting that Chris's mother continues to stay at Goldeneye on occasion. One wonders if she still dreams of the handsome Fleming and herself back in the heyday of their lives.

The most tangible reminder of Fleming in the house's interior is his red bulletwood desk where he wrote every one of his Bond books, "with the jalousies closed around me so that I would not be distracted by the birds and the flowers and the sunshine outside until I had completed my daily stint." Those beautiful jalousies are still open to let in the sweetly scented Jamaican air that Fleming referred to as the "Doctor's Wind." The former navy commander worked on his books only from January to March of each year, beginning in 1952, spending the rest of the year in England working for the Kemsley newspaper chain, which included the prestigious *Times* of London. At the end of the 1950s, Canadian Roy Thomson bought the print empire and became Fleming's ultimate boss.

By August 1964, when Ian Lancaster Fleming died at the age of 56, his books had sold more than 40 million copies and had been translated into nearly a dozen languages. Two films starring Sean Connery—*Dr. No* and *From Russia, with Love*—had already been made, with a third, *Goldfinger*, about to be released.

Today, the floors that Fleming would have rested his bare feet on at Goldeneye have been redone, the house now has bathrooms (and hot water!), the ceilings have been raised, and the furniture is made of comfortable and elegant Balinese cane. Noël Coward would be happy with Chris Blackwell's modifications to

Goldeneye; he never liked Fleming's austere taste in furnishings and decor.

Meanwhile, over at legendary Round Hill, the continuous procession of Hollywood and Wall Street glitterati continues. Recently the cottage colony gained international attention as the setting for the film *How Stella Got Her Groove Back*, based on the novel of the same name by Terry McMillan, who also penned *Waiting to Exhale*.

I sat in a chair in Coward's Round House cottage, imagining birds in the lush vegetation outside twittering the lyrics of his popular songs, maybe "Some Day I'll Find You" or "I'll See You Again." New ideas for plays probably germinated in his mind and fell like ripe coconuts right here, while Buhalla, his Jamaican maid, served him papayas, mangoes, and other tropical fruit. I could almost see him scanning the curve of ocean just beyond the green, flower-festooned bluff, perhaps thinking of returning to his beloved Firefly, no doubt distracted by the captivating chorus of breeze and birds trying to claim his attention. Just as now, a single Jamaican doctor bird, emerald tail feathers flowing like a lyrical after-thought, would have flown across his line of vision to land in a stately palm.

Musing about such things, I got up from the chair, which I had turned to

Before he built his swimming pool at Blue Harbour, Noël Coward had to take his dips in the surf and hope there weren't any sharks in the vicinity.

face the sea, and browsed through Coward's old bookshelf, now filled with the discarded paperbacks of previous guests: Arab romances, thrillers, and one lonely copy of *Private Lives*. Outside, Jamaica was calling, and I gazed at the distant sea, just as Coward would have, then looked back at the room's tiny desk, determined to write something, to capture this moment, now fully in the thrall of the island siren, inspired by the palpable presence of one of the 20th century's great authors. Taking a deep breath of perfumed air, I began.

(Note: As this book was going to the printer, the contents of Noël Coward's former house, Firefly, were auctioned off. There are plans to rent the home out for parties and weddings.)

The Writer's Trail

Following in the Footsteps

Destination: Jamaica inspires passion. For some, she is a temptress, a siren, a mistress. For others, the raucous, sometimes overzealous, personality of her independent, proud people can inspire annoyance, even fear. Be aware of your tolerance for this very real part of Jamaican culture. Some call it "higgling," others call it harassment. Many thrive on the contact. Either way, beware Jamaica's charms if you travel there. She may never let you go!

Tip: Jamaica's great resource is its people, and they love to chat. Conversing with them is mandatory for those who want to experience authentic island life. But if you feel uncomfortable or just don't feel like talking, simply say, "With respect, mon!" You'll be understood.

Location: Jamaica is located 90 miles south of Cuba in the Caribbean Sea. It is the third-largest island in the Greater Antilles.

Getting There: Air Jamaica and American Airlines have nonstop flights to Kingston or Montego Bay from most major North American cities: Air Canada ([416] 925-2311 or 1-800-268-7240 in Canada); Air Jamaica and Air Jamaica Express (1-800-523-5585); American Airlines (1-800-433-7300); and British Airways (1-800-247-9297).

Orientation: Goldeneye, Blue Harbour, and Firefly are located on Jamaica's northeast coast, approximately three hours' drive from Kingston, or two and a half hours from Montego Bay International Airport. Round Hill is a 20-minute drive from the Montego Bay Airport. Arrange in advance for your hotel to pick you up at the airport for an extra charge, or rent a car.

Noël Coward's former Round Hill cottage ably demonstrates the luxurious simplicity the resort's wealthy patrons sought eagerly then and now. Courtesy of Round Hill

Getting Around: Rental cars through the usual international companies (Avis, Hertz) are available for approximately $75 per day. As an alternative to the big agencies, try Island Car Rental in Kingston, Jamaica, at (876) 926-8861 or (876) 926-5991.

Literary Sleeps

Goldeneye: Media room with satellite TV, CD/cassette stereos, and CD selection; exclusive access to private beach. All-inclusive (all meals and drinks) daily rates for entire three-bedroom house (up to six persons). Tel.: 1-800-688-7678. Extremely expensive.

Round Hill: Weekly rates. Tel.: 1-800-972-2159. Extremely expensive.

Blue Harbour: Rates are negotiable, as they should be. Tel.: (505) 586-1244. Inexpensive.

Literary Sites

Firefly: Formerly a museum devoted to Noël Coward, the playwright's onetime house will now likely be rented out for parties and other social affairs. Tel.: (876) 997-7201.

Rose Hall Great House: Open to the public and available for private bookings. Hours: 9:00 a.m. to 6:00 p.m. daily. Admission: adults $15; children $10; group rates available. P.O. Box 186, Montego Bay, Jamaica, West Indies. Tel.: (809) 953-2323. Fax: (809) 953-2160.

Tip: If you choose to rent a vehicle and drive from Montego Bay or Kingston to Goldeneye, Blue Harbour, and Firefly, leave in the morning and start fresh. Jamaica's roads can be windy and potholed. They are also filled with wonderful natural and local sights that you may want to slow down or stop for. Don't forget to drive on the left-hand side of the road.

Icon Pastimes

As Ian Fleming loved to do, you, too, can snorkel Jamaica's world-class reefs. Wearing nothing but a snorkel and mask, Fleming would float over Goldeneye's reef every chance he got. "I learned about the bottom of the sea from the reefs around my property and that has added a new dimension to my view of the world," Bond's creator once said. After snorkeling, have a martini and watch the Jamaican sunset. The next day, spend an afternoon at James Bond Beach (in Oracabessa, close to Goldeneye), where you can visit the sports facilities or stop for a snack at the bar and grill. Or take a trip to Jamaica Safari Village and visit the crocodile farm where *Live and Let Die* was filmed. The village is located one mile west of Falmouth, about two hours' drive from Oracabessa, or 30 minutes from Montego Bay. Admission: adults $6.50; children $3. Tel.: (876) 954-3065.

Contacts

Jamaica Tourist Board: 2 St. Lucia Avenue, P.O. Box 360, Kingston 5, Jamaica, West Indies. Web site: *www.jamaicatravel.com*. Tel.: 1-800-233-4582 or (876) 929-9200. Fax: (876) 929-9375.

In a Literary Mood

Books

Bond, James, Don Eckelberry, and Arthur B. Singer. *Peterson Field Guides: Birds of the West Indies.* 5th ed. Boston: Houghton Mifflin, 1993. The most recent edition of Ian Fleming's bird Bible and still the definitive avian guide for the region.

Bond, Mrs. James. *How 007 Got His Name*. London: Collins, 1966. Odd but interesting, this 61-page curiosity was written by the wife of the real James Bond, an American ornithologist and author of *Birds of the West Indies*, whose name Fleming borrowed for his famous spy. Bond's wife chronicles the "revolutionary" effect Fleming's creation had on the couple's life. A handwritten inscription—"To the real James Bond from the thief of his identity"—and Fleming's signature grace the back cover of the book. Original illustrations of Jamaican birds from *Birds of the West Indies* adorn the volume's pages.

Cargill, Morris, ed. *Ian Fleming Introduces Jamaica*. London: Andre Deutsch, 1965. The romance and charm of Jamaica are lovingly invoked by Fleming in the book's introduction, which was adapted from the author's 1947 *Horizon* article.

Coward, Noël. *Autobiography*. London: Methuen, 1986. The playwright tells his own story. This volume includes his first two memoirs, *Present Indicative* and *Future Indefinite*, as well as the unfinished *Past Conditional*, with plenty of the great man's drolleries on his life in Jamaica.

_____. *Three Plays*. New York: Vintage, 1999. The umpteenth printing of three of Coward's best plays—*Blithe Spirit*, *Private Lives*, and *Hay Fever*—gives a pretty good taste of the author's comic style.

Fleming, Ian. *Dr. No*. London: Cape, 1958. This James Bond novel, with many scenes in Jamaica, shows Fleming at the height of his powers. It was the first of the Bonds to be filmed; appropriately, actual Jamaican locales were used.

_____. *Live and Let Die*. London: The Reprint Society by arrangement with Cape, 1956. SMERSH's Mr. Big battles Bond in New York City, Florida, and Jamaica. If you haven't read any Bond novels yet, this one (the second), which many critics think is among his best, is a good place to start.

_____. *The Man with the Golden Gun*. New York: New American Library, 1965. Unfinished at Fleming's death, this last Bond by the master (other writers, including Kingsley Amis and John Gardner, have since penned new Bond books) was published posthumously. Although probably the weakest in the series, the novel is worth a look for its author's final invocation of Jamaica.

Hoare, Philip. *Noël Coward: A Biography*. Chicago: University of Chicago Press, 1998. A recent biography that presents Coward's fascinating life in great detail.

Lesley, Cole. *Remembered Laughter: The Life of Noël Coward*. New York: Knopf, 1976. A full account of the life and times of the master playwright by his secretary and close friend.

Lycett, Andrew. *Ian Fleming*. London: Weidenfeld & Nicolson, 1995. An absorbing account of Fleming's Bond-style, real-life experiences, plots, and escapades during his days in British naval intelligence in the Second World War. The book also documents his important relationship to Jamaican socialite Blanche Blackwell.

Morley, Sheridan. *Out in the Midday Sun: The Paintings of Noël Coward*. Oxford: Phaidon, 1988. An excellent introduction to Coward's painterly side, with a good selection of prints of his paintings.

Pearson, John. *The Life of Ian Fleming*. London: Pan, 1968. An early biography still packed with plenty of insights into the man and his work.

Shacochis, Bob. *Easy in the Islands*. New York: Penguin, 1986. Feel the real Jamaica! Oozing with island-style sunlight and black humor, this fantastic collection of short stories picks you up and transports you not just to the Caribbean, but directly into the shoes of the most deeply fleshed-out characters you are ever likely to meet.

Tip: Nude swimming is de rigueur only in West End Negril, located on the western tip of Jamaica, or on lonely beaches.

Guidebooks

Luntta, Karl. *Jamaica Handbook*. 4th ed. Chico, CA: Moon Publications, 1999. This excellent guidebook gets at the real heart of Jamaica, and its author displays a deep knowledge and great love for the island. Indispensable.

Pariser, Harry S. *Jamaica: A Visitor's Guide*. Edison, NJ: Hunter Publishing, 1996.

Permenter, Paris, and John Bigley. *Adventure Guide to Jamaica*. 4th ed. Edison, NJ: Hunter Publishing, 1999.

Films/Videos

Bass, Ronald, and Terry McMillan (producers). *How Stella Got Her Groove Back*. Kevin Rodney Sullivan (director). 20th Century Fox, 1998. Fox Video. Cast: Angela Bassett, Taye Diggs, and Whoopi Goldberg.

Broccoli, Albert R., and Harry Saltzman (producers). *Dr. No*. Terence Young (director). United Artists, 1962. MGM/UA Home Video. Cast: Ursula Andress, Sean Connery, and Joseph Wiseman.

_____. *Live and Let Die*. Guy Hamilton (director). United Artists, 1973. MGM/UA Home Video. Cast: Yaphet Kotto, Roger Moore, and Jane Seymour.

Coward, Noël (producer). *Blithe Spirit*. David Lean (director). Cineguild, 1945. Cinema Classics (video). Cast: Constance Cummings, Rex Harrison, and Margaret Rutherford.

Franklin, Sidney (producer and director). *Private Lives*. MGM, 1931. MGM/UA Home Video. Cast: Una Merkel, Robert Montgomery, and Norma Shearer.

Risher, Sara (producer). *Wide Sargasso Sea*. John Duigan (director). New Line Cinema, 1993. New Line Video. Cast: Karina Lombard, Nathaniel Parker, and Michael York.

Web Sites

James Bond: *www.mcs.net/~klast/www/bond.html*; *www.commanders.com*; *www.007forever.com*. The last site is the definitive spot on the Net for 007 lore and news.

Noël Coward: *www.noelcoward.net*. The official site celebrating the 100th anniversary of Coward's birth.

Ian Fleming: *www.mcs.net/~klast/www/fleming.html*. Fairly detailed information on Fleming's life and art.

Jamaica: *www.jamaicatravelnet.com*; *www.fantasyisle.com*.

John Stephens and Frederick Catherwood
Mayan Adventure in Mexico

Joyce Gregory Wyels

THERE IS SOMETHING about catching your first glimpse of an ancient stone temple through dense vegetation that makes a gong go off inside your head. The temple rises darkly from a tangle of roots, vines, and trees growing out of its sides. Bromeliads cluster on the branches, and philodendron crown the carved surfaces.

Today, Yucatán's pyramids are as likely to be overrun by tourists as over-grown by vegetation. But a century and a half ago the once-glorious Mayan cities were so near collapse that early explorers feared for their survival. "In a few generations, great edifices, their facades covered with sculptured ornaments, already cracked and yawning, must fall and become mere shapeless mounds," wrote John L. Stephens and Frederick Catherwood.

In two long sweeps through southern Mexico and Central America, the duo braved civil wars, impenetrable jungles, intense heat, and tropical diseases to document these desolate monuments to a forgotten civilization. Their efforts resulted in two classics of travel literature: *Incidents of Travel in Central America, Chiapas, and Yucatán* (1841) and *Incidents of Travel in Yucatán* (1843), both written by Stephens and illustrated by Catherwood.

By the time he set off for the Mayan realm, writer John L. Stephens had already traced his journeys through exotic destinations in Europe and the Middle East in bestselling books. But his previous "Incidents" were only the prelude to Stephens's greatest accomplishment: unearthing the vestiges of the Western Hemisphere's most advanced civilization and jump-starting the new field of Mayan archaeology.

Stephens made it his goal "to snatch from oblivion the perishing but still gigantic memorials of a mysterious people." As a measure of his success, later travelers to the Mayan region used Stephens and Catherwood's books as travel guides, scholars studied the text and drawings, and armchair archaeologists then and now have vicariously hacked their way through the underbrush to admire long-abandoned palaces.

Equally important, Stephens and Catherwood spiked myths as rampant as the tropical vegetation surrounding the mysterious ruins—that they had been constructed by Egyptians, or one of the Lost Tribes of Israel, or refugees from the submerged continent of Atlantis. Academics argued that such noble buildings could hardly have emanated from the "savage races" of America.

Lively and engaging, the books are a good read. Better yet, Stephens's prose and Catherwood's fantastical sketches still entice contemporary adventurers to view for themselves these stone cities built more than a thousand years ago by the master architects of the Maya: ornate temples and pyramids, sacred wells, ceremonial centers filled with plazas, ball courts, palaces, and shrines.

My own Mayan wanderings start modestly enough with a vacation in Cancún. The latter-day tourist resort rates barely a mention in Stephens and Catherwood's books: "Kancune, a barren strip of land . . . we did not think it worth while to stay." Nor do I, eager as I am to forsake high-rise hotels for Mayan pyramids.

Just as Stephens promises, "Tuloom"—present-day Tulum—rises dramatically above the cliffs overlooking the Caribbean Sea. The former trading center and fortress sheltered inhabitants long after the classic Mayan sites had been abandoned. Now Tulum is one of the most visited of all Mayan sites, a condition abetted by its nearness to Cancún and verified by the exhaust from dozens of tour buses.

Cobá, a few miles inland, offers appealing isolation from crowds. But this is one set of ruins that Stephens and Catherwood bypassed: "They were all buried in forest . . . we concluded that it would not be advisable to go and see them." Although no longer buried, Cobá still has a natural, undisturbed look, only minimally excavated and restored. At one time all roads led to Cobá, the ceremonial center for a vast complex of Mayan villages. Brilliant blue butterflies flutter about the trail to Nohoch Mul, at over 100 feet the highest pyramid on the peninsula. Still, an anachronistic Club Med hotel rises only a short distance from Cobá's stark pyramids.

Just as Stephens and Catherwood had done on occasion, I decide to base myself in Mérida, an inviting city in its own right, and strike out from there to nearby Mayan sites. My friend Cindy joins me in the old colonial city which, despite increased population and traffic, continues to radiate charm. On Sunday, families stroll through the plaza, or pedal surreys with bright striped awnings around the *zócalo*, or promenade in horse-drawn carriages. "One fiesta was hardly ended when another began," Stephens writes approvingly, while admiring "the beauty

Close to Cancún and perched on the Caribbean Sea, Tulum has become one of the most popular, and accessible, Mayan sites to visit. Joyce Gregory Wyels

of the ladies of Mérida."

Chichén Itzá, the largest excavated city in Yucatán, lies between Mérida and Cancún. "Ever since we left home we had had our eyes upon Chichén," admits Stephens. Like our intrepid predecessors, we climb the pyramid called El Castillo by the Spaniards and look out over dozens of Mayan and Toltec structures. We peer into the sacred well, the cenote, whose depths have yielded the bones of sacrificial victims. Then we try to imagine knocking a ball through the vertical stone hoop high on the side of the great ball court, and gape at rows of human skulls carved in a stone wall.

From Mérida a short drive brings us to Uxmal, a classic Mayan city built about 600 A.D. "I had found the wrecks of cities scattered more numerously than I expected," writes Stephens in his second book. "Here [Uxmal] they still stood, tottering and crumbling, but living memorials, more worthy than ever of investigation and study . . . perhaps the only existing vestiges that could transmit to posterity the image of an American city."

When a wag speculated about deconstructing a tall pyramid for paving stones, Stephens touted its tourism potential: "We suggested that if he had it on the banks of the Mississippi, easy of access . . . it would stand like Herculaneum and Pompeii, a place of pilgrimage for the curious; and that it would be a much better operation to put a fence around it and charge for admission, than to sell the stone for paving streets."

The imposing temples of Uxmal enhance the Mayan reputation as "the Greeks of the New World"—talented artists, architects, astronomers, and mathematicians, creators of an accurate calendar and an advanced system of writing. The Palace of the Governors lives up to Stephens's praise: "If it stood this day on its grand artificial terrace in Hyde Park or the Garden of the Tuileries, it would form a new order . . . not unworthy to stand side by side with the remains of Egyptian, Grecian, and Roman art."

After a harrowing climb, Cindy and I finally scale the Pyramid of the Magician. Then, touring Uxmal's onetime suburbs, we discover that each smaller site offers its own gem of Mayan creativity, like Labná's ornate arch or the wall covered with masks of the rain god Chac at Kabah.

On a subsequent trip, another friend accompanies me in a drive across the peninsula, as we compile a litany of Stephens and Catherwood's greatest hits. I revel in the mystery of not-fully-deciphered glyphs, the unexplained demise of Mayan culture, the tragedy of Spanish book burnings, the underappreciated glory of Mayan art, architecture, and astronomy.

Still, I want to see Stephens and Catherwood's brooding stone temples ravaged by time and jungle vegetation, not neat restorations photographed by distracted cruise passengers. Although I am too late to "discover" Uxmal and Tulum and Chichén Itzá, I learn that hundreds of other sites lie hidden at the base of the peninsula, awaiting the occasional traveler who is willing to venture beyond tour buses and Club Med hotels.

"This trip is not for everyone," warns archaeologist Mary Lucas, ticking off necessary items: sleeping bag, tent, insect repellent, and flashlight. Indeed, only three other people join our guide Alfonzo and me at the rendezvous point in Mérida: Dell and her friend Roger, and John. The conversation centers around previously visited Mayan sites, a category in which I find myself hopelessly outclassed.

Leaving Mérida, we skirt the Mayan ruins of the Puuc Hills (*puuc* means "hill" in the local language), driving south through Muna, Ticul, Oxkutzkab, and Tekax, little towns where Alfonzo greets residents in Yucatec Mayan as well as Spanish. Stephens, too, passed this way. He writes glowingly of Ticul, where he once recuperated from a bout of fever and, on another occasion, "settled down at a fancy ball amid music, lights, and pretty women." At Yotolin we view a Catholic church where the original builders in the 1500s, through habit or rebelliousness, added symbols of the Mayan rain god Chac to the back of the church.

Chacmultún, a set of ruins on the crest of sun-baked hills, harbors no signs of life until an iguana darts out of the underbrush at my feet. I wonder whether

Chacmultún might be one of the "unnamed ruins" encountered by Stephens. Farther south, in Quintana Roo, we admire Kohunlich, the gardenlike setting for four-foot-tall stucco masks of the Mayan sun god.

Our ultimate destination is the Río Bec sites, Mayan cities from the classic period, 250 to 850 A.D., that are rarely visited because of the lack of tourist amenities. After one night at a truck stop in Xpuhil, Alfonzo arranges for us to camp at Becán, a grand Mayan ceremonial center about six miles down the road. When necessary, we return to Xpuhil to use the shower.

Our group sets up tents at Becán in the middle of a wide, grassy plaza bounded by pyramids on four sides. Wind whistles through our refuge at night (the breath of the gods), and our sleeping-bag view of the stars makes it easy to understand how the Maya came to excel as astronomers.

During the day, we venture to other sites in a flatbed truck, the kind that carries Mexican laborers to the fields. Parrots and great-tailed grackles soar overhead as skeletal tree branches slap at us. Strangler figs wrap themselves around victim trees, and *chicozapotes* wear chevronlike stripes where their trunks have been slashed for sap.

A veteran *chiclero* accompanies us to the ruins—Juan Briseño, renowned locally as the "rediscoverer" of Río Bec B. As Juan tells it, many years ago archaeologists stumbled upon an exquisite temple deep in the jungle, but by the 1970s the trail was lost to rampant growth. When they asked locals if they knew the location of Río Bec B, Juan, among others, shrugged no. Finally someone thought to show the old *chiclero* a photo of the temple they were looking for. *"Ah, sí,"* replied Juan, and led them to it. And he guides us to it, swinging a machete in a wide arc to clear a path for us to follow.

There, far from the tourist crowds, is the intricately carved facade of Río Bec B. The sense of stumbling across forgotten, seldom-visited ruins grows even more pronounced at Hormiguero and at foliage-shrouded Payán. That internal gong I hear is the thrill of discovery, however belated.

To enter the main temple at Chicanná, you step into the mouth of a monster, stone fangs curving over your head. Spiral eyes stare vacantly into the jungle, and stylized carvings of snakes flank the jaws. The squarish opening suggests the entrance to Xibalba, the Mayan netherworld. It's not hard to imagine eighth-century Mayan commoners watching in awe as Mayan priest-nobles emerged through these unearthly portals.

For our foray into Calakmul, we heave tents and sleeping bags onto the back of the flatbed truck, stash a cooler with beer and soft drinks, and climb in after them. Then we dodge branches snapping overhead as the truck bounces along the narrow track hacked out of the jungle like a green tunnel. Elias, Juan's son, cuts back branches and vines with his machete. Along the way, we glimpse foxes, deer, parrots, wild turkeys, *chachalaca*, and the endangered *curasao*.

As we explore the forest around our camp, a trio of spider monkeys chatters excitedly overhead. We laugh at their antics until a branch crashes to the ground at our feet. "Be careful!" warns Alfonzo. "When they're agitated, that's not all they drop!" Shielding our heads, we scurry back to the safety of the clearing.

Fading golden light illuminates an excavated temple at Calakmul. We hike to its base and crawl over it like lizards seeking the sun. It's impressive, but it represents only a small portion of this once-powerful city that extended over 40 square miles in its Mayan heyday.

The next morning we embark on the most treacherous climb of our trip, scaling the enormous, overgrown main pyramid at Calakmul. Not only is the ascent steep, but trying to get a foothold in the loose limestone proves unnerving. Above me, I hear John lose his footing and slide downward a few feet, grunt, then scramble upward again. Soon I hear only my own labored breathing and the gravelly sounds of my hiking boots on the incline.

At the top, I find the group's members resting on the pyramid's peak, staring across an invisible border into Guatemala. Alfonzo points out a hump on the flat horizon of the Petén: El Mirador, the nearest metropolis in the days when no arbitrary lines divided Mayan city-states.

Back at ground level, Elias, who once worked under the archaeologist at Calakmul, slashes his way through the underbrush to lead us to hidden places in the forest where a carved stone and a fallen stela lie. The carvings on the stones tantalize us with clues to the lives of rulers and captives whose stories are recorded here.

Alfonzo slakes our thirst for Mayan lore with one more "incident." He persuades Florentino García, the archaeologist at an early classic site, to allow us on the grounds while work proceeds. The one proviso: no photos.

Hands at our sides like well-behaved schoolchildren, we group ourselves in a semicircle around García. Behind him, workmen have excavated an ornately carved temple. A specialist applies preservative to the exposed stone as though he were restoring an oil painting. Above our heads, barefoot workers string together a bamboo scaffolding, the base of a protective cover that will shield the restoration during the coming rainy season.

Alfonzo asks García what he calls this site. "Balamku," he replies, pointing out the carved sacred jaguar heads on the temple's facade—"Temple of the Jaguar" in Mayan. This naming of archaeological sites intrigues me. I had heard that Chichén Itzá meant "Well of the Itzá," and Uxmal "thrice-built," but I had imagined the names were bestowed by the inhabitants, not by archaeologists.

Climbing Uxmal's pyramids can be hard going, but the rewards are many. Joyce Gregory Wyels

The night before our departure from Becán, Juan Briseño and his wife, Dora Alicia, prepare a hearty barbecue for us, with black beans and homemade tortillas. The meat is lamb, but for some perverse reason I picture the cute little goats across the road and eat sparingly.

We have one more stop on our itinerary, one that prompted Stephens to write: "In the romance of the world's history, nothing ever impressed me more forcibly than the spectacle of this once great and lovely city, overturned, desolate, and lost; discovered by accident, overgrown with trees, it did not even have a name to distinguish it." To reach Palenque, Stephens and Catherwood struggled for 10 days over hazardous trails, battered by drenching rains, oppressive heat, hunger, and exhaustion. We, on the other hand, simply drive to the parking lot, purchase our tickets, and walk through the gate into what is, for many, the most beautiful of all Mayan cities.

At your right, as you enter the gate, the majestic Temple of the Inscriptions soars upward from the jungle clearing, backed by luxuriant green foliage carpeting the hills behind it. In 1952 this temple was the site of one of the greatest archaeological discoveries ever, when Alberto Ruz dug through centuries of rubble to uncover the tomb at the bottom of a long inside staircase. Behind the magnificent sarcophagus and the jade mask lay the earthly remains of Lord Pacal, the seventh-century ruler whose image now symbolizes the site of Palenque and its home state of Chiapas.

Del and I scale the broad staircase leading up the front of the pyramid. At the top, the trapdoorlike entrance is open, the one Ruz's eye for detail noticed after 12 centuries of sealed silence. Dell and I follow the same path Ruz took, sharply downward to a landing, then a 180-degree turn and the rest of the way down to ground level. Moisture covers our bodies, as it does the slick surfaces of the walls and stairs, and the air becomes dank and stifling.

An eerie red light now illumines the crypt where Ruz found Lord Pacal, more than 1,200 years after he passed to the Mayan netherworld. The 12-foot sarcophagus cover shows Pacal in a reclining position, poised between this world and the next. Behind him, an exquisitely rendered cross represents the sacred ceiba tree, with roots in Xibalba, its trunk projecting through the world of the living, and branches supporting a celestial bird. One look at the enormous carved stone, and that gong goes off in my head again. I glance at Dell. She hears it, too.

The Writer's Trail

Following in the Footsteps

Destination: Yucatán is magnificent archaeological sites and little Mayan villages, beach resorts, and ecological preserves. Numerous unexcavated mounds hint at further explorations of the Mayan legacy.

Location: The Yucatán Peninsula, which comprises the states of Yucatán, Campeche, and Quintana Roo, extends northward into the Caribbean Sea from the southeastern coast of Mexico.

Getting There: Aeroméxico and Mexicana fly to Mérida from Miami. Airlines that fly to Cancún include Aeroméxico (1-800-237-6639), American Airlines (1-800-433-7300), Continental (1-800-523-3273), Mexicana (1-800-531-7921), and United Airlines (1-800-241-4322).

Orientation: Tulum and Cobá can be easily visited from Cancún. Mérida makes a good base for seeing Chichén Itzá (east), Dzibalchaltun (north), and the sites to the south in the Puuc Hills: Uxmal, Sayil, Labná, Xlapac, and Kabah. New facilities on the edge of the Calakmul Biosphere Reserve put travelers in the midst of the Río Bec sites.

Getting Around: Renting a car is the most convenient way to reach most archaeological sites. Driving is easy in the northern part of the Yucatán Peninsula, though still hazardous at night. Car rentals in Cancún run about $40 per day: Alamo (1-800-327-9633), Budget (1-800-527-0700), and Hertz (1-800-654-3131). Car rentals in Mérida may be a little less expensive than those in Cancún. Some local rental agencies are Mexico Rent a Car ([52-99] 27-4916), Mundo Maya ([52-99] 24-6521), Wider Car Rental ([52-99] 23-2277), and Uxmal Rent a Car ([52-99] 23-2070.

Tip: The sign Topes is a warning that you're approaching speed bumps, a jolt if you don't anticipate them.

Literary Sleeps

Club Med Villas Arqueológicas: These hotels, which can be found at Cobá, Chichén Itzá, and Uxmal, were originally built for the workers excavating the ruins. Each has comfortable rooms, a nice restaurant, and a refreshing pool. Tel.: Chichén Itzá (1-800-258-2633), Uxmal ([52-99] 28-0644), Cobá ([52-98] 74-2087. Moderate.

Mérida: Hotel Casa del Balam is pleasant, with dark-wood colonial furniture and a shady courtyard. 488 Calle 60. Tel.: (52-99) 24-8844 or 1-800-235-4079 in U.S. Expensive. The Gran Hotel was a favorite of Fidel Castro. The turn-of-the-century Italianate building has recently been restored, but something of the hotel's former glory remains in the high-ceilinged loggias, Corinthian columns, and arches. 496 Calle 60. Tel.: (52-99) 23-6963. Moderate. The Hotel Dolores Alba is also a good bet; this hotel operates another place in Chichén Itzá. 464 Calle 63. Tel.: (52-99) 28-5650. Inexpensive.

Southern Campeche: The Ramada Chicanná Ecovillage is a new lodging. The one- and two-story solar-powered stucco villas are handsomely decorated and beautifully landscaped. Good food, a refreshing pool, and tours to the nearby ruins, including Calakmul, add up to make this place extremely comfortable and convenient. Reserve through Ramada Campeche. Tel.: (52-98) 16-2233. Moderate to expensive.

Literary Sites

Chichén Itzá: This spectacular Mayan site is located in the northern part of the Yucatán Peninsula in Yucatán state, about a three-hour drive from Cancún or a two-hour drive from Mérida. Restoration began here in 1923 and still continues. So far 18 structures have been excavated. The highlights include the Temples of the Warriors, the Jaguar, and the Bearded Man; the Sacred Cenote (a well); Kukulcán (a pyramid); and the Observatory.

Palenque: Perhaps the most breathtaking series of ruins in the Yucatán, Palenque is found in the western part of the peninsula, perched on the edge of the lush green Sierra de Chiapas rainforest in Chiapas state. Among the must-see structures are the Temple of the Inscriptions and the unusual Palace, with its four-story tower.

Uxmal: Fifty miles south of Mérida in Yucatán state, Uxmal is the greatest Mayan city of the Puuc Hills. Highlights include the Houses of the Magician/Diviner and the Turtles, the Palace of the Governors, and the Great Pyramid. The latter is 100 feet high.

 Tip: Make sure you wear good walking shoes when climbing around Mayan ruins. Arrive very early. The weather in the Yucatán is unpredictable, and the crowds that tour buses bring usually hit the ruins later in the day.

Icon Pastimes

Far Horizons runs a tour called Hidden Maya Cities of the Yucatán (see **Contacts** for details). Besides surveying the Mayan ruins, John Stephens and Frederick Catherwood explored some of the limestone caves in the region, an activity that's open to today's visitors. Stephens, apparently more gregarious than his artist companion, also went off on little forays of his own to inspect a church here, a village there, attending fiestas and religious processions everywhere. You can, too. Be prepared for a lot of walking and hiking uphill.

Contacts

Far Horizons Archaeological & Cultural Trips: P.O. Box 91900, Albuquerque, New Mexico 87199-1900 U.S. Tel.: 1-800-552-4575 or (505) 343-9400. Fax: (505) 343-8076. Web site: *www.farhorizon.com.*

Mexican Government Tourism Office: United States: 450 Park Avenue, Suite 1401, New York, New York 10022. Tel.: (212) 755-7261. Fax: (212) 755-2874. Canada: 2 Bloor Street West, Suite 1801, Toronto, Ontario M4W 3E2. Tel.: (416) 925-0704. Fax: (416) 925-6061. Web site: *www.mexico-travel.com.*

In a Literary Mood

Books

Gallenkamp, Charles. *Maya: The Riddle and Rediscovery of a Lost Civilization.* New York: Viking, 1985. This book presents John Stephens and Frederick Catherwood's explorations in the context of what was previously known about the Maya and what has been learned since. A good overview of Mayan archaeology.

Hunter, Bruce C. *A Guide to Ancient Maya Ruins.* Norman, OK: University of Oklahoma Press, 1986. Detailed maps, descriptions, and photos of 10 archaeological sites in Guatemala, 13 in Mexico, and Copán in Honduras.

Perera, Victor, and Robert D. Bruce. *The Last Lords of Palenque*. Boston: Little, Brown, 1982. An amazing anthropologically oriented tale of life among one group of present-day Maya, the well-studied and beleaguered Lacandón Maya.

Stephens, John L. *Incidents of Travel in Central America, Chiapas, and Yucatán*. New York: Dover Publications, 1969. This unabridged republication of the two-volume work originally published by Harper & Brothers in 1841 recounts Stephens and Catherwood's first trip to Mesoamerica, in which they spent some nine months exploring Copán, Quirigua, and Palenque. Their visit to Uxmal was cut short when Catherwood contracted malaria.

_____. *Incidents of Travel in Yucatán*. Edited by Karl Ackerman. Washington, D.C.: Smithsonian Institution Press, 1996. This condensed version of the work originally published by Harper & Brothers in 1843 records Stephens and Catherwood's second excursion through Yucatán. Here they report on some 44 sites, including Uxmal, Kabah, Sayil, Labná, Chichén Itzá, and Tulum.

Wright, Ronald. *Time Among the Maya*. New York: Weidenfeld & Nicolson, 1989. A fascinating account of the author's odyssey through the Mundo Maya of Belize, Guatemala, and Mexico, overlaid by an awareness of the importance of time in the Mayan cosmos.

Guidebooks

Conord, Bruce, and June Conord. *Adventure Guide to the Yucatán*. Edison, NJ: Hunter Publishing, 1998. The authors travel well beyond the established archaeological circuit, providing insights and useful information for the independent traveler.

Mallan, Chicki. *Yucatán Peninsula Handbook*. 6th ed. Chico, CA: Moon Publications, 1998. The latest update of a popular, reliable guide to the peninsula.

Rider, Nick. *Yucatán and Southern Mexico*. London: Cadogan, 1999. Well-researched guide delves into the history of the dynasties that ruled each of the great Mayan cities and includes the life stories of John Stephens and Frederick Catherwood as well as practical information.

Films/Videos

Bick, Jerry, William S. Gilmore, and Taylor Hackford (producers). *Against All Odds*. Taylor Hackford (director). Columbia, 1984. Columbia Tristar Home Video. Cast: Jeff Bridges, Rachel Ward, and James Woods. Partly filmed in Chichén Itzá, this lukewarm remake of the classic film noir *Out of the Past* needs all the help it can get from Mayan ruins.

Wild, Nettie, Betty Carson, and Kirk Tougas (producers). *A Place Called Chiapas*. Nettie Wild (director). Documentary. CBC/Téléfilm Canada/NFB and others, 1998. Hit-and-miss agit-prop probe of long-running Zapatista Indian rebellion in Mexico's Chiapas state.

Web Sites

Mexico: *www2.planeta.com/mader/ecotravel/mexico/mexico.html*; *www.cancun.com*.

"It is the paradoxes in Yeats's

poetry that have lured me to this

emerald isle across the sea, a land

as passionate as the beating of a

bodhran drum, as peaceful as a

Celtic melody, as turbulent as

the moody Atlantic Ocean on a

Connemara shore, as magical as

a fairy ring on a moonlit eve."

5   Great Britain
      and Ireland

W. B. Yeats
Magic and Mystery in Ireland

Tanya Storr

CYCLING FROM SLIGO TOWN to Drumcliff in County Sligo, I reach William Butler Yeats's gravesite mid-morning, just as the sun warms the walls of the church. Apart from a lone rooster strolling along the top of the churchyard's low stone wall, the place is deserted. Off in the distance, Ben Bulben stands watch, an enigmatic sentinel hiding untold secrets within its slopes. I am in Ireland, land of magic and mystery.

It is the paradoxes in Yeats's poetry that have lured me to this emerald isle across the sea, a land as passionate as the beating of a bodhran drum, as peaceful as a Celtic melody, as turbulent as the moody Atlantic Ocean on a Connemara shore, as magical as a fairy ring on a moonlit eve. Proud nationalist, rejected lover, mystic visionary, and accomplished writer, Yeats personified the complexities of his homeland.

His poetry and plays, wrought from a foundation of myth and culture centuries old, won him the Nobel Prize for literature in 1923 and continue to earn him the praise of readers around the world. Like the legends that inspired them, Yeats's words illuminate the beauty of the Irish landscape and document the tempestuous heritage of his people. He speaks of noble beggars and saintly fools, violent clashes and unrequited love, ancient towers and great houses, and paints a picture of Ireland so compelling that I felt drawn to explore the places he loved.

Yeats was born in Dublin in 1865 but spent a good part of his childhood in Sligo, the county where his grandparents resided. Many of his early poems gleaned their inspiration from Sligo. Brimming with magic and pastoral imagery, these poems are a fitting tribute to an exquisite region. In his *Autobiographies*,

Yeats recalls his mother reminiscing about Sligo when the family was living in London: "it was always assumed between her and us that Sligo was more beautiful than other places." Yeats said that when he began to write he hoped to find his audience in Sligo. His brother, Jack B. Yeats, who became one of Ireland's best-known painters, once said he never completed a painting "without putting a thought of Sligo into it."

The border between mystical experience and tangible reality is blurred in Yeats's Sligo-based poetry. Fairies, druids, and legendary figures are as much a part of the population as are the Sligo townspeople. At picturesque Glencar Waterfall, Yeats envisioned fairies whispering in the ears of sleeping trout. In "The Stolen Child," the poet describes fairies dancing in the moonlight on the lovely beach at Rosses Point, where he spent many childhood summers: "Far off by furthest Rosses/We foot it all the night/Weaving olden dances/Mingling hands and mingling glances/Till the moon has taken flight . . ."

The beauty of the Sligo countryside is reflected in the natural imagery of Yeats's early poems. In "The Lake Isle of Innisfree," he immortalized a tree-covered island on Lough Gill, where he dreamed of building a small cabin and living "alone in the bee-loud glade." Across the water from this idyllic spot, Dooney Rock offers sweeping vistas of the lough and its enchanting islands. Here Yeats was inspired to write "The Fiddler of Dooney," a poem about a fiddler playing tunes so merry they incited folk to "dance like a wave of the sea."

Yeats was a frequent visitor to Lissadell House, the ancestral home of the Gore-Booth family on the northern shore of Sligo Bay. The Georgian mansion was built in 1830-35 for Sir Robert Gore-Booth, who mortgaged his estate during the Great Famine of the 1840s in order to provide food for everyone in the area. Designed by London architect Francis Goodwin, the house was built according to classical precedents. With its gray limestone exterior, Doric and Ionic columns, and porte cochere, Lissadell has an aura of stately grandeur. The mansion sits on a terraced lawn facing Sligo Bay and is surrounded by pretty woods.

Yeats first saw Lissadell from his grandmother's carriage as a child, and later received an invitation to visit the family when he was in his late twenties. He became a close friend of the Gore-Booth daughters, Constance and Eva, and traveled the winding, tree-lined road to Lissadell often. Constance, who chose a turbulent life as an Irish nationalist, was a key participant in the 1916 Easter Rising against the British and was sentenced to death for her part in it. However, her death sentence was later rescinded and she became the first woman elected to Britain's House of Commons, a seat she never took. Eva, on the other hand, was a strong supporter of social causes and a poet. Yeats wrote a poem in honor

Traditional currach boats are still commonly seen on Ireland's west coast. Courtesy of Irish Tourist Board

of the two sisters, "In Memory of Eva Gore-Booth and Con Markievicz," that is inscribed on a sign at Lissadell's entrance: "The light of evening, Lissadell/Great windows open to the south/Two girls in silk kimonos, both/Beautiful, one a gazelle."

Constance named her daughter after Maeve, the first-century warrior queen of Connaught who is a recurring figure in Celtic legends and in Yeats's poetry. According to popular belief, Queen Maeve is buried in the cairn grave on the summit of Knocknarea (1,083 feet high), west of Sligo Town. Archaeologists, however, assert that the large mound of stones probably marks a 3,000-year-old passage tomb. The grave has never been excavated, so its contents, buried beneath 40,000 tons of stone, remain a mystery. The top of Knocknarea is certainly a fitting place for the grave of a famous queen, with a wide-angle view encompassing the ocean, the surrounding mountains, and the farmland below.

After he moved away, Yeats visited Sligo regularly, and the poet's presence still seems to linger in the county's vibrant green hills and tranquil waterways. Yeats's final resting place is located, as he had wished, "under bare Ben Bulben's head." Before he died in Roquebrune, France, in 1939, Yeats asked that his body be buried there temporarily and then dug up and brought to Sligo a year or so after his death. Almost a decade later, his request was fulfilled and he was reinterred in quiet Drumcliff Churchyard in 1948, where his great-grandfather, John Yeats, had been rector from 1805 to 1846.

The poet's simple limestone headstone is inscribed with his own epitaph: "Cast a cold eye/On life, on death./Horseman, pass by!" Yeats's wife, George, is buried with him. An ornate 10th-century high cross stands opposite the grave, and the base of a round tower—all that remains of a monastery dating back to 575 A.D.—is situated across the road. Close by, Ben Bulben (1,730 feet high) stands watch over the small churchyard, its velvety slopes and flat summit changing hue as the clouds fling shadows across it. Ben Bulben, like Knocknarea, holds mythical status in Celtic lore. Yeats's poem "The Hosting of the Sidhe" was inspired by a folk legend about the Sidhe, or fairy host, riding on the wind between Ben Bulben and Knocknarea. According to the legend, the Sidhe live inside or under Ben Bulben and leave on horseback from a magic door in the side of the mountain.

While images of Sligo are prevalent in Yeats's early poems, his later works contain many references to people and places in County Galway. Coole Park, a Galway Georgian country home and estate owned by Lady Augusta Gregory, was a place the poet frequented. Yeats first visited Coole Park in 1896, and Lady Gregory, a fellow poet, playwright, and author, quickly became his patron and great friend. Widowed at age 44, Lady Gregory shared Yeats's strong interest in

Irish folklore. The two collaborated on many projects and were key figures behind the Irish literary and artistic revival.

Spending many summers as a guest at Coole Park, Yeats enjoyed the company of the other Irish literary and artistic intelligentsia who gathered there. The house became a magnet for several influential minds of the time, including the poet and artist George Russell (AE), Gaelic scholar Douglas Hyde, novelist George Moore, playwrights John Middleton Synge and George Bernard Shaw, patron of the arts Hugh Lane (Lady Gregory's nephew), and Yeats's brother, Jack.

Images of Coole Park are numerous in Yeats's poems, and he named two books of poetry—*In the Seven Woods* (1908) and *The Wild Swans at Coole* (1919)—after the beautiful estate. For Yeats, Coole was a place of refuge from the hurried pace of Dublin and London. He would walk "in the seven woods" and admire the "nine-and-fifty swans," ruminating about Irish politics and his torrid yet exasperating love affair with Maud Gonne.

Gonne, a six-foot-tall regal beauty with a revolutionary spirit, captured the poet's heart and inspired much of his love poetry. Championing the causes of Ireland's poor, she was a well-known and much-loved figure among the oppressed. In the poem "Her Praise," Yeats sings of both his own love for Gonne and that of the poor, "both old and young," who also cherished her. Born an English Protestant, Gonne had Irish Ascendancy roots on her father's side. Yeats met her in January 1889 and first proposed to her in 1891, as she waited for a train at Howth station, but was turned down then and on every occasion thereafter. In "The Old Age of Queen Maeve," Yeats likens Gonne to Queen Maeve: "For you, although you've not her wandering heart,/Have all that greatness . . ."

When Gonne married Major John MacBride in 1903 after converting to Catholicism, Yeats wrote a number of bittersweet love poems, among them "Never Give All the Heart" and "O Do Not Love Too Long." Gonne and Major MacBride moved to Paris, but the marriage quickly went sour and Gonne tried to sue MacBride for separation in 1905. He refused, and when Gonne attempted to return home to Ireland that same year, she was denied entry and forced to remain in exile. Gonne was finally freed from her marriage when MacBride was executed for his role in the Easter Rising, and she came home in 1917, using a fake passport provided by Yeats. Still smitten by his love for her, Yeats proposed to Gonne one more time and, once again, she said no.

After Gonne's final rejection, Yeats married Miss George Hyde-Lees in 1917. The poet's young wife (when they wed, she was 15; he was 52) shared his interest in mysticism and possessed the gift of automatic writing, her penmanship providing metaphors and symbols for Yeats's *A Vision* and other works. Yeats had bought a 13th-century Norman tower house, Thoor Ballylee, for 35 pounds a year before his marriage. Originally a fortified Norman house built for members of the Protestant gentry, the tower had changed hands several times over the centuries. At one time, the building, located only two and a half miles from Coole Park, was part of the Gregory estate. The Gregorys sold Thoor Ballylee and some land to the Congested Districts Board and, since no one else wanted it, Yeats was able to purchase the run-down tower for a low price in 1916.

He and George went to work renovating the tower with the help of local craftsmen, as these words carved on a stone near the entrance attest: "I, the poet William Yeats,/With old mill boards and sea-green slates,/And smithy work from the Gort forge,/Restored this tower for my wife George . . ." They managed to renovate all but the uppermost room, which they had hoped to turn into a study. The tower became the Yeatses' summer home for the next 12 years.

Situated on the banks of a bubbling millstream, the tower was both a domestic haven and an important poetic stimulus for Yeats. The structure and its winding staircase are recurring symbols in his poetry of the 1920s and 1930s, particularly in *The Tower* (1928) and *The Winding Stair and Other Poems* (1933). Yeats would climb the spiral stone staircase, rubbed smooth by the footsteps of several centuries of occupants, enter his "chamber arched with stone," and write by candlelight in front of a turf fire. Sometimes he would go up to the tower's rooftop and "pace upon the battlements," gazing at the countryside visible for miles around. Writing in 1926 to Olivia Shakespear, his first lover and lifelong friend, Yeats commented: "We are at our Tower and I am writing poetry as I always do here, and as always happens, no matter how I begin, it becomes love poetry before I am finished with it."

Life at Thoor Ballylee wasn't always completely peaceful, however. Sometimes fierce storms would sweep in from the Atlantic, bringing howling winds that buffeted the tower's walls and filled the poet's mind with fear for the years ahead. It was during one of these Atlantic gales, while watching his young daughter sleep, that Yeats wrote "A Prayer for My Daughter." And although the tower is located in an isolated spot out in the countryside, evidence of the Irish Civil War (1921-22) came close to home, as Yeats describes in "Meditations in Time of Civil War": "Last night they trundled down the road/That dead young soldier in his blood." Whether he was penning happy scenes of domestic bliss or brooding about predictions of apocalyptic times to come, one thing is certain: Yeats found Thoor Ballylee to be a wellspring of inspiration for his work.

Over the years, the poet spent a good deal of time in Dublin, the city of his birth. Vibrant, stimulating, and controversial, Dublin was a place where Yeats was able to realize some of his artistic visions. One of these visions was to build up a thriving national theater, using material drawn from Celtic folklore and

Sligo Town and environs is Yeats Country. This statue of the master poet, complete with his poetry tattooed on his stylized body, is found outside the Ulster Bank on Stephen Street. Tanya Storr

Irish culture. Together with Lady Gregory and the writer Edward Martyn, Yeats founded the Irish National Theatre Society in 1902, a major achievement in the history of Irish dramatic art. The three first discussed forming the society when visiting the home of Count Floribund de Basterot, south of Galway City near Ballyvaughan, in August 1897. Yeats composed the society's manifesto: "We propose to have performed in Dublin in the spring of every year certain Celtic and Irish plays, which whatever their degree of excellence, will be written with a high ambition . . ."

Yeats was president of the new society, and George Russell (AE) and Douglas Hyde were vice presidents. With great excitement, the society opened its first play, Yeats's *Cathleen ni Houlihan*, in May 1899. In 1904 a philanthropic Englishwoman named Annie Horniman bought the building that became Dublin's Abbey Theatre and gave it to the society, furnishing it with an annual subsidy. *Cathleen ni Houlihan* was also the first play performed there.

The Irish National Theatre Society helped playwrights such as J. M. Synge and Sean O'Casey gain notoriety, and greatly furthered the reputation of Irish theater in general. However, Dublin audiences weren't always totally receptive to the plays at the Abbey. The crowd's reaction to the 1907 premiere of Synge's *The Playboy of the Western World* was so disruptive that Yeats had to call in the police. In 1926, after the audience responded loudly and unfavorably to O'Casey's *The Plough and the Stars*, Yeats, bristling with anger, walked out on the stage and scolded the crowd.

When Yeats was spending time in Dublin, he resided in Merrion Square. Designed by architect John Ensor in the 1760s, the square is distinguished by its elegant Georgian redbrick houses, complete with fanlights over the doors and foot scrapers on the top steps. A pretty central park, tumbling wisteria, and innumerable flowers flanking its walkway add to the square's charms. Yeats, one of many well-known figures who lived in the square, first resided at 52 Merrion Square East and then, in 1922-28, at 82 Merrion Square South. Russell, or AE, worked at No. 84, while Yeats's brother, Jack, lived in nearby Fitzwilliam Square.

The original Abbey Theatre burnt down in 1951, but a new building was erected in 1966 to take its place. The Abbey remains a thriving center of Irish theater. A collection of portraits of the Abbey's founders, actors, managers, and playwrights hangs in the building. These include paintings of Lady Gregory, Russell, and Annie Horniman by Jack Yeats, and one of W. B. Yeats by Sean O'Sullivan.

Today Dublin is home to two museums with Yeats connections. The first, the Dublin Writers' Museum, is a must-see for Yeats aficionados. The museum contains first editions of the poet's works, several photographs and newspaper clippings, and busts of Yeats and other famous Irish writers. In the spring of 1999, the Yeats Museum opened in the National Gallery of Ireland. This museum is a permanent tribute to the artistic talents of the Yeats family, in particular John Butler Yeats (W.B's father, a famous portraitist) and Jack Yeats.

In the end, though, Sligo and Galway are the places where Yeats's heart resides. The legacy of the poet's connection to the former is readily apparent, both in Sligo Town and the country surrounding it. In fact, it's still possible to see most of the sites mentioned in his early poems, many of them essentially unchanged from when he knew them.

In Irish, Lough Gill means "Lake Beauty." According to local legend, a silver bell from the Dominican Abbey in Sligo was thrown into the lough, and only those who haven't committed any sins can hear its pealing. I take a boat tour on a balmy, late-spring afternoon. As we pass by Innisfree, Dooney Rock, and other places celebrated in Yeats's work, the captain reads some of the poet's verse over the loudspeaker in a thick Sligo brogue, while his son stands behind the boat's small bar and pours pints of stout and ale for the passengers.

West of Sligo Town, I hike up Knocknarea's windy summit and add a small stone to Queen Maeve's purported cairn grave to ensure her good wishes, as all those who visit there are advised to do. Looking out across the countryside toward Ben Bulben, I think of Yeats's fascination with the legend of the Sidhe and their ghostly horse ride on the wind between the two peaks.

In Sligo Town itself there are other points of interest for Yeats fans. The Yeats Memorial Building, located close to the corner of O'Connell Street at the Douglas Hyde Bridge, is the site of the Yeats International Summer School. An annual event, the school attracts Yeats scholars from around the world. The building hosts art exhibitions during the rest of the year. An unusual sculpture of Yeats, with every inch of his body tattooed in lines of his poetry, stands outside the Ulster Bank. The Sligo Museum, on Stephen Street, contains a Yeats room full of interesting photos, manuscripts, and articles about the poet.

In County Galway both Coole Park and Thoor Ballylee are now open to the public, although the house at Coole Park no longer stands. It was demolished in 1941, nine years after Lady Gregory's death. Yeats predicted the fate of the once lively gathering place in a poem entitled "Coole Park, 1929": "Here, traveller, scholar, poet, take your stand/When all these rooms and passages are gone,/When nettles wave upon a shapeless mound/And saplings root among the broken stone . . ." Now a national forest and wildlife park, the estate is still home to the Autograph Tree, a copper beech upon which many of Lady Gregory's famous guests carved their initials.

Yeats also predicted that Thoor Ballylee would fall into ruin. Indeed, the tower was in pretty bad shape when the Kiltartan Society formed in 1961. With the assistance of the Irish Tourist Board/Bord Failte and Ireland West Tourism, the society restored the tower and opened it officially as a tourist site in 1989. It now looks the same as it did when the Yeats family lived in it.

Following a lovely country road lined with hawthorn and primroses, I arrive at Thoor Ballylee on a sunny spring morning with just a hint of breeze. Situated on the edge of a stream next to an old stone bridge, the tower is the epitome of arcadian beauty. Inside, I watch an audiovisual presentation on Yeats's life before venturing up the famous winding stair to see the family's living quarters. A tape recording in each room (activated by pressing a button) is available in seven languages. The family's furniture and decor have been carefully replicated, and there are even turf bricks in the fireplaces. A resident kestrel has built a nest inside a tower window, just as one did when Yeats lived there. The view of the surrounding countryside as seen from the battlements stretches for miles around.

Once outside again, I walk along the stream until I reach the remains of an old mill that Yeats used to visit. The light breeze ripples the nearby water as I look back at the tower and smile. It's clear now what the poet meant when he wrote "To leave here is to leave beauty behind."

The Writer's Trail

Following in the Footsteps

Destination: Ireland is famous for its green fields, literary culture, and friendly pubs. If you go, be prepared to linger for a while in each place to truly soak up the atmosphere. Outside of the big cities, Ireland is rarely in a hurry. The Irish are known for their "gift of the gab" and generally love to talk to travelers, whether over a pint of Guinness or while sharing a long bus or train journey.

Location: Three hundred miles long and 150 miles wide, Ireland is an English-speaking island on the northwestern edge of Europe in the North Atlantic Ocean. The Republic of Ireland, with a population of about 3.7 million, fills three-quarters of the island and its capital is Dublin. Northern Ireland, with a population of around 1.6 million, takes up the remainder and is part of the United Kingdom. Its capital is Belfast.

Getting There: From North America to the Republic of Ireland, airlines either fly into Shannon International Airport near Limerick on the island's southwest coast or into Dublin International Airport on the central-east coast. Some airlines fly into both airports. Dublin's airport is six miles north of the capital's center. Airlines that fly direct from the United States to Ireland include the Emerald Isle's Aer Lingus (tel.: 1-800-223-6537; Web site: *www.aerlingus.ie*), Delta (1-800-241-4141), Continental (1-800-231-0856), and Russia's Aeroflot (1-888-340-6400). Air Canada ([416] 925-2311, 1-800-361-5373, or 1-800-776-3000) operates flights direct to Ireland. Airlines that fly from the United States and Canada to cities in Britain, with connections to Ireland, include Air Canada, American (1-800-433-7300), British Airways (1-800-247-9297), Continental, Delta, Northwest (1-800-447-4747), TWA (1-800-892-4141), and United (1-800-241-6522). Airlines that fly from airports in London, England, to Ireland include Aer Lingus, British Midland (1-800-788-0555), City Flyer Express (1-800-247-9297), and Ryanair (1-800-365-5563). By sea, you can take ferries from ports in the United Kingdom to ports in Ireland through Irish Ferries (Scots-American Travel: [561] 563-2856; Dublin: [353-1] 661-0511); Stena Sealink (Britrail Travel International: (1-800-677-8585 in the United States; 1-800-555-2748 in Canada); Norse Irish Ferries ([44-1232] 779090 in Belfast); Seacat Scotland ([353-1] 874-1231 in Ireland); P&O European Ferries (Scots-American Travel [561] 563-2856); Swansea/Cork Ferries ([44-1792] 456116 in Wales; [353-21] 271166 in Cork). Scheduled ferry services also run between France and Ireland.

Orientation: Dublin is situated on Ireland's east coast, approximately one hour by air from London, England. Sligo is located on the northwest coast of Ireland, approximately four hours' drive from Dublin. Galway is also on the west coast, approximately two and a half hours by car south from Sligo or four hours' drive west from Dublin.

Tip: If you travel around Ireland by bus, be prepared to join in on sing-alongs. The Irish like to interact in confined spaces, and you'll be expected to join in with a few verses. It can be great fun once you overcome your shyness.

Getting Around: Rental cars are available and cost approximately $300 per week in high season (July and August) and $200 per week mid-season (May to June, September). Agencies include Malone Car Rental (1-800-229-0984), Avis (1-800-331-1084), and Hertz (1-800-654-3131). Ireland has good train and bus systems linking towns and cities with convenient scheduled services. Toll-free calls in North America to Irish Rail and Irish Bus: (1-800-243-7687). In Ireland: Irish Rail ([353-1] 836-6222); Irish Bus ([353-1] 836-6111). If you want to try a unique method of transportation within Ireland, rent a horse-drawn caravan through Into the West Drawn Caravans ([353-1] 509-45147.

Literary Sleeps

All Irish cities and towns boast numerous bed-and-breakfasts and guesthouses, but here are a few hotels that have literary connections, are close to literary sites, or are just simply comfortable, centrally located lodgings.

Dublin: The height of elegance in the Republic of Ireland's capital is the 160-room Shelbourne Hotel, where you should at least experience the afternoon tea. St. Stephen's Green. Tel.: (353-1) 676-6471. Extremely expensive. Between Merrion and Fitzwilliam Squares is the 26-room Longfield's Hotel. 9-10 Fitzwilliam Street Lower. Tel.: (353-1) 676-1367). Expensive. The 70-room Wynn's Hotel is a few steps away from the Abbey Theatre. 35-36 Abbey Street Lower. Tel.: (353-1) 874-5131. Moderate. The 55-room Ormond Hotel on the Liffey River figured in James Joyce's *Ulysses* (see the plaque outside). Ormond Quay Upper. Tel.: (353-1) 872-1811. Moderate. On the other side of the Liffey, the 47-room Georgian House is equally close to St. Stephen's Green and Merrion Square. 20-21 Baggot Street Lower. Tel.: (353-1) 661-8832. Moderate. George Bernard Shaw lived in the 40-room Harcourt Hotel from 1874 to 1876. 60 Harcourt Street. Tel.: (353-1) 478-3677. Moderate.

Galway City: Those with a penchant for luxury should try the Great Southern Hotel, which takes up one entire side of Eyre Square. Tel.: (353-91) 564041. Expensive. Jury's Galway Inn, on the other hand, will be kind to your pocketbook. Quay Street. Tel.: (353-91) 566444. Inexpensive to moderate. Also, check out Doorus An Óige Youth Hostel, south of Galway City off the main road to Ballyvaughan. It's a good place to stay if you're visiting Coole Park and Thoor Ballylee. The historic building was once owned by Count Floribund de Basterot. W. B. Yeats, Lady Gregory, and Edward Martyn first discussed the possibility of founding a national theater society during a visit here in August 1897. Tel.: (353-91) 637512. Inexpensive.

Sligo Town: The Silver Swan is a cozy, friendly hotel in the town's center. Tel.: (353-71) 43231. Inexpensive to moderate. Another good economical bet is the Clarence Hotel. Wine Street. Tel.: (353-71) 62101. Inexpensive.

 Tip: The Irish pub experience, not to be missed and hard to avoid, is a good way to get to know locals, especially in small towns. Before you know it, you'll be supplying answers to the barkeep's crossword puzzle, sharing the "crack," or yarns, with barflies, or standing your new mates drinks in the Irish tradition.

Literary Sites

Dublin

Abbey Theatre: Located just north of the Liffey River on the corner of Marlborough Street and Abbey Street Lower, the Abbey opened for business in 1904 and is still a major showcase for Irish theater. The original building burned down in 1951; its replacement is unfortunately uninspired and drab. Check out news of upcoming performances on the theater's Web site at *www.abbeytheatre.ie*. Tel: (353-1) 878-7222.

Dublin Writers' Museum: This mecca for anyone interested in Irish writing features the Gallery of Writers, with busts and portraits of Ireland's leading literary lights, including W. B. Yeats. The museum also displays a sizable collection of authors' letters, photographs, and first editions. There's a good restaurant and a bookstore on the premises, and next door the Irish Writers' Centre provides a meeting and working place for practicing writers. Open Monday to Saturday from 10:00 a.m. to 5:00 p.m.; 11:30 a.m. to 6:00 p.m. on Sunday; June, July, August open until 7:00 p.m. Admission fee. 18 Parnell Square North. Tel.: (353-1) 872-2077.

Merrion Square: Situated south of the Liffey River and near Trinity College, this Georgian square dates back to 1762. The roll call of the famous who have lived here is quite impressive: W. B. Yeats, George Russell (AE), Sir William Wilde and Lady Wilde (Oscar's parents), Daniel O'Connell, Erwin Schrödinger, and Joseph Sheridan Le Fanu.

National Gallery of Ireland: Along with a great selection of paintings by Ireland's best artists, the museum features works by British painters such as Sir Joshua Reynolds, William Hogarth, Thomas Gainsborough, and J. M. W. Turner. There are also canvases by El Greco, Francisco Goya, and Pablo Picasso. One of the highlights of the gallery is the Yeats Museum, with works by W. B. Yeats's father (John B.) and younger brother (Jack). Open Monday to Saturday from 10:00 a.m. to 5:30 p.m. (to 8:30 p.m. on Thursday); 2:00 p.m. to 5:00 p.m. on Sunday. Guided tours are available. Admission free. West side of Merrion Square. Tel.: (353-1) 661-5133.

Galway

Coole Park: Lady Gregory's former estate (minus her stately home) is located south of Galway City, just outside the town of Gort. The park is now a national forest and is open daily from 10:00 a.m. to dusk. A visitor center is open from mid-April to October. Admission fee. Tel.: (353-91) 31804.

Thoor Ballylee: Located approximately one mile off the N18, the main Galway Limerick road, and one mile off the N66, the main Gort-Loughrea road, W. B. Yeats's former home is near Coole Park. Follow the signposts. Admission fee. Group rates are available. Open daily from Easter to the end of September from 10:00 a.m. to 6:00 p.m. Tel.: (353-91) 631436.

Sligo

Drumcliff: W. B. Yeats and his wife, George, are buried in the small Protestant churchyard, located north of Sligo Town and east of Lissadell House and Carney on the N15. Yeats's grave is on the left near the church. An ancient ruined round tower and a 10th-century high cross are found not far from the churchyard. Three miles from Drumcliff you'll find Glencar Lough and Waterfall.

Lissadell House: The ancestral home of the Gore-Booth family is situated near Carney, northwest of Drumcliff. Open June to September Monday to Saturday from 10:30 a.m. to 12:15 p.m. and 2:00 p.m. to 4:15 p.m. Guided tours are available. Visitors are also welcome to walk around the grounds. Admission fee. Tel.: (353-71) 63150.

Lough Gill: Two Yeats sites are found in the lough, which is situated southeast of Sligo Town. They include Dooney Rock in the southwest corner of the lough, and the Lake Isle of Innisfree, made famous by Yeats's poem, near the south-central shore. You can experience the lough by boat via the Wild Rose Water Bus, which is licensed for 72 passengers and departs from Dorley Park in Sligo Town (2:30 p.m. and 5:30 p.m.) and Parke's Castle in neighboring County Leitrim (12:30 p.m., 1:30 p.m., and 4:30 p.m.) daily from June to September. During other months of the year, phone ahead to confirm times. The water taxi's captain, George McGoldrick, recites Yeats poems while the boat passes by sites of interest such as Innisfree. Tel.: (353-71) 64266. Adult fares are approximately $9 for a two-hour tour and $8 for a one-hour tour. The fare for children is approximately $3 for either tour.

Sligo Town: In the town itself, near the corner of O'Connell Street at the Douglas Hyde Bridge, is the Yeats Memorial Building ([353-71] 42693). The Sligo Museum, with the Yeats Room, is on Stephen Street across the river. A stylized sculpture of Yeats, with his poetry tattooed all over it, is located outside the Ulster Bank. also on Stephen Street, between Markievicz Road and Holborn Street. Rosses Point, which W. B. Yeats visited frequently as a boy, is a picturesque seaside resort northwest of the town. Knocknarea, west of town, is a hilltop cairn grave popularly believed to house the remains of the legendary Queen Maeve. Surprisingly the cairn and its 40,000 tons of stone have never been excavated, even though some archaeologists speculate that a tomb the size and significance of Newgrange in County Meath may lie underneath.

Icon Pastimes

Spend time on Lough Gill, one of Yeats's favorite places, and admire the Lake Isle of Innisfree. Climb up Dooney Rock and contemplate the lough's beautiful islands from above. Stop by Glencar Lough and Waterfall. Visit Lissadell, ancestral home of the Gore-Booth family, where Yeats used to go for frequent visits. Climb Knocknarea and admire the view and the mountain's mythic stature. Visit Drumcliff Churchyard, where Yeats is buried, and observe Ben Bulben in the distance. Stop by the Yeats Tavern Restaurant, within walking distance of the poet's burial place, for a meal afterward. Go to Thoor Ballylee and climb up the famous winding stair to view the tower rooms and battlements. Stop in at nearby Coole Park and walk through the seven woods, as Yeats used to do during his summer visits there. Take in a show at the Abbey Theatre and stroll around Merrion Square in Dublin.

Contacts

Ireland Reservations Direct: To make reservations for hotels, bed-and-breakfasts, farm-houses, guesthouses, hostels, and self-catering accommodation, call 1-800-398-4376 or e-mail *gulliver@fexco.ie*.

Irish Tourist Board: 345 Park Avenue, New York, New York 10154 U.S. Tel.: 1-800-223-6470. Web site: *www.ireland.travel.ie*.

In a Literary Mood

Books

Browne, Frank. *Father Browne's Ireland: Remarkable Images of People and Places.* Dublin: Wolfhound Press, 1989. A book filled with fascinating black-and-white photographs of Ireland by Frank Browne (1880-1960), a Jesuit priest who captured the images during the first half of the 20th century. Browne's photos from each of the 32 counties offer a portrayal of Ireland as it looked in W. B. Yeats's time. While Yeats was writing about places in Sligo, Browne was photographing them. Browne also admired the pastoral beauty of Drumcliff Churchyard and took pictures of it some time before Yeats decided he wanted to be buried there.

Foster, R. F. *W. B. Yeats: A Life. I. The Apprentice Mage.* Oxford: Oxford University Press, 1997. This tome is a comprehensive and illuminating biography covering the poet's early years from 1865 to 1914.

Newby, Eric. *Round Ireland in Low Gear.* Hawthorn, Australia: Lonely Planet Journeys, 1998. First published in 1987, this is an inspiring and often humorous account of Eric and Wanda Newby's journey through Ireland by bicycle.

Uris, Jill, and Leon Uris. *Ireland: A Terrible Beauty.* New York: Doubleday, 1975. This coffee-table book contains more than 388 striking photographs of Ireland by Jill Uris, accompanied by insightful text by husband Leon. The book is divided into two parts: Book One focuses on the republic and Book Two documents the Troubles in Ulster. Jill's photos of gun battles in Belfast are a striking contrast to her dreamy scenics.

Yeats, W. B. *Autobiographies.* London: Macmillan, 1955. Yeats's memoirs allow the reader an intimate glimpse of the life of an extraordinary poet and intellect. *Autobiographies* also contains Yeats's 1923 Nobel Prize speech.

_____. *Fairy Tales of Ireland.* London: HarperCollins, 1990. Twenty Irish fairy tales collected by Yeats fill the pages of this volume. Yeats had a keen interest in Irish folklore, and many of his poems and plays draw upon this rich tradition.

_____. *W. B. Yeats Collected Poems.* Edited by Augustine Martin. London: Vintage, 1992. All admirers of Yeats should have a copy of this book close at hand. The introduction by Professor Martin of University College Dublin provides a fascinating overview of Yeats's work, and the notes to each poem at the back of the book are invaluable.

Guidebooks

Bence-Jones, Mark. *Burke's Guide to Country Houses: Volume I, Ireland.* London: Burke's Peerage Ltd., 1978.

Crowl, Philip A. *The Intelligent Traveller's Guide to Historic Ireland.* Chicago: Contemporary Books, Inc., 1990.

Fodor's 2000 Ireland. New York: Fodor's Travel Publications, 1999.

Fodor's Pocket Dublin. 1st ed. New York: Fodor's Travel Publications, 1998.

Ireland. 3rd ed. Hawthorn, Australia: Lonely Planet Publications, 1998.

Sullivan, Frank, and Fran Sullivan. *The Irish Bed & Breakfast Book.* Gretna, LA: Pelican Publishing, 1998.

Web Sites

Ireland: *www.ireland.travel.ie.*

W. B. Yeats: *www.fas.harvard.edu/~ndrose/yeats.html*; *www.panix.com/~wlinden/yeats.html*; *www.tally.demon.co.uk/sarah*; *www.geocities.com/Athens/5379/yeats_index.html.*

Jane Urquhart and the Brontë Sisters
Swept Away on the Yorkshire Moors

Donna Carter

WHEN THE WOODEN WAGON bearing the Brontë family rumbled into town in April 1820, the folk of Haworth couldn't have imagined that the newcomers would forever change the tiny village on the fringe of the West Yorkshire moors. Holding the reins and sitting high in the driver's seat was Patrick Brontë, the newly appointed curate of the community's Church of St. Michael and All Angels. Riding beside him was his beloved young wife, Maria, and in the back of the wagon rode their six children, all under the age of seven. What nobody could have foreseen—not the parents nor the people of Haworth—was that three of the young Brontë siblings were destined to become among the greatest writers in the history of literary expression.

As every student and aficionado of classic literature learns, Charlotte, Emily, and Anne Brontë eventually penned famous novels, including, respectively, *Jane Eyre*, *Wuthering Heights*, and *The Tenant of Wildfell Hall*. For 150 years their books and poetry have enchanted readers around the globe and have inspired contemporary writers such as award-winning Canadian author Jane Urquhart. Not surprisingly, the worldwide popularity of the Brontë novels ultimately turned Haworth into a literary shrine; today nearly a million people a year flock to the town's gray stone parsonage (now a museum) where the sisters' literary genius was shaped. Every year, by the thousands, Brontë buffs from the four corners of the planet walk the moorland hills, plodding over the bleak but arresting landscape that so influenced the writing of the three celebrated authors.

My own pilgrimage to Haworth in 1986 fulfilled a desire to look upon the barren but strangely beautiful West Yorkshire moors where I, like legions of others before me, came to walk the windswept paths and hills that once fueled the unrestrained imagination of Charlotte, Anne and, to a greater degree, Emily. Moreover, I wanted to explore the rooms of the parsonage museum where the close-knit trio lived and developed their remarkable abilities.

At the same time as my maiden encounter with Haworth, Jane Urquhart, who ultimately received Canada's Governor General's Award for her bestselling novel *Away*, had rented a small stone cottage on the edge of the Brontë moors where she was researching and writing *Changing Heaven*, her second book of fiction. Urquhart had already been praised for her first novel, *The Whirlpool*, and a book of poems entitled *Storm Glass*. During her months in what had once been a humble Haworth weaver's cottage, she discovered the source of inspiration for *Changing Heaven* in the form of a moss-covered gravestone marking the burial place of a liberated lady balloonist named Miss Lily Cove. The stunt-performing, hot-air balloon rider died in an accident over the moors in 1906, and her grave marker, into which is etched the likeness of a turn-of-the-century balloon, can be seen today in the Haworth municipal cemetery. In *Changing Heaven*, Urquhart composed a whimsical tale that linked the ghosts of Arianna Ether (Lily Cove) and Emily Brontë in a moorland fantasy about love and tragedy.

While Urquhart was contemplating the images that would become fodder for *Changing Heaven*, I was thoroughly engaged in my passion for the Brontës. Lodging was arranged at the Old Silent Inn, an establishment on the fringe of the moors just west of Haworth. The ancient inn, which is still in operation, is steeped in British charm and romantic lore that harks back to the days when Scotland's Bonnie Prince Charlie hid there from the British. Today the inn is on England's register of authenticated haunted places, a claim I found to be entirely true. Tinkling bells heard in the middle of the night are credited to the ghost of an 18th-century kitchen maid who once summoned cats off the moors for feeding by ringing a bell.

What was lovely about lodging at the Old Silent Inn—in addition to its friendly ghost—was that my window opened directly onto the Brontë moors. Here, spread before me like a magnificent carpet, were the special moorland places that stirred the sister authors to words—all within easy walking distance of both the inn and the village of Haworth. Almost without exception, Brontë buffs walk the moors on foot and climb to Top Withens, the hilltop farmhouse believed to have been the setting for Emily Brontë's only novel, *Wuthering Heights*, the fictitious home of the wild, mysterious Heathcliff. Last occupied in 1926, Top Withens today is a desolate stone ruin at the crest of a high hill overlooking a sweeping skirt of shaggy moorland.

This lonely windswept summit, where the view of the moors is superb, has a magnetic attraction for Brontë lovers worldwide. Legions of hikers and walkers

Now a ruin, Top Withens in the West Yorkshire moors served as a model for Wuthering Heights, the famous house in Emily Brontë's novel of the same name. Donna Carter

who follow the nearly four-mile path from Haworth to Top Withens take advantage of strategically placed wooden benches on which to sit and study the unique landscape that greatly influenced Brontë writing. In early April, before peak tourist season begins, you can have a bench to yourself on which to ponder the magic of the moors. Later on you'll have to take a number.

After Emily's early death at age 30, Charlotte wrote of her sister's passion for the undulating Haworth moorland: "My sister Emily loved the moors. Flowers brighter than the rose bloomed in the blackest of the heath for her; out of a sullen hollow in a livid hillside her mind could make an Eden. She found in the bleak solitude many and dear delights; and not the least and best loved was—liberty." Certain present-day people of Haworth are said to believe that "Emily must be spinning in her vault," over the violation of her beloved moors: tourists flocking in droves, groomed footpaths, direction markers, bridges, and signs that were never part of the Brontë environment.

Given Emily's particular penchant for privacy, this may well be true, yet the encroachment of those who come year after year to trace the footsteps of the famous sisters stems from a deeply felt homage and literary admiration. Brontë worshipers like myself possess a compulsion to scan the rolling moorland mantle

Today you can still stay in the Black Bull Hotel, the pub in Haworth where Branwell Brontë reputedly drank himself to death. The only Brontë son failed miserably as a writer and an artist. Donna Carter

of heather, bracken, bog, and peat. Furthermore, we seek to share the intense bond that existed between the Brontës and endless stretches of grass, gnarled scrub, low hollows, rocky valleys, and trivial streams.

A shorter walk than the route to Top Withens—said to be a favorite of the sibling geniuses—is a two-mile hike beginning at the Haworth parsonage. The path meanders past Brontë Falls, which is little more than a trickle except in early spring or following heavy rains. Walkers can trace the footsteps of the sister trio over Brontë Bridge, or visit Brontë Chair, a seat-shaped boulder where Emily is said to have written some of her poetry. Among the several Brontë walks detailed in route maps available from the Haworth Tourist Information Office is the path to Ponden Hall, purportedly Emily's model for Thrushcross Grange, home of the Linton family in *Wuthering Heights.*

Yet the Haworth path most traveled is the one that leads to the Brontë Parsonage Museum, just off Main Street. With a somber cemetery nearly surrounding the old Georgian parsonage, this was the home of the Brontë family from 1820 to 1861. It was here that the remarkable sisters, who were first published under the male pseudonyms of Currer, Ellis, and Acton Bell, cultivated their extraordinary literary gifts, along with brother Branwell, whose writing and very existence succumbed to years of desperate melancholia, alcoholism, and drugs.

It is in the parsonage museum that visitors are able to establish the greatest bridge to the period and elements that molded the lives of the Brontë sisters and their exceptional talent. Museum guests can wander through the rooms where the budding Brontës began their writing, inventing make-believe kingdoms, battles, and relationships. Some of the juvenilia—tiny, early books made and written by the children—are on display along with a collection of original manuscripts, paintings, and furniture. Not all Brontë fans are aware that the sisters also possessed extraordinary painting and sketching talents and that their chief subject was often the life and landscape of the moors.

Most are amazed that such literary and artistic skills could have flourished in a remote corner of England during an era that was fraught with poverty, loss of jobs to a withering weaving industry, political upheaval, foul living conditions, and an unreceptive attitude toward female authorship. The Haworth of the period was a grim, dark place where the quest for survival represented an all-consuming challenge. Disease was rampant, and frequent outbreaks of cholera, dysentery, and typhus resulted in an average life expectancy of 25 years, while infant mortality nudged 50 percent. Just a year after the Brontës moved into the parsonage, death took the mother, Maria, and two elder daughters. Yet it was in this harsh environment that the legend of the remaining three sisters was shaped.

Today the parsonage is filled with period furniture, although not all of it belonged to the Brontës. In the dining room, however, there is a black settee on which Emily is said to have died on December 19, 1848, from what may have been chronic pneumonia or tuberculosis. Stoic to the end and without medical care, she attempted to fulfill daily chores until she finally lay down on the settee and passed away. As she lay dying, Charlotte was on the moors searching for a sprig of heather to cheer her sister. However, the room in which the flame of Emily's life last flickered likewise had a history of happier times. The dining room was also the spot where the girls walked nightly, arms linked, around and around the table discussing writing projects and creating plots.

Wandering from room to room in the former home of the great literary icons evokes both wonder and sadness. Although the parsonage today is similar to what it was during the Brontë period, visitors are reminded that until Charlotte's books began generating substantial income, the house had no carpets, curtains, or wallpaper. In the front parlor is the piano on which all of the Brontë children played, with the exception of Charlotte, and upstairs is the bedroom where, as youngsters, the children spent countless hours developing what they called, "scribblemania." This budding talent produced avalanches of words that eventually ripened into the great works for which the women are famous. On display in the museum is Emily's writing box along with other Brontë memorabilia such as Patrick's Bible, Anne's writing desk, original sketches and watercolors, Charlotte's wedding bonnet, and numerous other family treasures.

From the front windows of the imposing stone parsonage, the Brontës' view consisted of an enveloping sea of gravestones, some standing and some lying down. Nowadays the graveyard engenders an eerie sensation with its gray-green, moss-tinged stones marking the resting places of people who generally died too young of diseases that, for the most part, have long been eradicated from England and other developed countries. The big difference between the cemetery now and then is trees. During the Brontë era, the graveyard was a stark, treeless stretch of yard between the parsonage and the church where Curate Patrick delivered his sermons. Currently there are clumps of tall, full-grown trees shading the parsonage graveyard through which the Brontë women walked to church and Sunday school.

Indeed, the church where Patrick preached for decades—where his family worshiped and his daughters taught Sunday school—is an important element of almost all Brontë pilgrimages. It is here, in a crypt under the floor, that all members of the family, with the exception of Anne, are buried. The youngest daughter was sent to Scarborough, on England's east coast, in the hope that the climate there would cure the same ailment that had taken the life of sister Emily. But it was not to be so. On a May evening in 1849, Anne passed away in a small room that overlooked the North Sea. Her grave lies just beyond a stone fence in the shadow of Scarborough Castle.

Many Haworth pilgrims are also unaware that the village church is, except for the tower, a rebuilt version of the original. Although there was tremendous community upheaval over the issue, the old building was demolished in 1879 to make way for the construction of the church as it stands today. Several graves under the floor were removed (for hygienic reasons) and relocated to various spots in the graveyard. The Brontë vault, however, was left intact; today it is marked by a bronze plaque on the floor.

Although it is common knowledge that original oak pews from the old church—in all likelihood including the exact one that seated the Brontë sisters—were carted away by scavengers during the demolition process, and although the parsonage has from time to time been the victim of souvenir hunters, these invasions have failed to dull the aura of Charlotte, Emily, and Anne. Every year new Brontë fans—and perhaps a novelist or two, like Jane Urquhart, with a penchant for the English authors—are born. For the most part, their insatiable curiosity about this remarkable family of writers will only be satisfied by personal pilgrimages to the West Yorkshire moors—that blustery blanket of land that was home to three of the greatest literary icons of all time.

The Writer's Trail

Following in the Footsteps

Destination: On the edge of the wild and windswept West Yorkshire moors, the hilltop village of Haworth is clustered around cobblestone streets, and although it looks quite different today than it did during the Brontë period, it, together with Emily, Charlotte, and Anne's beloved moors, provided unlimited inspiration for some of the greatest novels ever written.

Location: England is in the southern portion of the island of Great Britain, which is found between Ireland and northwestern Continental Europe in the Atlantic Ocean. Haworth is located in West Yorkshire, about 125 miles north of the United Kingdom's capital, London. The closest major center to Haworth is Leeds.

Getting There: Since the North Atlantic is the planet's busiest air corridor, there is an astounding array of travel choices from North America to London, England, where your pilgrimage to Brontë country will likely begin. Some of the commercial airlines that offer nonstop flights to Britain's major London airports, Heathrow and Gatwick, include British Airways (1-800-247-9297), American Airlines (1-800-433-7300), Continental (1-800-231-0856), TWA (1-800-892-4141), Virgin Atlantic (1-800-862-8621), and Air Canada ([416] 925-2311 or 1-800-361-5373 or 1-800-776-3000). Not surprisingly, you can also get to London, England, and other British destinations by air from a number of major cities in Continental Europe. Check with your local travel agent for information on routes and carriers. If you're already on the Continent, you might want to take a ferry or hovercraft (with train/bus connections; consult a travel agent for details) across the English Channel or the North Sea to England. P&O/Stena Line ([44-990] 980980) operate combined frequent daily ferries between Dover, England, and Calais, France, that take 75 minutes to cross the channel, while Hoverspeed ([44-990] 240241) runs hovercraft and catamarans on the same route that take 35 minutes to cross. P&O/Stena also offer boat service several times a day between Newhaven, England, and Dieppe, France, a four-hour trip by ferry, half that by catamaran. Between Cherbourg and Le Havre, France, and Portsmouth, England, P&O ([44-990] 980555) operates daily ferries. This trip takes five to eight hours, depending on the time of day. Brittany Ferries ([44-990] 360360) offers a daily sailing from Caen and St. Malo, France, to Portsmouth, which takes about six hours (from Caen), and connects Roscoff, France, to Plymouth, England, by ferry, as well. Brittany also operates a weekly service between Santander, Spain, and Plymouth or Portsmouth. The Plymouth crossing takes approximately 24 hours; Portsmouth about 30 hours. Not to be outdone, P&O offers ferry service between Bilbao, Spain, and Portsmouth. Scandinavian Seaways ([44-990] 333000) operates ferry service from Gothenburg, Sweden, to Newcastle, England, or from Esbjerg, Denmark, and Gothenburg to Harwich, England. Norway's Color Line ([44-191] 296-1313) features ferry service between Stavanger, Haugesund, and Bergen in Norway to Newcastle. A new ferry company, Sally Direct ([44-845] 600-2626), offers an extremely cheap service between Ostend, Belgium, and Ramsgate, England, but it takes four hours. Scandinavian Seaways operates ferries between Hamburg, Germany, and Harwich or Newcastle, while Stena Line ([44-990] 707070) offers service between Hook of Holland, Netherlands, and Harwich. From Ireland there is a daunting selection of ferry possibilities. Check with your local travel agent for routes, companies, and other information. Finally, if you're driving or taking a train or bus from the Continent, you can travel *under* the English Channel via the Channel Tunnel, or "Chunnel," which connects Calais, France, with Folkestone, England. Eurotunnel ([44-990] 353535) and Eurostar ([44-990] 300003) operate, respectively, vehicle and passenger trains through the Chunnel. Vehicles travel through the tunnel on special shuttle trains; foot passengers on high-speed trains between London and Paris (three hours) or London and Brussels, Belgium (two hours and 40 minutes). In London trains arrive at and depart from Waterloo Station. Everyone has to use one of these services; if you're driving, you can't just drive your car through the tunnel.

Orientation: Haworth is eight miles west of the town of Bradford and three miles south of Keighley.

Getting Around: If you're not driving or flying from London, there are two ways to get to Leeds, the main transportation hub in West Yorkshire. You can take one of the hourly trains from London's King's Cross Station, or you can take one of nine buses that leave London daily from Victoria Coach Station. The famous Leeds–Settle–Carlisle line connects Leeds to Keighley. To get from Keighley to Haworth, there are two options: transfer to the Keighley & Worth Valley Railway ([44-1535] 645214), a private line that goes directly to Haworth, or catch a Keighley & District bus ([44-1535] 603284; bus numbers 663, 664, or 665). The Haworth train station is a ten-minute walk from the Brontë Parsonage Museum. BritRail Passes and Flexipasses allow unlimited train travel (within a consecutive-days time period for BritRail; within a month for Flexipass) throughout England, except on the London Underground. Various durations and prices apply to passes. For example, an adult eight-day BritRail Pass sells for $259; an adult eight-day Flexipass for $315. Senior and family discounts apply. There are also numerous types of bus passes, so consult your local British Travel Authority for details (see **Contacts**). BritRail/Drive Passes, which combine a Flexipass with the use of a Hertz rental car for side trips, are also available. Or you can simply rent a car by itself. Rates begin at about $40 per day for an economy vehicle. However, that doesn't include a hefty tax on rental-car fees, which is about 17 percent. Agencies include Alamo (1-800-327-9633), Hertz (1-800-654-3001 in the U.S.; 1-800-263-0600 in Canada), and Budget (1-800-527-0700).

Tip: If you opt to buy a BritRail Pass or BritRail/Drive Pass, make your purchase before you arrive in England. The passes must be bought in your country of origin. Contact the British Tourist Authority in your country for further details. Holders of BritRail, Eurail, and Euro Passes qualify for discounted fares on Eurostar trains from Paris or Brussels to London. Eurail Passes can't be used in Britain. If you decide to do without a rail pass, make sure you check into discounted train fares. The same applies for bus tickets.

Literary Sleeps

Apothecary Guest House: Across from the Black Bull Hotel, this comfortable lodging has a range of rooms, most with bathrooms. Main Street. Tel.: (44-1535) 643642. Inexpensive.

Black Bull Hotel: If you want to get intimate with Branwell Brontë's chief haunt in Haworth, this is the place for you. The hotel has two doubles with private bathrooms and decent food. Main Street. Tel.: (44-1535) 642249. Inexpensive.

Manor House: If you want to get away from the hubbub of Main Street, this comfortable bed-and-breakfast is still close enough to the center of things. Changegate. Tel.: (44-1535) 642911. Inexpensive.

Old White Lion Hotel: This old coaching inn is the place where the fallen-angel parachutist Lily Cove (a main character named Arianna Ether in Jane Urquhart's, *Changing Heaven*) stayed during her brief stint in Haworth before she plunged to her death on the moors. West Lane. Tel.: (44-1535) 642313. Inexpensive.

Tip: Although there are lots of places to stay in Haworth, it's prudent to book ahead in summer.

Literary Sites

Brontë Parsonage Museum: Surrounded by a picturesque garden, this Georgian house served as the Brontës' home when they lived in Haworth. All the Brontës died relatively young, except for Patrick, the father, who passed away in the parsonage at the ripe old age of 84. Open daily (except Christmas and New Year's Day) from April to September from 10:00 a.m. to 5:30 p.m., and from October to March from 11:00 a.m. to 5:00 p.m. In August the museum closes on Wednesday at 8:00 p.m. Admission fee. Off Main Street. Tel.: (44-1535) 642323.

Schoolhouse: Charlotte Brontë once taught school here; now the building, opposite the village church just off Main Street, houses a restaurant that features a pretty good ploughman's lunch.

Tip: *Brontë Way* by Marje Wilson describes 11 circular walks, including the demanding nine-mile hike from the Brontë Parsonage Museum to Colne/Laneshawbridge via Top Withens (Wuthering Heights), Ponden Hall (Thrushcross Grange), and Wycoller Hall (Ferndean Manor). The booklet is generally available from the Haworth Tourist Information Centre (see **Contacts**).

Icon Pastimes

Other than writing novels and poetry, the Brontë sisters' only other pastime was walking on the moors. Visitors with the time and energy will want to take the various walks frequently followed by Anne, Emily, and Charlotte. The Haworth Tourist Information Centre (see **Contacts**) hands out free trail maps outlining the walks to Brontë Falls, Brontë Bridge, and Brontë Chair, as well as to Top Withens, an Elizabethan farmhouse (now a hilltop ruin) that served as Emily's inspiration for *Wuthering Heights*. Brother Branwell's favorite pastime, however, seemed to be drinking. Indeed, it is said he drank himself to death in the Black Bull Hotel on Haworth's Main Street. Opposite the Black Bull, the Museum Bookshop once served as a drugstore during Branwell's days of self-destruction. It was here that he also purchased opium to further fuel his need for escape.

Contacts

British Tourist Authority: United States: 551 Fifth Avenue, New York, New York 10176-0799. Tel.: 1-800-462-2748. Canada: Suite 120, 5915 Airport Road, Mississauga, Ontario L4V 1T1. Tel.: 1-800-VISIT UK or (905) 405-1840. Fax: (905) 405-1835. Web sites: *www.bta.org.uk* or *www.travelbritain.org*.

Haworth Tourist Information Centre: Haworth's tourist office has lots of maps, walking-trail brochures, and books about the Brontës and the moors. Staff here can also help with accommodation bookings. Open daily during summer from 10:30 a.m. to 4:30 p.m. 2-4 West Lane, Haworth, England. Tel.: (44-1535) 642329.

In a Literary Mood

Books

Brontë, Anne. *Agnes Grey*. New York: Oxford University Press, 1998. Based on the author's experience as a governess and first published in 1847, the novel focuses on the rector's daughter of the title, who is employed by the Murray family, is badly treated, and relieves her unfortunate state by indulging in the kindness of Weston, the village curate, whom she eventually marries.

_____. *The Tenant of Wildfell Hall*. New York: Oxford University Press, 1998. Anne's second, more ambitious novel was first published in 1848. It traces the story of Helen Graham, the tenant of Wildfell Hall, and her difficult romance with a neighboring farmer named Gilbert Markham.

Helen is thought to be a widow but, as it turns out, is actually married to Arthur Huntingdon, a dissolute drunk. The realistic portrait of Huntingdon is undoubtedly based on the life of Anne's brother, Branwell.

Brontë, Charlotte. *Jane Eyre*. New York: Penguin, 1996. One of the great novels in the English language, *Jane Eyre* first appeared in 1847. Jane takes up a position as governess at Thornfield Hall, where she has one charge, the ward of Edward Rochester. Most of the novel concerns Jane's star-crossed romance with Rochester and her own self-determination as a woman.

_____. *Shirley*. New York: Oxford University Press, 1998. Originally published in 1849, this novel is set during the Luddite riots and the last days of the Napoleonic Wars. The tale concerns the tangled relationship between Shirley Keeldar and brothers Robert and Louis Moore. The character of Shirley is thought to be based on Charlotte's sister, Emily.

_____. *Villette*. New York: Penguin, 1980. First published in 1853, *Villette* uses material from Charlotte's earlier unpublished novel, *The Professor* (which was finally published after her death). Lucy Snowe, an English girl, is hired by a girls' school in Villette, Belgium. The novel details her relationships with two men, Dr. John Bretton, the son of Lucy's godmother, and Paul Emmanuel, a professor.

Brontë, Emily. *Wuthering Heights*. New York: Penguin, 1996. Emily's sole novel, a masterpiece, was first published in 1847. Its tortured, tragic tale of Heathcliff's machinations, plots, and manipulations, set against the wild backdrop of the Yorkshire moors, was ahead of its time. The novel's psychological complexity and demonic but compelling protagonist profoundly shocked many of Emily's contemporaries.

Hewitt, Peggy. *These Lonely Mountains*. Huddersfield, England: Springfield Books, 1985. This charming "biography" of the Brontë moors is written in a style and depth that could only be detailed by an author who spent her lifetime living and observing moorland life and sensing the all-encompassing literary effect the Brontë sisters had on the West Yorkshire moors and the world.

Urquhart, Jane. *Away*. Toronto: McClelland & Stewart, 1993. Set in 19th-century and present-day Ireland and Canada, Urquhart's bestselling tale of a family's tortuous, haunted past is compelling and resonant.

_____. *Changing Heaven*. Toronto: McClelland & Stewart, 1990. This imaginative, tragic love story about a balloonist (modeled on real-life aeronaut Lily Cove) weds the wraiths of Arianna Ether (Cove) and Emily Brontë while capturing all the mystique of the West Yorkshire moors.

Wilkes, Brian. *The Brontës*. London: Hamlyn Publishing Group, 1975. Innumerable tomes have been written about the Brontës by authors whose research offers different perspectives on the various family members, but this comprehensive historical study of the clan from early beginnings through hardship, success, and death is one of the best.

Guidebooks

Fisher, Robert I. C., ed. *Fodor's Upclose Great Britain*. 2nd ed. New York: Fodor's Travel Publications, 2000. This book features a chapter devoted to Brontë country and provides a host of practical details about the area, along with useful information about the rest of Britain.

Thomas, Bryn, Tom Smallman, and Pat Yale. *Britain*. 3rd ed. Hawthorn, Australia: Lonely Planet Publications, 1999. There are a lot of general guides to Britain, but this one may be the best. It offers all the usual Lonely Planet expertise.

Varlow, Sally. *A Reader's Guide to Writers' Britain*. London: Prion Books, 1997. A sprightly journey through the literary landscapes, shrines, and haunts of Britain's famous writers

Films/Videos

Gasser, Yves, Klaus Hellwig, and Yves Peyrot (producers). *The Brontë Sisters (Les Soeurs Brontë)*. André Téchiné (director). Action Films/France 3 Cinéma/Gaumont International, 1979. Cast: Isabelle Adjani, Isabelle Huppert, and Marie-France Pisier. Sumptuous French rendition of the lives of the Brontë sisters and brother Branwell. Where else can you get three of France's finest actresses together in one movie playing three of England's most tragic authors?

Goetz, William, and Kenneth Macgowan (producers). *Jane Eyre*. Robert Stevenson (director). 20th Century Fox, 1944. Fox Video. Cast: Joan Fontaine, Margaret O'Brien, and Orson Welles. Much-adapted for the screen (silent versions in 1914 and 1921; talkies in 1934 and 1996; TV takes in 1961, 1970, 1973, 1983, and 1997), this classic 1944 outing is still arguably the best, although the British TV miniseries in 1983 gets high marks, too. Welles sinks his prodigious acting teeth into Rochester, and Elizabeth Taylor pops up in a brief supporting appearance. Fontaine makes a fine Jane.

Goldwyn, Samuel (producer). *Wuthering Heights*. William Wyler (director). Samuel Goldwyn Company, 1939. MGM/UA Home Video. Cast: David Niven, Merle Oberon, and Laurence Olivier. Oberon as Cathy and Olivier as Heathcliff—who could ask for more? Well, maybe cinematographic genius Gregg Toland's camera artistry, which won him an Oscar. Like Charlotte Brontë's *Jane Eyre*, Emily's novel has been adapted for film and TV many times: a silent version in 1920, talkies in 1970 and 1992, TV adaptations in 1958 and 1999, and foreign offerings in 1953 (Mexican, directed by Luis Buñuel) and 1985 (French). Wyler's 1939 moody stunner is still the best, even though it stops at chapter 17, dispensing with a good portion of the novel.

Mann, Delbert (director). *Brontë*. Ireland/U.S., 1983. Cast: Julie Harris. Compelling made-for-TV drama adapted by William Luce from his own radio script. Harris is superb as Charlotte Brontë in this one-woman play that recounts her life and family troubles through first-person monologues, taken largely from Charlotte's own writings.

Web Sites

Brontës: *www.bronte-country.com*. There are scores of Web sites devoted to the Brontës, but this one is a good place to start. It has plenty of pictures and information about Haworth and environs in connection with the Brontës.

A. A. Milne

Winnie-the-Pooh in Ashdown Forest

Yvonne Jeffery Hope

ONE NEVER REALLY *intends* to become lost. It just sort of happens, a small, niggling doubt that grows and grows until, having attained the size of a Heffalump, it forces you to admit you have no idea where you are.

Actually I knew where I was in a general way: somewhere on the edge of Ashdown Forest, 35 miles south of London, England, in Sussex. The trouble was that I didn't know where I was in a really specific way.

It had all seemed so simple at first. My trail would lead from London Zoo to Ashdown Forest, where I would drive to the hilltop known as Gill's Lap (Galleons Lap to Pooh fans) for a leisurely walk around the sites that feature so prominently in A. A. Milne's *Winnie-the-Pooh* and *The House at Pooh Corner*. That I didn't have a map of those sites was a small detail, I thought. I would Discover them as I walked, just as Pooh and his friends Discovered them. Besides, when I arrived at the small car park, I found a low tablet that provided a map, and I quickly sketched a copy of it into my notebook. Rather handy, that.

Apparently, however, I'd lost something in the translation. The entire circular walk was supposed to be three miles long and, by my guess, I should have arrived at the memorial stone to Milne and illustrator E. H. Shepard, even at my ambling pace, 30 or 40 minutes earlier. Evidently I had turned left in the wrong spot.

To make matters worse, dark gray clouds chose this time to begin spattering down large drops of rain. In a distinctly Winnie-the-Poohish way, I began to wonder if striding over Ashdown Forest on a blustery October day was really such a good idea. I wasn't concerned about coming across Hostile Animals, such as Woozles or possibly Jagulars, but I did have an idea that I was in danger of becoming rather late for lunch.

Pooh fans will know that lunch, like all meals and even snack times, is Not To Be Missed, and I was, after all, in Pooh territory. When Milne's stories and Shepard's illustrations turned a bear of very little brain into a worldwide phenomenon, they also, from the Lone Pine to Poohsticks Bridge, brought Ashdown Forest into our lives.

While it's called a forest, more than half of Ashdown's 6,500 acres are actually open country, one of the few areas of lowland heath left in Europe. Here swaths of bracken, a type of fern, and tough evergreen heathers flourish in peaty soil. What isn't heath is mainly outcrops of small woods, with beech, birch, oak, and pine predominating.

To the literary traveler's delight, the forest looks much the same today as it did in 1925 when Milne bought nearby Cotchford Farm. Although the family—which consisted of Milne; his wife, Daphne; their four-year-old son, Christopher Robin; and Christopher's nanny—lived in London's Chelsea district during the week, Cotchford became their weekend and holiday home, and Ashdown Forest their adventure ground.

Of course, the story of Winnie-the-Pooh begins a little earlier than this. Until 1923 Milne had been known for his humor in *Punch* magazine, for his plays, and for his novel, *The Red House Mystery*. But Daphne had sent to *Vanity Fair* a poem Milne had written for her about a little boy saying his evening prayers. When the magazine published "Vespers" that January, the poem captivated audiences on both sides of the Atlantic Ocean.

Later in 1923, during a wet summer holiday in Wales, Milne escaped the too-close comfort of a group of family and friends by repairing to a nearby summerhouse. Eleven rainy days later, he had 11 sets of children's verses, the genesis of *When We Were Very Young*, subsequently published in 1924.

In the collection of verse, the bear that Christopher had received as a present on his first birthday makes several appearances: in the poem "Teddy Bear" where he's also known as Edward Bear, and in the Shepard illustration for "Vespers."

About the same time, Christopher and his father were visiting a Canadian black bear named Winnie at London Zoo. While in Ontario, Canada, en route to England during World War I, Lieutenant Harry Colebourn of the 34th Fort Garry Horse Regiment of Manitoba (and the Canadian Army Veterinary Corps) had purchased a bear cub. He had named her Winnie for his hometown of Winnipeg and left her in the care of London Zoo while he served in France. In 1919 he officially gave her to the zoo, where she later left a strong impression on the young Christopher. (The zoo still treasures the connection: a statue of Winnie the Bear, sculpted by Bill Epp, was presented to London Zoo by the people of Manitoba, Canada, in July 1995. Look for it near the Children's Zoo.)

Canadian Lieutenant Harry Colebourn poses with Winnie the Bear, who lent her name to Winnie-the-Pooh.
Courtesy of London Zoo

Again in *When We Were Very Young*, you'll spy a regal white swan in the poem "The Mirror." The Milnes saw the swan while on a pre-Cotchford holiday in Angmering, Surrey, and named it Pooh, on the principle that if it didn't come when you called it, you could pretend, exclaiming "Pooh!" dismissively, that you hadn't really called it at all. And so, under the influence of a Canadian bear and an English swan, Teddy Bear, aka Edward Bear, became Winnie-the-Pooh.

By this time, Eeyore had arrived in the nursery as a Christmas present, together with Piglet, a gift from a neighbor in London. (Kanga and Roo were purchased later, specifically for their potential for the stories, as was Tigger.) The toys traveled with the Milnes from London to Cotchford, where Ashdown Forest would create the prefect setting for their Brand New Adventure.

When Milne was asked to write a children's story for the Christmas 1925 issue of the *Evening News*, Daphne—who would later provide voices for the toys as she read Milne's stories aloud—suggested one of the bedtime stories her husband had told Christopher. Milne dismissed all of the stories but one, about Christopher and his bear, and the forest near Cotchford. That simple story of honey-chasing would subsequently become the first chapter of *Winnie-the-Pooh*, published in 1926. Before Milne turned once again to other writing, he would complete another collection of verse, *Now We Are Six* (1927), and another book of Pooh stories, *The House at Pooh Corner* (1928).

Milne drew inspiration from Ashdown Forest for the settings of the stories, the adventures within them, and even for the characters of Owl and Rabbit. When Shepard visited the Milnes at Cotchford, Milne took him to the forest sites the family loved, including Gill's Lap.

Consequently, in Shepard's illustrations you see the prickly leaves and bright, ever-present yellow flowers of the gorse bush (Winnie-the-Pooh's special nemesis, as prickles in one's nose are simply not nice), the Scots pine on the higher forest elevations, blown into leaning shapes by the wind, great oak trees perfect for climbing, and the heather and heath stretching out over hills and valleys.

It was past the pines that I'd made my way this morning, through the gorse and over the heather, down from Gill's Lap along a firebreak, leaving the dog-walkers and bird-watchers well behind me. Now, faced with an uncertain route and an even more uncertain sky, I felt distinctly Pooh-ish—that is, muddled—and wished I had the company of bouncy Tigger, the heroic-in-spite-of-himself Piglet, or even little Roo. Rabbit, I suspected, was with me already, judging by the rustling in the bushes. It was either Rabbit or a Jagular and, frankly, I preferred to assume it was Rabbit.

Perhaps just five more minutes, I thought. I'll walk along this firebreak for another five minutes, and if it doesn't come out somewhere recognizable, I'll turn around.

And that's how I Discovered the Poohsticks Bridge car park.

"Oh," I said out loud, as if to Rabbit. Then, "Oh," again, as I realized I had walked well past all of the sites on and around Gill's Lap and had found the car park to which I'd intended to drive after my ramble. But, since I was so obviously close to the bridge now, I followed the wooden sign that pointed from the car park into a treed area called Posingford Wood.

Twenty minutes (and some further doubts about my route) later, along a bridle path lined with wild holly, the unmistakable wood framework of Poohsticks Bridge awaited me. Originally built in 1907, and a favorite playground for Christopher, the bridge was restored in 1979. Erosion, helped along by thousands of pairs of feet, has required reinforcing the banks with concrete blocks. Fences also protect the stream's banks on either side of the bridge, in addition to saving overeager youngsters from accidental baths. The bridge itself, however, remains completely recognizable, a beacon for anyone looking to recapture part of their childhood. Shaded by the moss-covered branches of huge oak trees, the bridge still spans the stream Milne wrote about as a river: today, full and muddy from recent gales, the stream rushed along, chattering to itself as it disappeared under my feet.

Only a little self-conscious (I wasn't the only adult clutching sticks in my hands), I dropped two sticks into the water on the upstream side of the bridge. I dashed across to the downstream side, just in time to see them appear, neck and neck, until one was caught in a small eddy, leaving the other one to surge downstream, off to parts unknown.

Did I play Poohsticks? You bet I did!

Having found the bridge, I knew that Cotchford Farm was a bit of a walk beyond, with a right turn down the lane. Sure enough, there it was: a farmhouse of vaguely Queen Anne vintage, featuring an angular, almost jumbled appearance from having been three houses turned into one. It's still a private home, and not at all appropriate for bursting in on, so I peeked instead at Shepard's illustration for the poem "Buttercup Days" in *Now We Are Six*. In it Christopher and his good friend from London, Anne Darlington, are playing in front of the house, and it's easy to imagine a little boy and girl still playing there now.

Thus encouraged, I headed back to Gill's Lap, a steady, breath-stealing climb up the firebreak, retracing, I now realized, the footsteps of Milne and Shepard in 1926. Although the wind still had a distinct chill to it, blue sky to the south heartened me and I strode on with a delightful sense of discovery. The horizon stretched for miles, with the occasional white-walled farmhouse sheltering on a hillside the only sign of civilization. Ancient farming techniques—grazing, and

Gill's Lap in Ashdown Forest is called Galleons Lap in the Winnie-the-Pooh stories. Yvonne Jeffery Hope

the gathering of peat and bracken—created this quilted mix of heath and forest, where the grass and bracken in the open showed the russet and gold of autumn's first frosts. With Gill's Lap the highest point in sight, the hills around it seemed no more than gentle folds in the landscape, their valleys anchored with beech and birch, their tops swept bare by the wind, save for the hardy pine occasionally silhouetted against the sky.

As I finally neared the top of the hill, several low-set stones off to the right of the firebreak caught my attention. I detoured over and discovered the memorial I'd originally been looking for, a large, flat stone looking out over the forest, a simple plaque set into it: "Here at Gill's Lap are commemorated A. A. Milne (1882–1956) and E. H. Shepard (1879–1976), who collaborated in the creation of Winnie-the-Pooh and so captured the magic of Ashdown Forest and gave it to the world."

I looked east, down onto the treetops of the Five Hundred Acre Wood, known better to me as the Hundred Acre Wood. Closer to the memorial, just below me, was the mound on which Rabbit's myriad friends and relations played. And at the very top of the hill, where kites now dipped and bobbed against a rapidly clear-ing sky, a small, dark copse of pine trees swayed in the wind. The Enchanted Place, at last, where no one had ever been able to count whether the trees numbered

63 or 64. I didn't even try, content to rest within the shelter created by the over-lapping branches. Slightly more overgrown now than when Pooh paused here, it's still a calm, peaceful place, perfect for thoughts and imagination.

I've treasured Pooh even through the messy, complicated years of adult life: in his simplicity and his acceptance of the days as they unfold are lessons worth reviewing with a cup of hot cocoa in hand. I'm obviously not the only one who thinks so: Pooh has rocketed out of the children's bookshelves into the adult world, with Pooh-centered Latin, philosophy, Taoism, and business books paying homage to him. He has even scaled the heights of academia: in 1999 the University of California at Berkeley placed Pooh on their freshmen summer reading list.

His appeal isn't difficult to fathom. Who among us can't identify with a slightly addled bear whose fondness for sweets leads him not only into adventure, but also into difficulty touching his toes with his paws?

For Milne and his son, Christopher, however, the phenomenal success of Winnie-the-Pooh was a double-edged sword. The father would remain frustrated for most of his life that he couldn't shake the world's new view of him as a children's author; the son, as he entered the world of boarding-school teasing and press attention, would discover a world reluctant to allow him to grow up.

Today's Ashdown Forest mirrors this conundrum of success. While its Pooh connections have helped protect the forest from development and oil exploration, and while Pooh-seekers are welcomed, the abundance of visitors threatens the popular areas with overuse and can infringe on nearby residents' privacy. Hence the small, low-key wooden signs that mark the car parks, and the reliance on maps, not signs, in the forest itself.

And that, really, is the joy of walking in Ashdown Forest: the freedom to imagine. The lack of signs that had helped me lose my way leaves the forest blessedly free of anyone else's interpretation. The enchanted places are here, but it's up to you to find them. When you do, armed if you like with a dog-eared, yellowed copy of Pooh in paperback so as not to mind if the rain sprinkles the pages, you almost expect to bump into the bear and his friends around the next gorse bush.

You won't, of course, find Pooh and Tigger rambling together over the heather that in July and August colors the hillsides purple. As Milne himself emphasized, the stories are fictional, the combination of a father's observations of his son, the memories of his own childhood and, ultimately, his imagination. But because there's a little piece of Winnie-the-Pooh in all of us, there's a piece of our childhood in Ashdown Forest. To find it, you just need sturdy walking shoes for the muddy bits, and a smidgen of imagination.

Following in the Footsteps

Destination: Ashdown Forest lies in southeast England and offers one of the last remaining areas of open countryside in the region. Once a royal hunting ground, the forest today sports the designations for an Area of Outstanding Natural Beauty, a Site of Special Scientific Interest, and a Special Protection Area for birds—a collection of capital letters that wouldn't look out of place in their own Pooh book.

Location: Hartfield is an hour's drive south of London, about halfway between East Grinstead and Tunbridge Wells. The Pooh area of Ashdown Forest is just south of Hartfield.

Getting There: See **The Writer's Trail** in **Jane Urquhart and the Brontë Sisters** for details on getting to England.

Orientation: To reach Ashdown Forest, use the A264 either from East Grinstead or Tunbridge Wells and turn south onto the B2026. Stay on the B2026 through Hartfield Village (the road bears to the right). Stop at Pooh Corner, on the right just before you leave the village, to obtain walking maps. To find Poohsticks Bridge, leave the village on the B2026 (it forks to the left) and turn right at the sign to Marsh Green and Newbridge. The car park is on your right. The walk to Poohsticks Bridge takes 20 minutes one way. To find Gill's Lap and the other walks around Winnie-the-Pooh's territory, remain on the B2026 after Hartfield Village. Gill's Lap Car Park is at the intersection of the B2026 and the road to Coleman's Hatch.

Getting Around: Ashdown Forest has limited public transportation, so renting a car is advised. Arrange to pick up the car at one of the London airports, or in a sizable center such as Tunbridge Wells. Expect to pay approximately $40 to $90 per day. Agencies include Hertz (1-800-654-3131) and Avis (1-800-331-1212).

Tip: The British drive on the left-hand side of the road, so this puts the gearshift on your left. Since driving in Britain often involves small roads, tight bends, and heavy traffic, opting for an automatic may lessen your stress.

Literary Sleeps

All English towns and villages have economical bed-and-breakfasts, inns, and country homes that offer comfortable lodging. Check with the British Tourist Authority office in your country for a list of possibilities (see **Contacts**). You can base yourself in London, of course; stay in a large town such as Tunbridge Wells in Kent (east of Ashdown Forest) or Lewes in East Sussex (south of the forest); or check into a bed-and-breakfast in East Grinstead. What follows is a short list of typically English places to stay that aren't too far from Pooh's slice of Ashdown.

Antioch House: Located in Lewes, East Sussex's handsome, ever-so-English county town, this Jacobean town house boasts attractive gardens. 104 High Street, Lewes, East Sussex. Tel.: (44-1273) 473057. Moderate.

Ashdown Park: This splendid, well-run hotel is situated in a building that was once home to a community of nuns. It features a chapel with fine stained-glass windows and a working organ and has big, homey rooms. Wych Cross, Forest Row. Tel.: (44-1342) 824988. Expensive.

Royal Wells Inn: One of the grand old hotels of Tunbridge Wells's glory days as a spa, this place will have you believing A. A. Milne himself, or one of his contemporaries, could pop out of a room. Common, Tunbridge Wells, Kent. Tel.: (44-1892) 511188. Expensive.

Swan Hotel: A little less expensive than the Royal Wells, this other venerable Tunbridge Wells lodging is pretty plush, too. Pantiles, Tunbridge Wells, Kent. Tel.: (44-1892) 541450. Moderate.

Literary Sites

Ashdown Forest: From Gill's Lap, a three-mile walk leads past the Enchanted Place, the memorial stone, Roo's sandy pit, the North Pole, and Eeyore's sad and gloomy place. A longer, seven-mile walk leads from Gill's Lap to Poohsticks Bridge; you can add the loop across to the North Pole and Eeyore's place if you're energetic. Cotchford Farm is located past Poohsticks Bridge, down the lane to the right (the east). You can stroll by, but it's privately owned and not open to the public.

Hever Castle: A. A. Milne's first published writing, at age eight, mentions a walk in Ashdown Forest, followed by a visit to this small castle in nearby Kent, once the home of Anne Boleyn. The moat and gatehouse date to around 1270, and the gardens, with a traditional yew hedge maze, make for a beautiful stroll. Take the A264 and turn north onto the B2026, then follow the signs. Open daily March to late November from noon to 6:00 p.m. Admission fee. Near Edenbridge, a few miles west of Tonbridge. Nearest train station is Hever on the Uckfield line. Tel.: (44-1732) 865224.

London Zoo: It's one of the world's oldest zoos and still one of the places you should visit in London. When you go, leave your car outside the city to avoid London's traffic and take the train or the Underground (tube). The zoo is in Regent's Park; the nearest tube station is Camden Town. Open daily March through September from 10:00 a.m. to 5:30 p.m. and daily October to February from 10:00 a.m. to 4:00 p.m. Admission fee. Tel.: (44-171) 7223333.

Icon Pastimes

There's no better way to enjoy the Ashdown Forest of A. A. and Christopher Milne than to walk it as they did. To aid your exploring, visit the Ashdown Forest Information Centre. Turn right off the B2026 at Gill's Lap car park, then turn left toward Wych Cross (at the Hatch Inn). The center is along the road, on the right, and features an interesting exhibition barn. Leaflets, including walks on Ashdown Forest, are about $3 each (your only cost, as access to the forest is free). Further afield is Tunbridge Wells, just east of Hartfield. It was a popular place for royalty and society in the 1600s and 1700s, thanks to the local mineral waters. To try the water, head to the historic, colonnaded main street known as the Pantiles. Christopher Milne mentions Tunbridge Wells as a place to shop, particularly around the time of his birthday!

Contacts

Ashdown Forest Centre: Wych Cross, Forest Row, East Sussex, England RH18 5JP. Tel.: (44-1342) 823583.

British Tourist Authority: United States: 551 Fifth Avenue, New York, New York 10176-0799. Tel.: 1-800-462-2748. Canada: Suite 120, 5915 Airport Road, Mississauga, Ontario L4V 1T1. Tel.: 1-800-VISIT UK or (905) 405-1840. Fax: (905) 405-1835. Web sites: *www.bta.org.uk* or *www.travelbritain.org.*

Pooh Corner: Pooh Corner, High Street, Hartfield, East Sussex, England TN7 4AE. Tel.: (44-1892) 770453. Web site: *www.poohcorner.co.uk.*

In a Literary Mood

Books

Milne, A. A. *Autobiography*. New York: E. P. Dutton 1939. Milne's autobiography was published in England as *It's Too Late Now*, a reference to his belief that childhood and early adulthood make the man—and provide the most interest. Indeed, he does focus on his early days, devoting barely 10 out of 315 pages to the writing of his children's books.

_____. *The Complete Tales and Poems of Winnie-the-Pooh*. New York: Dutton Children's Books, 1996. *When We Were Very Young*, *Winnie-the-Pooh*, *Now We Are Six*, and *The House at Pooh Corner* in one volume and illustrated by E. H. Shepard. What more can one say?

Milne, Christopher. *Beyond the World of Pooh*. New York: Dutton Books, 1998. Christopher Milne also published three other memoirs: *The Path Through the Trees*, *The Hollow on the Hill*, and *The Open Garden*. Selections from all four books are collected in this volume, an excellent introduction to the man the boy became.

_____. *The Enchanted Places*. London: Eyre Methuen, 1974. A. A. Milne's son offers an honest, yet charming, memoir filled with the Pooh detail that his father's autobiography lacks.

Thwaite, Ann. *A. A. Milne: The Man Behind Winnie-the-Pooh*. Toronto: Random House Canada, 1990. Thwaite provides a definitive biography, simultaneously readable and revealing.

_____. *The Brilliant Career of Winnie-the-Pooh*. London: Methuen, 1992. A fun collection of illustrations, articles, and photos all pertaining to Winnie-the-Pooh's career, from A. A. Milne's early days to Pooh's popularity today.

Guidebooks

England: The Rough Guide. 3rd ed. London: Rough Guides Ltd., 1998. You'll find more detail on Sussex in this guide than in Lonely Planet's book, but still nothing much about A. A. Milne, Pooh, or Ashdown Forest.

Thomas, Bryn, Tom Smallman, and Pat Yale. *Britain*. 3rd ed. Hawthorn, Australia: Lonely Planet Publications, 1999. It's hard to get good, hard guide information on Ashdown Forest or A. A. Milne, but Lonely Planet's all-purpose compendium is still a good repository of things British.

Varlow, Sally. *A Reader's Guide to Writers' Britain*. London: Prion Books, 1999. This delightful hike through literary Britain has a pretty good section on Sussex and Kent, with a short commentary on A. A. Milne and Ashdown Forest.

Films/Videos

There are innumerable Winnie-the-Pooh animated movies on celluloid and video, but the two Walt Disney shorts made in the 1960s are still the best of the bunch.

Disney, Walt (producer). *Winnie-the-Pooh and the Blustery Day*. Wolfgang Reitherman (director). Walt Disney Productions, 1968. Disney Video. Voices: Sebastian Cabot, John Fiedler, and Sterling Holloway.

_____. *Winnie-the-Pooh and the Honey Tree*. Wolfgang Reitherman (director). Walt Disney Productions, 1966. Disney Video. Voices: Sterling Holloway and Ralph Wright.

Web Sites

East Grinstead: *www.egnet.co.uk.*

East Sussex: *www.eastsussexcc.gov.uk/ashdown.*

Southeast England Tourist Board: *www.southeastengland.uk.com.*

Winnie-the-Pooh: *http://chaos.trzinc.com/jmilne/Pooh.*

Agatha Christie and Jane Austen
Trekking Through Southern England

Susan Kostrzewa

A SERENE SILENCE pervades the Hampshire afternoon, punctuated only by soft gusts of wind through chestnut trees and the scuffle of feet against a narrow, dusty lane. Ahead, nestled behind dark greenery, the worn stone of a Norman church peers out expectantly.

I am walking the road to Steventon rectory, a road left unblemished by time, a road well-known by Jane Austen, who lived in the area for 25 years. The echo of her here, haunting and insistent, transforms me. Eagerly I scan the surrounding fields for her tall, slim form, striding into the distance. I am disappointed not to see her, so entrenched am I in her world.

As I trace the paths of Jane Austen and Agatha Christie through such dramatic English environs as Devon, Somerset, Hampshire, Dorset, and Wiltshire, I experience an adventure that is a communion of past and present, and a hands-on education about the life and times of both literary icons. When I explore the windswept coastal towns, historic cities, and pastoral villages that figure dramatically in Austen's and Christie's novels, the pervading presence of each author arrests the senses. By visiting locations so well-known to the writers themselves, the most intimate connections between reader and novelist are formed.

Although she later developed a taste for mystery and the macabre, Agatha Christie's early years were swathed in the genteel shelter of Torquay, her beloved hometown in Devon. "What has one really enjoyed most in one's life?" she once wrote wistfully. "For my own part . . . it seems that it is almost always the quiet moments of everyday life."

Dubbed the English Naples years ago due to its balmy climate, seaside location, and shimmering white villas, Torquay was a wealthy and fashionable seaside
resort when Christie was born here in 1890. The commodious Georgian and
Victorian mansions still dotting its seven green hills give testament to the
"lovely, safe, yet exciting world of childhood" and privilege that Christie would
later idealize. Her beloved childhood home, a spacious villa called Ashfield, is
sadly no longer among those relics, having been pulled down in the 1960s to
make way for a group of small houses. Fortunately most of the sites and buildings
associated with Christie's often idyllic Victorian childhood are still standing.

As I explore the Royal Pavilion (a once-famous concert hall) and have high tea
at the Imperial Hotel (elegant setting of *Peril at End House* and *The Body in the
Library*), Christie's presence is unmistakable. Gazing at the creamy stonework and
Art Deco iron detailing of the pavilion, I can easily envision an insistent Archie
Christie escorting a calm Agatha Miller from a Wagner concert in 1913. His hasty
marriage proposal that night was in part fueled by his impending departure for
the battlegrounds of World War I. The romantic strains of *Tristan and Isolde* are
mentally summoned while standing on the main floor of the building and admiring the original plaster work and pillars, still evocative of the turn-of-the-century
era despite the modern shops now occupying the hall.

Countless Victorian afternoons of roller-skating by the sea are imagined
when walking along Princess Pier, which was opened to the public in 1894 and
was the scene of many teenage Christie flirtations and hijinks. "You fell down
a great deal," she remembered later, "but it was great fun." Although roller-
skating on the pier is now strictly prohibited, it's still possible to envision the
energetic Christie, decked in long skirts and extravagant hat, speeding up and
down the boards, boyish admirers in hot pursuit.

Similarly the sometimes humorous ironies of Christie's Victorian era resurface
when passing the Royal Torbay Yacht Club, once a favorite haunt for Christie's
father and his cohorts. Overlooking a beach called Beacon Cove where Agatha
herself bathed as a young girl, the front window of the club is still a perfect
vantage point from which to view the secluded beach. The thrill of that view
was more significant in Agatha's time, as gentlemen peered slyly through opera
glasses at the supposedly private women's bathing beach below.

Although additional visits to the picturesque towns of Paignton, Dartmouth,
and Cockington Village also paint a vivid picture of Christie's life and works,
other scenes more effectively capture her presence. A foray to nearby Dartmoor,
a desolate tableland set dramatically in lush Devon, brings to life the image of

When traveling in Agatha Christie country, it's quite common to come across places that invoke the mystery author's fiction such as this bar, Poirot's, in Dartmouth. Susan Kostrzewa

26-year-old Agatha retreating to the Moorland Hotel at Hay Tor to write her first novel, *The Mysterious Affair at Styles*. Christie reputedly took long walks along the moors as she muttered aloud the workings of her plot, intent on isolating herself from other guests. The writer used escapes like this when writing all of her future novels, although the idea was initially her mother's.

Travelers experience the decadent romance of Christie's twenties and thirties when staying at the Burgh Island Hotel, an Art Deco jewel frequented by the author in the late 1920s. Nestled on the tidal Burgh Island off the coast of Devon near Bigbury-on-Sea, the 15-room hotel was once a private home owned by Christie's eccentric London theater acquaintance, millionaire Archibald Nettleford. Nettleford was famous for his rollicking house parties, to which Christie and her second husband, archaeologist Max Mallowan, were often invited. The island's brooding charm intrigued Christie so much that she set two of her novels there: *Evil Under the Sun* and *And Then There Were None*.

From the gleaming, mirrored palm court to the vintage sea-view rooms, Burgh Island Hotel provides the perfect opportunity to saunter straight into one of Christie's mysteries. Intimate yet isolated, the hotel has a lazy, languid feel that effectively conjures up the 1920s and early 1930s era. Although modern stars

The citizens of Torquay, Devon, Agatha Christie's birthplace, are quite proud of the bestselling novelist, as this memorial to her attests. Susan Kostrzewa

such as Mick Jagger and Whoopi Goldberg frequent the hotel nowadays, it is the images of such bygone legends as playwright Noël Coward and the infamous Duke of Windsor and Mrs. Wallis Simpson that really stalk its labyrinth of corridors. Surrounded by dramatic cliffs and ominous mist, the hotel evokes the kind of foreboding loneliness so ideally suited for a murder mystery.

Guests are zealous to get "in the mood," donning evening dress consisting of tuxedos, flapper gowns, broaches, and feather boas. Gramophone-style music crackles in the background as course after sumptuous course is laid out on tables draped in crisp white linen. One night, as we lounged around sipping cocktails under an intricate Art Deco aviary, we giggled wickedly at the notion that we were to suffer the same fate as Mr. Owens's guests. Who would be left alive, we wondered, when the cold and windy night was through?

Peaceful cliffside walks around the 28-acre island also leave one expecting to run into Hercule Poirot snooping around in his white duck suit, or Christie marching purposefully with pen and paper in hand.

Even Burgh Island's rustic and romantic Pilchard Inn (established 1336) has a story and is reputedly haunted by smuggler Tom Crocker. When I took shelter from a brisk night over pints of cider, it was easy to imagine a sea-worn Crocker kneeling by the fire, a bowl of fish soup in hand. The drama of pirates and smugglers led Christie to christen the place "Smuggler's Island" in *Evil Under the Sun*. "That kind of address tickles you up, you know," she wrote.

Rewinding another 130 years in time to the subtle elegance and rural charms of Jane Austen's early 19th-century England, travelers are whisked into the very private author's intimate and exclusive fold. Like Christie, Austen was specific about the towns, streets, and buildings she wrote about, making it possible for explorers to follow the trails of the novelist and her characters to the minutest detail. Although some sites from Austen's life have been seriously altered by nearly 200 years of progress and expansion, it is still possible to relive the stylized world of Regency England that she so incisively satirized.

In Lyme Regis, a small town settled along the cliff-lined Dorset coast, we follow the steep main street used by the Austens when visiting the then-tiny port in 1804. Described by Austen as "almost hurrying into the water," the scenic entrance into town would have been even more dramatic to the Austens than to a modern visitor, since the brakes on their horse-drawn carriage were less reliable than those of our Peugeot minivans and Honda Civics. Austen adored the area and wrote emotionally about it in *Persuasion*, published originally in

1818: "Its sweet retired bay, backed by dark cliffs, where fragments of low rock among the sand make it the happiest spot for watching the flow of the tide, for sitting in unwearied contemplation . . . must be visited, and visited again . . ."

Making our way along a windy, medieval stone pier called the Cobb, we reach the infamous Granny's Teeth. The teeth are rough-hewn slab steps offering a perilous descent from the upper level of the Cobb to the lower and were the scene of flirtatious Louisa Musgrove's near-fatal jump in *Persuasion*. The site was also used in the 1995 film version of the novel.

Unlike Louisa, I have no gallant soldier waiting at the foot of the teeth, so I grab on to the wall and clumsily clamber down. Although eager to imagine myself in Austen's story, getting concussed on the hard stone of the Cobb is hardly my idea of romance. I do, however, wonder how any Regency woman clad in flimsy shoes, a cumbersome bonnet, and three layers of dresses billowing in the wind could ever find her way down the steps without tumbling headlong to the bottom.

The town literally heaves with the presence of Austen and the immortal characters of *Persuasion*. A cluster of tidy cottages near the Cobb display names such as "Benwick" and "Harville," and images of a convalescent Louisa being wooed by melancholic Captain Benwick and his readings of Lord Byron add a poignant drama to the otherwise quiet dwellings. While bracing myself against the brisk sea wind and gazing along the rocky shore, it's easy to understand why Austen was so touched by the vigor and romance of such a place.

Although Lyme Regis affords some close encounters with Austen's real and imagined world, it's in Bath that visitors are most immersed in her life. The bustling spa town wasn't particularly beloved by country girl Austen (she was forced to move there in 1801 when her clergyman father retired from the Steventon living), but neither was she oblivious to its charms. *Northanger Abbey*'s Catherine Morland arrives for the first time in Bath "all eager delight; her eyes were here, there, every where, as they approached its fine and striking environs . . . she was come to be happy, and she felt happy already." The town's stately, neoclassical symmetry proves an effective backdrop for *Northanger Abbey* as well as for *Persuasion*.

Austen protested "all the hot, white glare of Bath" (sun reflected off the pale sandstone of its Georgian buildings) and the "vapour, shadow, smoke and confusion" of its busy streets, but it had been a fashionable watering hole long before she arrived. In the 18th century, Bath was an affordable substitute for London society and a haven for those suffering from gout and rheumatism. By the time Austen arrived in 1801, it was slightly less exciting, being a favorite retirement community for ex-naval officers, while fashionable families had

Montacute House in Somerset was used as a backdrop for Marianne Dashwood's frenzied decline in the film version of Jane Austen's *Sense and Sensibility*. Susan Kostrzewa

moved on to Cheltenham or Brighton. Nevertheless, 40,000 visitors that year and a 20-week social season ensured some society.

Appropriately lodged in a renovated Georgian manor overlooking the city, I spend one whirlwind day reveling in the sites and sounds of Austen's Bath. At the elegant Assembly Rooms, I stand in the vast, empty ballroom flanked by fireplaces and exquisite chandeliers. A room once throbbing with the vitality and pageantry of Austen's era, the ballroom now evokes a loneliness that makes the passage of time seem somberly final. Bringing to mind Austen's own disappointment at the sparsely attended Bath balls of 1801 (private parties had become de rigueur), I wonder where the dancers have gone. Later, downstairs at the Museum of Costume, I look at the sweeping skirts and empire waists of authentic Austen-era dresses.

On chaotic Milsom Street, I try to guess in which building Austen bought her bonnets, and am shown the site of Molland's Confectionery Shop, from which a surprised Anne Elliot spied Captain Wentworth trudging through the rain in *Persuasion*. I even "test the waters" at the Pump Room, where glasses of the Roman Bath's iron- and mineral-laden water can still be had, and an elaborate divan chair (once used to carry the elite to the higher ground of the Crescent) continues to hold court in the dining room.

I am also allowed a unique entrance into the Austens' first lodging at 4 Sydney Place, now owned privately by a Mr. and Mrs. Davis. Over a glass of sherry, I talk with Mrs. Davis in Mr. Austen's former study, the original marble fireplace exuding a welcome warmth from the chill Bath night.

Later she shows me a heavy leaden safe in the old dining room and tells me that the only way to open it is to use explosives and damage the wall, so the safe remains untouched. Fantastically I imagine an unpublished novel hiding in its impenetrable depths, and my mind reels after the visit.

Touring Montacute House, a magnificent Elizabethan manse decorated with Austen-era furniture, also evokes Austen's real and imagined worlds. The estate was used as the Palmer residence and scene of Marianne's breakdown in the 1995 film version of *Sense and Sensibility*. Its grotesquely misshapen Brain Hedge provided a surreal backdrop for the character's frenzied decline.

Another stately manor that greatly impressed and intimidated Austen was the Vyne in Hampshire, which was owned by a friend of her brother, James. The house was handed over to the National Trust fully furnished and remains much as it looked when Austen attended dances there in the late 18th century, vermilion silk damask walls and all. The grandeur and sophistication of the Vyne would serve as Austen's model for the great houses and wealthy families she later wrote about.

While the Vyne's Tudor Gallery would have been ideal for a long minuet or spirited country dance, Austen probably danced in one of the smaller drawing rooms, with the carpets flung back for easy movement. Judging from the draft in the larger chambers, it's no wonder the muslin-clad women preferred the more concentrated blaze of a drawing-room fire.

Although Austen moved to Chawton Cottage (now the Jane Austen Museum), Hampshire, in 1809, her failing health in 1817 forced her to move closer to her doctor in Winchester. From the street, I regard the window from which Austen's devoted sister, Cassandra, watched her funeral pass, and I, too, feel the loss of the talented woman who died at age 41 of Addison's disease.

By journey's end, I've forged an intimate acquaintance with both Austen and Christie. In reflecting on their lives, it's inevitable that I contemplate my own. In Christie's own words, I have "been on a journey. Not so much a journey back through past as a journey forward—a starting at the beginning of it all—going back . . . to [ourselves]."

The Writer's Trail

Following in the Footsteps

Destination: Megalithic remains, Roman ruins, magnificent medieval cathedrals, impressive stately homes, dramatic coastlines, rolling hills, relatively untouched forest and moors, and quaint little English towns characterize Hampshire, Wiltshire, Dorset, Somerset, and Devon, the counties that constitute Agatha Christie and Jane Austen country.

Location: Sandwiched between Cornwall on the west; Gloucestershire, Oxfordshire, and Berkshire on the north; and West Sussex and Surrey on the east, the five counties with connections to Agatha Christie and Jane Austen are southwest of London.

Getting There: See **The Writer's Trail** in **Jane Urquhart and the Brontë Sisters** for details on getting to England.

Orientation: Part of what is known as the English Riviera, Torquay is on the South Devon coast, between Plymouth and Exmouth, just south of Exeter. Lyme Regis, east of Torquay, is also on the English Channel coast, near the Devon-Dorset border. Dartmoor National Park, which includes some of England's wildest and bleakest landscape, is northwest of Exeter. Bath is 12 miles southeast of Bristol. Winchester is in central Hampshire, while Chawton is northwest of Winchester and Basingstoke is northeast of the cathedral city.

Tip: The South West Coast Path is Britain's longest national trail. A domesticated hike, it follows the West Country coastline through various villages from Minehead in North Devon all the way through Cornwall, around Land's End, and up the southern coast to Poole in Dorset. The South West Way Association ([44-1364] 73859) publishes an accommodation guide as well as detailed descriptions of routes.

Getting Around: Trains link London, Bristol, Bath, Salisbury, Weymouth, Exeter, and Winchester. A branch rail line runs from Newton Abbot, via Torquay, to Paignton. For more information, call the 24-hour national rail inquiry line at (44-345) 484950. National Express ([44-990] 808080) buses connect the main centers in southwest England. The Key West Explorer bus pass provides unlimited travel in South Devon and Cornwall for three/seven days for about $22/$38, or you can purchase a one-day Explorer pass for about $8 (for example, the Wiltshire Day Rover features unlimited travel in that county—Salisbury, Avebury, Bradford-on Avon, et cetera—as well as to Bath). The number X46 bus runs hourly from Exeter to Torquay. Number 100 operates along the coast from Paignton and Brixham to Torquay. The best way to get around, though, is to rent a car, especially if you want to tour out-of-the-way stately homes, hamlets, and Dartmoor National Park. All the usual rental-car agencies—Hertz (1-800-654-3131), Avis (1-800-331-1212), Budget (1-800-527-0700)—are represented in England.

Literary Sleeps

Burgh Island Hotel: The tides make it necessary for guests to arrive via sea tractor, so call ahead. Bigbury-on-Sea, South Devon. Tel.: (44-1548) 810514. Expensive.

Olde Churston Court Inn: An eccentric Saxon manor complete with roaring hearths and affectionate mastiff dogs, this inn exudes atmosphere and was frequented by Agatha Christie, who was a close friend of Lord Churston. The church next door displays a stained-glass window donated by Christie. Churston, Brixham, Devon. Tel.: (44-1803) 842186. Moderate.

Paradise House Hotel: This Georgian house, built in the 1720s, is reputedly haunted by myriad ghosts. There are excellent views of Bath and a beautiful garden to stroll in. Jane Austen would likely have passed the home on her way into town, since it's built on the old Roman road (and coaching route). Holloway, Bath. Tel.: (44-1225) 317723. Moderate.

Royal Crescent Hotel: If you've got the cash, this 46-room lodging is the place to stay in Bath. It's decorated with period furnishings and is just down the street from 1 Royal Crescent, the grand Palladian town house that is the epitome of genteel early-19th-century Bath. 15-16 Royal Crescent, Bath. Tel.: (44-1225) 739955. Expensive.

Royal Hotel: In the heart of Winchester, this establishment is down a peaceful street and has a lovely garden. St. Peter Street, Winchester, Hampshire. Tel.: (44-1962) 840840. Moderate.

St. Michael's Hotel: Centrally located in Lyme Regis, this pleasant hotel features nice views and rooms with baths. Pound Street, Lyme Regis, Dorset. Tel.: (44-1297) 442503. Inexpensive.

 Tip: If you decide to explore Dartmoor National Park, don't feed the semiwild ponies found there. You'll encourage them to stray dangerously close to the roads. Also, in the park's northwestern Ministry of Defence (MOD) training area, where the hiking is great and the tors (high rocks) are highest, walking is restricted when there's live firing. Notice boards and red-and-white posts mark the main approaches. Red flags (red lights at night) indicate when firing is under way. You can check firing schedules by calling MOD at (44-1392) 270164.

Literary Sites

Book Museum: The museum features rare Jane Austen books and prints. Several first editions of her works are on display with other novelties such as the sketchbook of her sister, Cassandra. Open Monday to Friday 9:00 a.m. to 1:00 p.m. and 2:00 p.m. to 5:00 p.m.; Saturday 9:30 a.m. to 1:00 p.m. Manvers Street, Bath. Tel.: (44-1225) 466000.

Jane Austen House: Austen lived here from 1809 to her death in 1817 (though she actually died in Winchester). The museum has a good deal of Austen memorabilia on display. Admission fee. Open daily March through December from 11:00 a.m. to 4:30 p.m.; weekends the rest of the year. Call to verify times. Chawton, Alton, Hampshire. Tel.: (44-1420) 83262.

Montacute House: Featured in the 1995 film version of Jane Austen's *Sense and Sensibility*, this impressive Elizabethan mansion was built in the 1590s for Sir Edward Phelips, a Speaker of England's House of Commons. The Long Gallery showcases Tudor and Jacobean portraits on loan from London's National Portrait Gallery. Formal gardens and a landscaped park encircle the house. Admission fee. Open daily April to October from noon to 5:00 p.m. (except Tuesdays). Twenty-two miles southeast of Taunton and four miles west of Yeovil in Somerset. Tel.: (44-1935) 823289.

St. Nicholas's Church-Steventon: The parish church of Steventon, once the Reverend George Austen's living, can still be visited. It's suggested that visitors contact the church to arrange an appropriate time to view it. The site of Jane Austen's childhood home, Steventon Rectory, is within walking distance, but the only remaining remnant is the original water pump. Write care of Charles Elderfield, School Cottage, Steventon, Basingstoke, Hampshire RG25 3BH, England.

Torquay Natural History Society: The museum is home to an extensive exhibit on Agatha Christie's life and works. Christie's father was elected a member of the society in 1894, and she would have known the building well. Admission fee. Open Easter through October Monday to Saturday from 9:30 a.m. to 6:00 p.m.; Sunday from 1:30 p.m. to 4:45 p.m. Open November to Easter Monday to Friday from 10:00 a.m. to 4:45 p.m. 529 Babbacombe Road, Torquay, Devon. Tel.: (44-1803) 293975.

The Vyne: Recently renovated, the Vyne hosted dances attended by Jane Austen in her youth. Call or write for opening times. Sherborne St. John, Basingstoke, Hampshire RG24 9HL. Tel.: (44-1256) 881337.

Icon Pastimes

Agatha Christie enjoyed picnics in Dartmoor from early childhood until old age, when she brought her daughter, Rosalind, and grandson, Matthew, here to relax. Spreading out a large blanket, feasting on cold chicken, and sipping champagne from silver cups pleased Dame Agatha to no end. Christie often traveled on the picturesque Paignton and Dartmouth Steam Railway from Churston Station, which was mentioned in both *Dead Man's Folly* and *The ABC Murders*. The route between Paignton and Kingswear is serviced by steam trains running every 45 minutes. Call (44-1803) 555872 for more information. Jane Austen was a spirited walker and spent many after-noons exploring the environs around Steventon. One regular route was from Steventon Rectory to the inn (now called the Wheatsheaf) where her letters were posted and delivered. Facing the road from the Steventon water pump, turn right and follow the road (keeping right) a few miles until you reach the Wheatsheaf on the left. Although part of the experience is imagining oneself in the sheltered and isolated valley of Austen's time, don't forget to watch for traffic on the nar-row, country lanes!

Contacts

British Connection: 1166 Oxford Road, Atlanta, Georgia 30306 U.S. Tel.: 1-800-420-2560 in the U.S. E-mail: *Britcon777@aol.com*.

British Travel Authority: United States: 551 Fifth Avenue, New York, New York 10176-0799. Tel.: 1-800-462-2748. Canada: Suite 120, 5915 Airport Road, Mississauga, Ontario L4V 1T1. Tel.: 1-800-VISIT UK or (905) 405-1840. Fax: (905) 405-1835. Web sites: *www.bta.org.uk* or *www.travelbritain.org*.

English Riviera Tourist Board: Dept. ACR, The Tourist Centre, Vaughan Parade, Torquay, Devon TQ2 5JG, England. Tel.: (44-1803) 211211. Fax: (44-1803) 214885. Web site: *www.torbay.gov.uk*.

In a Literary Mood

Books

Austen, Caroline. *My Aunt Jane Austen*. Winchester, England: Sarsen Press, 1952. Although not the only memoir of Austen to be written by a family member, Caroline's modest recollection of her Aunt Jane's last years at Chawton Cottage affords the kind of firsthand, realistic account of the mannerisms, routine, and lifestyle so hard to find on the private Austen.

Austen, Jane. *Northanger Abbey*. London: Penguin, 1972. A satire of the Gothic novels so popu-lar with Austen-era women, the novel is set almost exclusively in Bath.

_____. *Persuasion*. New York: Bantam, 1984. An introspective and contemplative tale of love lost and found, *Persuasion* is set in memorable locales such as Bath and Lyme Regis.

_____. *Sense and Sensibility*. London: Penguin, 1995. Austen's first novel tells the story of two sisters whose different approaches to life result in some surprising twists and turns of fate.

Cannadine, David. *Aspects of Aristocracy*. London: Penguin, 1994. Although Jane Austen writes almost exclusively about the English gentry, her characters often aspire to, and occasionally mix in, the soci-ety of English aristocrats. Cannadine's study of that world is valuable in understanding 19th-century aristocratic hierarchies and beliefs.

Christie, Agatha. *An Autobiography.* New York: Berkley Publishing Group, 1977. An essential read for anyone interested in Christie's life, times, and work, this book is a candid reflection on the episodes that would eventually lead to her writing career (as well as those that occurred after the career began). The book's intimate narrative tone gives one a true sense of what the author must have been like: witty, warm, but proudly opinionated.

_____. *And Then There Were None.* New York: Berkley Publishing Group, 1995. Considered by many to be Christie's best mystery, it tells the story of 10 strangers who are lured to a Native American island and are eventually murdered one by one. The setting was inspired by Christie's visits to Burgh Island off the Devon coast.

_____. *The Mysterious Affair at Styles.* New York: Berkley Publishing Group, 1991. Christie's first mystery novel and the public's introduction to fastidious Hercule Poirot. Written at the dramatic Moorland Hotel in 1917, it marked the beginning of the author's prolific writing career.

_____. *Peril at End House.* New York: Berkley Publishing Group, 1996. After four murder attempts on the young mistress of End House, it's time for Hercule Poirot to step in. Scenes of Poirot at the Majestic Hotel (actually the Imperial Hotel) in Torquay can be relived in a visit to the terrace overlooking the sea.

Myer, Valerie Grosvenor. *Jane Austen: Obstinate Heart—A Biography.* New York: Arcade Publishing, 1997. An account of Austen that deftly deflates the cherished image of the author as a prim and precious Regency sweetheart. Myer's Austen is an energetic, flirtatious, satirical woman whose tongue often gets the better of her in polite society. Letters between Austen and her sister, Cassandra, that were once protected by the family appear here in all of their humorous and sometimes bittersweet glory, revealing the human side of a woman so talented and incisive that she would inevitably feel out of place in her own time.

Sales, Roger. *Jane Austen and Representations of Regency England.* London: Routledge, 1994. A valuable discussion of the "hot topics" of Austen's day as they apply to her letters and novels.

Guidebooks

Gerrard, David. *Exploring Agatha Christie Country.* Leyburn: Trail Publishing, 1996. Bite-size reference guide of all major and lesser-known sites associated with Christie's life, from the pavilion in Torquay to her final home, Greenfield. The book includes pictures and detailed directions to relevant Christie sites..

Nicolson, Nigel. *The World of Jane Austen.* London: Phoenix, 1991. A gorgeous picture book of the places associated with Jane Austen's life, from the grand houses to the cheerful rectory cottages in which she lived and/or played. Excellent photos are accompanied by period drawings, engravings, and maps of the relevant places. Readers are completely immersed in Austen's world.

Rivière, François. *In the Footsteps of Agatha Christie.* London: Ebury Press, 1997. A highly detailed textual and pictorial guide that beautifully captures the allure of Christie's picturesque South Devon. While the photos transport the reader to the romantic Christie era, the text educates on every level, discussing her novels, personal history, and the history of the places with which she is associated.

Thomas, Bryn, Tom Smallman, and Pat Yale. *Britain.* 3rd ed. Hawthorn, Australia: Lonely Planet Publications, 1999. Lonely Planet's all-purpose compendium is a good repository of everything British. There are some references to Jane Austen; check the book's index.

Films/Videos

Numerous films have been made from the novels of Jane Austen and Agatha Christie. Here are a few notable ones.

Aukin, David, Sarah Curtis, and others (producers). *Mansfield Park*. Patricia Rozema (director). BBC and others, 1999. Cast: Johnny Lee Miller, Frances O'Connor, and Harold Pinter. Canadian director Rozema melds Jane Austen's most ambitious novel with extracts from the writer's journals and letters to present an artful, visually stunning foray into early 19th-century English mores and manners. Some may object to the nudity, opium indulgence, and the overt political correctness and feminism. Playwright Pinter is superb as Sir Thomas Bertram.

Brabourne, John, and Richard N. Goodwin (producers). *Evil Under the Sun*. Guy Hamilton (director). EMI Films/Titan Productions, 1982. Republic Video. Cast: Colin Blakely, Maggie Smith, and Peter Ustinov. Ustinov tries his hand at the much-attempted role of Hercule Poirot in this star-studded pirouette through murder and mayhem in a resort hotel.

Bronston, Samuel, René Clair, and Henry M. and Leo C. Popkin (producers). *And Then There Were None*. René Clair (director). 20th Century Fox, 1945. VCI Home Video. Cast: Barry Fitzgerald, Louis Hayward, and Walter Huston. Remade three times, this classic take on one of Agatha Christie's best novels has a great script by Dudley Nichols, helped out by outstanding visuals.

Finlay, Fiona (producer). *Persuasion*. Roger Michell (director). BBC and others, 1995. Columbia Tristar Home Video. Cast: Ciarán Hinds, Corin Redgrave, and Amanda Root. Made for British television, this exquisite rendering of Jane Austen's novel about a young woman's tumultuous relationship with a sailor is well acted and beautifully shot.

Pollack, Sydney, James Schamus, and Laurie Borg (producers). *Sense and Sensibility*. Ang Lee (director). Columbia, 1995. Columbia Tristar Home Video. Cast: Hugh Grant, Emma Thompson, and Kate Winslet. Thompson does double duty as screenwriter (she won an Oscar) and star in a delightful, memorable interpretation of Jane Austen's novel about two newly impoverished sisters—one spontaneous and flirtatious, the other constantly disappointed in life and love.

Stromberg, Hunt (producer). *Pride and Prejudice*. Robert Z. Leonard (director). MGM, 1940. MGM/UA Home Video. Cast: Greer Garson, Laurence Olivier, and Maureen O'Sullivan. As with most of Jane Austen's novels, this book, about five husband-hunting sisters in early 19th-century England, has been filmed many times. MGM's classic version, cowritten by Aldous Huxley, is still one of the best Austen renderings on celluloid.

Web Sites

Jane Austen: *www.pemberley.com*; *www.geocities.com/Athens/Aegean/9140*; *www.hants.gov.uk/austen/index.html*; *www.jasna.org*. The first site is a necessity for Austen fanatics. The second site features a collection of links devoted to Austen and the Regency era. The third site is the Hampshire Web page, with visits to places associated with Austen's time in the area. The last site belongs to the Jane Austen Society of North America.

Agatha Christie: *www.goblinmarket.com/index.html*; *www.aber.ac.uk/~jgs/ag4.html*. The first site is *Miss Marple's Mystery Magazine*—for fans of Christie and the mystery novel. The second site has valuable related Christie links.

"We were on Haholmen, a bleak and beautiful island that lies about 60 miles southwest of Trondheim: icy blue water, a rocky inlet weathered by wind and tides, mountains that seem to drift in and out of the ever-shifting clouds. In Norway, although time can move slowly, the sky is never still."

6   Continental Europe

Knut Hamsun
Inner and Outer Journeys in Norway

Tom Henighan

ON A VISIT TO NORWAY a few years ago, I asked a leading Scandinavian television reporter about one of my favorite writers. "Hamsun," I said. "What do you think of Knut Hamsun?"

The setting was spectacular. We were on Haholmen, a bleak and beautiful island that lies about 60 miles southwest of Trondheim: icy blue water, a rocky inlet weathered by wind and tides, mountains that seem to drift in and out of the ever-shifting clouds. In Norway, although time can move slowly, the sky is never still.

At that moment, if nature was relatively calm, my reporter friend was not. Despite the fact that Hamsun had been a Nobel Prize winner and remained Norway's greatest novelist, the man seemed surprised, even agitated, by my question. He clutched at his drink, took a puff of his cigarette, and glared at me across the table. "Hamsun!" he growled finally. "I hate him. A great writer, no doubt about it. But I hate him. Let me tell you something!"

I sat back to listen. Not entirely to my surprise, the reporter proceeded to recount his firsthand experience of the Nazi invasion of Norway in 1940. He spoke of a courageous effort by his countrymen to block the airfield at Oslo against the Germans, of heroic resistance elsewhere, and of the formation of one of Europe's most effective underground movements. Hamsun, I knew, had not been part of that. To his shame, the great writer, in his extreme old age, had sided with Adolf Hitler.

I looked around at the Norwegian landscape. Haholmen is the private estate of Ragnar Thorseth, an explorer and national hero, and it is a setting fit for a descendent of Vikings. Forming part of the reticulated coastline and its myriad islands lying between Trondheim and Bergen—two of Norway's largest cities—the island seems far from urban life, Europe, and the whole modern world. The houses, modeled on 200-year-old fishermen's shacks, are painted a pleasing red. They are snug and comfortable, and yet in their simple construction and honest craftsmanship, might almost be medieval. Tied up at the dock nearby, next to a small ancient sailing cutter, I saw a full-size replica of a Viking long ship, one that would soon cross the Atlantic Ocean to L'Anse aux Meadows, Newfoundland, where those intrepid Norsemen had landed long ago.

Norway is a strange country, incredibly *there*, yet at the same time hidden. It is a country still close to nature, to the sea, to earth, rock, and glacier, as well as to the realities of peasant life. The country prides itself on "progress," yet plays up its traditional virtues. This is the country of the Vikings, the epitome of aggressive physicality, and the country of Edvard Munch, whose *The Scream* has become so famous as to be almost a clichéd image of paralytic neurosis. It seems quite appropriate that Knut Hamsun, the great, tortured genius of the north, should be Norwegian.

Hamsun was born Knud Pederson in 1859, son of a village tailor and crofter in Garmo on Lake Vaga in the upper Gudbrandsdal region of south-central Norway, about halfway between Lillehammer, where the 1994 Winter Olympics took place, and the Atlantic Ocean. Knut was the fourth of seven children, and the family was poor and without much distinction, although his mother may have been descended from medieval Norwegian kings. Later, neither the Norwegian literary establishment nor the city burghers let Hamsun forget his humble origins.

When he was only three, the boy was taken to the far north, to the so-called Nordland above the Arctic Circle, a majestic world of sea, islands, and mountains. He grew up on a farm called Hamsund at Hamaroy, a rocky islet on the edge of the Lofoten Islands. Here he enjoyed what he remembered as idyllic times, until at about age nine he was sent inland as house servant and farm helper to a cruel and demanding uncle. Not until he was 14 did he gain his release from this bondage, and years later, when he was on trial for treason, the Norwegian state psychiatrists attributed some of his erratic behavior to the cruelty he suffered in those early days.

The real Hamsun emerged at about age 16 when, after a trip to his birthplace, he began his career as a wanderer, day laborer, and traveling peddler. Although he began writing fiction shortly afterward, his path to fame was slow and tortuous. Like many Norwegians of those days, he virtually gave up on his country and sought to make his fortune in the new world. He immigrated to America, where he worked as a farm laborer in Wisconsin and in a lumberyard in Minnesota.

Norway in reality, and as seen by Knut Hamsun in his fiction, is a land of mountains, rocks, clouds, and water.
Tom Henighan

He returned from this first trip thinking he was dying of tuberculosis. Six or seven hard years were to follow (he was often close to starvation) and another trip to America ensued before, at the age of 31, Hamsun finally published *Hunger*, the book that made him famous.

Hamsun's career began in Oslo, or—as it was known in his day—Christiania, and this is where your trip to Norway should begin. It is a wonderful city, but not warmhearted, extroverted, or jolly. It is clean, cool, and northern, a city where few appear to be at loose ends, where everyone seems to have somewhere to go. How well Hamsun conveyed this in *Hunger*, a book in which his starving protagonist watches but cannot participate in the well-oiled machinery of bourgeois life!

In *Hunger*, Hamsun hardly refers to the harbor, except when the hero decides to leave, but one of your first impressions of Oslo may be the exhilarating sight of a forest of masts, of ships of all descriptions down in the Pipervika or the Bjorvika, the main harbors of the capital. The visitor to Oslo could do worse than to follow this maritime theme. At Byngdoy, nearly four miles west of the city, you can see the Viking Ships Museum, the Thor Heyerdahl Museum with the *Kon-Tiki* and the *Ra*, or Fram House, which holds the ship in which the great explorer Fridtjof Nansen drifted across the North Polar Sea in the 1890s.

You may not want to begin there, but it would be unthinkable to miss these sights, or to pass up a chance to inspect the charming models (displayed in the Maritime Museum) of the interiors of classic coastal steamers, one of the main forms of transport in Norway from Hamsun's time to ours, and one that is referred to constantly in his writings.

It's a fascinating theme, this notion of a country always facing the sea, yet it might be better to begin your Oslo experience a little closer to the center, with two other great Norwegian revealers of the inner states of the human psyche, Edvard Munch and Henrik Ibsen, both of whom have strong connections with Hamsun. In fact, you might want to head straight to the Munch Museum on Toyengate 53, which contains over a thousand paintings by Hamsun's countryman. In the National Gallery (although there is much fine Norwegian, Scandinavian, and world art on display), you can also find a Munch room. (These Norwegian creators are prolific!) A reviewer of the time compared Munch and Hamsun, declaring that the work of both was marked by "twisted imaginations, atmospheres swimming in delirium, sick and feverish hallucinations."

Hamsun spent some part of his early career attacking what one of his characters called Ibsen's "dramatized pulp." The playwright, already a world figure, pretended to ignore the upstart, yet his drama *The Master Builder* seems to be partially a response to Hamsun's critiques of his art. If you walk over to the National Theater, northwest of Eidsvollplas, you'll find the spot where Hamsun met his second wife, Marie. He stood on the steps of the building and stared at the 26-year-old actress. "My God, child," he said, "how beautiful you are!" He dragged her away for a conversation and the next day sent her two dozen and two roses. Much later, in 1925, Hamsun came to Oslo to stay in the Victoria Hotel (which also figures in one of his best fictions, *Under the Autumn Star*, but unfortunately no longer exists). The purpose of his visit was not literary but to get himself psychoanalyzed; he was, perhaps appropriately, the first in Norway to go through this Freudian ritual.

The National Theater, with its prominent statues of Ibsen and writer Bjornstjerne Bjornson (not Hamsun!), the university (with some murals by Munch), the Historisk Museum, containing many Viking treasures, and the National Gallery cluster at one end of Karl Johansgate, the historical central thoroughfare of Oslo, where you'll certainly want to do some shopping. If you stop also for a snack, try not to think of *Hunger* and Hamsun's starving hero! Walking south from the theater area, you soon come to City Hall, with its striking twin towers, which are especially impressive as seen from the harbor. This enormous building, built between 1931 and 1950, is well worth a visit. And here, if you wish, you can take a motor launch to Byngdoy to inspect the maritime treasures mentioned above.

Oslo has much more that is of interest, and many more connections with Hamsun, but if you want to follow the track of the novelist and to see more of the "real Norway," you must head north. You might want to stop at Lillehammer, the 1994 Olympic village, where you can find some good hiking and fishing and imagine yourself to be one of Hamsun's peripatetic heroes. Hamsun himself was a restless wanderer, not a homebody, and his many books reflect this, some even in their titles: for example, *Vagabonds*, *The Road Leads On*, *A Wanderer Plays on Muted Strings*, *Under the Autumn Star*. A repeated pattern in a Hamsun novel sees an outsider upsetting things in a settled community, and perhaps getting himself killed in the process, either through his indifference to survival, or because of his inability to conform. Yet, ironically, it was *Growth of the Soil*, a celebration of rural rootedness and simplicity, that helped Hamsun win the Nobel Prize in 1920. Near Lillehammer, on Peer Gynt Road at Aulestad, you may stumble on the house of Bjornson, an important Norwegian literary figure whom Hamsun idolized but who didn't succeed in helping the younger writer when he needed it most. It was at Lillehammer, too, in 1895, that Hamsun convalesced after completing his first five important novels.

From the Olympic town, you can drive right through the heart of Gudbrandsdal, the very pleasant agricultural region of Hamsun's birth. Norway has, understandably, been slow to celebrate Hamsun, but there is a museum at Lom, once considered his birthplace, as there is at Hamsund in the far north, while Norholm, his farm in the south, bought with Nobel Prize money, is preserved by the writer's family. Hamsun is a writer whose spirit is best recalled in the atmosphere of the country and in the psychic life of the people he both loved and hated, yet he is no regionalist. So don't linger in Gudbrandsdal, but drive on to tackle some of the hair-raising Norwegian highways that lead over the mountains down into the fjords. Sognefjord, Geiranger fjord (with the Seven Sisters Waterfall), and Hardangerfjord, among many others, are the stuff of legend, with mountains rising sheer from channels cut deep in the ancient rock, a panorama of light, airy heights, shining glaciers, villages and farms clinging to the cliffs. Most visitors find that the word *spectacular* takes on a new meaning after a tour of this region. It is not really Knut Hamsun country, however, for— with one notable exception, described below—he alludes to the breathtaking mountain scenery of Norway not with the superlatives of the tourist but with the casual familiarity of the native who has struggled to survive in a harsh climate and an unfriendly and seemingly alien social milieu.

To experience the real Norway, the visitor must take a coastal steamer, or— if this exceeds your budget—at least some of the ferries that run between the fjords, the islands, and the Atlantic towns. There are a number of choices, but your trip should take you to some of the sights on the marvelous stretch of coast that runs between the Art Nouveau town of Alesund and the ancient city of Trondheim. In the cabin of one of the ships or on the deck of a ferry, you'll relive the experience of many a Hamsun hero, and of Hamsun himself, for— even after his greatest successes—the writer often scoured the western coast in search of a quiet hotel where he could write (and drink) outside of the trammels of the "domestic bliss" he shared with the beautiful Marie, or with his first wife, Bergljot.

The most memorable destination of your Norwegian trip, however, may well be the splendid Lofoten Islands, which are part of the Nordland where Hamsun spent his youth, and about which he wrote his most lyrical and descriptive novel, *Pan*. The Lofotens, located well north of the Arctic Circle, are easily accessible these days by steamer or by air. There are four main islands, set close together, with cliffs rising more than 3,000 feet straight from the water.

These islands are surrounded by hosts of islets and skerries. In winter the climate is mild and the landscape quite varied: you see sheer rock everywhere, rising steeply to snow-clad Alpine heights, while meadows, swamps, and tarns encircle the many villages from which fishing fleets have sailed for centuries. Here the northern lights are eerie in winter and the midnight sun is visible on many a memorable midnight vigil. Trollfjord, a narrow channel surrounded by towering mountains, has to be seen to be believed, and not far away is Trollfjordvann, a mountain lake that is almost always frozen: a hike around the latter will take you back to the beginning of creation when the Norse gods contended with the Frost giants for dominion over the primeval earth.

One of the most beautiful towns in the Lofotens is Reine. You may also want to visit the Refsvikhula Cave, with its 3,000-year-old paintings, and to experience the Maelstrom, a coastal tide made famous as the irresistible whirlpool in one of the best-known stories of Edgar Allan Poe. Around the Lofotens, too, during July and August, you can see many whales. Interestingly enough, the Norwegian government has recently resumed controlled whaling, much to the dismay of environmentalists around the world. It is ironical that this country, with its love of nature, is at odds with so many over this issue, yet is also part of the perversity that connects Norway and Hamsun. The writer would surely have loved the inconsistencies implied in Norway's new policy. Nature and Vikings, protection and slaughter, a perverse streak in the heart of all this healthiness. It is worthy of Norway's greatest novelist.

Hamsun, as mentioned earlier, grew up in the Nordland and celebrated it in *Pan*, which has been described by his biographer Robert Ferguson as "one of the most beautiful short novels ever written, an experience rather than a book."You won't want to visit the Lofotens without a copy of it in your suitcase or rucksack, just so you can savor passages like this:

> It was quiet and hushed everywhere. I lay the whole evening looking out
> of my window. An enchanted light hung over field and forest at that hour; the
> sun had set and coloured the horizon with a fatty, red light, motionless like oil.
> Everywhere the sky was open and pure. I gazed into the clear sea and it was as
> if I lay face to face with the depths of the earth, and as if my beating heart went
> out to those depths and was at home there. God knows, I thought to myself,
> why the horizon clothes itself in mauve and gold tonight; or perhaps there is
> some celebration above the world, a celebration in grand style, with music from
> the stars and boat trips down the tides. . . .

Only in his breathtakingly beautiful narrative, *Victoria*, which Thomas Mann, great German novelist and himself a Nobel Prize winner, called one of the greatest love stories ever written, does Hamsun write as lyrically as this. In *Pan* he evokes the Nordland in an unforgettable way, capturing with unmatched precision and fervor the essence of the northern lights, the midnight sun, and the wild and endlessly changing ocean and sky. It's rather sad—but, in some perverse way, quite appropriate—that the only monuments to Hamsun in the area he immortalized in his prose are a tiny museum at his home farm and a dusty, deserted road near Presteid called (perhaps with some irony) Knut Hamsun's Way.

The Lofotens and the north should be the climax of your trip to Norway, unless it's the great fjords to the south. But there are other superb destinations: Bergen, European culture city in the year 2000, which has little to do with Hamsun and much to do with the great composer Edvard Grieg; Trondheim, a most pleasant ancient place; and Norway's south coast where, near Grimstad, one can find Norholm, Hamsun's beloved estate at which he died in 1952. There Hamsun's remains are encased in a memorial statue by Wilhelm Rasmussen.

It is not uncommon to discover that some of the greatest writers and artists are notably cantankerous and even perverse human beings, but Hamsun would surely rank near the top of any such list. Mann wrote of him: "Never has the Nobel Prize been awarded to one worthier of it."Yet Hamsun sent his Nobel Prize medal to Nazi propagandist Joseph Goebbels with an admiring letter, while in a private interview he growled at Hitler and complained about the details of the occupation of Norway. Hamsun was so outspoken in the presence of the Fuehrer that the wary translator refused to put his Norwegian phrases into

Old fishing villages dot the rugged, fjord-riven coast of Norway. Little seems to have changed in places like this since Knut Hamsun's time. Tom Henighan

accurate German.

For his tragic mistake in supporting the Nazis, Hamsun was condemned and stripped of his assets by a Norwegian court in 1948, but excused from execution and jail as having "permanently impaired faculties." Yet with "permanently impaired faculties," at age 90, he published one of his most memorable books, *On Overgrown Paths*, which everyone should read for its memorable rendition of what the experience of extreme old age is like. And one of the notable tributes to Hamsun comes from the Jewish writer, Isaac Bashevis Singer, who rightly observed that "Hamsun belonged to that select group of writers who not only interested a reader but virtually hypnotized him." Singer wrote that "the whole modern school of literature stems from Hamsun." He notes that the Norwegian influenced Franz Kafka, Arthur Schnitzler, Maxim Gorky, Boris Pasternak, Andrei Bely, André Gide, Robert Musil, Ernest Hemingway, and Henry Miller, among many others. Modern fictional narrative would not have been the same without him.

As I have indicated, a trip around Norway can be much enriched with

Hamsun's books in hand. At this point, you won't be surprised to learn that Hamsun despised the idea of Norway becoming a tourist country. He spoke disparagingly of the Swiss tourist industry and urged his countrymen not to follow a similar path. His scornful reaction was very similar to that of the Orson Welles character Harry Lime in the film *The Third Man*: "Two thousand years of peace and what has Switzerland produced? The cuckoo clock!" Hamsun despised the idea that Norwegians should spend their time catering to tourists, selling—if not cuckoo clocks—then toy trolls, "Viking" spoons, and frumpy sweaters. It is superfluous to say that many Norwegians disagree with this attitude and that hordes of tourists and visitors, this writer included, thank their lucky stars they touched down in Norway.

For many reasons, some of them obvious, Norway still officially ignores Hamsun—although some signs of a thaw have been in evidence recently. But in his complexity of character, his inwardness, his appreciation of nature, Hamsun is Norwegian to the core. And he would be quite happy, I believe, to know that his presence still rankles, that he is far from accepted in his native country. He wrote as follows: "Once upon a time I was like my comrades. They have kept pace with the times. I have not. Now I am like no one. Unfortunately. Thank God."

I suggest that you pick up copies of *Pan*, *Victoria*, and *Mysteries* and head north. You won't be disappointed on any count.

Following in the Footsteps

Destination: Norwegians are efficient, polite, and never effusive. In recent years, the facilities for tourism have multiplied and generally improved. One of the main problems of visiting Norway over the years has been the sheer expense of everything there, although special discounts and passes are helping in a small way to counteract this.

Location: Norway is one of the five Scandinavian countries located in the far north of Europe. About the size of California, it has a relatively small population of about 4.5 million people. The country is long, narrow, and mostly mountainous, with an extensive and much-reticulated coast-line, which makes possible the country's most famous geographical wonder—its fjords.

Getting There: Various airlines serve Norway. Oslo is the usual point of entry. SAS, or Scandinavian Airlines (1-800-221-2350), flies out of Newark, New Jersey, with connecting flights that can be arranged from almost any large Canadian or American city. Finnair (1-800-950-5000) flies from New York City, San Francisco, and Toronto to Helsinki, Finland, and thence by connecting flight to Oslo. On Icelandair (1-800-223-5500) you can fly to Oslo, with a stop in Iceland, year-round from several major U.S. cities, or from Halifax, Nova Scotia. Most major European airlines have flights from European capitals to Oslo. You can also get to Norway by ferry, particularly from Britain. Norway's Color Line ([44-191] 296-1313 in England) connects Stavanger, Haugesund, and Bergen in Norway with Newcastle, England. Check with the Scandinavian Tourist Board, or the Norwegian embassy or consulate in your country (see **Contacts**), for further details on air and ferry travel or on international rail and bus service.

Orientation: Oslo and the Lofoten Islands are the two "musts" for a Hamsun-related visit, although to go to Norway without seeing the fjords would be rather foolish. Your best bet might be a stay in Oslo, followed by a drive to the fjord region. You can take some ferry trips there, then continue north to the Lofotens by car or by coastal steamer. A steamer trip should be arranged in advance. These are very expensive but spectacular. The Norwegians are past masters at this kind of thing and maintain a fleet of ships of different eras to meet the needs of various travelers. Get in touch with the Norwegian embassy or consulate in your area for more information (see **Contacts**).

Tip: Terrific for shorter trips in Scandinavia is the Scanrail Pass or a combination Scanrail Pass with a car rental, much less of a commitment than a Eurail Pass, which you have to buy in North America before you fly to Europe.

Getting Around: Don't rent a car in Norway if you have anything resembling vertigo. The roads are well engineered but are sometimes simply hair-raising. On the other hand, Norway is well set up to accommodate physically challenged travelers. Car-rental agencies include Auto-Europe (1-800-223-5555), Avis International (1-800-331-1212), and Hertz (1-800-654-3131).

Literary Sleeps

The old Victoria Hotel, associated with Knut Hamsun, doesn't exist. Hotel prices in Oslo are steep, and at the large international palaces prices can go through the roof. In the north, it is recommended that you rent a fisherman's cottage in the Lofoten Islands. This will cost between $85 and $150 per night. When you get there, you can rent a bicycle and a boat and transport yourself back in a twinkling to Hamsun's Norway. Arrangements for cabins can be made with the following tour companies, among many others: Nordic Saga Tours (1-800-848-6449) and Scantours (1-800-223-7226). What follows, however, are three hotels in Oslo for various budgets.

Hotel Continental: This place has some traditional character and is rather suave. Stortingsgaten 24-26. Tel.: (47-22) 824040. Expensive.

Anker Hotel: This rather functional place has a hostel and student lodging connection and expands in summer. It's conveniently located. Storgata 55. Tel.: (47-22) 997510. Moderate.

Hotel Foenix: This establishment is a seemingly typical Norwegian lodging, although it has a Cajun restaurant attached! Dronningsgaten 19. Tel.: (47-22) 425957. Moderate.

Tip: Make use of Norway's camping, youth hostel, and bed-and-breakfast facilities. You can stay on a farm or in a guesthouse or get private accommodations. If you're determined to stay in a three- or four-star hotel, use the Scan-Cheque system, which gives you vouchers valid for any such hostelry—you choose the time and place. For more information, call 1-800-843-0602.

Literary Sites

Knut Hamsun doesn't have a large public presence in Norway. If you're really keen to see Norholm, where Hamsun is buried, you'll have to apply for permission (and may not get it). This is probably best arranged by contacting your local Norwegian embassy or consulate in the United States or Canada. It is suggested, however, that you concentrate on traveling the western coast by steamer or ferry and then staying for a while in the Lofoten Islands. There, at Hamaroy, you can drop in on the privately run Hamsun Museum (inquire locally about the visiting hours). More to the point would be hikes through the Lofotens with a copy of *Pan* in your pocket. Lillehammer is another good place for hiking and has, as noted, some Hamsun connections.

Icon Pastimes

Given the importance of *Hunger* in Knut Hamsun's output, and the writer's terrible battle with poverty—and taking into account his ironic sense of humor—it's tempting to suggest that you starve yourself in Oslo! More likely, however, you'll want to walk around the capital and hike in the Lofoten Islands or at Lillehammer.

Contacts

Royal Norwegian Embassy: United States: 2720 Thirty-fourth Street NW, Washington, D.C. 20008-2714. Tel.: (202) 333-6000. Fax: (202) 337-0870; Canada: Royal Bank Centre, 90 Sparks Street, Suite 532, Ottawa, Ontario K1P 5B4. Tel.: (613) 238-6571. Fax: (613) 238-2765.

Scandinavian Tourist Board: P.O. Box 4649, Grand Central Terminal, New York, New York 10163-4649 U.S. Tel.: (212) 885-9700. Fax: (212) 885-9710. Web site: *www.goscandinavia.com*.

In a Literary Mood

Books

Ferguson, Robert. *Enigma: The Life of Knut Hamsun*. New York: Farrar, Straus & Giroux, 1987. A marvelous biography, but in terms of recent Hamsun studies it's a little outdated.

Hamsun, Knut. *Growth of the Soil*. New York: Vintage, 1992.

_____. *Hunger.* Translated by Robert Bly. New York: Noonday, 1998. Or check the new translation by Sverre Lyngstad (New York: Penguin, 1998).

_____. *Mysteries.* New York: Noonday, 1998.

_____. *Night Roamers and Other Stories.* Seattle: Fjord Press, 1992.

_____. *On Overgrown Paths.* New York: Eriksson, 1967.

_____. *Pan.* Translated by James MacFarlane. New York: Noonday, 1956. Or read the new translation by Sverre Lyngstad (New York: Penguin, 1998).

_____. *Victoria.* Los Angeles: Sun and Moon Press, 1994.

_____. *Under the Autumn Star.* Los Angeles: Sun and Moon Press, 1998.

_____. *Wayfarers.* Los Angeles: Sun and Moon Press, 1995.

Naess, Harald S. *Knut Hamsun.* Boston: Twayne, 1984. A very good introduction to Hamsun's fiction by a leading Hamsun scholar.

Naess, Harald S., ed. *Knut Hamsun: Selected Letters.* Norwich: Norvik Press, 1990.

Guidebooks

Baedeker's Touring Guide: Scandinavia. Freiburg: Baedeker, 1963. This old Baedeker's, if outdated in some ways and useless for hotels, et cetera, is wonderful. If it says a 12th-century church will appear on the left at the next turn, it always does!

Swaney, Deanna. *Norway.* Hawthorn, Australia: Lonely Planet Publications, 2000.

Films/Videos

Bernard, Vannick, and Matthijs van Heijningen (producers). *Mysteries.* Paul de Lussanet (director). Sigma Film Productions, 1978. Cast: Rutger Hauer, Sylvia Kristel, and David Rappaport. This Dutch production is available (if you can find it!) on video in an English-dubbed version. It's an intriguing film, but no masterpiece.

Carlsen, Henning, Bengt Forslund, and others (producers). *Pan.* Henning Carlsen (director). Zentropa Entertainments/Dagmar Films, 1995. Cast: Marit Andreassen, Stein Bjorn, and Sofie Grabol. *Pan* and *Victoria* seem to be the favorite Hamsun novels to film. The former has been the basis for four movies, but this version is your best bet.

Kolvig, Lars, and Hans Morten Rubin (producers). *Hamsun.* Jan Troell (director). TV2-Norge/Norsk Filminstitutt, 1996. First Run Features (video). Cast: Anette Hoff, Ghita Norby, and Max von Sydow. This terrific biopic focuses on Hamsun's support of Nazism and his subsequent trial after the war. Von Sydow is excellent as Hamsun, as is Norby as his wife.

Lindgren, Göran (producer). *Hunger.* Henning Carlsen (director). Svenska Film Institutet/Sandrews, 1966. Studio Connoisseur/Meridian Films (video). Cast: Birgitte Federspiel, Gunnel Lindblom, and Per Oscarsson. Swedish actor Per Oscarsson apparently starved himself to portray Knut Hamsun's struggling protagonist in an Oscar-quality performance in this haunting film.

Widerberg, Bo (producer and director). *Victoria.* Bo Widerberg Film/Corona Film/Svensk Filmindustri, 1979. Cast: Erik Eriksson, Gustaf Kleen, and Amelie von Essen. There are three film versions of this quintessential Hamsun novel, but this Swedish production is easily the best.

Web Sites

Knut Hamsun: *members.aol.com/wpwinter/hamsun*; *www.nrk.no/hamsun*. The second site is maintained by the Norwegian Broadcasting Corporation.

Henrik Ibsen: *www.ibsen.net.*

Edvard Munch: *www.oir.ucf.edu/wm/paint/auth/munch.*

The Lost Generation

American Expatriates in Paris

Suzie Rodriguez

IF I COULD CLIMB into a time machine, twirl a few dials, and zip anywhere in the past I wanted to go, one of my top five choices would be Paris in the 1920s.

It's hard to believe now, but the good life in Paris cost almost nothing back then—if you weren't French, that is. The franc was in a pitiful state for most of the decade, and foreigners from more robust economies quickly learned they could thrive on just a tiny income from home. Not surprisingly, the City of Light was awash in expatriates.

Drawing them was a single truth: if you cared anything at all for the arts, Paris was *the* place to be at that particular time. It was, after all, the absolute epicenter of Modernism, having already gifted the world with the Cubism of Pablo Picasso and Georges Braque, the ballets of Sergei Diaghilev, the liberating movement of Isadora Duncan, the streamlined sculpture of Constantin Brancusi, the atonal music of Erik Satie, the discordant sounds of Igor Stravinsky, and the radical writing of Gertrude Stein.

While Americans dominated the expat scene, other nations added spice and texture to the mix. The most colorful group may have been the newly impoverished Russian nobility, recently fled from the revolution. Counts and princesses could be seen regally waiting tables, driving taxis, and toiling as seamstresses. There were also many British, Canadians, Japanese, Argentines, Swedes, Finns, Romanians, Poles, and Australians . . . They came from everywhere, really. What expats tended to have in common was youth and—at least in the decade's early years—artistic or literary leanings.

One day, dismissing these newcomers in her characteristically opinionated manner, Gertrude Stein proclaimed to Ernest Hemingway: "You are all a lost generation." He transformed her stinging remark into the leading epigraph of his first novel, *The Sun Also Rises*—and the rest, as they say, is history.

But let's not merely talk about the past . . . let's visit! After years of tinkering, I've managed to invent a workable time machine that we can pilot straight into 1920s Paris. Unfortunately, since the primitive technology allows only a single 24-hour stay, we can't sample the decade selectively. But I've stumbled onto a workable solution, a VirtualTime visit that takes bits and pieces from the entire decade to create a representative day. While in RealTime Josephine Baker's triumphant entry into Paris occurred four years after Ernest Hemingway and Hadley, his first wife, resided in that little place above the *bal musette*, VirtualTime allows both events (and much else) to occur on the same day.

Flawed, I know, but better than nothing. Are you interested in joining me? All right, then: jump in and let's go!

After a whirlwind trip, we land in a hidden corner of Montparnasse Cemetery, home of the famous dead. It's exactly seven in the morning on what promises to be an excellent late-spring day. We hop out, pull our vehicle up to poet Charles Baudelaire's gravestone, disguise it as an evil floral offering, and step back to take our bearings.

I realize with a shock that our clothing has been transformed while en route: I'm now clad in a straight, short dress with a dropped waist, have a long rope of pearls knotted around my neck, and on my feet are some fairly amusing T-strap shoes with small heels. As for you . . . well, don't ask.

The trip from the future has made us ravenous, but we realize with despair that we have no money. Just then a clutch bag appears in my hand. Inside I find a big wad of old-style franc notes. Relieved, we leave the cemetery and head over to Boulevard du Montparnasse, which is very quiet at this time of the morning. A waiter is briskly sweeping the sidewalk in front of the Rotonde, and the Dôme doesn't appear to be open, so we take a table at the Sélect and order a café au lait and croissants.

Montparnasse supported dozens of cafés in the 1920s, but these three were by far the most popular with the literary expat set. Each was different, and simply by crossing the street from one to the other you could drastically alter the tempo of your day. At the Dôme people pushed tables together and took boisterous command of the sidewalk. The Rotonde, on the other hand, was the place to go for a quiet, intense conversation.

And the Sélect? It was wildly popular. In large part that's because it stayed open late, providing sustenance and booze long after its neighbors had closed. But a lot of its appeal lay in the fact that it was a place people loved to hate. The always-scowling Madame Sélect guarded the cash register zealously, was

Okay, you can't get more touristy, but gliding down the Seine River in a *bateau-mouche* has always been a great way to take stock of the City of Light. M. R. Carroll

thought to be a police spy, and battled violently with her customers, whom she disliked intensely. They returned the sentiment, taking great pleasure in goading her. The insults of writer-publisher Robert McAlmon were legendary: one night he made Madame Sélect quiver with rage by announcing that her welsh rarebit tasted like a toilet. She once had the poet Hart Crane literally dragged off to jail, kicking and screaming, when he couldn't pay for his drinks. In his memoirs, writer Harold Stearns called the Sélect "a seething mad-house of drunks, semi-drunks, quarter drunks, and sober maniacs." He should know. He was the inspiration for Harvey Stone in *The Sun Also Rises*, the character forever drunkenly sprawled at one of the café's outdoor tables.

Glancing over at the Rotonde, I notice a pretty woman sit down, order something, and begin scribbling a letter. It's poet Edna St. Vincent Millay, who eats there every day when she's in Paris (she's mad for the *choucroute garnie*). She's in good company: others who have frequented the place include Guillaume Apollinaire, Picasso, Amedeo Modigliani, and Max Jacob. The Dôme, I know, was once a big Lenin/Trotsky hangout and is now popular with American writers. It was here, one day in 1924, that novelist Sinclair Lewis, who in 1930 would win the Nobel Prize for literature, was insultingly and loudly dismissed before a delighted crowd as a mere "bestseller."

At the moment, though, little is happening on the boulevard. We decide to go strolling about in hopes of catching a glimpse of writers we admire.

Over on nearby Rue Delambre, we discover At the Sign of the Black Manikin (Rue Delambre 4), a bookstore opened by Edward Titus in 1924. Two years later Titus founded the Black Manikin Press, whose memorable books included *The Education of a French Model*, the racy memoirs of Man Ray's longtime lover, Kiki of Montparnasse. Even more controversial was the second edition of D. H. Lawrence's *Lady Chatterley's Lover*. The first edition of 1,000 copies had been privately printed by Lawrence in Italy because British and American publishers, fearful of obscenity charges, wouldn't touch it.

Continuing up Rue Delambre, we stand for a moment outside the Dingo Bar (Rue Delambre 10, but now gone)—the very watering hole in which Hemingway and F. Scott Fitzgerald met for the first time on a late-April day in 1925. Hemingway was drinking with an Englishwoman, Duff Twysden, and her boyfriend, Pat Guthrie (both would soon be infamously transformed into Lady Brett Ashley and Mike Campbell in *The Sun Also Rises*). Suddenly the trio was approached by an elegantly dressed man whose half-handsome, half-pretty face made Hemingway uneasy. It was Fitzgerald, who was 28—three years older than Hemingway—and a highly successful novelist.

Fitzgerald introduced himself and generously praised *In Our Time*, Hemingway's recently published volume of short stories. The macho Hemingway, whose personal rules of etiquette apparently included the phrase "real men don't compliment other men," considered the praise akin to insult. Even worse was the fact that Fitzgerald couldn't hold his liquor: he soon became so drunk on champagne that the bewildered and slightly disgusted Hemingway helped the bartender pour him into a taxi. Despite this shaky beginning, a friendship of sorts would gradually take hold between the two men.

That particular bartender, by the way, was so popular among the expats that whenever he changed jobs a bar's entire clientele would move along with him. An ex-flyweight boxer from Liverpool, his name was James Charters, but he was known simply as Jimmy the Barman. Aside from the intelligent and gentle Sylvia Beach, Jimmy may have been the only other expat who knew and got along with everybody. Friendly, pugnacious, and generous, he loved his work and wrote all about it later in his high-spirited memoirs, *This Must Be the Place*. "I had never been in a madhouse before I went to Montparnasse," he confided. "I had never seen people drink to get drunk; never seen artists, writers, nobles, American sailors and doubtful women mingle on equal terms without reserve." Perhaps they were helped along by the renowned Jimmy Special, a mixture of equal parts cognac, Pernod, Amer-Picon, mandarin, and kirsch, which he guaranteed to be a surefire aphrodisiac.

"Yecch!" you exclaim, practically spitting. It's clear from your expression that the Jimmy Special would do little to tempt *your* virtue. I quite agree.

We head off to look for Ernest Hemingway. Although he had many homes in Paris, we aim for the one in which he was probably the happiest: an old sawmill (now replaced by a brand-new building) set in a cobblestoned court-yard at Rue Notre-Dame-des-Champs 113. In 1924 at the top of its rickety wooden stairs, Ernest and Hadley Hemingway lived with their baby, John, nicknamed Bumby. While living here Ernest decided to stop writing journal-ism for newspapers back home and work full-time at fiction. For a while the family's only income was provided by Hadley's small trust. They were so poor that Ernest often captured pigeons in the Luxembourg Garden, bringing them home for dinner. His short stories received many rejections and he was often discouraged, but he never gave up. Finally, while still at this address, he wrote a novel based on his experiences in Paris and on a trip to Pamplona, Spain. The publication of *The Sun Also Rises* in 1926 transformed him, almost overnight, into a legend.

Farther up the street (Rue Notre-Dame-des-Champs 70 bis), we find the home of the highly influential American poet Ezra Pound, who lived for most of the decade on the second floor of a small *pavillon* (a detached house) with his wife, Dorothy. They, too, were poor. To furnish their digs, Pound built chairs of rough-hewn boards and canvas and made tables from packing crates. But the place had good light, a nice garden view, and lovely Japanese paintings on the wall.

Shortly after moving to Paris in 1920, Pound persuaded his friend, James Joyce, to move there, too, thus placing the world's three major proponents of modern literature—Gertrude Stein, Joyce, Pound—in the same city. Pound soon became involved with every aspect of Paris-based Modernism, befriending the writer Jean Cocteau, the sculptor Brancusi, and the musician Stravinsky. He espoused the ideals of Dadaists and their stepchildren, the Surrealists. But his real love lay in promoting the work of his fellow Americans. He was tireless in his efforts on behalf of other writers.

The *pavillon* door opens and out come Hemingway and Pound. Odd as they seem together—the somewhat flamboyant older writer and the burly young bear of a man beside him—they are good friends. Ernest is teaching Ezra how to box; Ezra is helping Ernest promote his work. "Ezra was kinder and more

Boulevard du Montparnasse has no shortage of venerable cafés with 1920s credentials, but Le Sélect has always had a certain intimacy many of the others lack. Sip a Pernod, read a little Gertrude Stein, and watch the Parisian parade pass by. Suzie Rodriguez

Christian about people than I was," Hemingway would write much later. "So kind to people that I always thought of him as a sort of saint." As they walk by, they are deep in conversation and don't notice us. I have always adored Hemingway and can't resist the temptation to talk to him. But the moment I run after them, they fade away and we are swept into a vortex.

Suddenly we are standing before a small, respectable-looking apartment house at Rue de Fleurus 27. Through the entranceway we can see a courtyard garden in the rear, as well as a *pavillon* and a smaller studio, or atelier. Both buildings are occupied by Gertrude Stein and her companion, Alice B. Toklas. The *pavillon*, their residence, contains a dining room, study, kitchen, two bedrooms, and a bath. Miss Stein writes and holds her salon in the atelier, which is, in fact, our destination.

We step into a large room comfortably decorated with solid Italian antiques— a rather bourgeois backdrop for the stunning and explosive paintings hung row upon row, eye level to ceiling: works by Picasso, Henri Matisse, Pierre Auguste Renoir, Paul Cézanne, Eugène Delacroix, Pierre Bonnard, Henri de Toulouse-Lautrec, and Félix Vallotton.

To my great shock, one of the artists is actually in the room. Although he visits far less now than before the Great War, the mighty Picasso sits beside his hostess at the room's far end. He talks and gesticulates in his expansive way, while she sits quietly and Buddha-like, enthroned in a well-padded Renaissance chair, directly beneath his 1906 *Portrait of Gertrude Stein*. The other guests stand at a respectful distance. I spot composers Virgil Thomson and George Antheil, painters Juan Gris and Georges Braque, and quite a few writers, including Djuna Barnes, Ford Madox Ford, William Carlos Williams, Sherwood Anderson, H.D., Jean Cocteau, Pound, Margaret Anderson, Bob McAlmon, and Janet Flanner.

The exotic-looking Miss Toklas sits at the tea table beside a heavy silver teapot, an inviting platter of petit-fours, and thimble-size glasses of fruit liqueur. She is chatting politely with Mrs. Anderson while simultaneously monitoring every detail of the salon. Her eyes are on us from the moment we step through the door, and you can practically hear her thought process as she tries to figure out who we are. Somehow we manage to imbibe a refreshing cup of tea and a few pastries before she comes right out and asks us.

And just like that—before I can even shake Miss Stein's hand—we disappear in a puff of smoke!

We land atop hard cobblestones, pick ourselves up, and take a look around. We appear to be in some sort of courtyard. There's a nice, very old residential building to our left. Past the courtyard we see another *pavillon* and, somewhat amazingly, a small Greek temple. Both buildings are nearly buried in a lush wood copse.

You look dazed. "Are we still in Paris?" you ask.

I know where we are: the temple is a dead giveaway. "We're smack dab at the center of town," I reply, "in its pure and ancient heart."

For it's clear that we've arrived at the Rue Jacob 20 salon of Natalie Clifford Barney, also known as the Wild Girl from Cincinnati, the Amazon, and countless other nicknames—Flaxen-Flower, Flossie, Moonbeam, to cite a few—bestowed by an army of lovers and friends. All the lovers, incidentally, were women notable for being great beauties, great intellects, great talents, or all three. Men were consigned, often against their wishes, to the realm of friendship; they included some of the greatest literary minds of Europe and America.

Born in 1876 to a wealthy Ohio family, as a young woman Barney possessed long and billowing masses of blond hair, a slender figure that she refused to corset, a grand intelligence, and amused blue eyes. From an early age she could ride a horse like nobody's business and was incapable of making a commonplace statement. She moved to Paris early on, where her uninhibited and emancipated life scandalized society, transformed her into the thinly disguised heroine of at least six novels, and made her a major entrant in scores of memoirs and biographies from the Belle Epoque to the present day. In 1909 she moved to Rue Jacob, a historic and ancient street in the Latin Quarter, and instituted a weekly literary salon—acknowledged by most French literary historians as the most important of the 20th century—which would last for the next 60 years. There was something magical about Barney's chosen backdrop. The elegant *pavillon* with its ironwork balconies was beautiful enough, but the overgrown woods surrounding her were perhaps the last remnants of a forest that once covered the southern banks of the Seine River. And in their midst was that mysterious little Doric-columned temple, inscribed over the entrance with the words *"à l'amitié"*—to friendship.

The nature of Barney's salon changed over the years. In her very young days—before coming to the Rue Jacob—she once hired Mata Hari to ride naked through her gardens on a white horse harnessed with turquoises. Those were the days, too, of open-air performances of racy playlets written by herself or friends such as Colette and Pierre Loüys. Very late in life, in her eighties and nineties, the salon was extremely subdued, though it remained intellectually vibrant and attracted young writers such as Truman Capote and Françoise Sagan.

And in the 1920s? What little we get to see of the salon is lively indeed. Djuna Barnes stands just inside the door, engaged in conversation with Ezra Pound. Colette and Marie Laurencin laugh uproariously, Sylvia Beach listens intently to George Antheil while Virgil Thomson tries to put his two cents in.

Janet Flanner is there again, trading sardonic quips with Solita Solano. And I notice André Gide, Jean Cocteau, James Joyce, Paul Valéry, Rainer Maria Rilke, and many others.

And there, sitting calmly by the punch bowl, is our hostess. Grown stout now, no longer the sylphlike beauty of earlier years, she nonetheless possesses the kind of magnetism that rivets the attention of her guests. She rarely speaks, but when she does conversation stops. Her voice is soft and low—she can't bear people who talk loudly—adding impact to the delivery of her witty, sometimes cruelly accurate bon mots.

I head directly toward her to learn the answer to a question that has longed puzzled me. "How did you," I want to ask, "a woman born into a proper Victorian home, find the wherewithal not just to rebel against society, but to thumb your nose at it?"

But I never get to ask. The thing about the time machine, you see, is that those who ride it can never do anything to alter history. If you try, you land on your rump somewhere else. Barney was incredibly self-centered but not at all self-aware; if I had asked her a question that necessitated looking within, perhaps—who knows?—she might have altered her course. She might have ended up in a nunnery like her former lover, the illustrious Belle Epoque courtesan Liane de Pougy.

And so, once again, we are yanked away just as things start getting good.

It is time for dinner and we land in Trianons (Place du 18-Juin-1940 5, but no longer in business), the favorite restaurant of James Joyce. He used Trianons as both an office and a dining establishment, keeping a permanent table on reserve. Even when he had no money Joyce insisted that his guests eat and drink whatever they liked. He himself preferred white wine to anything, and he wasn't fussy about its quality. He was quite shy, but after a second bottle of Chablis he usually livened up. He liked singing Irish songs and Italian opera. His trained tenor voice was considered quite beautiful.

Alas, he doesn't sing the night we dine at Trianons, nor even drink too much. We spy on the Joyce table surreptitiously while downing our roast partridge, *pommes frites*, and *salade frisée* (with cheese and fruit for dessert) but little happens. He, his pretty wife, Nora, and their lovely daughter, Lucia, talk quietly. Every once in a while Nora bursts out in a big guffaw, her curly red hair swinging back and forth as she laughs. It is obvious that the intellectual Joyce adores his robust, earthy wife—and she him. Ford Madox Ford, the British writer and *Transatlantic Review* editor, comes in with his companion, Stella Bowen. They stand in the aisle, conversing with the Joyces, but eventually take their own table.

After dinner, as we linger on the sidewalk outside Trianons, we debate what to do next. We consider dancing at a *bal musette*, browsing in Sylvia Beach's bookshop, trying to gain entry to Brancusi's white stone studio. Nothing really grabs us, though, until you suggest the theater.

We immediately set off to the Right Bank, strolling over the Pont-Neuf, through the Tuileries, past the Place de la Concorde, and up to the leafy Champs-Elysées. Turning down a side street, we come to stand before the Théâtre des Champs-Elysées (Avenue Montaigne 15). We examine the stunning Antoine Bourdelle sculpture of Isadora Duncan, which is part of the facade. Then, caught up by the excited, glamorous crowd pushing past, we go inside and take seats in the orchestra.

The curtain goes up. A sensuous jazz beat rises above the noise. The audience, suddenly quiet, turns its full attention to the stage. A massively built black man appears in the wings, pauses dramatically, and begins walking slowly forward. Atop his back, carried upside down, is a beautiful nude black woman with a pink flamingo feather between her limbs. At center stage the giant stops and, in a long, slow movement, turns the woman right side up so that she stands—magnificent, flawless—before the breathless crowd. There is a long silence until suddenly an ecstatic scream fills the theater and the entire audience jumps to its feet in tribute. I spot *New Yorker* journalist Janet Flanner again, scribbling away like mad. Her next column will discuss this night, this Parisian triumph of a young American dancer named Josephine Baker.

The curtain descends, the lights go out; the curtain rises, the lights come back up. The audience has changed into a more intellectual crowd. I see Joyce, T. S. Eliot, Brancusi, Harry and Caresse Crosby, Barney, Pound, Barnes, William Carlos Williams, Diaghilev, and Sylvia Beach. I glance at the stage, which contains not only a full orchestra, but eight pianos, a player piano, oil drums, anvils, automobile horns, and two airplane propellers. The last "instruments" cinch it: this can only be the official premiere of George Antheil's infamous *Ballet Mécanique*.

The performance proves to be strident, a disturbing cacophony of sound that doesn't please everyone. Beach, writing many years later, remembers that "the music was drowned out by yells from all over the house." People rise from their seats, screaming and demanding their money back. One or two fistfights break out. At one point Pound, a close friend of Antheil, jumps onstage to shout the audience down and ask them to exhibit basic manners, but by then most of the crowd has stormed out. Near the concert's end, the propellers whir so loudly and kick up such a forceful breeze that a man's toupee is jerked from his head and flies toward the back of the theater. The floating toupee seems to put everyone who remains (except its owner) in a happy mood. I notice Janet Flanner taking notes again (she will describe the concert as "good but awful"). I want to ask her how I can get a nifty job like hers, but she, along with the

These days La Coupole is all spiffed up and crammed with tourists, but if you close your eyes and use your imagination, you just might glimpse the ghosts of Ernest Hemingway and F. Scott Fitzgerald at a nearby table. Suzie Rodriguez

entire theater, suddenly disappears, and we hurtle through space once more.

"Wow!" you shout in my ear. "And I thought it got wild at a Rolling Stones concert!"

Right about now things start getting really crazy. For a while we are back on Boulevard Montparnasse, sitting in the Dôme. English painter Nina Hamnett strums a guitar and belts out a risqué sailor's song that has the patrons laughing hysterically. Man Ray's lover, Kiki, walks through the door, her face painted white with two big scarlet beauty marks added for emphasis; her eyebrows have been shaved off and penciled back on in thick bright jade swoops. She pauses dramatically and lowers her heavy eyelids to reveal daubed-on eyeballs.

The crowd breaks into an ecstatic clamor.

Suddenly we are jolted from our seats and set down hard in Le Boeuf sur le Toit, Jean Cocteau's stunningly popular cabaret (now gone), at Rue Boissy-d'Anglas 28. The bandleader, a black American saxophonist named Vance Lowry, draws crowds of Parisians who love to Black-Bottom and Charleston to American jazz. For a while, Le Boeuf was the favorite hangout of writer Bob McAlmon. Deciding to fake a Charleston, we stand and move to the dance floor.

But then pow! zap! yoweeee! Just like that we're high in the stands of the Velodrome d'Hiver (long gone) at Boulevard de Grenelle 6, mingling with a crowd captivated by cyclists riding round and round in circles. It's the annual six-day bicycle races, in which the riders make only brief stops for nourishment, the toilet, and a few minutes' shuteye. All of Paris turns out for this event—everybody from princes to *poules*—and the most popular time to come is after midnight. We spot Hemingway and John Dos Passos nearby, and Sylvia Beach, and . . .

But we're gone already! And surrounding us now is a rampaging mob of naked orgiasts. This could only be the annual Quatz'Arts Ball, sponsored by the students at the Ecole des Beaux-Arts and patronized by many Americans. In fact, I can see the founders of Black Sun Press, Harry and Caresse Crosby. Riding topless on the back of an elephant, Caresse carries away the night's first prize for costume. ("My breasts helped," she admits later.) As for Harry, what can you say about a guy who wears a necklace of dead pigeons and carries a bag filled with snakes?

We end up in Bricktop's (alas, no more, but likely once located on Rue Fontaine), a smoky cabaret with an illuminated glass dance floor, banquette-lined walls, and the hottest jazz in Paris. The charming owner/hostess who gave the place her name, a light-skinned black woman with oodles of freckles and red hair, seems to be everywhere at once. She croons soulful tunes, tallies up champagne bills, jokes with special friends such as Cole Porter and the Prince of Wales, and keeps a wary eye out for trouble. When it arises, she quells it—immediately.

Musicians visiting Paris often stop by, and Bricktop's has been honored with the presence of, among countless other luminaries, Louis Armstrong, Sidney Bechet, Alberta Hunter, and Duke Ellington. American writers who frequent the place include Kay Boyle, Bob McAlmon, T. S. Eliot, Scott and Zelda Fitzgerald, and Ernest Hemingway.

Hungry and tired, we grab a banquette, order a bottle of champagne and some of Bricktop's famous corned-beef hash, and lean back to enjoy an impromptu performance of piano playing and singing by Noël Coward, who just happened to stop by. Our time here is sheer heaven. The food's good, the music's great, and the people are fascinating. We're among the last to leave at about 5:30 in the morning.

"What a night!" you enthuse, and then you do a little jig in the middle of the street. It's been fun watching you gradually loosen up in devil-may-care Paris. But suddenly you stop and look up, concerned. "We better head back toward the cemetery, don't you think? We don't want to miss our ride back."

"We won't," I say. "We've got plenty of time, and there's one last thing we have to do before we can really say we've been to 1920s Paris. We've got to hit Les Halles for onion soup as dawn breaks."

You seem perplexed. "Onion soup? For breakfast?"

"Of course! All the expats do it."

"Well, then," you say, "what the hell!"

And away we go.

Sadly Les Halles, the gigantic wholesale produce, seafood, and meat market held for decades in the center of Paris, was relocated years ago and largely replaced by an insipid modern mall (though the nearby Centre Georges-Pompidou, another relatively new building, houses one of the world's premier modern art galleries). Here at dawn came everyone, from housekeepers to the finest chefs, seeking the best and freshest foodstuffs. Surrounding the markets were inexpensive restaurants frequented by gangsters, pimps, prostitutes, slumming socialites, and expats, all on their way home from various festivities of the night. So many writers penned memories of onion soup at dawn in Les Halles that it became the quintessential expat experience.

But we see only ordinary folks on this quiet daybreak—no fancy socialites, no cynical writers, no flamboyant sculptors. We duck into Au Père Tranquille (Rue Pierre-Lescot 16), make our way through the pimps and *poules* to an empty table, and order two bowls of *soupe à l'oignon*. It comes quickly, and it's delicious. All the essence of 1920s Paris seems captured in my bowl: the fragrance, the flavor, the slight bite, the fleeting—too fleeting—pleasure. I place the last spoonful in my mouth and close my eyes, reluctant to finish.

I have no choice, though. Before I know it, we're back in the cemetery, standing before Baudelaire's grave. I glance at my watch: it's 6:58—we've just made it! With a snap of my fingers, the evil floral bouquet reverts to a time machine. We hop in, and I twirl the dials into position and poise my finger above the go button . . .

But somehow, for some reason, I can't bring myself to press it. I turn to look at you. We've had quite an adventure in the past 24 hours, and I've come to appreciate your quirky nature.

"I'm so sad to leave," I say.

"I know."

"It was fun here. A little disjointed maybe, but fun. It was a good time, Paris in the 1920s."

"Yeah," you say, nodding slowly. "But it was *their* time, wasn't it?"

You're right, of course. It *was* their time—and now it's gone. I press the button, and so are we.

Roast Chicken à la Alice B. Toklas

You might find it difficult to whip up this delicious concoction while you're in Paris. But if you're able to, pack it in a picnic hamper and head for the Bois de Boulogne. Otherwise, try it at home. Whether you add Alice's infamous hash brownies for dessert is entirely up to you! You can check out her "recipes" in The Alice B. Toklas Cookbook *(New York: Lyons Press, 1998).*

2 tablespoons of butter
1 chicken, cut in eighths
freshly ground black pepper
1 cup of port wine
1 cup of orange juice
dash of soy sauce
1 cup of cream
zest of 1 orange
1 cup of chopped Italian parsley
1 large round loaf of French bread

Heat oven to 350 degrees Fahrenheit. Melt the butter in a cast-iron skillet and brown chicken pieces. Sprinkle with pepper. Pour the port wine, orange juice, and soy sauce over the chicken. Put the chicken on a pan and bake in oven until done (30 to 45 minutes). Transfer the chicken to a dish and return the pan to stove. Pour the cream into the pan drippings and add half of the orange zest. Reduce slightly over medium heat. Return the chicken to the pan and stir each piece in the mixture until coated. Slice off the top of the bread loaf and remove the bread within. Fill the hollowed loaf with the chicken mixture. Sprinkle the parsley and the remaining zest over the chicken. Replace the top of the bread and wrap in tea towels. Serves four.

The Writer's Trail

Following in the Footsteps

Destination: It's long been called the City of Light, perhaps because it's a place of sun-drenched springtimes and dazzling dreams. It's known as the birthplace of modern art, the exemplar of culinary excellence, and the world's most romantic destination. Vincent Van Gogh summed it up long ago. "There is but one Paris," he wrote. And few would, or have ever, disagreed. Oscar Wilde called Paris the place all good Americans go to when they die. To Ernest Hemingway a sojourn here was a movable feast, an experience that stayed with you for the rest of your life. So captivating was the city to World War I Yankee soldiers that a popular song on the homefront worriedly demanded, "How you gonna keep 'em down on the farm after they've seen Paree?" If you've been here, you understand; if you haven't, you will. It's as simple as that.

Location: Paris, the capital of France, straddles the Seine River in the north-central region of the country.

Getting There: Paris has two major airports: Roissy-Charles de Gaulle, 14 miles to the north, and Orly, 10 miles to the south. The latter is for domestic flights. Most international airlines fly to Paris. They include Air France (1-800-237-2747 in the United States; 1-800-667-2747 in Canada), British Airways (1-800-247-9297), United Airlines (1-800-538-2929), Delta Airlines (1-800-241-4141), Continental (1-800-231-0856), and Air Canada ([416] 925-2311 or 1-800-361-5373 or 1-800-776-3000). Air France bus shuttles, public-transport buses (RATP), private minibuses, RER trains, and taxis are available to and from the airports. Of course, if you're already in Europe, you can also take a train or a bus to Paris from practically anywhere on the continent. Paris has six mainline stations: Gare du Nord (for northern France, United Kingdom, Belgium, Holland, Denmark, Germany, and Scandinavia); Gare de l'Est (for eastern France, Austria, Germany, and Luxembourg); Gare de Lyon (for eastern and southern France, the Alps, Greece, Italy, and Switzerland); Gare d'Austerlitz (for western France, Portugal, and Spain); Gare Montparnasse (for western France); and Gare St-Lazare (for regional lines to northwest France). Eurostar operates regular departures from London (Waterloo Station) to Paris (Gare du Nord) via the Channel Tunnel. For general information and reservations on all trains, call (33) 8 36 35 35 35, 7:00 a.m. to 10:00 p.m.

Tip: All train tickets have to be validated prior to boarding a French train, on the day of travel, in one of the orange automatic date-stamping machines found on the way to platforms. For a place on the TGV (*train à grande vitesse*), seats must be prebooked.

Orientation: Divided into 20 *arrondissements*, Paris is built on a series of low hills, most notably Montmartre, which is topped by the splendidly white church known as Sacré-Coeur. The Seine River splits the city into the Left Bank, where the Latin Quarter, Montparnasse, the Luxembourg Garden, the Eiffel Tower, and the Musée d'Orsay are found; and the Right Bank, where the Bois de Boulogne, the Arc de Triomphe, the Champs-Elysées, the Louvre, the Tuileries Garden, the Opéra, the Centre Georges-Pompidou, Père-Lachaise Cemetery, and Montmartre are located. Notre-Dame Cathedral is on Ile de la Cité in the Seine right in the middle of everything.

Tip: When you've had enough of the cafés of Montparnasse and the Latin Quarter, head over to Ile St-Louis in the Seine next to Ile de la Cité. Here you'll find a wonderful neighborhood of 17th-century stone town houses once inhabited by bankers, lawyers, and nobles, but now favored by writers, artists, and lovers of a bygone Paris. The main street of the island is Rue St-Louis-en-l'Ile, which is crowded with art galleries, bookshops, and créperies.

Getting Around: Most people staying in Paris don't rent a car: parking is difficult, and driving is even worse. Besides, the inexpensive subway system, the Métro, whisks you quickly to every corner of town. You'll find a system map at the entrance to every station (you'll probably want to buy one of your own, though). Some stations have maps with indicator buttons that light up when you press your destination. It's hard to get lost. Buy your tickets at any Métro station—a one-way trip takes one ticket, and you get a bargain price by buying 10 tickets (a *carnet*) at a time. The Paris taxi system is also efficient. Even better, Paris is probably the best walking city in the entire world. It's a sheer pleasure to amble from your hotel to dinner, from the restaurant to a jazz club, and so on.

Literary Sleeps

L'Hôtel: A beautiful boutique hotel with its own luxurious restaurant (Le Bélier), L'Hôtel is a Left Bank lodging that has the distinction of being the place (room 16) where Oscar Wilde died in 1900. Rue des Beaux-Arts 13, St-Germain-des-Prés Métro. Tel.: (33) 1 44 41 99 00. Expensive.

Hôtel d'Angleterre: This nice old hotel has a long and noble history with American writers, dating clear back to Washington Irving! More recent denizens have included Ernest and Hadley Hemingway and Sherwood Anderson and his wife. And it's just a few doors from Natalie Barney's former home at Rue Jacob 20. St-Germain-des-Prés Métro. Tel.: (33) 1 42 60 16 93. Moderate.

Hôtel Istria: Popular with impoverished artists and writers in the 1920s and 1930s, this 26-room, family-run Montparnasse establishment is still kind to the pocketbook. Once upon a time, Marcel Duchamp, Rainer Marie Rilke, Tristan Tzara, and Francis Picabia, among others, called it home. Rue Campagne-Première 29, Raspail Métro. Tel.: (33) 1 43 20 91 82. Moderate.

Hôtel St-Germain-des-Prés: This hotel is another great Left Bank locale. The rooms are small but charming, with antique wooden beams. Janet Flanner lived here for many years. Henry Miller was a guest in the 1930s. Rue Bonaparte, St-Germain-des-Prés Métro. Tel.: (33) 1 43 26 00 19. Moderate.

Literary Sites

Brasserie Lipp: Ernest Hemingway wrote a good deal of *A Farewell to Arms* in this eatery, which first opened its doors in 1880. Nowadays French TV celebrities, journalists, and politicians gather for coffee on the small glassed-in terrace off the main restaurant. Boulevard St-Germain-des-Prés 151, St-Germain-des-Prés Métro.

Café du Dôme: Pablo Picasso and Lenin, as well as a stellar list of Lost Generation writers, once hung out here. Although now transformed into a trendy brasserie, you can still get just a café au lait or a drink. Boulevard St-Germain-des-Prés 108, Vavin Métro.

La Clôserie des Lilas: Copper plates commemorate the literary famous who once came here. If you care to look, you'll spot the names of Ernest Hemingway and André Breton, among others. Boulevard du Montparnasse 171, Vavin Métro.

La Coupole: Refurbished in the late 1980s, this venerable writers/artists haunt still attracts a pretty big crowd of tourists every night. The cast of characters who used to come here is impressive: Erik Satie, Jean Cocteau, Max Jacob, Ernest Hemingway, Igor Stravinsky, Guillaume Apollinaire. The columns in the café were painted by, among others, Marc Chagall and Constantin Brancusi. Boulevard du Montparnasse 102, Vavin Métro.

La Rotonde: There was a time—in the 1920s, of course—when you could walk into this place and spy a who's who of modern art: André Derain, Amedeo Modigliani, Maurice de Vlaminck, and Kees van Dongen, among many others. Boulevard du Montparnasse 105, Vavin Métro.

Le Sélect: As soon as it opened in 1924, this relatively quiet, intimate Montparnasse bar became a popular stopoff for soon-to-be-famous literary and artistic lights, including Isadora Duncan and Hart Crane. Boulevard du Montparnasse 99, Vavin Métro.

Les Deux Magots: Arthur Rimbaud, Paul Verlaine, Stéphane Mallarmé, Oscar Wilde, and the Surrealists all frequented this still-lively café. These days, though, you'll be rubbing elbows with tourists instead of intellectuals and artists. Boulevard St-Germain-des-Prés 170, St-Germain-des-Prés Métro.

Montparnasse Cemetery: If you're into places where the literary and otherwise famous are buried, this graveyard, along with Père-Lachaise on the Right Bank (where Honoré de Balzac, Colette, Sarah Bernhardt, Gertrude Stein, Alice B. Toklas, and the Doors' Jim Morrison are buried), is the spot to visit. Here you'll find the tombs of Charles Baudelaire, Guy de Maupassant, Jean-Paul Sartre, Simone de Beauvoir, and Man Ray. Boulevard Edgar-Quinet, Raspail Métro.

Icon Pastimes

The obvious thing to do while on the trail of Lost Generation authors is to hop from café to café in Montparnasse and St-Germain-des-Prés. Drink a little coffee, sip a bit of Pernod, knock back a brandy or two, sample some oysters, or, well, just write or sketch, if you're into that. Or you could visit the bookstore Shakespeare and Company (Rue de la Bûcherie 37, St-Michel Métro). It has absolutely no relationship to Sylvia Beach's original bookstore, but it's a charming, one-of-a-kind place and it carries a huge selection of used English-language books. And if you're in a shopping mood, head out to Le Marché aux Puces St-Quen flea market (Porte de Clignancourt Métro) on the northern boundary of Paris. The century-old maze of alleys is crammed with antique dealers' booths and junk stalls that stretch for more than a square mile. Make sure you bargain, though, when you spy that print you just have to own. Prices can be steep if you don't haggle. When you've had enough wheeling and dealing for one day, try a lunch of mussels and fries at one of the market's many rude-looking cafés.

Contacts

French Tourist Office: United States: 444 Madison Avenue, 16th floor, New York, New York 10022. Tel.: (212) 838-7800. Fax: (212) 838-7855; Canada: 30 St. Patrick Street, Suite 700, Toronto, Ontario M5T 3A3. Tel.: (416) 593-4723. Web site: *www.francetourism.com.*

Office du Tourisme de la Ville de Paris: Avenue des Champs-Elysées 127, Paris, France. Tel.: (33) 1 49 52 53 54 or (33) 1 49 52 53 56 (for recorded information in English). Web site: *www.paris.org.*

In a Literary Mood

Books

Beach, Sylvia. *Shakespeare and Company.* New York: Harcourt, Brace, 1959. Beach's English-language bookstore, Shakespeare and Company, was the expats' home away from home. She knew and was loved by everybody. Even Ernest Hemingway, who rarely had a kind word for anyone, praised her. These quietly humorous memoirs are a must for any serious student of the Lost Generation.

Callaghan, Morley. *That Summer in Paris.* New York: Penguin, 1979. After Ernest Hemingway's memoir of 1920s Paris, *A Moveable Feast,* Callaghan's reverie is the best thing ever written in

English about being young and literary in the City of Light in the good old days. Callaghan's account of the fabled boxing match between him and Hemingway, with F. Scott Fitzgerald as the timekeeper, is worth the price of the book alone. An added plus is that Callaghan is a lot more trustworthy than Hemingway when it comes to veracity.

Charters, James. *This Must Be the Place: Memoirs of Montparnasse.* Edited by Morrill Cody, with an introduction by Ernest Hemingway. London: Herbert Joseph, 1934. Jimmy the Barman's singular view of 1920s Paris from behind the bar is a hoot.

Fitch, Noel Riley. *Sylvia Beach and the Lost Generation: A History of Literary Paris in the Twenties and Thirties.* New York: W. W. Norton, 1985.

Flanner, Janet. *Paris Was Yesterday.* New York: Viking, 1972. Beginning in the early 1920s, Flanner covered Paris for the *New Yorker* for many years. In a wry, witty way, she wrote about her friends and fellow expats, as well as about major and minor events. This book, a compilation of her "Letter from Paris" for the years 1925 to 1939, is enthralling.

Glassco, John. *Memoirs of Montparnasse.* Toronto: Oxford University Press, 1995. Canadian writer Glassco was a well-known figure in 1920s Montparnasse. In *Death in the Afternoon*, Hemingway etched a pretty caustic, thinly disguised portrait of the flamboyantly gay writer. You can't really believe everything in Glassco's devilish account, but you'll have fun reading it, especially if you're sipping pastis in one of the grand old cafés on Boulevard du Montparnasse.

Hemingway, Ernest. *A Moveable Feast.* New York: Touchstone, 1996. Published posthumously in 1964, this memoir of Paris in the 1920s is often mean-spirited. Even so, it's brilliant and evocative and displays some of Hemingway's best writing.

_____. *The Sun Also Rises.* New York: Scribner, 1996. This fast-paced, brilliant first novel (originally published in 1926) was a roman à clef whose four leading characters were easily identifiable on the streets and in the bars of Montparnasse. One of them, Harold Loeb—the book's Robert Cohn—threatened to kill Hemingway the next time they met.

Stein, Gertrude. *The Autobiography of Alice B. Toklas.* New York: Vintage, 1990. If you have time to read only one book listed here, read this. Strictly speaking, it covers most of Stein's life, not just the 1920s, but somehow it all blends together. Don't let your fear of the author's prose style keep you away. This book, originally published in 1933, is not only completely comprehensible, it's great fun!

Guidebooks

Fitch, Noel Riley. *Walks in Hemingway's Paris: A Guide to Paris for the Literary Traveler.* New York: St. Martin's Press, 1992.

Haight, Mary Ellen. *Walks in Gertrude Stein's Paris.* Salt Lake City: Peregrine Smith Books, 1988.

Hansen, Arlen J. *Expatriate Paris: A Cultural and Literary Guide to Paris in the 1920s.* New York: Arcade Publishing, 1990. Haight presents actual walking tours.

Morton, Brian N. *Americans in Paris.* New York: Morrow, 1984. A street-by-street, building-by-building history of Paris.

Paris. 3rd ed. Watford, England: Michelin Travel Publications, 1998. If you've used a Michelin green guide before, you're probably a great fan. These slender, no-nonsense books tell you what you want to know about the sights and they weigh hardly anything.

Wells, Patricia. *The Food Lover's Guide to Paris*. 4th ed. New York: Workman Publishing, 1999. If you love to eat, you absolutely *must* have this book in hand the next time you visit Paris. Wells's entertaining-but-meticulous reviews of eateries, from the low-budget to the ridiculously expensive three-star, are interspersed with recipes, photos, a food glossary, and much more.

Films/Videos

Blocker, David, Shep Gordon, and Carolyn Pfeiffer (producers). *The Moderns*. Alan Rudolph (director). U.S., 1988. Cast: Keith Carradine, Geraldine Chaplin, and Linda Fiorentino. Rudolph, a disciple of director Robert Altman, tries hard to capture the essence of 1920s Paris but falls short. Still, this tale of a painter (Carradine) who dabbles in forgery does have its moments. Even watching Kevin J. O'Connor turn in the worst interpretation of Ernest Hemingway ever seen on film has a certain fascination.

Law, Lindsay, and others (producers). *Waiting for the Moon*. Jill Godmilow (director). Channel Four Films/American Playhouse, 1987. Cast: Linda Bassett, Linda Hunt, and Bruce McGill. Movies seem to have a hard time capturing Gertrude Stein effectively on celluloid. This film pairs Bassett as Stein and Hunt as Alice B. Toklas, with McGill as Hemingway. How anyone can make those three insipid and boring is a mystery. It's a shame, too, because Hunt is just who you would imagine playing Alice B.

Weinstein, Henry T. (producer). *Tender Is the Night*. Henry King (director). 20th Century Fox, 1962. Cast: Joan Fontaine, Jennifer Jones, and Jason Robards. Not as good or as outrageous as director King's earlier take on Hemingway's *The Sun Also Rises*, but this adaptation of F. Scott Fitzgerald's tragic, often funny novel of the relationship between a psychiatrist and his wife (read Scott and Zelda) in 1920s Europe gets an A for effort.

Zanuck, Darryl F. (producer). *The Sun Also Rises*. Henry King (director). 20th Century Fox, 1957. Cast: Ava Gardner, Errol Flynn, and Tyrone Power. Still the quintessential Hollywood film about 1920s Parisian expatriates and their madcap exploits. Who better to personify Lost Generation dissolution than real-life aging rakes Flynn and Power at the end of their short, not-so-happy careers and lives?

Web Sites

Natalie Barney: *www.natalie-barney.com*.

Ernest Hemingway: *www.lostgeneration.com/hrc.htm*. A Hemingway resource center linked with an online bookstore devoted to Lost Generation authors.

James Joyce: *http://rpg.net/quail/libyrinth/joyce*. The site's called *The Brazen Head: A James Joyce Public House*, and it's one of the better literary Web pages on the Net. There's lots of links to keep you hopping through a veritable joycerinthian maze.

Ezra Pound: *www.lit.kobe-u.ac.ip/~hishika/pound.htm*. Great resource center for Pound, with plenty of links.

Gertrude Stein: *www.ionet.net/~jellenc/gstein4.htm*. A reasonably good site that provides biographical information on Stein and pictures of places and people associated with her, including some shots of Paris.

Mary Shelley
Frankenstein's Mother in Geneva

Mavis Guinard

NOT FAR FROM Geneva, Switzerland, *Frankenstein* was born of a waking night-mare and uneasy foreboding. And, practically since Mary Wollstonecraft Shelley set down the first words of her story, "the miserable wretch" has stolen the show.

Then, as now, unusual weather was the rule in Geneva. The summer of 1816 went on record as the wettest and the coldest of the entire 19th century. To while away rainy days, a small group of friends on vacation in Cologny read ghost stories, then competed to write one. Percy Bysshe Shelley, her husband, and Lord Byron got bored with the parlor game and never completed theirs. Mary Shelley, then 19, had a hard time starting hers.

Although she racked her brain for a Gothic horror, it was in vain. Each morning she felt humiliated when she was asked politely, "Have you thought of a story?" The reply was always a mortifying "No!"

In the evenings around the fire, she listened spellbound as the two poets discussed the theories of Jean-Jacques Rousseau, or talked of mesmerism, of automatons that acted like living creatures, and of experiments that pushed the borders of science. As they watched electrical storms rage over Lake Léman and the Jura Mountains, the poets evoked weird experiments on galvanism and spoke of Erasmus Darwin, "who preserved a piece of vermicelli in a glass case till by some extraordinary means it began to move with voluntary motion."

Byron and Shelley speculated about "the principle of life" and wondered if it could be sparked into a "manufactured creature." How far could science venture? How could it be controlled?

Mary Shelley soaked up the poets' views with the same enthusiasm with which she had already learned philosophy, literature, and several languages from her father, philosopher William Godwin. The talented youngster worshiped but had never known her mother, Mary Wollstonecraft, the first English feminist writer, who died scant days after Mary's birth.

As Mary described it later, the idea for *Frankenstein* came from the right side of the brain. That night, in a twilight zone between sleep and thought, she saw "the pale student of unhallowed arts kneeling beside the thing he had put together . . . saw the hideous phantasm of a man stretched out, then on the working of some powerful engine, show signs of life and stir with an uneasy, half vital motion."

Any movie fan can fill in the rest: the horror-stricken scientist flees, but the "horrid thing" follows to his bedside, "opening his curtains and looking on him with yellow, watery, but speculative eyes."

Mary Shelley opened her own eyes in terror, relieved to see her familiar room at Montalègre, "the dark parquet, the closed shutters with the moonlight struggling through and the sense of the glassy lake and the white, high Alps beyond." She realized that she held a story "that would make the reader dread to look round, to curdle the blood and quicken the beatings of the heart."

To the routine breakfast question, she replied she had thought of a story, and drafted a few pages on the evil unleashed by an uncontrolled scientific experiment. But Percy Shelley insisted the story should be a full-length book; literary London expected much of Mary, the offspring of two famous writers. On July 24, 1816, she first entered in her journal: "Wrote my story." For the next 10 months, despite family grief, money problems, and another pregnancy, Mary padded out her tight little plot to 24 chapters as loosely stitched as the Monster. She assembled a patchwork of social and educational theories, emerging political ideas, and voyages of discovery to the Arctic. Two London publishers rejected the manuscript before a third accepted it.

The book came out in January 1818, prefaced by Percy Shelley. Three editions appeared during Mary's lifetime. In 1823 *Frankenstein* jumped onstage in a moralizing play that greatly amused Mary. But with the movies, the Monster got his big chance when he turned up on a one-reel Edison film in 1910. In more than 40 movie and TV versions since, the plot has run away with the text. The story was spoofed by Abbott and Costello (*Abbott and Costello Meet Frankenstein*) and Mel Brooks (*Young Frankenstein*) and was blown up into grisly sensationalism by Terence Fisher (*Frankenstein Created Woman, Frankenstein Must Be Destroyed*) and Paul Morrissey (*Andy Warhol's Frankenstein*) before receiving more attentive treatment in Kenneth Branagh's *Mary Shelley's Frankenstein*.

Over the years, Mary's agile eight-foot Monster who could scale Mont Salève in one bound has become clumsy. The reasoning creature corrupted by society

The Romantics, including Mary and Percy Shelley and Lord Byron, loved the wild scenery of the Swiss Alps around Chamonix, which hasn't changed much since their day, although the red rack-railway to Montenvers is something they weren't able to take advantage of. Courtesy of Chamonix-Tourisme

that aroused some compassion has turned subhuman. The hideous features she never described took on the lidded forehead, sutures, and electrode bolts first imagined in 1931 by Universal's makeup man, Jack Pierce, for Boris Karloff.

But there is more to the book than the Monster. Mary was thrilled by Geneva. The Shelleys arrived in May 1816 after braving a snowstorm over the Jura Mountains. The very next day the brilliant sun, the lake, and the mountains made her feel like an uncaged bird. In serene contrast to her cautionary tale, she conjured up the background of that carefree summer. After Shelley's untimely death by drowning, the young widow reminisced, "the pages speak of many a walk, many a drive and many a conversation when I was not alone."

Mary Shelley never forgot Geneva, but the city did forget her. Yet, if there was a *Frankenstein* tour, it would lead to some of the most scenic spots around this international city. Sadly, though, not one plaque, not one street name recalls the author.

The Writer's Trail

Following in the Footsteps

Destination: Geneva, in French-speaking Switzerland, is home to the United Nations and various international organizations that lend the uptight bankers' and watchmakers' town a vividly exotic look. Mary Shelley came to a highly intellectual ancient city on a hill, topped by a Calvinist cathedral and walled by ramparts. In the Romantic poets' time, the town gates closed at night, so the Shelleys and Lord Byron chose to stay in nearby Cologny in order to have freedom of movement. These days you won't have to worry about that!

Location: Geneva lies on the western end of Lake Léman. Continental Europe's largest lake, carved out by vast glaciers, lies snug against the Alps, tapering into Geneva where its waters spill into the Rhône River, bound for the Mediterranean Sea. Hemmed in by mountains, Geneva is so close to the French border that its airport, two miles from downtown, has custom gates to France as well as to Switzerland.

Getting There: Swissair has one daily direct flight from New York to Geneva. Other airlines land at the Swiss hub of Zurich, with shuttle flights to Geneva within an hour. These include Swissair (1-800-221-4750), Delta (1-800-221-1212), British Airways (1-800-247-9297), and Air Canada (1-800-776-3000 in the United States; 1-888-247-2262 or [416] 925-2311 in Canada). If you're already in Europe, more than 30 high-speed Eurocity trains link Switzerland with many European countries.

Orientation: Geneva spreads around the lake along two banks linked by bridges. On the north bank, you'll find Cointrin Airport, the railway and tour-bus stations, most hotels, quays, and flower parks. The boat landing is Pâquis. On the south bank, you'll find downtown banks, boutiques, the old town's steep streets, quays, and a floral clock. The boat landing is Jardin Anglais.

Tip: The most pleasant way to cross the bay in summer is not over the flag-bedecked bridge or the two pedestrian crossings but by Mouettes motorboats, which shuttle below the Jet d'Eau to the south bank.

Getting Around: Cointrin Airport connects to Geneva's main railway station and beyond by train. All the major car-rental agencies are represented in Geneva, including Hertz (1-800-654-3131) and Avis (1-800-331-1212). There are many bus lines in the city. Maps and information are available at the train-station information desk, Rive bus stop, or from hotel concierges.

Tip: It's far cheaper to rent a car before leaving North America. Avoid Pont du Mont-Blanc during heavy commuter hours: 8:30 a.m. to 9:30 a.m. and 5:00 p.m. to 6:30 p.m.

Literary Sleeps

Hôtel d'Angleterre: Spoil yourself. Recently refurbished, this Edwardian-style hotel has 45 rooms and air-conditioning and is soundproofed. There is a lake view from Bertie's restaurant-conservatory. The restaurant features sepia photos of British royalty, maps, and engravings on the walls and serves afternoon tea. Quai du Mont-Blanc 17, north bank. Tel.: 1-800-228-3000 in Canada and the United States or (41-22) 906 55 55. Fax: (41-22) 906 55 56. Extremely expensive.

Hôtel Cornavin: Fans of the beloved fictional French children's hero Tintin will recognize this 118-room hotel. It figures in *Affaire Tournesol*, one of the character's most famous adventures.

Boulevard James Fazy 23, north bank. Tel.: (41-22) 716 12 12. Moderate to expensive.

Hôtel du Midi: Located off Quai des Bergues and surrounded by twisting, narrow streets, this 89-room hotel is a good launching point for explorations of Geneva's old town. Place Chevelu 4, south bank. Tel.: (41-22) 731 78 00. Fax: (41-22) 731 00 20. Moderate to expensive.

Hôtel La Tourelle: Four miles from Geneva, beyond Cologny, this comfortable 23-room lodging offers the relaxed country life that delighted Mary Shelley. Ask for room 11 with its pink quilts. The room is particularly charming and overlooks a shady garden. The hotel offers breakfast only, but there are small restaurants nearby. A taxi from the Geneva airport to La Tourelle is about $40. Route d'Hermance 26, Vésenaz. Tel.: (41-22) 752 16 28. Fax: (41-22) 752 54 93. Web site: *www.geneva.Yop.ch/hotels/la_tourelle.* Moderate.

Literary Sites

Cologny: Two miles from Geneva, a once-simple farm village perched on a hill has been divvied up into lush estates where celebrities like singers Petula Clark or Charles Aznavour or former Olympic skiers like Jean-Claude Killy live behind the double protection of ironwork fences and clipped hedges. Even so, the village center does retain its old-time charm. From the Mairie de Cologny bus stop, head along Chemin de Ruth. In minutes you'll reach an open field where Lord Byron's name is carved on a boulder facing the view of lake, city, and Jura Mountains. Back in Cologny, one of the Geneva area's best restaurants, the Lion d'Or, enjoys the same view. Choose a table by the picture windows or under the plane trees outside the simpler bistro. Both places operate from the same kitchen. Chefs Tommy Byrne and Gilles Dupont like fish specialties, even bouillabaisse (the Mediterranean Sea may be far away, but the airport is close). The restaurant is located at Place Gautier 5 in Cologny (tel.: [41-22] 736 57 80).

Musée d'Histoire des Sciences: In La Perle du Lac, the Villa Bartholoni, an exquisitely renovated Palladian mansion, houses a museum devoted to 18th- and 19th-century science. Among frescoed walls and marble floors, it displays the superb brass instruments used, collected, or invented by Genevese scientists—Mary Shelley's models for Victor Frankenstein. One room is devoted to the barometer and other paraphernalia that Horace-Benedict de Saussure loaded in 1787 on the backs of 18 guides for his observations at the top of newly conquered Mont Blanc. In an array of quadrants, astrolabes, microscopes, telescopes, marine compasses, surveying tools, and prints of early electrical experiments are a few instruments Dr. Frankenstein would have found handy to assemble the Monster: dissection kits, suture needles, and electromagnetic apparatus. Admission free. Open daily from 1:00 p.m. to 5:00 p.m. (closed Tuesday). Rue de Lausanne 128, Geneva. Tel.: (41-22) 731 69 85.

Villa Diodati: Lord Byron and Mary and Percy Shelley spent the summer of 1816 here. From its terrace, Mary may have seen "those vivid flashes of lightning, illuminating the lake, making it appear like a large sheet of fire." Unfortunately the privately owned villa can't be visited. A carefully mown slope, Pré Byron, has replaced the vineyards where Mary's stepsister, Claire Clairmont, once lost a slipper after a late tryst with Byron. Tourists and tour buses park here by day but, after dark, drug addicts also like this secluded spot. Byron's ghost wouldn't care, though. He was into laudanum, alcohol laced with opium. Just off Chemin Byron, a quiet lane peters out by a mossy stone wall, all that remains of the Maison Chapuis, the house the Shelleys rented close by. One can imagine the two sisters waiting, Mary's baby William between them, watching sails skim the lake, impatient for the poets' return from their hazardous trip to Chillon.

Tip: The best time to travel in Switzerland is from May to October. However, in August the country is crowded with tourists and the weather can be quite hot. During that month, side trips on Lake Léman or a trip to Chamonix's tremendous glacier are cool choices.

Icon Pastimes

Below Cologny lake boats cruise along scenes that Mary Shelley loved. She had Victor Frankenstein and his doomed bride follow the same route. Years later she would recall: "Those were the last moments of my life during which I enjoyed the feeling of happiness. . . . At a distance we saw, surmounting all, the beautiful Mont Blanc and the assemblage of snowy mountains that try to emulate her." She enjoyed sailing on a lake that, as the poets realized on their trip to Chillon, may be at times treacherous. From April to October, stately white paddlewheelers zig and zag around Europe's largest lake. The plush ambience below decks is a far cry from the rustic fishing boats in which the Shelleys and Lord Byron sailed. Smaller motorboats whip around parks, allow passengers to gawk at famous residences, or shuttle across the bay below Geneva's 500-foot Jet d'Eau, a plume of water as high as New York City's United Nations Building. Boats can be rented from Les Corsaires ([41-22] 735 43 00), Quai Gustave Ador 33 (near Rue des Vollandes); SwissBoat ([41-22] 732 47 47), Quai du Mont-Blanc 4; and Mouettes Genevoises ([41-22] 732 29 44), Quai du Mont-Blanc 8. The Compagnie Générale de Navigation's eight large paddlewheelers leave from two landings: Pâquis on the north bank and Jardin Anglais, by the floral clock, on the south bank. The company offers a variety of trips: midday cruises, brunch cruises every Sunday, round-the-lake cruises (about five hours to Chillon), and dance cruises. Another excellent excursion while in the Geneva area is to do as the Shelleys did (traveling through valleys and pine forests on foot and by mule): visit Chamonix and Mer de Glace in France. Today you reach the glacier wedged between helmeted Alpine climbers via rack-railway and cable car. On that tremendous glacier flowing from the Mont Blanc massif "like the waves of a troubled sea," Mary Shelley set a dramatic confrontation. As "icy and glittering peaks shone in the sunlight over the clouds," Victor Frankenstein faced the Monster advancing with superhuman speed. An odd octagonal stone building, a temple dedicated to nature in 1795, still stands. Chamonix guides would bring their clients here to warm up and rest, providing benches and a bottle of ink to sign the guest book. A stone plaque by the fireplace records famous names: Byron, of course and, a few lines below, Percy but not Mary Shelley. Now a tiny museum, it's open in July and August from 10:00 a.m. to 7:00 p.m., and there's an admission fee. Buses leave every day for Chamonix and Mer de Glace at 8:30 a.m. from Geneva's Gare Routière, Place Dorcière, a couple of blocks from Cornavin Railroad Station. Chamonix may also be reached by train or car (60 miles). The red train for Montenvers/Mer de Glace leaves every 20 minutes from 8:00 a.m. to 6:00 p.m. in July and August; every half hour in May, June, and September from 8:30 a.m. to 5:30 p.m. A huge old-time mountain refuge, Hôtel Refuge du Montenvers ([33] 450 53 12 54), provides rustic overnights at budget prices.

 ## Contacts

Geneva Tourist Office: Rue du Mont-Blanc 18, P.O. Box 1602, CH-1211 Geneva, Switzerland. Tel.: (41-22) 909 70 70 or 909 70 00. Fax: (41-22) 909 70 75 or 909 70 11. Web site: *www.geneve-tourisme.ch.* Note: the Information Office is at Rue du Mont-Blanc 3.

Swiss Embassy: United States: 2900 Cathedral Avenue NW, Washington, D.C. 20008. Tel.: (202) 745-7900; Canada: 5 Marlborough Avenue, Ottawa, Ontario K1N 8E6. Tel.: (613) 235-1837.

Swiss National Tourist Office: United States: Swiss Center, 608 Fifth Avenue, New York, New York 10020. Tel.: (212) 757-5944; Canada: 926 The East Mall, Toronto (Etobicoke), Ontario M9B 6K1. Tel.: (416) 695-2090. Web site: *www.switzerlandtourism.ch.*

In a Literary Mood

Books

Bennett, Betty T. *The Letters of Mary Wollstonecraft Shelley.* New York: Johns Hopkins University

Press, 1980-88. Unknown facets of Shelley, such as her relationships with other women, turn up in this abundant and well-footnoted collection of letters.

Byron, George Gordon. *Byron's Poetry*. Edited by Frank McConnell. New York: W. W. Norton, 1980. Includes "The Prisoner of Chillon" text, letters, and journals.

Nichie, Elizabeth. *Mary Shelley, Author of Frankenstein*. New Brunswick, NJ: Rutgers University Press, 1953.

Shelley, Mary. *Frankenstein*. London: Oxford University Press, 1969. Originally published in 1818, Shelley's first book was twice rejected and appeared anonymously with a preface by her husband, Percy.

_____. *The Journals of Mary Shelley*. Edited by Paula R. Feldman and Diana Scott-Kilvert. Oxford: Clarendon Press, 1987.

_____. *The Last Man*. London: The Hogarth Press, 1985. The author of *Frankenstein* again uses an Alpine background—this time for a futuristic novel set in 2073. The plot concerns a lone survivor in the chaos of a world wiped out by plague.

Shelley, Mary, and Percy Bysshe Shelley. *History of a Six Weeks' Tour*. London: T. Hookham and C. & J. Ollies, 1817. A joint account of the Shelleys' summer tour of 1816.

Shelley, Percy Bysshe. *Poems*. New York: Alfred J. Knopf, 1993.

Spark, Muriel. *Mary Shelley: A Biography*. New York: Dutton, 1987. A scholarly account of Shelley's life, told with sensitive insight by novelist Spark.

Guidebooks

Honan, Mark. *Switzerland*. 2nd ed. Hawthorn, Australia: Lonely Planet Publications, 1997. The third edition of this generally excellent guide should be available soon.

Switzerland. 3rd ed. Watford, England: Michelin Travel Publications, 1999.

Films/Videos

Asher, E. M., and Carl Laemmle Jr. (producers). *Frankenstein*. James Whale (director). Universal, 1931. MCA Universal Video. Cast: Mae Clarke, Colin Clive, and Boris Karloff. There have been dozens of movie and television adaptations of Mary Shelley's classic novel, but this one, though a bit creaky, is the one firmly established in our minds, for better or worse. J. Searle Dawley did the first silent version in 1910, and since then directors as varied as Roy William Neill, Paul Morrissey, Howard Koch, Jack Smight, Mel Brooks, Roger Corman, and Kenneth Branagh have taken turns, while actors Bela Lugosi, Michael Sarrazin, Peter Boyle, Robert De Niro, and Randy Quaid, among others, have stalked the celluloid world as the Monster. Nevertheless, Karloff's classic portrayal of Dr. Frankenstein's creature in this film (and a number of sequels) is surprisingly effective, even after all these years. In many ways, *Bride of Frankenstein* (1935), which Whale also helmed, is much better than the director's original film. Elsa Lanchester does double duty as the unforgettable Bride and as Mary Shelley in a captivating prologue. Throughout the movie there's a delicious dry wit at play, likely thanks to Whale.

Barker, Clive, Sam Irvin, and others (producers). *Gods and Monsters*. Bill Condon (director). Regent Entertainment, 1998. MCA Universal Home Video. Cast: Brendan Fraser, Ian McKellen, and Lynn

Redgrave. A sympathetic look at the last days of Hollywood director James Whale. Flashbacks to his classic *Frankenstein* and *Bride of Frankenstein* curiously entwine Monster and filmmaker.

Clark, Al, Robert Devereux, and Penny Corke (producers). *Gothic.* Ken Russell (director). Virgin Vision, 1986. Vestron Video. Cast: Gabriel Byrne, Natasha Richardson, and Julian Sands. This filmic re-creation of the night in the summer of 1816 that Mary Shelley, in company with Lord Byron, Percy Shelley, and Dr. John Polidori (who wrote *The Vampyre*), concocted the idea for *Frankenstein* is over the top as only Russell can be, complete with overheated sex, eye-popping hallucinations, and some pretty bad acting. The same material was treated a little better in *Haunted Summer* (1988), directed by Ivan Passer and based on Anne Edwards's novel.

Web Sites

Romantics: *www.rc.umd.edu/indexjava.html.* The University of Maryland's excellent Romantic Circles site has links to articles about every facet of the Romantics, including the Shelleys and Lord Byron.

Mary Shelley: *www.desert-fairy.com/maryshel.shtml; www.english.udel.edu/swilson/mws/mws.html.* The first site has a wealth of information about Shelley and the novel *Frankenstein*, with lots of good links. The second site is a pretty good all-purpose compendium of Shelley resources, biographical material, and links.

Biographies

Victoria Brooks is editor in chief of the travel webzine *www.greatestescapes.com* and creator and general editor of the Literary Trips series. A member of the Society of American Travel Writers and the American Society of Journalists and Authors, she has authored numerous travel features in North American magazines and worldwide Internet publications.

Marda Burton, based in New Orleans, has written hundreds of articles for publications that include *Saturday Evening Post, Cosmopolitan, Travel & Leisure, Southern Living,* and *American Artist.* At present she works on assignment as travel editor for *Veranda* magazine.

M. R. Carroll, series editor of *Literary Trips*, has been a book editor for more than 15 years. He lives in Vancouver, British Columbia, and has written on a variety of subjects, from art and literature to sports and jazz, for publications that include the *Globe and Mail*, the *Georgia Straight*, and the *Vancouver Sun*. Recently he published his first novel, *Dead False*, a literary mystery.

Marilyn Carson lives in Ottawa, Ontario, where she works as a freelance writer and special-education teacher. Her interests include gardening, turn-of-the-century decor, visual arts, female singers, and Jungian psychology.

Donna Carter, the sister-in-law of author Jane Urquhart, is an Ontario-based freelance writer who specializes in leisure and corporate travel, golf, and sailing. She is a former editor of *Sailing Canada, Travel à la Carte,* and *Century Home* magazines. In 1998, she won the Travel Media Association of Canada award for best international travel story.

Margaret Deefholts lives in Surrey, British Columbia, but grew up in India. Many of her award-winning short fiction works are set within an Indian framework. She is vice president of the B.C. Association of Travel Writers.

Elaine Glusac has published articles in *American Way*, *Shape*, *Coastal Living*, *Travel & Leisure*, and *Reader's Digest*. She also reviewed more than 200 restaurants for *CityGuide Chicago*.

Mavis Guinard was born in the United States but grew up in Milan, Paris, and Buenos Aires, where she worked as a reporter. She has coauthored a book on Lausanne and now works as a freelancer based in Switzerland.

Tom Henighan, who is a professor of English at Carleton University in Ottawa, Ontario, has published a novel, two collections of stories, and a volume of poetry. He is also the author of *The Presumption of Culture* and *The Maclean's Guide to Canadian Arts and Culture*.

Yvonne Jeffery Hope is an award-winning freelance travel writer based in Ottawa, Ontario. Her travels have taken her across Canada and as far afield as Cambodia. However, England, where she grew up, remains one of her favorite places to explore.

Jennifer Huget is a former publicity director for Mark Twain House in Hartford. Currently she is a freelance writer based in East Granby, Connecticut.

Susan Kostrzewa, a literature and travel enthusiast, lives in Tiburon, California. She is the managing editor of *Specialty Travel Index*, and when she's not buried under bluelines and production schedules, looks for inspiration in places like the remote beaches of Costa Rica or the grasslands of South Africa.

Kathryn Means once followed the path of Don Quixote across the plains of La Mancha in Spain. Since then she has continued to follow authors' trails wherever she goes, and has published articles with newspapers and magazines from Texas to Singapore.

Eric Miller is a writer who specializes in cities. He has a master's in urban studies from the University of Akron and lives in San Francisco.

Suzie Rodriguez is the author of *Found Meals of the Lost Generation*, a book devoted to the more free-spirited writers, artists, and hangers-on of 1920s Paris. Currently she is working on a biography of literary salonist and writer Natalie Clifford Barney.

Bob Shacochis is the author of the American Book Award–winning collection of short stories *Easy in the Islands*. He was also nominated for the National Book Award for his first novel, *Swimming in the Volcano*, and most recently published *Immaculate Invasion*, a nonfiction eyewitness account of the 1994 American intervention in Haiti.

Tanya Storr calls Quadra Island, British Columbia, home. She is a freelance writer and photographer and is a member of the Periodical Writers Association of Canada.

Richard Taylor has published a novel, a collection of short stories, and feature articles on subjects as diverse as Lord Byron, open-water swimming, surfing, and the perils and pleasures of being a househusband. He lives in Ottawa, Ontario, and teaches English literature and creative writing at Carleton University.

Nancy Wigston wrote her doctoral thesis on Aldous Huxley. She began it in Cambridge, worked on it in Montreal, finished it in Malaysia, and defended it in Toronto. She belongs to the Society of American Travel Writers and to the Periodical Writers Association of Canada.

Joyce Gregory Wyels, a Southern Californian, has brought back stories and photos from six continents for airline in-flight magazines, travel anthologies, and publications such as *Civilization, Historic Traveler,* and *Coastal Living.*

Index

Page numbers in italics refer to photographs

Notes

Travel…and Reading About It
Life's GreatestEscapes!

GreatestEscapes.com Publishing is a multimedia company that produces online content as well as traditional books. We are passionately devoted to the very finest in travel writing, seeking to inspire the wanderlust of our readers rather than simply giving them a list of sights, restaurants, and hotels. Read the GreatestEscapes travel webzine (*www.greatestescapes.com*), a monthly compendium of award-winning travel stories from around the globe.

Literary Trips 2
Following in the Footsteps of Fame
edited by Victoria Brooks
ISBN: 0-9686137-1-3
$19.95 U.S.; $29.95 Canada

If you liked the critically acclaimed *Literary Trips: Following in the Footsteps of Fame*, be sure to check out the second volume, *Literary Trips 2*. Following the same format, it's packed with 22 stories about famous writers and the locations around the world they're associated with, including Graham Greene's Vietnam, Robert Louis Stevenson's Hawaii, Jack London's Northern California, Henry David Thoreau's Walden Pond, Robertson Davies's Ontario, Pablo Neruda's Chile, Beatrix Potter's England, Franz Kafka's Prague, and much more. The distinguished science-fiction writer Sir Arthur C. Clarke, the subject of an essay in the book, also wrote the foreword, and noted travel writer Christopher Ondaatje penned the introduction.

Literary Trips 2: Following in the Footsteps of Fame is available online at *www.literarytrips.com* (in whole or by the chapter), in bookstores across North America, and by calling 1-877-474-6743 (toll-free in North America). To order by phone outside of North America, call 604-683-1668.

GreatestEscapes.com
PUBLISHING

Available Fall 2001

Red Dream
an exotic novel
BY VICTORIA BROOKS

ISBN 0-9686137-2-1
$13.95 U.S.; $19.95 Canada

- Part historical novel, part romance. Part fact, part fiction. An Asian *Gone with the Wind* set against a seething, exotic background of love and sex, intrigue and war.
- Melodrama pitched into the bloody palette of Vietnam's history. Vietnam when it was French Indochina. Vietnam when it was a country divided.
- A story punctuated with Communists and coups, politicians and spies.
- A text spiked with simple poetry that reads like the modern lyrics of a song.
- Pages subtly laced with visual images.

The Characters

- *LA DOCTORESSE* JADE MINH, an exquisitely beautiful woman with a hole for a soul and a secret in her past.
- THE MYSTERIOUS CHOU, the South Vietnamese embassy's slippery legal eagle who dabbles in skullduggery with the dangerous other side. A man who lusts after the delectable Jade Minh with a creative perversion. A man who makes secrets his business.
- THE LOVELY SUZETTE, illegitimate child from a star-crossed union. Born half-French, half-Vietnamese, though she'd never stepped a foot in Asia. Abandoned by her alcoholic father at a Catholic orphanage near Paris. Adopted into a fearful America during the leadup to the Vietnam War. A runaway looking for love. A young woman trying to discover her identity. Her only clue: an old photo she finds secreted in her father's things. Her search in Saigon for the real mother she's never seen, and her love for THANH, a young government official drafted into the Army of the Republic of South Vietnam.

And The War That Ruins Everything!

Available Fall 2001 in bookstores everywhere.
Signed copies will be available online at *www.literarytrips.com* or by calling 1-877-474-6743.

Interested U.S. retailers can call Words Distributing (toll-free) at 1-800-593-9673.
Interested Canadian retailers can call Sandhill Book Marketing at 1-800-667-3848.